D1500312

# THE GREEN COUNT OF SAVOY

# The
# Green Count
# of Savoy

## AMADEUS VI
## AND TRANSALPINE SAVOY
## IN THE FOURTEENTH CENTURY

EUGENE L. COX

PRINCETON, NEW JERSEY

PRINCETON UNIVERSITY PRESS

1967

Maps by Federal Graphics, Washington, D.C.

Printed in the United States of America

by Princeton University Press, Princeton, New Jersey

*To the memory of*

*SIDNEY PAINTER*

# Preface

IN THE corner of the European continent where France, Italy, and Switzerland come together, the Graian and Pennine Alps reach their culminating points in the Mont Blanc and the Monta Rosa. For nine hundred years these lofty mountains with their passes and adjoining plains were in large measure dominated by the princes of Savoy. The efforts of these princes to create a great and unified state where nature has created innumerable Alpine barriers make one of history's most intriguing success stories. Yet the world of English-speaking scholars has remained remarkably unintrigued; the only full-length scholarly study in English on Savoy in the Middle Ages is Professor Previté Orton's *The Early History of the House of Savoy 1000–1233* (Cambridge, 1912). Even French and Italian scholars have not been drawn into the history of medieval Savoy in the numbers which the abundance of archive material warrants. Aside from such landmarks in Savoyard institutional history as the works of Chiaudano and Tallone, and some excellent local studies, the only histories of medieval Savoy to appear during the past seventy years have been popular rather than scholarly in character. Within the past decade, the medieval states of Burgundy and Geneva have been the objects of original research and fresh points of view; neighboring Savoy merits equal attention.

The present volume on the "Green Count" is hopefully a contribution toward a better understanding of social and political life in the Western Alps through a study of the transalpine state of Savoy and its role on the international scene during the fourteenth century. The book is also intended as a portrait of a rather remarkable personality, Count Amadeus VI, who fully deserves to take his place beside the great princes of his age. Amadeus VI can truly be called the architect of the medieval Savoyard state at its height, for his grandson, Amadeus VIII, under whom medieval Savoy attained its territorial apogee, largely reaped where his grandfather had sown. It was Amadeus VI who finally stabilized the western frontiers of Savoy and, except for the county of Geneva, brought within the fabric of his state the major lay and ecclesiastical baronies which had hitherto escaped comital control. Then, while perfecting the machinery of centralized administration for his greatly enlarged dominions, Amadeus VI firmly oriented his policies toward expansion on the Italian side of the Alps. The growing power of France and Burgundy had removed the opportunities for expansion westward, and Amadeus VI marked out instead the pathways to domination in Italy which his distant descendants would achieve.

Amadeus VI was more than an accomplished statesman and warrior; he was also a model of Christian knighthood, as his surname, "the Green Count," suggests. He was the child of an age of transition from medieval chivalry toward Machiavellian realism, and the conflict of ideals can be clearly traced in his career. He had been raised in the more conservative tradition of northern Europe, a tradition which emphasized Christian piety and respect for the Church, as well as the classic virtues of knighthood "without fear and without reproach." From his youth Amadeus VI dedicated himself to the ideals of chivalry and Christianity and sought to cover himself with glory through distinguished service to both. As he grew older, however, he began to perceive obstacles to the realization of his ideals. Particularly, as he came into increasing contact with hardheaded and opportunistic Italian neighbors armed with ready cash and easy consciences, the Green Count discovered that neither the rules of chivalry nor those of Christianity were adequate guidelines for success in affairs of state. Gradually he learned to adapt to an environment of sharp political opportunism without sacrificing his carefully constructed image of the illustrious Christian prince. It was a virtuoso performance which won him a special place in the annals of his dynasty, and which deserves a place in the histories of his era.

In preparing this study over the past five years, I have relied principally upon the archives at Turin, Chambéry, and Dijon, where a great wealth of documents on medieval Savoy and its rulers await more extensive investigation than I have sometimes been able to give them. For what I have been able to accomplish, I am much indebted to Dr. Matteo Sandretti, Dr. Augusta Lange, and the staff of the *Archivio di Stato* at Turin for their generous assistance, as well as to M. André Perret and the staff of the *Archives départementales de Savoie* at Chambéry. Special thanks are due also to M. Louis Binz of the *Archives de l'Etat de Genève* and to M. Jean-Jacques Bouquet of Lausanne, who very kindly read through the chapter on the Green Count's crusade.

I am also grateful to the Faculty Awards committee of Wellesley College, whose moral and financial support over the years has made this book possible, and to Dr. Owen Jander, who laboriously proofread much of the manuscript. Finally, my special thanks to Professor Frederic C. Lane of the Johns Hopkins University for his reading and criticism of the manuscript and for his advice and encouragement during the final stages of the project.

Eugene L. Cox

*Turin*
*February 1965*

# Contents

# Contents

# Contents

*CHAPTER XI · THE LAST CAMPAIGN · 1382–1383*

# Illustrations

## Illustrations

Drawing by Fornazeris, dated 1589, showing the basin of Lake Geneva and the Alps of Chablais and Faucigny. Original in Bibliothèque publique et universitaire de la Ville de Genève. Photograph by Jean Arlaud, Geneva.

Artist's view of the canyons of the Rhône, approaching Savoy from the southwest. In his last will and testament, dated 27 February 1383, Amadeus VI ordered the foundation at his castle of Pierre-Châtel of a Carthusian monastery in honor of the Order of the Collar. The community was to consist of fifteen monks representing the fifteen joys of the Virgin, just as the Order of the Collar had consisted of fifteen knights at its foundation. This picture shows the Abbey-fortress on the cliffs above the Rhône as it looked to Claude Chastillon, *Topographie française* (Paris, 1691). Photograph by Studio Guy, Chambéry.

View of the Abbey of Hautecombe on the shores of Lake Le Bourget opposite Aix-les-Bains. Hautecombe was the burial place for the princes of the House of Savoy throughout the Middle Ages. Taken from the *Théatre des Etats de S.A.R. le Duc de Savoie* (The Hague, 1700). Photograph by Studio Guy, Chambéry.

MAPS

THE GREEN COUNT OF SAVOY

# ABBREVIATIONS

| ADCO | Archives départementales de la Côte d'Or (Dijon) |
| ADI | Archives départementales de l'Isère (Grenoble) |
| ADS | Archives départementales de la Savoie (Chambéry) |
| AEG | Archives de l'Etat de Genève (Geneva) |
| AHS | *Archives héraldiques suisses* |
| ASI | *Archivio Storico Italiano* |
| ASL | *Archivio Storico Lombardo* |
| AST | Archivio di Stato di Torino (Turin) |
| BSBS | *Bollettino Storico Bibliografico Subalpino* |
| BSI | *Bibliotheca Storia Italiana* |
| MARS | *Mémoires de l'Académie royale de Savoie* |
| MAS | *Memoria della Reale Accademia delle Scienze* |
| MASBAS | *Mémoires de l'Académie des Sciences, Belles-Lettres, et Arts de Savoie* |
| MDG | *Mémoires et Documents de la Société d'histoire et d'archéologie de Genève* |
| MDR | *Mémoires et Documents de la Société de l'histoire de la Suisse Romande* |
| MDSS | *Mémoires et Documents de la Société savoisienne d'histoire et d'archéologie* |
| MHP | *Monumenta Historia Patriae* |
| MSI | *Miscellanea di Storia Italiana* |
| MSRS | *Mémoires de la Société royale académique de Savoie* |
| RIS | *Rerum Italicarum Scriptores* (ed. Muratori, 1730) |

# The Mountains and the Men

## GEOGRAPHICAL INTRODUCTION

MEDIEVAL SAVOY was rather a dream than a state, a dream in the minds of the family which carried the name. The state was centered on the *combe de Savoie* in the valley of the Isère, but the dream included all of the innumerable valleys of the Graian and Pennine Alps from the Mont Cenis to the Monta Rosa. To outsiders, Savoy was a terrifying obstacle which lay between where they were and where they wished to be. Eustache Deschamps, a fourteenth-century poet, frankly declared that anyone who made the journey through the Savoyard Alps for any reason short of urgent necessity was out of his mind. Yet of all the great mountain ranges of the world, the Alps are among the most accessible. Unusually deep valleys penetrate to the interior of the chain and permit the traveler a relatively easy approach to even the loftiest pass. These same valleys channel a surprisingly mild climate to the interior lowlands, and despite the warnings of Eustache Deschamps and others who found the trip equally exhausting, through the centuries a steady stream of outsiders have trod the Alpine trails and settled in Alpine valleys. From Roman times onward, empire-builders, missionaries, and traders have crossed the giant barrier between Italy and northwestern Europe, determined to unite a continent which nature seemed determined to separate.

The principal Alpine passes controlled by the medieval princes of Savoy were the Mont Genèvre, the Mont Cenis, the Little St. Bernard, the Great St. Bernard, and the Simplon. The Mont Genèvre and the Simplon passes were located beyond the limits of Savoyard territory, but the Savoyards dominated the Piedmont approaches to the former and the Valais approach to the latter. Francis I, whose mother was a Savoyard princess, was perhaps

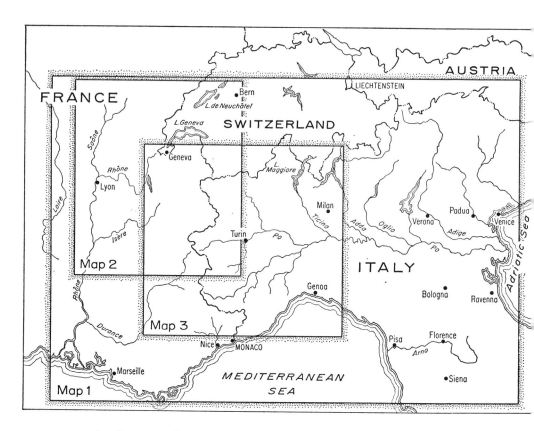

the first to refer to the rulers of Savoy as the gatekeepers of the Alps, a role which meant both fortune and disaster for the dynasty over the centuries. From the Roman conquest of Gaul, the passes which later came under the sway of the house of Savoy were vital links in the network of routes connecting the Mediterranean and western provinces of the Empire. The era of barbarian invasions disrupted the flow of international trade, but the economic recovery beginning in the eleventh century was the dawn of a more prosperous age for the people of the Alps. Italian merchants and bankers carried their enterprises across the mountains to every part of Europe; the Italian peninsula, spiritual seat of the medieval "Roman Empire" and of the medieval papacy, became again the great magnet of the western world, drawing not only traders, but emperors, armies, churchmen, pilgrims, and adventurers from far and near. The tempo of movement on the great transalpine thoroughfares began to quicken, and as the passes increased in importance, so did the dynasty that controlled them.

The cradle of that dynasty was the "combe de Savoie," the geographical nucleus of what later became the county of Savoy.

4

Savoy centered then, as it does now, upon the wide arm of valley separating the Bauges Mountains from a semicircle of ranges between the Mont du Chat on the west and the Belledonne on the south. In this geographical "arm," Lake Le Bourget lies at the shoulder, Montmélian at the bend, and St-Pierre-d'Albigny at the wrist. The whole forms a giant corridor, some 1,000 feet above sea level, between the basin of Lake Geneva to the north and the Isère valley routes to Italy. These routes continue east of St-Pierre-d'Albigny, where the corridor divides, the Tarentaise curving more to the north, following the Isère toward the pass of the Little St. Bernard into the Val d'Aosta. This was the preferred route between cisalpine and transalpine Gaul during the centuries of Roman domination. In the Middle Ages the more frequented route was the second corridor, the valley of Maurienne, which turns sharply to the south at St-Pierre-d'Albigny and follows the arc, bending eastward to the pass of the Mont Cenis into the Val di Susa.

In the opposite direction, the canyons of the Rhône between Lake Geneva and the confluence of the Rhône and the Guiers formed the western boundary of Savoy proper, but the mountainous country between the Rhône and the Ain (Bugey and Valromey) was also ruled by the house of Savoy from an early period. Further west of the Ain, the mountains melt into verdant plains rolling gently toward the banks of the Saône. This was the land of Bresse, acquired in the thirteenth century, the one place where the frontiers of the Savoyard state bordered those of the kingdom of France. The dominions of the house of Savoy were thus a patchwork of principalities stretching from the banks of the Saône to the plains of the Po. But the center of the patchwork remained the valley of Le Bourget and the "combe de Savoie," where the principal routes from western Helvetia to the cities of the lower Rhône intersected the major thoroughfares to northern Italy.

The Alps of Savoy may be unusually accessible, but before the age of modern tunnels, motor highways, and railroads, they remained a formidable obstacle nevertheless. Narrow trails, sometimes hardly more than footpaths, followed the difficult valley edges in order to escape the lowland marshes. Bridges more often of wood than of stone spanned the rocky chasms and rivers, but could not always be depended upon to withstand the annual on-slaught of floods and avalanches. As recently as the eighteenth century, travelers unaccustomed to Alpine heights were often frightened by their encounters with these towering ramparts of rock and snow, and several well-known writers of that period have recorded their impressions. To Joseph Addison the Alps presented "snow-prospects" that were pretty enough, but they were "broken into so many steps and precipices, that they fill the mind with an agreeable kind of horror, and form one of the most irregular misshapen scenes in the world."[1] For Thomas Gray, traveling through Savoy some decades later, the mountains in-spired the same mixed reaction of dread and admiration. Arriv-ing from Lyon at Les Eschelles on a visit to the monastery of the Grande Chartreuse, Gray described "all the beauties so savage and horrid a place can present you with; Rocks of various and uncouth figures, Cascades pouring down from an immense height out of hanging Groves of Pine-Trees, and the solemn Sound of the Stream, that roars below, all concur to form one of the most poetical Scenes imaginable."[2] Later he wrote to a friend that on the journey to that part of Savoy he found "Not a preci-pice, not a torrent, not a cliff, but is pregnant with religion and poetry." The pass of the Mont Cenis, which he declared to "carry the permission mountains have of being frightful rather too far," was not without its beauties, but the dangerous crossing gave him little time to reflect upon them.

Canon Paradin of Beaujeu, writing in the mid-sixteenth cen-tury, furnishes other vivid geographical descriptions of the Alps in the opening chapters of his chronicle. He was particularly im-pressed by the "exceeding high and prodigious mountains and rocks," with summits eternally covered with ice and snow, "scarce distinguishable from pure crystal."[3] When the thaws set in after the long winter, the land of silent snow and ice becomes a roar-ing, living thing, marvelous and terrible to behold. "Innumerable streams and rivers rush down the mountains and valleys with

[1] Joseph Addison, "Remarks on Several Parts of Italy, Etc.," *Miscellaneous Works of Joseph Addison*, ed. Guthkelch (London, 1914), II, 202.

[2] Cited from *Correspondence of Thomas Gray*, ed. Toynbee and Whibley (Oxford, 1935), I, 122, note 1. Subsequent citations above are *ibid.*, pp. 128–129.

[3] This and following quotations are from Guillaume Paradin, *Cronique de Savoye* (Lyon, 1552), Chapters I and II. My translation.

great abundance of water, and in narrows and straits through the rocks they make such a great roar that two men walking together can scarcely hear each other speaking; between these concurrent rocks and stony chasms so dreadful is the din set up by water tumbling from cataract to cataract . . . that not only do the waters become spray, but even resolve into clouds from such impetuous agitation."

The mountains were fearful to contemplate because of their size and the extreme cold which they generated in winter, but the lowlands and valleys were often "delectable prairies," rich in all things requisite for human life. The good Paradin was struck by the extremes which characterize this country, affirming it to contain both the best and the worst in soil. The Piedmont on the Italian side and several regions in the west were very good and fertile, "as much in good grains, wines, livestock, as in other good things." Yet many other parts of the country were so "bad, poor, and unfertile that they never produce anything of great profit, and the greater part nothing at all, so that it is a perfect wilderness." Moreover, the canon continues, the "reverberations of their long coldness, perpetual in several places, spoil and retard the fruit produced in nearby regions, so that it is still unripe two or three months after the others, and sometimes never."

In those days wildlife was far more abundant in the Alpine region than it is today. Paradin remarked upon strange goats of marvelous agility which "leap from rock to rock as if moved and tossed by some engine or machine"; and white rabbits "which are thought to graze upon the snow during the winter, for in truth no sooner are the snows melted than [the rabbits] take on a reddish color." There were also "mighty large bears in great numbers" inhabiting the heights and the dense forests which still blanketed so much of the region. As late as 1770, Charles Burney was dissuaded from inspecting a glacier on the Mont Cenis when his muleteers told him that "wild Bears and Wolves in great numbers" inhabited those wastes in the summer.[4]

---

[4] Charles Burney, *Dr. Burney's Musical Tours in Europe: An Eighteenth Century Musical Tour in France and Italy*, ed. P. A. Scholes (Oxford, 1959), I, 51. One of Gray's most impressive experiences crossing the Mont Cenis in November 1739 occurred in broad daylight when a "great wolf" suddenly rushed out from the pines along the road and carried off Walpole's spaniel, which was running along beside the chaise. Gray, I, 125–126.

7

BOURGOGNE
Bern
AIN
VAUD
Lausanne
Mâcon
SAÔNE
BRESSE
Bourg
Gex
GEX
CHABLAIS
Sion
BEAUJEU
BUGEY
Genève
VALAIS
GENEVOIS
FAUCIGNY
Grand-St-Bernard
Lyon
Annecy
Aosta
RHÔNE
SAVOIE
TARENTAISE
VAL D'AOSTA
Petit-St-Bernard
CANAVESE
LOIRE
Vienne
Chambéry
ISÈRE
MAURIENNE
FRANCE
DAUPHINÉ
Montcenis
Grenoble
Susa
VAL DI SUSA
Torino
ISÈRE
Pinerolo
Die
PO
Montgenèvre
Saluzzo
SALUZZO
RHÔNE
Cuneo
Mondovi
Avignon
VAR
Albenga
DURANCE
Monaco
Nice
PROVENCE
Marseille

Territories controlled
by Amadeus VI ca. 1382

Savoy-Achaea

INN

ADIGE

Bergamo

Vimercate

Milano

TICINO

Pavia

ADDA

Cremona

Brescia

OGLIO

PO

Verona

Mantova

ADIGE

Venezia

sandria

Parma

Modena

Ravenna

nova

Bologna

Firenze

Pisa

ARNO

Siena

ean Sea

ITALIA

## The Mountains and the Men

The population of Savoy is usually described by eighteenth-century observers as ragged and poverty-stricken. Both Gray and Burney found the men who made their living carrying travelers over the Mont Cenis a veritable race of savages, "in all respects, below humanity," often living in one room which "serves the whole family, Mules, Asses, Cows, and Hogs included."[5] While conditions may have been somewhat better during the Middle Ages, when the population was smaller and the rulers still made these valleys the center of activity, life could never have been very easy for most of the inhabitants.[6] Paradin characterized them as "strong and rude by nature, hardworking, enduring all hardships and labor marvelously . . . good-humored, faithful, and of mild disposition." Savoyard folktales ascribe the qualities bred into the people by the rigors of Alpine life to a common progenitor, Japheth, an intractable son of Noah. When the Flood began to recede, the mighty Ark came to rest upon the Dent du Nivolet and the Mont Revard, which still frown loftily above Lake Le Bourget and Chambéry. Japheth made up his mind to disembark and, despite Noah's protests, remained with his wife to people the land with a hardy race of mountaineers as stubborn as he.[7]

The capital of Savoy in the fourteenth century was Chambéry, which lies in the geographical arm of Savoy between Lake Le Bourget and Mount Granier, the culminating point in the massif of the Grande Chartreuse. Six hundred years ago, this small Alpine capital, boasting some 2,000 inhabitants, was enclosed by earthen ramparts and high stone walls pierced by nine gates, each with a drawbridge to span a moat formed by the waters of the Albane.[8] Chambéry was overshadowed by its mountain setting and almost lost to invading forests, but its location on the routes to Geneva and the Mont Cenis ensured a fairly continuous stream of both local and foreign traffic. The toll stations of Chambéry in the time of Count Aymon (1329-1343) brought in between 300 and 400 gold florins each year, and merchants from Flanders,

---

[5] Burney, I, 49–50.

[6] Cf. Raymond Rousseau, *La Population de la Savoie jusqu'en 1861* (Paris, 1960), p. 124, on population growth since the Middle Ages.

[7] Cf. Jean Portail, *Contes et Légendes de Savoie* (Paris, 1960).

[8] Timoléon Chapperon, *Chambéry à la fin du XIVe siècle* (Paris, 1893), p. 35, counts 435 *foci* in the town in 1331 and 1,440 *foci* in the castellany of Chambéry, which he estimates to mean a population of 2,175 and 7,220 respectively.

France, and the Germanies appear regularly in the *péage* rolls, along with merchants from Italy.[9] A "bonne ville et marchande" was the judgment of a Flemish traveler in 1518, and his impression was generally shared by those who have left some record of their passage through the town.[10] In addition to merchants, clerics and pilgrims over the centuries frequently made Chambéry a stopping place on the long journey to and from Rome, for writers such as Matthew Paris and Albert de Stade had placed the town on their recommended itinerary for those planning a trip to Italy.[11] For many a weary traveler who had just spent several days among "montes asperrimos" on "the worst roads that ever were since the world began," Chambéry seemed a positively beautiful place with an importance far exceeding its modest size.

THE BIRTH OF AMADEUS VI

Amadeus VI was born in the castle of Chambéry on a January night in 1334. His birth was an exceptionally important event for the dynasty of Savoy because Count Aymon was forty-three and his marriage was thus far without children. His older brother and predecessor, Count Edward, had died five years before without male heirs. Since then, only Aymon's own life had preserved the direct legitimate male line in Savoy from extinction. Had he died without a son, the disintegration of the Alpine state which he and his forebears had labored for centuries to build might very well have followed.

These Savoyard counts were not unlike the mountains they lived among: obstinate, niggardly, enduring, patient. For centuries they had been the gatekeepers of the Alps, and they had taken on something of the ruggedness of the passes they guarded. Mountain country is not easy country, either to traverse or to make a living in; the rocky pastures and forested valleys yielded but grudgingly to the axe and plow. The world, like the mountains, was often dangerous and inhospitable, but it too could be made to yield to relentless activity and endless patience. By the end of

---

[9] Cf. Léon Ménabréa, *Histoire de Chambéry* (MS dated 1846 in *ADS*), p. 153; Thérèse Sclaffert, "Comptes de péage de Montmélian 1294–1585," *Revue de Géographie Alpine*, XXI (1933), 591–605.

[10] Max Bruchet, *La Savoie d'après les anciens voyageurs* (Annecy, 1908), p. 34.

[11] Cf. Joseph Bédier, *Les Légendes épiques*, 4 vols. (Paris, 1926–1929), II, 152ff.

the thirteenth century, the princes of Savoy had brought their dynasty to the brink of greatness, but sons were required if their dreams were to be realized. Without sons to carry forward the banners of conquest and unification, the accomplishments of centuries would be lost. A daughter would not suffice, for females were excluded from the succession.

Count Aymon had not married earlier, for during the life of his older brother he had been destined for a career in the Church. The Savoyard chronicles affirm that he was at Avignon in attendance upon Pope John XXII at the time of Count Edward's unexpected death in 1329.[12] Ambassadors from Savoy had sought him out at the papal court and had begged him to be their new count. Aymon was supposedly so reluctant to abandon the joys of the spiritual estate for the hardships and vanities of the temporal that the ambassadors had recourse to the pope himself. John was implored to "have pity on the poor desolate land of Savoy," and to release Aymon from his vows. The pope was reportedly so impressed by the "grande affeccion" shown by the Savoyards for Lord Aymon that he ordered Aymon to accede to their humble petition.

Chroniclers are better romancers than historians, and their accounts are often more entertaining than accurate. Aymon had already demonstrated that his aversion for temporal affairs was not insuperable. He had commanded the war engines at the siege of Corbières in 1321, and he had ruled in person his appanage of Bresse ever since the death of his father, Amadeus V, in 1323.[13] His acknowledged paternity of half a dozen illegitimate children, while in no way rendering him a "bad man" by medieval standards, does permit some doubt as to the intensity of his spiritual vocation. Thus it was probably not with overwhelming reluctance that Aymon left the precincts of sanctity in 1329 to become the sixteenth count of Savoy. The following year he married the daughter of Marquis Teodoro I of Montferrat, whose dominions

[12] Jehan Servion, *Gestez et Croniques de la Mayson de Savoye*, ed. F-E. Bollati di Saint Pierre, 2 vols. (Turin, 1879), II, 35–38. See Commentary, I, following text, for a discussion of the chronicles of Savoy.

[13] *ADCO*, series B, Bressan castellany accounts for 1323–1329; A. C. N. *Lateyssonnière, Recherches historiques sur le département de l'Ain*, 4 vols. (1838–1843), III, 207; L. Ménabréa, "L'Organization militaire au Moyen Age," *MARS* (2nd series, I, 1851), 191.

bordered those of the house of Savoy in the Piedmont; and with energy, if not enthusiasm, he took on the "hardships and vanities" of the temporal estate.

For four years the newly married couple remained childless, however, and their anxiety increased with each year that passed. Aymon had sired strong sons before his marriage, but his youthful bride, Violante de Montferrat, seemed unable to bear children. Both the count and his wife made every effort to placate an apparently angry deity with prayers, pilgrimages, and pious works. The countess made a special journey across the mountains of Bugey to visit the shrine of the Virgin Mary in the parish church of Bourg-en-Bresse, who enjoyed a great reputation in the region for her power to make fruitful marriages. At last the countess had conceived, and the answer to the family prayers came at about midnight on 4 January, when "Madame la Comtesse fist ung biau fils."[14]

Early the next day the happy news reached the town, where the citizens in their delight rang bells and lit bonfires. A week later in the Sainte-Chapelle, which was still under construction within the castle walls, the child was baptized by the bishop of Maurienne in the presence of a great host of dignitaries. The child's name was probably chosen in honor of his illustrious grandfather, Amadeus V "the Great." Amadeus was held at the baptismal font by his youthful first cousin, Count Amadeus III of Geneva. Other cousins, including Louis II, baron of Vaud, and his family, came down from the northern shores of Lake Geneva to be present for the occasion.[15]

As soon as Violante de Montferrat was able, she crossed the mountains again to visit the Virgin of Bourg-en-Bresse, this time with gifts of thanksgiving. If she prayed for the life and health of her son and implored the favor of more children for the increase of the dynasty, her prayers again did not go unanswered. Two years later at Chambéry she had a daughter, christened Blanche, probably in honor of Blanche de Bourgogne, widow of Count Edward, who may have been living at the court of Savoy

[14] Servion, II, 43.

[15] Cf. Jean Cordey, *Les Comtes de Savoie et les Rois de France pendant la Guerre de Cent Ans* (Bibl. de l'Ecole des Hautes Etudes, fasc. 189, Paris, 1911), p. 65; also documents in Dino Muratore, "Bianca di Savoia e le sue nozze con Galeazzo II Visconti," *ASL*, VII (1907), 5ff.

at the time. Then, in 1338 at the castle of Voiron, another son, Jean, was born, to be followed during the succeeding four years by Catherine and Louis, both of whom lived only long enough to be named. Violante had given her husband two fine sons, however, and the future of the dynasty now seemed assured.

The household of the count now took on a new character, for the children were provided with servants, nurses, guardians, and masters almost at once. It was customary for the rulers of Savoy to take their illegitimate children into their households and to bring them up along with their legitimate offspring until they were old enough for independent establishments. Just how many such brothers and sisters young Amadeus grew up with is difficult to determine. The dates of their births are usually unknown, and their whereabouts are often indicated only by rare and scattered references. Two of them, Humbert and Ogier, make frequent appearances, for both served Amadeus VI in important administrative and military posts throughout their lives.[16] Of the other *illegitimati* far less is known, but some of them were clearly alive and present during the years of Amadeus' childhood. There was an illegitimate Amadeus who lived with the family and was reared with his brothers and sisters until his death in 1346.[17] In 1339-1340 there is mention of one Benoît, "bastard of the lord count," and another, Jean la Mitre, "knight and bastard of Savoy," was castellan of Tarentaise and Entremont in 1343–1345.[18] Another Jean, bastard of Savoy, was a canon in the cathedral chapter of Lausanne in 1349, and cantor in that of Geneva.[19] A daughter, Marie, was affianced in 1335 to Master André Boncristiani of Pisa, knight, a treasury officer and castellan of Rossillon

---

[16] See Commentary, II, on Humbert and Ogier de Savoie.

[17] *ADCO*, B 7345 (Bresse, judicature, 1343–1346). He was buried in the Franciscan monastery of Chambéry on 16 May 1346. *AST*, inv. 38, folio 43, doc. 2.

[18] *ADCO*, B 9592 (St.-Germain-d'Ambérieux); *AST*, inv. 38, folio 43, doc. 2; *ADS* (castellany), Montmélian, 1348; *ADS* (castellany), Le Bourget, 1347–1349. Jean was also seigneur of Cuine in the Maurienne. He died and was buried at Montmélian in 1348. He was called "La Mitre" because he was the bastard of Pierre de Savoie, archbishop of Lyon in 1307–1312 and 1322–1332. Cf. Félix Bernard, *Histoire de Montmélian* (Chambéry, 1956), p. 136, note 1.

[19] Marie-José, *La Maison de Savoie: Les Origines, Le Comte Vert, Le Comte Rouge* (Paris, 1956), genealogical table, pp. 60-61. This Jean is mentioned in Aymon's will.

in 1331-1336.[20] Two other girls, Donata and Huguette, were made nuns at Bons-en-Bugey, and there may have been a third daughter, name unknown, who married a noble of the Chablais, Louis de Lucinge.[21]

The illegitimate children were thus considered part of the family, and the family was a very important entity. Anyone with the blood of the mountain dynasty in his veins was a God-given member, regardless of the irregularities surrounding his birth. No resentment seems to have been felt by the countess toward these children, for she gave them presents and looked after their needs exactly as she did for her own offspring. Indeed, the title of "bastard of Savoy" was a source of pride, not shame, and that epithet, testifying to such illustrious paternity, was commonly employed in official documents. The counts married their bastard sons to noble heiresses and sought posts for them in the state or in the Church, as their status and opportunities allowed. When Bastard Humbert de Savoie began to have illegitimate sons of his own, they too were received as part of the family by the count and countess and were destined for military and political posts when they grew up.[22] Blood kinship was often relied upon in the mountains of Savoy to supply what underdeveloped political institutions could not: a binding sense of loyalty to the head of the family as head of the state.

## THE DYNASTY OF SAVOY

When young Amadeus first looked out upon the world, the first thing he saw was the castle of Chambéry. It was a bristle of battlements situated on a low hill overlooking the town and separated from its walls by a moat. In the shadow of the massive entrance towers stood a platform upon which malefactors were exposed to public scorn. Access to the castle was provided by a

---

[20] *Ibid.*; *ADCO*, B 9390 (Rossillon).

[21] Marie-José, *op.cit.* It was not always possible to keep track of the family bastards even in the fourteenth century. In 1352–1353 (*AST*, inv. 38, folio 21, doc. 60) a gift of two florins was made "to a certain bastard claiming to be a bastard of the [late] Count Aymon."

[22] For example, Pierre, bastard of Humbert de Savoie, was castellan of Cusy in 1345-1352. See also *ADCO*, B 7444; *ADS* (castellany), Chambéry, 1357; and *AST*, inv. 38, folio 43 (1345–1353).

ramp, which curved under two battlemented gateways and emerged upon a spacious courtyard. In the center of the courtyard, a large fountain supplied fresh spring water piped from the hills south of town in wooden conduits built by Count Edward in 1328.[23] In a small pond nearby, carp, tench, pike, and trout were kept alive until they were wanted for the count's table.

Three great towers divided the buildings grouped around the courtyard and provided vantage points from which to survey the surrounding country. At the foot of one of them, the "Great Tower," were the count's falconry, kennels for his hunting dogs, and cages for his bears, wolves, lynxes, and occasional lions.[24] The principal building of the castle stood between the Great and Prison Towers, and a staircase led from the courtyard into a large hall, the "camera paramenti" or parade hall. This hall boasted a rose window and four lattice windows, all with colored glass painted by one Master Johannet in 1302–1303. The interior was decorated with carved woodwork and paintings (probably frescoes) by Georges de Aquila, a Florentine student of Giotto who had been brought by Amadeus V to the court of Savoy, where he lived and worked until his death in 1348.[25] The windows of the hall opposite those on the court overlooked a garden, which apparently occupied a sort of terrace formed by the great earthen ramparts. Beyond the parade hall in the same building were at least two other large rooms, one called the "room of the great stove," and another that was known as "the emperor's chamber" after 1365.[26]

Another large hall and the kitchens communicated with the parade hall, and on the other side of the Great Tower were the apartments of the count and countess and living quarters for members of the household. The ceiling of the "camera domini et dominae" also was decorated by Georges de Aquila in 1315, and separate additional rooms for the count and countess were also frescoed. Near the count's chamber was a bathing room, the

[23] Descriptive details on the castle can be found in the Chambéry castellany accounts in *ADS* and in the scholarly studies of Chambéry by Chapperon and Ménabréa, previously cited.

[24] Cf. *ADS*, castellany accounts for 1340, 1353.

[25] Chapperon, pp. 98–99; Ménabréa, *Chambéry*, p. 362.

[26] Probably because Emperor Charles IV was lodged there during his visit in 1365.

"camera balnearum." Elsewhere in the castle was a private chapel for the family and accommodations reserved for familiars of the count and officers of state.

From the very first, young Amadeus had to learn to travel, for in his lifetime he would be obliged to ride literally thousands of miles on horseback. Within a few weeks of his birth, he was placed in the care of his nurse and taken to the castle of Le Bourget near the lake, where the road from the valley of Chambéry begins to climb the Mont du Chat. Like most ruling families of the Middle Ages, the count and countess moved constantly from castle to castle, accompanied by their entire households. Political reasons required such continuous traveling of the count, but economic considerations were also important. The great quantities of foodstuffs owed annually by the peasants of the count's scattered estates posed serious problems of transportation. These could be solved in part by visiting the estates with some regularity, so that the produce could be consumed on the premises.

The political advantage of this constant movement was that the count could oversee in person the administration of his properties, enquire into the conduct of his officers, and make certain that his rights were respected. The journeys also permitted the common folk of the various regions to see the ruler and his family and to develop a personal basis for loyalty to their "natural seigneur," who thus demonstrated knowledge of and concern for their grievances. The castellany accounts abound with examples of the count's personal intervention, whether in the correction of his officers, in the remission of dues in a disaster area, or in the granting of pardons to those condemned for some infraction of the laws. This direct personal contact between the count and his subjects helped to foster mutual respect and gave a kind of unity to the mosaic of Alpine baronies under Savoyard rule.

The origins of the house of Savoy and of Savoyard domination in the Western Alps are shrouded in legend and scholarly speculation. The masters who made Amadeus conscious of his lineage may have begun, as Savoyard chroniclers sometimes do, with the year 242 A.D., when supposedly there lived a Pope "Fabien XIX," an Emperor "Giordain," and a king of Cologne named Ezeus. Ezeus was described as a "moult grand signieur" who held sway over "the Rhine and Saxony and as far as the sea of Flanders."[27] He and his wife, "Helayne," had a son named Theseus, who was born a hunchback but was miraculously made straight by the Virgin Mary when he was fifteen. After many extraordinary adventures, Theseus won the hand of the Emperor Giordain's daughter and succeeded to the throne of Saxony. Servion, and perhaps Amadeus' masters, implied that King Theseus was the progenitor both of the dynasty of Saxon Holy Roman Emperors and of the house of Savoy. One Berauld of Saxony, a warrior hero in the best chivalric tradition who settled in Savoy, was identified as a nephew of Emperor Otto III. Berauld joined with the king of Arles and, on behalf of his suzerain, swept outlaws and invaders from the Alps and brought the inhabitants under his sway.

Thus far, storytellers at the court of Savoy would have had the tale all to themselves, unhampered by historical facts. Only with the son of Berauld, Humbert I "Whitehands," would they enter at last the realm of historically identifiable characters. Even Humbert Whitehands and his career are sometimes barely visible through the controversy which surrounds the handful of documents concerning him, but at least it is certain that he existed and was active during the second quarter of the eleventh century.[28] It is also certain that he held extensive lands and jurisdiction in the kingdom of transjurane Burgundy, one of the fragments into which the Carolingian Empire had disintegrated by the end of the ninth century. By the early eleventh century, the kingdom of Burgundy was itself disintegrating, and Humbert Whitehands (whose sobriquet remains a mystery) was a prominent supporter of the Burgundian monarchy. His loyalty to Rudolf III, the last king of an independent Burgundy, was one key to his success, and his support of Rudolf's successor, Emperor Conrad II, after 1032, was another.

Just how and when Humbert acquired his Alpine valleys, and from whom, remain open questions. It is clear that during the last decade of Rudolf's reign (993–1032) "Humbertus Comes" was busily extending his holdings in the region south and west of Geneva. He held the counties of Belley and Aosta and was probably ruler of Savoy, although it may not have been important

[27] Servion, I, 9ff.

[28] C. W. Previté Orton, *The Early History of the House of Savoy* (Cambridge, 1912), p. 21. For a thorough discussion of the problem of the origins of the house of Savoy, the reader is referred to this excellent study.

enough at this time to form a county by itself.[29] Members of Humbert's family in episcopal sees at Lyon, Belley, Sion, Aosta, and perhaps elsewhere were often in a position to further the interests of the dynasty. Humbert's alliance with Conrad II, who wanted the Great St. Bernard route in friendly hands, seems to have led to the family acquisition of the great abbey of St-Maurice-d'Agaune, along with extensive jurisdiction over the Chablais. With kinsmen holding the sees of Sion and Aosta, Humbert Whitehands thus controlled both approaches to the Great St. Bernard, as well as the northern approach to the Simplon pass. Acquisition of the county of Maurienne may also belong to this period, and when a fortunate marriage alliance subsequently added the marquisate of Susa, the family's domination of the Mont Cenis route was assured on both sides of the Alps.

To the young Amadeus, Humbert Whitehands would have been known, however vaguely, as a great warrior, the founder of the family's transalpine state. More specific lessons in state-building might have been found in the career of a more recent ancestor, Pierre II, the "Little Charlemagne," who died in 1268. The Savoyard chroniclers devote far more space to Pierre than to Humbert Whitehands, and it is reasonable to suppose that much of the fact and fiction they record was already repeated at the court of Savoy in the time of Count Aymon. Pierre was the sixth of eight sons, and his prospects for more than a very modest inheritance were fairly remote. He was accordingly destined for a career in the Church, beginning as a canon of the cathedral of Lausanne and provost at Aosta and Geneva. He became administrator of the church of Lausanne and seemed likely to be its next bishop by the time of his father's death. No sooner was his father dead, however, than Pierre put aside his clerical garb and set about to make up for so slender a share of the paternal heritage.

In 1234, Pierre married the sole heiress of Aymon II, baron of Faucigny, whose dominions comprised the watershed of the Arve from the shores of Lake Geneva to the slopes of the Mont Blanc.

---

[29] *Ibid.*, p. 100. The title of "count of Savoy" does not clearly supersede that of "count of Maurienne" until after the reign of Count Thomas (1189–1233). Cf. pp. 421–422. A county of "Saboia" is mentioned as early as 806 in Charlemagne's division of his inheritance at Thionville. Cf. Francesco Cognasso, *Umberto Biancamano* (Turin, 1937), p. 13.

Having acquired this strong territorial base, Pierre energetically set out to create a principality for himself in the Pays de Vaud, the Chablais, and the Valais. It was he, rather than his less vigorous older brother, Count Amadeus IV, who established Savoyard influence in the city of Geneva, who built the famous castle in the lake at Chillon, and who extended his rule over the peoples of the upper Rhône valley as far as Sion. By 1253, Pierre had acquired most of the Pays de Vaud, from the northern shores of Lake Geneva to Morat and Lake Neuchâtel, and had made himself protector of the city of Bern. He is then supposed to have appeared before the emperor to do homage for his lands wearing a garment part silk and part chain mail and, thus prepared for either peace or war, declared that his title was and would remain his sword.

In Savoyard tradition Pierre II is above all the mighty warrior, but he was much more than that. His niece, Eléonore de Provence, was queen of England; and her sister Marguerite, queen of France.[30] Pierre's English connections and the esteem in which he was held by Henry III furnished him with men and money when he needed them most. But he seems to have brought more than just men and money back to the Alps; he also brought ideas. He introduced a new type of castle architecture (featuring the large circular donjon) in the Pays de Vaud and the Valais.[31] And when, on the death of his nephew in 1263, he became count of Savoy, he introduced administrative reforms as well. He divided the territories of Savoy into bailliages made up of castellanies, which were jurisdictional units centering on castles directly under control of the count. The *baillis* and castellans were accountable only to him in military and political matters and to a new *chambre des comptes* at Chambéry in financial matters.[32] In 1264 or 1265, Pierre issued the earliest of Savoyard comital statutes, an attempt to do in the realm of justice what he had already done

---

[30] There were four sisters, daughters of Béatrice de Savoie, wife of Count Raymond-Berengar of Provence, who married two pairs of brothers: Henry III and Richard of Cornwall, elected king of the Romans in 1256; and Louis IX and Charles of Anjou, who became king of Sicily in 1266.

[31] Cf. Louis Blondel, "L'Architecture militaire au temps de Pierre II de Savoie," *Genava*, XIII (1935), 271–321.

[32] Cf. Laurent Chevailler, *Recherches sur la Réception du Droit romain en Savoie des Origines à 1789* (Annecy, 1953).

in finance and administration toward the creation of centralized government for his widespread dominions. If Humbert White-hands had laid the territorial bases upon which his successors would build, Pierre II laid the foundation for the government and defense of those territories.

The peak of territorial expansion achieved under the "Little Charlemagne" could not be maintained. Pierre's only child was Béatrice, who inherited the barony of Faucigny from her mother and transmitted it to the descendants of her husband, the dauphin of Viennois, a dangerous rival of the Savoyards. Efforts to recover the barony were unsuccessful, and the dauphins thereafter had a foothold in the very heart of the Savoyard Alps. Other setbacks followed the death of Pierre's successor, Philippe, in 1285. Philippe was succeeded by his nephew, Amadeus V (1285–1323), who found himself opposed by both his brother Louis and his nephew Filippo,[33] count of Piedmont. Filippo had claims of his own to the succession in Savoy, and Amadeus secured the grudging withdrawal of those claims only by allowing his nephew virtual independence in the Piedmont. As for brother Louis, he was equally annoyed with the succession arrangement and utilized the weakness of Amadeus' position to secure a generous appanage. Amadeus was forced to enfeoff Louis with nearly all the territories acquired by Pierre II in the Pays de Vaud. Thus, by the time of Count Aymon, two considerable regions, Piedmont and the Pays de Vaud, were in the hands of cadet branches of the house of Savoy. Although both cadets were held to the senior line by the strictest bonds which kinship and honor could impose, both remained in a position to create separate states of their own.

On his own account, Amadeus V was able to make up for some of the losses of the previous half-century. The land of Bresse and adjoining castellanies in the Revermont were obtained by marriage and war, and footholds across the Alps in the Val d'Aosta and Canavese were strengthened and multiplied. For his assistance to Emperor Henry VII, whose wife's sister, Marie of Brabant,

[33] Hereafter, the Italian form will be used for the names of the Savoy-Piedmont line, in order to distinguish them the more readily and to emphasize the Italian orientation of that part of the Savoyard holdings. After Filippo's marriage to Isabelle de Villehardouin in 1301, he and his successors always styled themselves "princes of Achaea" in cognizance of Isabelle's claim to that principality in Greece.

was Amadeus' second wife, the count received the county of Asti,[34] although he never succeeded in making good his claims. It was rather the scope of his activities and the grandeur of his ambitions that earned Amadeus V the sobriquet of "Great" in the chronicles of Savoy. In 1310, Chablais and Aosta were raised to the rank of duchies; in 1311, Henry VII made Amadeus V his vicar-general in Lombardy and confirmed his official status as a prince of the Empire.[35] This dignity strengthened the count's position in relation to neighbors and rivals by placing him under the direct authority of the emperor. The career of Amadeus V was a sort of blueprint which his dynasty, and particularly his grandson, would follow long after he was gone. Both his expansionist policies in Italy and the great web of international alliances created by his enterprising marriage diplomacy drew his successors irresistably toward goals which he envisioned but could not fully attain.

Intermarriage with powerful European families had always been important for Savoyard prestige and dynastic ambitions, and young Amadeus VI had an army of relatives that bore comparison with any dynasty of the times. Amadeus' great-great-grandfather was also the great-great-grandfather of Edward III of England, of Robert of Naples, and of Marguerite de Valois, mother of Philippe VI of France. The more recent marriages of Amadeus' uncle and eight aunts, the children of Amadeus V, had created more immediate ties. Edward had married the sister of Eudes IV of Burgundy, and the only child of this marriage was Jeanne, wife of Jean III of Brittany. Marie was wed to Hugues de Viennois, baron of Faucigny and brother of the dauphin, probably with the hope of recovering the long-lost barony of Faucigny through inheritance. Agnes became countess of Geneva and mother of the present Count Amadeus III, Eléonore married Guillaume de Châlon and became countess of Auxerre, while Bonne married a brother of Othon IV, count-

---

[34] Cf. W. M. Bowsky, *Henry VII in Italy* (Lincoln, 1960), p. 196.

[35] The 1310 text is in Samuel Guichenon, *Histoire généalogique de la Maison royale de Savoie* (Lyon, 1660), III, *preuves*, 137–139; Bowsky, p. 94; Giovanni Tabacco, *Lo Stato Sabaudo nel Sacro Romano Impero* (Turin, 1939), Chapter III. The oft-repeated assertion that Emperor Frederick II made the Chablais into a duchy in favor of Amadeus IV in 1238 is without documentary foundation.

palatine of Burgundy.[36] The other four aunts of Amadeus VI were bestowed upon more distant and illustrious princes: Marguerite was wed to the marquis of Montferrat; Catherine to Leopold of Habsburg, landgrave of Alsace; Beatrice to Leopold's brother Henry, duke of Carinthia; and Jeanne to Andronicus III Paleologus, emperor of Byzantium.[37]

These far-flung dynastic ties would one day be as important to Amadeus VI as the similar ties closer to home. In addition to affecting foreign policy, such relationships also formed part of the internal fabric of the Savoyard state. Cousin Filippo, lord of the Piedmont and titular prince of Achaea, died the year of Amadeus' birth, but he left a numerous progeny on both sides of the Alps. The eldest son, Giacomo, succeeded to his father's titles, while three of his four brothers went into the Church, where they would one day be extremely useful to Amadeus VI as bishops of Maurienne, Turin, Belley, Sion, and Tarentaise. Two of Giacomo's sisters married barons of the Maurienne, thus bringing a pair of potentially dangerous magnates into the dynastic fold.[38] Two other sisters were wed to powerful nobles on the western frontiers of Savoy, Humbert of Thoire-Villars and Amadeus de Poitiers, sire of St-Vallier on the Rhône. A fifth sister married Manfredo di Saluzzo-Cardé, a younger son of the marquis of Saluzzo, whose family had often been rivals of the house of Savoy in the Piedmont. This was another match designed to accomplish by marriage what could not be accomplished by war.

### SAVOY AND THE DAUPHINÉ, 1333–1342

The early years of Count Aymon's reign were chiefly occupied by the wars with Guigues VIII, dauphin of Viennois, which Ay-

---

[36] Cf. Marie-José, pp. 60-61. Eléonore successively married Dreux de Mello and Jean, count of Forez.

[37] Violante de Montferrat was the granddaughter of Marguerite de Savoie's husband's sister, Violante, empress of Byzantium. Cf. *ibid.*, pp. 220–221. Leopold and Henry of Habsburg were younger brothers of Frederick the Handsome, duke of Austria. Cf. marriage treaties in Guichenon, IV, *preuves*, 158–160. No sons resulted from the Habsburg marriages, but one of Catherine's daughters married Enguerrand de Coucy and her famous warrior son, Enguerrand VII, later fought for Amadeus VI in Italy. Jeanne de Savoie, empress of Byzantium, was called Anna by the Greeks. She died in 1360. Cf. George Ostrogorsky, *History of the Byzantine State* (New Brunswick, 1957), p. 515.

[38] They were Antelme de Miolans, sire of Urtières, and Jean de la Chambre, viscount of Maurienne.

mon had inherited from his father and brother. Philippe VI of France, who was as eager as his predecessors to extend French influence and control in the kingdom of Arles, had attempted to mediate between the count and the dauphin on several occasions.[39] The king's efforts were not notably successful until 1333 when Guigues VIII was killed during the siege of the Savoyard castle of La Perrière. In 1334, Aymon and the successor of Guigues VIII, Humbert II, agreed upon a treaty which at least provided for a peace based upon the maintenance of the status quo, although it did nothing to resolve the frontier questions that lay at the base of relations between Savoy and the Dauphiné. The treaty of 1334 served the purpose of peace chiefly because the attention of both parties was preempted over succeeding years by the activities of the arbiter, the king of France.

The designs of the French monarchy to expand into the territories of the Holy Roman Empire were nothing new. For at least a century, as the power and prestige of the emperors declined, French interference beyond the Saône-Rhône frontier had steadily increased in the county of Burgundy, in the Dauphiné, in Provence. For nearly half a century following the Savoyard acquisition of Bresse, the count's castellans there had been forced to battle ceaselessly against the encroachments of the French royal *baillis* of Mâcon.[40] More dangerous still, the French kings had on several occasions been on the verge of securing, from emperors too weak to resist, the grant of regalian powers over the entire kingdom of Arles. This kingdom had been little more than a geographical expression for more than a century, but it theoretically comprised both Savoy and the Dauphiné. If the French king ob-

[39] The kingdom of Arles was the name traditionally applied to the part of the Holy Roman Empire bounded roughly by the Saône, the Rhône, the Alps, and the Mediterranean (that is, including the county of Burgundy, the dominions of the count of Savoy west of the Alps, the Dauphiné, and Provence). The Holy Roman Emperors theoretically ruled the kingdom of Arles (or Arles-Vienne), but in reality their power there had been purely nominal for centuries. Cf. Paul Fournier, *Le Royaume d'Arles et de Vienne 1138–1378* (Paris, 1891).

[40] For examples, *ADCO*, B 6740 (Bâgé, 1294); B 7337 (Bresse, 1309): "librata de mandata domini Edouardi in expensis commissarum regis Franciae missis ad requisitionem domini comitis apud Matisconem pro negotiis . . . non edificii facienda juxta turrim pontis"; Bâgé, *liasse*, B 564, paq. 8, doc. 21 (1345); Mâcon, B 654, paq. 15, docs. 3–6.

tained the right to exercise royal power in the kingdom of Arles, the semi-independence of all of the principalities which composed that kingdom would be very seriously threatened.

In 1333 the princes of the kingdom of Arles had been startled by just such a project. It was apparently conceived by Pope John XXII, who, by establishing the seat of the papacy at Avignon, had become a prince of the kingdom of Arles himself. For many years, John XXII had been engaged in a struggle to humble or depose the emperor, Louis IV of Bavaria. In fact, if not in theory, the scheme which the pope evolved in 1333 would have delivered into the hands of the pope's protector and ally, the king of France, the bishopric of Cambrai and the territories "bounded by the Rhône, the Saône, the Alps, Lombardy, and the sea"—in other words, the kingdom of Arles, including the possessions of the house of Savoy.[41]

Fortunately, there were others more influential than the count of Savoy who were as disturbed as he by this proposal. Among them was Robert d'Anjou, king of Naples, who was French in blood but not sufficiently French in sentiment to sacrifice his own interests as count of Provence to those of his Valois cousins. The regional opposition to the pope's scheme reinforced the hand of opponents of the project at the court of Louis IV, who had at first accepted it as the price of peace with the papacy. In July 1334 the emperor withdrew his support, and when John XXII died some months later, the whole scheme died with him.

The pro-French project for annexing the kingdom of Arles was soon followed by an imperial project equally dangerous in the eyes of the count of Savoy. The emperor was unable to exercise any real authority in the kingdom of Arles, but the plan of 1333 awakened him to the need for some kind of defensive measures against the expansionist designs of the French king. Louis IV decided that his best move would be to resurrect the royal title of the kingdom of Arles and to bestow it upon a candidate of his own choosing. The moment seemed propitious, for the French scheme had just failed, and Louis's archenemy, John XXII, was dead. Moreover, the pro-French dauphin of Viennois, Guigues VIII, had just been replaced by Humbert II, who had lived for some years at the court of Naples.[42] Louis IV apparently

[41] Details in Fournier, pp. 391–399.
[42] Guigues VIII had married Isabelle de France, daughter of Philippe V.

hoped that the new dauphin shared the Angevin distrust of the French, for the emperor now offered to make Humbert II king of Arles.

Such an offer could not fail to alarm the count of Savoy. The dauphins were hereditary enemies of the house of Savoy, and all-too-recent events had strengthened that enmity. Only nine years before, at the battle of Varey, the Savoyards had been disastrously defeated at the hands of the dauphin, and Count Edward had barely escaped with his life. A Savoyard had shot the crossbow bolt that struck and killed Guigues VIII in 1333. Any royal title endowing a dauphin of Viennois with regalian rights over the possessions of the count of Savoy would mean an immediate revival of the bloody wars of the past century.

Everything depended upon the character of the new dauphin. Although Humbert was less warlike than his brother had been, he was nevertheless proud and unpredictable. During his youth he rather fancied himself destined for a life of ease and comfort, for the affairs of the Dauphiné were in the capable hands of his energetic older brother. Humbert had been given the barony of Faucigny in the mountains of Savoy as an appanage, but he had preferred to leave it to his officers while he sojourned in the gentler climate of Naples. Robert d'Anjou was Humbert's uncle, and he welcomed the young man at his rich and cultivated court. The king secured for the future dauphin the hand of one of the royal nieces, Marie de Baux, and not long after the marriage settled upon him a handsome annual pension.[43]

The unexpected death of Guigues VIII without heirs suddenly altered Humbert's prospects for a comfortable and carefree existence and inaugurated a new era of tension and uncertainty in the kingdom of Arles. The new dauphin had no sooner arrived than he encountered the emperor's proposal, with all of its vast implications for himself and his dynasty. There is little doubt that Humbert was tempted to accept. Royal rank suited his notions even better than the princely dignity to which he had succeeded, and as a devoted friend of the Angevins, he probably did oppose the further extension of French influence beyond the

---

[43] Fournier, p. 408, note 1. J. J. Guiffrey, *Histoire de la Réunion du Dauphiné à la France* (Paris, 1868), contains more than one hundred pages of documents from which both the course of events and the personality of the dauphin can be studied.

Rhône. But Humbert was not a bold man, and he did not feel able to accept the opportunity which Louis IV was offering him. With his own authority not yet firmly established in the Dauphiné, Humbert did not care to provoke the wrath of the French king, antagonize his own neighbors, and offend the new pope, who had not yet freed the emperor from the sentence of excommunication laid upon him by John XXII. The dauphin seized upon this fact as a pretext and replied that he could not consider the emperor's proposal until Louis IV had made his peace with the Church.

The next eight years were characterized by increasing French pressure on the dauphin, who became increasingly indecisive. At first Humbert followed the example of his late brother and the count of Savoy in an effort to convince the French that their interests would be better served by making an ally, rather than an enemy, of him. The dauphin went to Paris in the summer of 1335 with the object of settling peaceably a dispute over the frontier town of Sainte-Colombe on the Rhône. The matter was settled peaceably, but in a manner which indicated all too clearly the course of future events. Humbert lost Sainte-Colombe in exchange for a large annual pension on the royal treasury. Since the dauphin had never been able to live within his means, Philippe VI thereby increased Humbert's dependence upon the French perhaps more than either of them realized at the time. In August 1335 the bonds were made stronger by the betrothal of Humbert's two-year-old son, André, to a princess of the royal house, the daughter of the king of Navarre. At the same time, the dauphin renewed his homage to the king for fiefs in Normandy and Auvergne and induced Philippe VI to grant him his late brother's Paris hotel on the Place de Grève. But the era of good feeling between Humbert and the French was short-lived. In 1336 the hopes for a marriage alliance were lost with the death of the infant André, and soon frontier quarrels with the French drove the dauphin back to his former attitude of hostility.

At this point the attention of the French king was diverted from his eastern neighbors by the steady deterioration of relations with the English. The various causes of the Hundred Years War need not detain us here; suffice it to say that by the spring of 1337 both Philippe VI and Edward III were recruiting supporters among neighboring princes.[44] As early as August 1334, English ambassadors had come to Savoy in an effort to persuade the count that his duty lay on the English side in the impending conflict. Aymon was reminded of the close relations formerly existing between Savoy and the Plantagenets in the time of Henry III, and of the count's kinship with Edward III. Certain English fiefs once held by Aymon's forebears were promised to him now, arrears and all, if he would do homage and join the English cause.[45] Aymon remained noncommittal at the time, and in early April 1337, messengers arrived from Paris with letters requesting him to honor his obligations as a vassal of the French crown.[46]

Typically, the count of Savoy decided to take advantage of the situation. He replied to the king's envoys that he could not leave his dominions because of a quarrel with the dauphin over frontier jurisdictions. Philippe VI hastened to assure the count that the matter would be arranged to his satisfaction, and royal emissaries were dispatched at once to pacify the disputes.[47] In May the French king declared Edward III of England a contumacious vassal and decreed the confiscation of Gascony. Almost without delay hostilities began on the northern frontiers of Aquitaine, and the French fleet made an attack on the island of Jersey. Neither side was able to sustain a full-fledged campaign at this point, but the "Hundred Years War" had begun.

The outbreak of war between France and England initiated a new era in the relations between France and the princes of the Rhône valley. The Valois never abandoned their expansionist ambitions, but they were forced to change tactics. Philippe VI's need for allies against the English naturally made him careful not to offend those with armies and influence on his eastern boundaries. The destiny of both Savoy and the Dauphiné was significantly affected by French involvement in the Hundred Years War, but with completely opposite results. For the Savo-

[44] For a full account of the events leading to the Hundred Years War, see Edouard Perroy, *The Hundred Years War* (Bloomington, 1959).

[45] Cordey, *Les Comtes*, p. 40.

[46] Since the time of Amadeus V, the counts of Savoy held the viscounty of Maulevrier in Normandy as a fief of the French crown.

[47] Beaujeu was the present bone of contention. The sire of Beaujeu was a vassal of both Savoy and the Dauphiné for territories lying on the imperial side of the Saône. Disagreements as to who owed whom homage for what were frequent causes of hostilities among all three.

yards, alliance with the French meant enhanced prestige and a more prominent role on the international scene; for the Dauphinois, the French alliance meant the gradual loss of their independence.

Once peace with the dauphin had been established through the French king's good offices in 1337, the count of Savoy proved a loyal ally. In August 1339, Aymon made his first appearance in France with a sizeable company of Savoyards, and during the three years which followed, he frequently participated in the campaigns which Philippe VI organized against the English. The dauphin's attitude toward the French, however, was somewhat equivocal. Humbert was in no mood to comply with the letters requesting his appearance with troops for Philippe's campaign in 1337, particularly when, in July of the same year, letters came from the emperor ordering the dauphin to support Edward III. To ignore these demands for long was impossible, even for one so practiced in the arts of procrastination, but early in 1337, Humbert appears to have conceived a wholly new plan of action which would free him forever from political opponents and creditors. He had resolved to sell his principality, and he had approached Robert of Naples as a possible purchaser.

This was an extraordinary resolution, but Humbert II was an extraordinary personality. The death of his only child in 1336 and his apparent decision to have no others (he was only thirty-five) removed the most important reason for remaining in a position which he had come to despise. He declared himself weary of worldly ambitions and professed religious sentiments that justified his distaste for public affairs. Humbert's piety was probably real enough, and his display of it reflects in a curious way the spread of religious reform ideas among laymen disgusted with the worldliness and corruption of the Church, and particularly of the papacy, in the fourteenth century. But is is difficult to believe that in Humbert's case "religious vocation" was more than a respectable pretext for abandoning his temporal responsibilities. Certainly he was no believer in a return to apostolic poverty, as were many of the truly reform-minded groups active at the time. The terms which Humbert proposed to Robert of Naples included elaborate provisions to ensure that the remainder of the dauphin's life would be comfortable and carefree.

In Robert's eyes these provisions were too elaborate. After much wavering, the king decided that the sale price was too high, especially since Humbert also demanded an annual pension of 3,000 florins for life, a castle in Provence, and the right to make whatever bequests he chose in his will, provided that he did not divide the principality or alienate the rights pertaining to it.[48] Robert of Naples has been bequeathed to posterity with the sobriquet "the Wise," but it is difficult to see much wisdom in his refusal of this offer. It was the perfect opportunity to thwart his French cousins and, by annexing the Dauphiné to his county of Provence, to lay the foundations for a new Angevin empire in the Rhône valley. But Robert proved penny-wise and pound-foolish: he offered 100,000 florins and objected to Humbert's fringe benefits. The dauphin was predictably offended, and negotiations were sharply broken off.

Between 1337 and 1342, Humbert made various halfhearted attempts to fight off French encroachments along the Rhône frontier, while Philippe VI busily drew increasing numbers of Dauphinois nobles into his service. With pensions and fiefs he created a great web of vassalage from which even the dauphin would find it hard to extricate himself.[49] Finally, in 1342, Humbert made another attempt to sell his principality, this time to the pope. But Benedict XII died in April, and on 7 May he was succeeded by Pierre Roger, former archbishop of Rouen. Roger, who took the title of Clement VI, was wholly devoted to the interests of the French monarchy in the Dauphiné affair. With papal blessings, French agents labored to persuade the dauphin that there was only one buyer able to satisfy all of his requirements—the king of France. Humbert at last agreed, and in January 1343 the first of three treaties regulating the "transport" of the Dauphiné to France was drafted. On 10 January 1343, Robert of Naples, the other possible buyer, died, leaving a daughter preoccupied with other problems. For Humbert there was no turning back now.

### THE DEATH OF COUNT AYMON

How much the count of Savoy knew about the negotiations concerning the Dauphiné is not certain, but the frequency of Ay-

---

[48] Cf. Fournier, pp. 422–423, for details. The proposed sale price was 120,000 florins.

[49] Cf. Guiffrey, p. 19ff.

mon's contacts with the principal figures involved in the project between 1340 and 1342 makes it extremely probable that he knew what was afoot even if he did not know the details.[50] The acquisition of so important a principality as the Dauphiné by so formidable a neighbor as the king of France could hardly have been a pleasant prospect for the count of Savoy. The Savoyard bailliage of Viennois lay in the very heart of the Dauphiné,[51] just as the dauphin's barony of Faucigny lay in the heart of transalpine Savoy. It was one thing to dispute border territories with Guigues VIII and Humbert II, and quite another to do so with a dauphin of the royal house of France. The Savoyards had no illusions about the territorial appetite of the French Goliath.[52]

Time did not allow Count Aymon the opportunity to react to developments in the Dauphiné. In June 1342 he went to France in response to Philippe VI's summons for a muster at Arras, but later in the summer the count received news that all was not well in Savoy. Violante was seriously ill, and Aymon decided to return to his Alps. By early November he was back in his territories where he spent a sorrowful winter with his family. All attempts to restore the countess' health were in vain, and on the day before Christmas 1342, Violante died in childbirth, losing the child as well. She was scarcely thirty years old at the time of her death. The countess was buried in a small chapel which she had had built for that purpose in the abbey of Hautecombe, perched on the rocks above the dark waters of Lake Le Bourget.

Count Aymon himself survived his young wife by only a few months. In February 1343 he was absorbed in frontier disputes with the dauphin; in May he was at St-Georges-d'Esperanche, a few miles east of Vienne in the Dauphiné, probably in order to follow more closely the progress of the all-important negotiations going on not far to the south. His health now began to fail, however, and on 11 June he made up his last will and testament in the *maison-forte* of Pierre Mareschal at "Crestum" near Mont-

[50] Aymon joined the French host at the siege of Tournai in the summer of 1340, and in 1342, when Jean of Normandy was en route to Avignon, Aymon accompanied him for at least part of the way. Cf. *AST*, inv. 38, folio 21, doc. 48.

[51] See Commentary, III, on the bailliages of Savoy.

[52] *ADCO*, B 6765 (Bâgé, 1342–1343), for example, records the expenses of men-at-arms sent "to destroy the constructions built by the *gentes regis Franciae* on the bridge at Mâcon."

mélian. Scarcely two weeks later, on 22 June, the count died at the castle of Rossillon in Bugey at the age of fifty-one.[53] His body was taken to the Sainte-Chapelle at Chambéry and placed in a coffin covered with cloth-of-gold and black taffeta. There it remained for three days and three nights, so that his family and subjects might pay their last respects during the day, and during the night the Franciscans might offer prayers for his soul. On the fourth day, amid a great crowd of mourners, a funeral cortege bore the count's body down across the castle drawbridge, through the town, and northward along the road to the shores of Le Bourget. From there it was carried in a black-draped barge across the waters and laid to rest beside that of Violante in the burial vault of the abbey of Hautecombe.

[53] For the place and date of Aymon's death, which are repeatedly misrepresented, see *ADCO*, B 6766 (Bâgé, 1343–1344), and *AST*, inv. 38, folio 1 (1343). Details of the funeral are in *AST*, *ibid.*

# Ⅱ

# The Regency

## 1343-1348

### THE REGENTS AND THE COUNCIL OF SAVOY

THREE small children—Jean, Blanche, and Amadeus, aged five, seven, and nine respectively—accompanied the casket draped in black and gold to its final resting place in the abbey chapel, then returned to the castle of Chambéry. On the very day of Aymon's funeral, young Amadeus was seated upon a tall wooden *fauteuil* in the great hall of the castle to receive the homage of his late father's vassals. The ring of Saint Maurice, patron saint of the house of Savoy, was placed upon the boy's finger.[1] Then he was solemnly proclaimed Amadeus VI, count of Savoy, duke of Chablais and Aosta, lord of Bâgé and Coligny, and marquis in Italy. Amadeus' two cousins, Amadeus III of Geneva and Baron Louis II of Vaud, had been designated by Aymon's will as regents during his minority. They were the first of those present to kneel at the boy's feet, place their hands in his, and swear to be loyal and faithful "against all who may live or die," so long as both shall live. The regents were followed by Edward of Beaujeu, Hugard of Gex, Humbert de Savoie, and twenty-eight other knights and barons from the neighboring region. Over the next year, hundreds of vassals from the Pays de Vaud, the Viennois and Bresse, the

---

[1] Cf. *Cronica latina Sabaudiae* in *MHP*, III, and "Scriptores," I (Turin, 1840), col. 610; Servion, I, 267-268. Tradition identified Saint Maurice as the leader of a Christian legion in the Roman army, the "Theban Legion," which had distinguished itself in many campaigns. Maurice and his men were supposedly massacred at the order of a brutal pagan general in the third century for refusing to abandon their faith and salute the deities of Rome. According to the chroniclers, Count Pierre II, before his accession to the throne of Savoy, was the first to commend himself and his family to the protection of Saint Maurice and to take his ring as the symbol of sovereignty in the dynasty.

Tarentaise and Maurienne, and from distant Italy, would do homage and take the oath of fidelity to Amadeus, sixth of the name and seventeenth count in Savoy, to borrow the phraseology —if not the numbering—in the chronicles.[2]

While apartments in the castle of Chambéry were being prepared for the count of Geneva and the baron of Vaud, the two regents came to an agreement regulating their joint conduct of affairs.[3] The agreement is recorded in a document which not only reflects the administrative structure of the Savoyard state, but which also reveals overtones of mutual suspicion brought to the fore by the count's minority. The regents decided that neither one of them would issue commands except with the concurrence of the other, or of his duly authorized representative. No change of "Baillif, juge, chastelain ne procurour" could take place except by joint action. Neither regent might receive on his own the homage of "nobles homes," bestow or alienate noble fiefs valued at 100 *livres viennois* or more, alienate any jurisdiction, adjudicate jurisdictional disputes, or "compose" any serious crime. The *censae* owed by the Jews and Lombards were to remain untouched, and the movable property of Monseigneur was to be "preserved" (no doubt from being pawned to Jews and Lombards). The possessions of deceased usurers were to be confiscated without composition, as provided by law, unless valued at less than 100 *livres viennois.*[4]

These and other clauses concerning administrative policies were followed by regulations of procedure. Everything was to be put in written form so that it might be subject to review, not only by the other regent, but also by a council which met regularly. Each regent was to have with him at all times a "clerc bon et souffisant," chosen from among the secretaries of Monseigneur.

[2] Servion, II, 67, calls him "Ame V et conte XIIIᵉ en Savoye." If Previté Orton's genealogy is correct in listing a Count Oddo II (*op.cit.*, end chart), then Amadeus VI would be the eighteenth count. Since Previté Orton was in doubt on this, I have followed the more recent genealogy given in Marie-José, pp. 36–37, 60–61.

[3] Text in Cordey, *Les Comtes, pièces justificatives*, doc. 22.

[4] "Composition" refers to the *banna concordata*, in which the offender was permitted to avoid the usual penalties for his offense by paying a sum of money agreed upon between him and the count's representatives sitting in judgment upon him. This was a widespread practice in Savoy.

These clerks were to draw up all letters "perpetuax et temporax" concerning business transacted, and to make a register of them to be submitted to the council whenever a "parlement" was held.[5] If the secretary entertained doubts about any of the business transactions, he was to consult the chancellor of Monseigneur, a member of the council, or the other regent or his representative. The regents were permitted to retain the emoluments arising from the discharge of their administrative and judicial duties, but all such revenues and perquisites ("druelies") had to be recorded by the secretaries and divided evenly, with one-half going to the two regents and the remainder to the members of the council. The regents, when traveling on the count's business, were permitted to stay at the count's castles; and the expenses of themselves and a retinue of not more than eighteen horses would be defrayed by the castellan. If this income proved insufficient to maintain the regents in their dignity, the deficiency would be made good by the count's treasury upon petition to the council.

The council of Savoy which exercised so much authority along with the regents was the *curia* of the late count, expanded for purposes of the regency to include major personages from all of the Savoyard territories. Since the late thirteenth century, part of the count's *curia*, the group of counselors who followed him wherever he went, had been detached to form a resident council at Chambéry.[6] This body gradually subdivided in turn, according to its different functions. One became a *chambre des comptes* to receive the count's moneys and to audit the annual accounts, while another concerned itself chiefly with judicial matters and acted as a kind of supreme court of appeals.[7] This latter body was the council of Savoy, or *conseil résident*, which served as the nucleus for the council of regency instituted by Count Aymon's will.

The regency council included representatives from the various

---

[5] Cordey, *Les Comtes*, p. 301. The clerk's registers were to be presented "au temps du parlement."

[6] Cf. Etienne Dullin, *Les Châtelains dans les domaines de la Maison de Savoie en deçà des Alpes* (Grenoble, 1911), pp. 20–21.

[7] The resident council received statutory recognition in 1327, and the *chambre des comptes* in 1351, but the castellany accounts for Bresse, among others, prove the latter body existed as a separate entity at least as early as 1285. Cf. my thesis, "Social and Political Institutions in Bresse, 1250–1350" (Johns Hopkins University, 1958), pp. 126–127.

territories of Savoy as well as from the most influential baronial families. Six regional groups can be distinguished. Four knights represented Savoy: Guillaume, sire of Entremont; Pierre, sire of Urtières; Pierre Mareschal (of Montmélian); and Pierre de Montgelat. Seven nobles were named from the Viennois.[8] From the nobility of Bresse and Bugey, Aymon had selected members from four of its most prominent families: the Palud-Varembon, Saint-Amour, La Baume, and Corgenon.[9] From the mountains of Chablais and the Valais came Bishop Guichard Tavel of Sion, Pierre de Saillon, and Rodolf de Blonay, who represented probably the most powerful baronial clan in that region. The duchy of Aosta was represented by its bishop and Pierre de Challant, coseigneur of Montjovet; and the marquisate of Susa sent the abbot of San Michele della Chiusa, and Guillaume, coseigneur of Rivalta. The regency council was to survey the acts of the regents and, on the "lundi gras" of each year, received the revenue and expense accounts of the castellans, *baillis*, and judges of the count's dominions. No homages from vassals of the lord count could be received, no buildings not already under construction could be built, no great affairs could be undertaken by either of the regents without the consent of the council. Aymon was clearly counting upon the traditional loyalty of his nobility to safeguard the interests of his dynasty from any encroachment which his cousins might be tempted to make.

In the selection of the two regents, Aymon had displayed considerable insight. The choice of Louis II of Vaud, the son of the first baron of Vaud, was no surprise. In his mid-fifties in 1343, Louis II was the grand old man of the dynasty in wisdom and experience. Much of his life had been spent outside the dominions of Savoy in the service of various European sovereigns. In 1308 he had been among the Savoyards present at the coronation of

---

[8] The act establishing the regency is published in Guichenon, IV, *preuves*, 175. From the Viennois were: Hugues, sire of Maubec; Amadeus, sire of Miribel, and Guillaume de Miribel, sire of Faramans; Amadeus de Beauvoir; Pierre de Montbel, seigneur of Les Echelles; "Godonarius de Failo," and "Guinus," or Girin, de St. Symphorien.

[9] Pierre de la Palud, sire of Varembon; Jean, sire of Saint-Amour; Jean de la Baume, sire of Fromentes, and Galois de la Baume, sire of Valusin; and Jean, sire of Corgenon.

Edward II at Westminster Abbey.[10] Two years later in Italy, he was made a senator of Rome, "magnificus vir Ludovicus de Sabaudia Dei gratia Romae Urbis senator illustrissimus," and he worked diligently for the cause of Emperor Henry VII during that monarch's Italian expedition of 1310–1313.[11]

The baron of Vaud had served Amadeus V equally well, leading armies against the dauphin in the campaigns of 1314–1322, and in 1322 the count had appointed him lieutenant-general of the Canavese, on the Italian side of the Alps. From 1330 onward, Louis was a member of the council of Savoy without, however, abandoning activities of broader scope. He spent most of 1331 in Lombardy assisting Jean of Luxembourg in his abortive effort to create a new Lombard kingdom. When Jean installed his sixteen-year-old son, the future Emperor Charles IV, as his vicar of Lombardy, he named Louis of Vaud as the boy's chief counselor. This was an honor which the Savoyard chose to forego, however, since his daughter had just married Azzo Visconti, lord of Milan, and Louis wished to avoid a conflict of interests. After the outbreak of the Hundred Years War, the baron of Vaud was frequently in France commanding Savoyard troops in the service of Philippe VI.

The choice of Amadeus III of Geneva as the other regent was a calculated risk. The counts of Savoy and Geneva had been traditional rivals for centuries. The territories comprising the Genevois were almost surrounded by those of Savoy, which gave rise to ceaseless disputes over frontier rights and jurisdiction. The Savoyards might naturally have expected that a count of Geneva would seek to profit as fully as possible from the weakness of their position during a minority. Amadeus III himself had not always been the friend and ally of Savoy. As recently as 1325 he had joined the coalition formed by Dauphin Guigues VIII against Count Edward, and he had participated in the great victory of

---

[10] For a fuller account of the life of Louis II, see A. de Gerbaix de Sonnaz, "Mémoire historique sur Louis II de Savoie, sire de Vaud, sénateur de Rome (1310–1312), de 1275 à 1349," *MARS* (5th series, 1908), I. The recent research of Mr. Olivier Dessemontet of the *Archives cantonales de Vaud* requires modification of much that has been previously written on the barons of Vaud. Louis II was born sometime between 1283 and 1294, not in 1269, as has been affirmed heretofore.

[11] Cf. Bowsky, *op.cit.*, and Marie-José, pp. 75-82.

37

the Dauphinois at the battle of Varey. A truce had been arranged in 1326 by emissaries from the king of France, who was anxious for the military support of both counts in his Flemish campaign of 1327–1328.[12] But a treaty actually designed to settle the points of difference between Savoy and Geneva was not achieved until January 1329. It was then that Aymon "le Pacifique," as the chroniclers have labeled him, succeeded his belligerent brother and persuaded the count of Geneva to abandon the traditional policy of his forefathers. Amadeus III was of less warlike disposition than his predecessors, and the same could be said of the new count of Savoy. In 1329, Aymon and Amadeus had jointly established a commission to investigate their conflicting claims to the territory between Duingt and Faverges, and in 1338 similar commissions were set up in an attempt to deal amicably with other boundary questions. Although several of these investigations continued for years, neither count cared to substitute haste for thoroughness or warriors for jurists. After 1337 both rulers were frequently absorbed with the task of raising armies for campaigns in France, where they were often comrades-in-arms.

This friendship of long standing, partially the result of Amadeus' gentle and relatively unambitious nature, was undoubtedly what had induced Aymon to select him as one to whom his young son could be entrusted after his death. Perhaps a count of Geneva at the very helm of the Savoyard state might sufficiently identify himself with its interests to forget his own, at least temporarily. Aymon had indeed gambled, for had he misjudged his man, the consequences might have been disastrous. There is some indication that certain Savoyard barons did not entirely trust the count of Geneva,[13] but their fears were groundless. There is no evidence during the six years of the regency that the Genevan cousin ever betrayed his trust. The Savoyard blood he had inherited from his mother proved a stronger bond than the interests of his own principality.

### THE POLITICAL ORGANIZATION OF THE SAVOYARD STATE

The government with which the young count had to become familiar had its seat at Chambéry. Besides the resident council with its extensive administrative and judicial attributes, it con-

---

[12] Cf. Duparc, p. 267.    [13] See Chapter III, note 1.

sisted of a supreme court of appeals, a chancery, and the *chambre des comptes*. The post of judge of appeals had been created in 1340 to assist the resident council in coping with questions of high justice, which had greatly increased in volume as the count's jurisdiction had expanded. In 1330, Aymon had created the office of chancellor, whose task was to oversee the drafting and sealing of official documents, particularly those concerned with comital rights and properties. The keystone of the count's administrative organization, however, was the *chambre des comptes*, where auditors and "masters of accounts" received the annual reports of receipts and expenditures prepared by every collector of revenue in the count's far-flung dominions. No clear distinction was made between public and private income, and the *chambre des comptes* handled accounts from household, manorial, and public officials.

At the death of Aymon, the Savoyard state was divided into eight bailliages, of which the *baillis* were usually the castellans of the principal town or fortress. The bailliage of Savoy was the most important, containing seventeen castellanies scattered through the Maurienne, the Tarentaise, and the region around Chambéry.[14] Equally extensive was the bailliage of Chablais, comprising the south and eastern shores of Lake Geneva, the Rhône valley to the bend at Martigny, and the route of the Great St. Bernard. West of Savoy lay the two bailliages of Bugey and Bresse, with the bailliage of Novalaise situated chiefly between the chain of the Mont du Chat and the Rhône. Beyond the confluence of the Rhône and the Guiers was the bailliage of Viennois with nine castellanies scattered almost as far as Vienne. The remaining two bailliages were across the Alps in Italy: the Val d'Aosta and the marquisate of Susa.

Superimposed upon the bailliages were the "judicatures," the districts of the itinerant judges, who held between six and eleven assizes each year in the principal castellanies of their circumscriptions. These judges took cognizance of criminal and civil cases that exceeded the competence of the castellans. The most important cases, however, were the province of the *judex major*,

[14] Luigi Cibrario, *Storia della Monarchia di Savoia* (Turin, 1844), III, 47, says there were eighteen but does not list them. Dullin, p. 27, gives seventeen, with which my own findings agree. See list of castellanies and bailliages in Commentary, III.

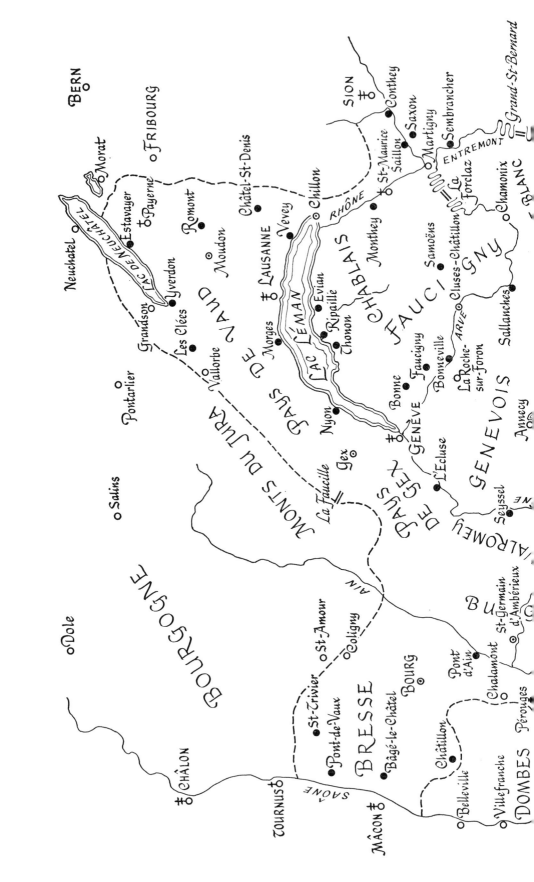

The region of Genevois, as shown on p. 8, was not ruled by the House of Savoy.

Pinerolo

Avigliana ⊙

Susa  DORA RIPARIA

Montcenis

Montgenèvre

Briançon

DURANCE

Lanlebourg

St-Jean-de-Maurienne

ARC

Bourg-St-Maurice

TARENTAISE

‡MOÛTIERS

ISÈRE

Salins

Aiguebelle

La Chambre

‡St-Jean-de-Maurienne

MAURIENNE

La Rochette

ISÈRE

Montmélian

SAVOIE

Le Bourget

CHAMBÉRY

‡La Grande Chartreuse

GRENOBLE

GENEVOIS

VALAIS

GUIERS

St-Laurent-du-Pont

St-Genix

Les Abrets

Pont-de-Beauvoisin

La Tour-du-Pin

Voiron

DAUPHINÉ

St-Symphorien-d'Ozon

VIENNOIS

St-Georges d'Esperanche

La Côte-St-André

‡VIENNE

St-Jean-de-Bournay

ISÈRE

‡VALENCE

RHÔNE

Territories Ruled by the
House of Savoy in the 14th Century
on the French side of the Alps

‡ Seat of Bishopric or Archbishopric
† Abbey
● Castellany Belonging to Savoyard Princes
⊙ Seat of a Savoyard Bailliage
-- Approximate Boundaries of Savoyard Dominion
‖ Pass

or *juge-mage*, at the head of each of the judicatures.[15] Accompanying each judge was a procurator charged with looking after the interests of the count. Above the *juge-mages* were the appellate judge at Chambéry and the resident council; and, of course, the count himself could decide any case brought before him personally during his travels. An exceptional situation existed in the Val d'Aosta, where the count presided over *Audiences générales* every seven years. When this assembly was in session, it constituted the final court of appeals for all cases, save those under episcopal jurisdiction.[16]

The "jack of all trades" in comital administration was the castellan. There were about eighty of them in 1343, and their duties were extremely varied. Their judicial and financial responsibilities distinguished Savoyard castellans from those in France, and their judicial attributes made them different from castellans in Burgundy.[17] There was, however, a pronounced trend toward specialization of function in the fourteenth century. Castellans were generally high-ranking nobles whose military and diplomatic duties elsewhere required the appointment of lieutenants and vice-castellans for the conduct of local affairs during their absence. Officers called *receptores* gradually replaced many castellans in the collection and accounting of castellany revenues, and after 1331 the collectors of subsidies were often special agents delegated for that purpose.[18]

The principal duty of the castellan was to see that his castle was well-fortified and in good repair, and that its garrison was adequate and well-supplied with weapons and missiles. He also recruited the men-at-arms for the count's armies and sent them at the appointed date to the town where the *bailli* was assembling

---

[15] In 1343 there were eight judicatures: Savoy, Chablais, Tarentaise-Maurienne, Val di Susa, Novalaise, Bresse, Bugey, and Val d'Aosta. Often the *juge-mage* served in that capacity for more than one district. Cf. *ADCO*, series B, Bresse and Bugey judicatures.

[16] Further details on the Val d'Aosta are provided later in Chapter III, part 2.

[17] Cf. Dullin, p. 33.

[18] Even when the collector of a subsidy was the local castellan, after 1331 he had to account for the subsidy separately, instead of including it in the castellany rolls as before. Cf. castellany and subsidy account series in *ADS*. This innovation appears to have been Count Aymon's idea, and it was intended to permit more rapid auditing and more effective measures to cope with delinquency in payments.

the host. The castellan's judicial functions were equally important, for most criminal cases in the castellany came before his court, only the most important ones falling to the *juge-mage*. It was the castellan more often than any other officer of the count who competed on the local level with the lords spiritual and temporal who also ruled in the valleys of Savoy. Since the great majority of castellans were nobles,[19] they could match in pride and temper the contentious disposition of noble neighbors; and the backing of the count gave them a great advantage. The more enterprising castellans repeatedly filled their courts and prisons with subjects who claimed to belong to someone else and their coffers with taxes supposedly owed to somebody else. When disputes over these activities reached the count, he usually denounced them and ordered his officers to cease and desist. Yet cease and desist they rarely did, and protest was apt to be a constant recourse for barons and bishops whose authority was encroached upon. In the end it was sometimes easier to sell to the count those rights which could no longer be effectively exercised. In the fourteenth century, the castellans were the chief instruments of the count's expanding jurisdiction, particularly in conflicts with ecclesiastical lords.

Probably most of the villages and hamlets in the Savoyard Alps were governed by the castellans' subordinates, to whom various local revenues were farmed out annually at a fixed rate. These lieutenants went by various titles, *prévôts, constabularii, blaerii*, and served as chiefs of police and tax collectors for their superiors.

Some castellanies, however, such as those of Tarentaise and Maurienne, present a different picture of local government. These castellanies comprised entire regions centering on a major valley with a widely scattered population in upland hamlets and numerous small lateral valleys. There most of the inhabitants were grouped into rural "communes," led by the heads of families and syndics, who were chosen from among the "prudhommes" of the village.[20] Not everyone who lived in the village belonged to the commune. Only the *comparsonerii*—those who had participated in the act of association—enjoyed that privilege, which was heredi-

[19] On the role of the nobility in the count's administration in the fourteenth century, see Commentary, IV.

[20] See study of rural communes by Gabriel Pérouse in the introduction to *Inventaire sommaire des Archives départementales de la Savoie antérieures à 1793, Archives communales.* I (Chambéry, 1911), iii–xcix.

tary and could sometimes be acquired only by marriage. The rural commune, in other words, was a legal, not a territorial, entity. A stranger who moved into the valley and acquired property there had no right, merely by virtue of his domicile, to membership in the commune. The commune had its origins in the arrangements made among the inhabitants of the area for the common exploitation of pastures, forests, waters, and other natural resources belonging to their common overlord. If the population and resources of a valley belonged to more than one seigneur, there was more than one commune, since each group of *comparsonerii* held in common the properties of a given seigneur. As the villagers put it on one occasion, the "conservation of our mountain and of the poor folk of the place" required a rigorous control of the number of persons with rights of exploitation, just as the rights themselves were strictly limited.[21] Each *communier* had the right to pasture only as many animals as he could carry through the winter, and the right to gather only as much wood in the forest as he needed to keep his cottage warm.

The inhabitants of the commune determined the customs of the valley and mountain themselves and depended upon the seigneurial officers to help enforce their regulations. The castellan had to be informed of all meetings of the commune, however; otherwise they were considered "rebellions." When the village churchbell convoked the heads of house or of family to a meeting, the castellan or his lieutenant was expected to be present (he was paid for his trouble), and it was the commune, not the castellan, which decided when a meeting would be held. Each officer of the count, be he castellan or mestral or other, had to swear to observe the customs and liberties of the commune before he was received in his office, and the villagers did not hesitate to appeal to the count against any infringement of their privileges.[22] In some regions the rural communities even enjoyed the authority to punish infractions of the law committed by members of the commune.[23]

[21] *Ibid.*, p. lxxii.

[22] On 25 March 1344 the regents issued a blanket confirmation of the franchises of the communes of the Tarentaise, and among other things, specifically revoked all concessions and *albergamenta* granted by comital officers there to individuals at the expense of the community. Pérouse, p. lxiii.

[23] Cf. Victor de Saint-Genix, *Histoire de Savoie* (Paris, 1868–1869), I, 313ff., for examples.

Not all rural communities were subject to the authority of the counts, however, and any discussion of political conditions in fourteenth-century Savoy requires some mention of those who could challenge Amadeus' power even within his own dominions. There were still a great many noble families whose lands enjoyed almost complete fiscal and judicial immunity, and where the officers of the count had very little opportunity to intervene. The counts of Savoy had sought to cope with this situation in two ways. One was to insist upon the best established of all baronial obligations, that of military service. Long years of campaigning under the war-banners of Savoy fostered the habit of loyal service among the barons and left them with less time for their own enterprises. Many others became officers in the counts' administrations, which had something of the same effect as continuous service in comital armies. Administrative obligations promoted a sense of responsibility and gave the counts considerably more control over their nobles than a purely feudal relationship permitted.[24]

An equally serious rival of comital sovereignty in the Alps was the Church. Besides the great lay magnates were abbots and bishops armed with formidable charters dating from the centuries when centralized government was disintegrating, and guarantees of salvation were to be had in return for gifts of power as well as land. By the fourteenth century, the bishops in Savoyard dominions were no longer the virtually independent sovereigns that some of them had once been, but several were still powerful enough to be dangerous. The bishops of Belley and Aosta had lost most of their temporal authority and many of their properties to the counts of Savoy by the end of the thirteenth century, and Pierre of Savoy had wrested comital authority over the Pays de Vaud from the bishop of Lausanne.[25] But that prelate still held the preponderance of power in the city of Lausanne, and Savoyard encroachments there were rather modest thus far. In the Maurienne the situation was similar. The bishops there had claimed temporal sovereignty over their very extensive diocese since its foundation in the sixth century. They were never fully able to enforce these claims, but it was not until 1327 that the balance of power in the valley definitely shifted in favor of the counts of

[24] See Commentary, IV.
[25] Cf. Previté Orton, p. 265.

Savoy. That was the year of the "Révolte des Arves," a rebellion of the bishop's subjects which forced the prelate to seek the aid of Count Edward. The count restored the bishop to his see, but in return for his assistance Edward appropriated half of all episcopal revenues and all temporal authority in the diocese.[26]

At Geneva, Sion, and in the Tarentaise, the situation was less satisfactory from the count's point of view. The bishops in these dioceses possessed imperial charters conferring upon them the status of princes of the Empire and freeing them from any other secular authority. Capable and obstinate bishops in all three sees had preserved these immunities more or less intact, although they were compelled to ceaseless vigilance against Savoyard encroachments. At Geneva in 1287, Amadeus V, after fourteen weeks of siege, captured the castle of the Ile in the middle of the Rhône, the essential link between the city and points north. This triumph led to a peace treaty in which the count of Geneva received the castle of the Bourg-du-Four (in the center of the city near the cathedral) in fief "reddabile" to the count of Savoy. By late 1288, Amadeus V had seized the *vidomnat* of Geneva and had bestowed that office upon his castellan of the Bourg-de-l'Ile.[27] Over ensuing decades the bishops recovered most of their control in the diocese of Geneva and obtained considerable power in the city itself, but the Savoyard foothold, based upon the Bourg-de-l'Ile and the *vidomnat*, remained solidly entrenched.

At Sion the firm stand taken by Bishop Aymon III de la Tour (1323–1338) had forced Count Aymon to be satisfied with a mutual act of homage in which the bishop recognized holding only the *via publica* and the fief of Mörel from Savoy, but not the *regalia* of his see or the *chancellerie*.[28] Nevertheless, Savoyard hopes for recovering the dominion once exercised by Pierre II in the Valais were raised in 1342 when Count Aymon secured the

[26] For a fuller account, see Adolphe Gros, *Histoire du Diocèse de Maurienne* (Chambéry, 1948), II, 32ff.

[27] The *vidomne* at this time was supposedly an episcopal officer who exercised important police and judicial functions. He enjoyed unlimited authority in civil cases, low justice in criminal cases, and powers of enquiry in matters of high justice, which were to be decided by the bishop's court. Duparc, pp. 208–209.

[28] The *chancellerie* was the right to register public acts. Cf. Victor van Berchem, *Guichard Tavel, Evêque de Sion* (Extr. *Jahrbuch für Schweizerische Geschichte*, 1899), pp. 51–59.

promotion of one of his staunchest supporters, Guichard Tavel of Geneva, to the see of Sion.

In the Tarentaise the authority of the archbishop, buttressed though it was by imperial charters of 1196 and 1226, seemed on the verge of new setbacks. A series of quiet usurpations had been going on for many years, but a great crisis occurred in the fall of 1335, when an armed battle took place between the count's castellan of Salins and the inhabitants of Moûtiers, the archiepiscopal seat.[29] The result of this fray, which had arisen from the castellan's pretension to jurisdiction over foreigners in the town (contrary to the municipal franchises), was the siege of Moûtiers by the count's army. The town was forced to surrender, and its fortifications were destroyed. Throughout this struggle Archbishop Jacques de Verloz de Salins had been unable to protect his subjects of Moûtiers against the count's officers. He died in 1341 at the papal court, where he had gone to defend himself against accusations that his election had been irregular and that he had alienated the property of his see.

The counts of Savoy in the fourteenth century were thus distinctly on the offensive, constantly working to extend their jurisdiction and to consolidate their power. It would be erroneous to suppose, however, that they had sought allies only among the nobility in their efforts to achieve these ends. The bourgeois were also cultivated by the counts, particularly as towns grew in importance. The bourgeois appear more often than before in administrative posts, and a few achieved noble rank in the count's service. Dozens of charters of liberties were granted to towns in Savoyard dominions; the counts regarded such charters as sources of revenue, and any town sufficiently prosperous to pay for a charter was likely to receive one. In some cases, such as in the Piedmont, where the town population was considerably larger than elsewhere in Savoyard territories, the counts granted municipal liberties with a view to increasing their political influence among the bourgeois. In the Pays de Vaud the establishment of "free towns" by the Savoyard princes of the thirteenth and early fourteenth centuries was often intended to reduce the influence of the bishops of Lausanne.

[29] For a full account of this subject, see Jacqueline Roubert, "La Seigneurie des Archevêques-comtes de Tarentaise du Xe au XVIe siècles," in *MASBAS* (6th series, V, 1961), 103ff.

The bourgeois in Savoy at this time were very different from the wealthy, enterprising multitudes in the cities of Italy, who demanded political privileges more in conformity with their new economic preeminence. In the count's dominions by the mid-fourteenth century, there were very few towns which numbered over 2,000 inhabitants, and most were much smaller. The enfranchisement movement in the Savoyard towns does not seem to have been a struggle for emancipation on the part of a large and restive business community. The charters which the bourgeois sought and acquired were principally concerned with regularizing and simplifying the obligations of an essentially rural community toward its overlord. Only in this light can the franchises of most Savoyard towns be considered at all liberal, for compared with the charters of the great free cities of France and the Empire, their privileges seem meager indeed.[30] The citizens were always freed from tallage and corvées, and maximum penalties were fixed for lesser offenses. A few charters permitted the bourgeois annual elections of syndics (from two to four in number) to represent them in the conduct of public affairs.[31] But the count's castellan, although his authority was limited by the franchises, remained the real ruler of the town in his master's name.

The citizens enjoyed the status of the vassal class and were referred to as "dilecti et fideles," rather than as "subditi" in official documents. To the count they did homage honorably by kissing his thumb or the top of his hand.[32] The bourgeois still owed military service to the count, although it was limited in duration and distance, and they were still subject to financial contributions from time to time. The town syndics, or simply the "prudhommes" if there were no syndics, always negotiated as low an assessment as possible, then undertook to apportion its payment as equitably as possible among the population. The community was expected to maintain the fortifications of the town and pay the watchmen;

---

[30] The franchises of Chambéry are published in Chapperon, pp. 378–382; those of Montmélian in Bernard, pp. 43ff. Cf. also F. Forel, "Chartes communales du pays de Vaud," in *MDR* (XXVII, 1872).

[31] The charter of Moudon in the Pays de Vaud, considered the most liberal in that region, did not provide for any municipal organization at all. Cf. Charles Gilliard, "Moudon sous le Régime savoyarde," in *MRD* (2nd series, XIV, 1929), pp. 62ff.

[32] Ménabréa, *Chambéry*, p. 141.

but police and judicial power remained largely in the hands of the count's officers.

At Chambéry the heads of each family assembled in the chapter hall of the Franciscan monastery when decisions were to be made and voted viva voce in the selection of their syndics, if at least two-thirds of the citizens were present.[33] Ebony staves ornamented with silver were the insignia of the syndics, who then chose their counselors, sometimes as many as a hundred. Meetings of syndics and counselors took place in the refectory of the Franciscan monastery, and on these occasions copious dinners were sometimes provided. Now and then the castellan was invited to attend such banquets, in the hope of inclining him favorably toward petitions brought before him by the town fathers. The officers of the municipal government included an attorney, a notary, a doctor, a captain of the watch, gatekeepers, a master of fountains, a carpenter, a mason, and various "servitores villae."[34] In 1377 when the count had the first mechanical public clock in the region constructed, the post of "magister horologii" was created to provide for its upkeep.

The resources of Chambéry were not very extensive. They consisted chiefly of the revenues from the wine ban,[35] rent from the town ovens and from fishing rights in the moats, and the receipts of the offering boxes at St-Léger and the chapel of Sainte-Marie every year on Good Friday.[36] These and other miscellaneous revenues barely sufficed to meet the routine expenses of town government. Whenever unusual expenses arose, the community assembled at the Franciscans' and, "the rich helping the poor," assessed a hearth tax on the households of the town and its *mandamentum*.[37] The assessments were always voted, but the business

[33] *Ibid.*     [34] *Ibid.*, pp. 113–114.

[35] This amounted to four *solidi* per *setier* of wine sold in retail in the parishes of Lémenc, St-Léger, and St-Pierre-de-Mâché. J. H. Costa de Beauregard, "Documents inédits pour servir à l'histoire de la ville de Chambéry," *MSRS*, XI (1843), 191–192.

[36] *Ibid.*

[37] The *mandamentum* was the district outside the walls which fell under the jurisdiction of the town. Exemptions from the assessment of 1375–1377 included the children of Jean Barbier, whose house had collapsed; Sophie Panicet, "who is a poor woman without resources"; Berthet de Pré-Joppé, whose house had burned down; Jean Payen, "because he is the *rector scolarum*"; Girard d'Estrées,

of collecting them was not always easy. If someone refused to pay, the officers of the castellan (or of the town, if they could get there first) arrived, forced open the door, and carried off the contents of the house. Furniture, dishes, glassware, clothing—anything that might have value at the pawnshops of the Jews and Lombards was seized and carried off to be pawned for the amount of the tax. Nor was this the lot only of those who really could not afford to pay. In 1358 when an assessment was being collected to pay for a new dike to protect the town from the annual spring floods, the syndics undertook to break and enter several noble dwellings. Lord Pierre de Châtillon lost the ornamental bridles for his charger, and Humbert, seigneur of Clermont, had his boots and a white fur carried away and deposited with the Lombards.[38]

These assessments were fairly frequent, for the citizens of Chambéry, in addition to maintaining walls, dikes, bridges, and canals, were expected to contribute presents to visiting dignitaries, including members of the house of Savoy when they visited the town for the first time. Fresh fish from Lake Le Bourget, fat beeves, barrels of fine wines, good mutton—all were suitable but expensive offerings. Any particularly costly enterprise of the count of Savoy would lead to a request for a contribution from his "dilecti et fideles," even if they had to borrow the money, which was not infrequently the case. The citizens of Chambéry owed one man per hearth for the count's armies in any major campaign on their side of the Alps. They also owed a contingent of *gentes armorum* (mounted warriors of noble rank, fully armed), the number to be determined in each case by the castellan and four "prudhommes" from the town. This little regiment had its own banner—red with the white cross of Savoy and an eight-pointed gold star in the upper left quarter—and when the men of Chambéry marched off to battle behind their trumpets and bagpipes,[39] they made as proud a sight as any of the good and loyal subjects of the count of Savoy.

### EDUCATION AND EARLY YEARS OF AMADEUS VI

The prince who would govern such subjects needed education of many kinds. The Savoyards had always been warlike, and they

---

chancellor of Savoy, who sealed without charge certain letters for the town. Ménabréa, *Chambéry*, pp. 209–210.

[38] Costa de Beauregard, pp. 201–202.   [39] Ménebréa, *Chambéry*, pp. 147–149.

were surrounded by warlike neighbors. If the young count's success in ruling his dominions depended upon the development of his mind, his success in defending them depended upon his physical strength and endurance. The sight of hard mountain warriors kneeling and swearing oaths of loyalty could not have failed to carry its own lesson to the boy upon the throne; the new count also had to learn to bear the weight of steel. As soon as he was old enough, he was put on the back of a horse to learn the kind of master horsemanship that could mean the difference between victory and defeat. For hours each day his masters taught him how to handle weapons, beginning with small, lightweight arms, until he was strong enough to take up the weapons of men. As Servion remarked, the count's masters "put him to the exercise of his person, to joust, to fight, to leap, to dance."[40] Fortunately, Amadeus was of athletic constitution and temperament, and he both delighted and excelled in the noble profession of arms.

But physical training was only part of his education. In the fourteenth century it was no longer possible for the ruler of an important state to remain ignorant of letters. The administration of his far-flung territories required the services of a literate bureaucracy, and if the count hoped to be master in his own dominions, he must learn to write and read at least well enough to oversee those who served him. In 1337 the household included not only "masters of the count's children," but more specifically one "Jacobus de Syvriaco," identified as "doctor Amadei, filii principis quondam."[41] By the time Count Amadeus was thirteen, his household accounts record the salary of Master Jean Berrot, who taught him and his brother Jean to read and write ("instruenti literaliter").[42] The accounts for 1347 record the purchase in Paris of two learned treatises: Vegezio's *De Re Militari*, to instruct the young count in the art of war; and Aegidius Colonna's *De Regimine Principum*, to acquaint him with the qualities necessary to the statesman.[43] Servion was doubtless essentially correct when he declared that Amadeus was brought up "moult vertueusement"

---

[40] Servion, II, 70.

[41] *AST*, inv. 38, folio 21, doc. 44 (1337). The Amadeus mentioned here is not the count, but the item does reveal the existence at that date of instructors for the children of the count at the court of Savoy.

[42] *AST*, inv. 16, doc. 14 (1346–1349).

[43] Fernand Hayward, *Histoire de la Maison de Savoie* (Paris, 1941), I, 132.

to live "em bonnes moeurs et de tenir et croyre conseil," and that in the matter of reading and writing, he was soon "clerc entendant et bon lattinieux."[44]

The young count was also instructed in other matters besides reading and writing. Gray was perhaps wiser than he knew when he declared that every rock and torrent of these Alpine highlands was "pregnant with religion and poetry." In the fourteenth century most of the poetry was in the religion, and the facts of nature—always so dramatically present in a land of mountains—fostered the religious inclinations of the inhabitants. Amadeus' private chaplain was Jean Albi of Evian, and within a year of his father's death, the count requested and obtained from Pope Clement VI the special privilege of a portable altar.[45] This privilege had been accorded to his predecessors, along with the right to have mass celebrated wherever they were, even if the locality was under interdict—but only at dawn, and only when the pressure of affairs absolutely prevented attendance at regular services. This curious favor reflects in a rather unexpected way both the itinerant life of the counts of Savoy and their attention to religious duties. Throughout his life Amadeus remained faithful to habits learned from both parents in earliest childhood. When he was still very young, his piety apparently reached such a pitch that "ex quodam devotionis fervore" he took a vow to fast every Friday and Saturday and to abstain from meat on Wednesdays. Later, when the moment of passionate conviction which had prompted so extreme a resolution had passed, he wrote to Innocent VI begging to be absolved from his vow, "for this manner of abstinence and fasting was too debilitating physically." The pope obliged by substituting ten *Pater Nosters* and ten *Aves* every Friday, Saturday, and Wednesday, and by requiring the count to feed twelve poor people every Sunday and to clothe anew and also feed twenty more every year at All Saints.[46]

Amadeus' attention to his religious obligations is further exemplified by the manner in which he carried out the pious and charitable provisions in his father's will. Funds were allocated for

[44] Servion, II, 70.

[45] Cf. Carlo Cipolla, "Clemente VI e Casa Savoia," *MSI* (3rd series, V, 1900), *documenti*, docs. XV, XVI.

[46] Luciano Scarabelli, "Paralipomeni di Storia Piemontese dall'Anno 1285 al 1617," in *ASI*, XIII (1847), 71–72. The pope's letter is dated 20 June 1360.

masses for the souls of parents and ancestors, as Aymon had directed, and money was given to the Franciscans at Chambéry to assist them in reconstructing buildings destroyed by floods.[47] The late count had also ordered a hospital built at St-Genix-d'Aoste, and by 1347 the house of Guichard Ponzard of St-Genix had been purchased and was being altered for that purpose.[48]

No princely court of the fourteenth century would have been complete without instructors in the "gay science" as well as instructors in the "True Faith," and the court of Savoy was no exception.[49] Several "menestrerii" were attached to the young count's household, and they probably played an important role in developing the taste for chivalric pageantry and practice that was so prominent a feature of Amadeus' later years. During Lent, when the musicians were not allowed to perform, the Savoyard minstrels frequently gathered at Bourg-en-Bresse or at Geneva for some kind of training sessions called "scolas." In 1347 one of the count's minstrels was given three florins "pro subsidio," for his expenses "proponens ire ad scolas sue menestrerie." Two years later Gautier, one of the count of Geneva's minstrels, received a gift from Amadeus VI to enable him also to go "ad scolas."[50] There were also painters attached to the court during these years. Among them were Rodolph of Fribourg, who died between 1347 and 1349; one Master "Royde," who received ten *solidi gros tournois* per year as long as he resided at Chambéry; and Master Hugonin Frenier, who decorated the new hall at Le Bourget when the old one burned down on St. Vincent's Day 1347.[51]

Young Amadeus was to need all the moral and intellectual training he could get, for hardly had he recovered from the loss of his father when troubles began. The most pressing matter had to do with a rival claimant to the throne of Savoy, Jeanne de Savoie, duchess of Brittany. As the sole surviving child of Count Edward, Jeanne had laid claim to the inheritance of her father on his death in 1329. Aymon, with the full concurrence of the council of barons

---

[47] *AST*, inv. 16, doc. 14 (1346–1349). Amadeus' order was dated 4 January 1347.

[48] *Ibid.*    [49] *Ibid.*

[50] *Ibid.* An item in the accounts for Bourg-en-Bresse (*ADCO*, B 7132, 1377–1378) mentions expenditures in oats for the horses of the count's minstrels, who were holding their "scola" at Bourg during Lent.

[51] *AST*, inv. 16, doc. 14. The new hall at Le Bourget also had glass windows.

and prelates, had replied to her ambassadors that it had always been the custom in Savoy for the inheritance to pass to the nearest male relative of the late count, and to a woman only if no males were living.[52] The duchess was not satisfied with this reply, nor was her husband, Jean III, who immediately concluded an offensive alliance with Dauphin Guigues VIII. This alliance became much more dangerous in January 1330, when Philippe VI gave it his support, in keeping with his general policy of interfering in the affairs of his neighbors beyond the Rhône.

Several months later Count Aymon had sent a delegation to Bruges, where the duke of Brittany was staying at the time, in an attempt to negotiate a peaceful settlement. No agreement appears to have been reached, however, and it was not until 1339, when the outbreak of war with England had removed any prospect of aid from Philippe VI, that Jean, deeply involved in the preparations against the English invasion, was able to induce his wife to abandon her claims.[53] At Vincennes on 22 November 1339, Jeanne de Savoie resigned her claims to the succession in Savoy in return for a life rent of 6,000 *livres tournois* annually.[54]

Jeanne appears to have accepted this compromise reluctantly, but she had no alternative. In April 1341 her husband died without heirs, giving rise to a bloody war of succession in Brittany between the late duke's niece, Jeanne de Penthièvre, and his younger brother, Jean de Montfort. Jeanne appealed for assistance to the king of France, Jean, to the king of England—thus con-

[52] Servion, II, 33, phrases the Savoyard reply to Jeanne's ambassadors as follows: " . . . sachiez que par bellez constitucions sont faitz decres et ordonnances par tous les signeiurs de Savoye, que tant quil ly aura enffans masle du nom et des armes de Savoye, soit de frere ou de cosin ou de propinque, que nulle fillie ne femme ne doibt heriter." Cabaret, p. 121 *dorso* has essentially the same version. Saint-Genix, I, 325, note 1, traces this exclusion of females back to the *lex burgundina*. In fact, however, there was no statutory provision for the succession in Savoy until 1414.

[53] Considering Jeanne's subsequent behavior, I think it more likely that she, and not her husband, was the chief instigator of this action, contrary to the suggestion of Cordey, *Les Comtes*, p. 5.

[54] Four thousand *livres* were to come from royal pensions then owed annually by the king of France to the count of Savoy, and the remaining 2,000 *livres* were to come from the revenues of Bresse. Cf. *ibid*; p. 6. It was provided, however, that Jeanne was not to receive the Bressan revenues until after the death of her mother, Dowager-Countess Blanche, which means she never got them at all, since she predeceased her mother.

tributing to a fresh outbreak of hostilities in the Hundred Years War. Under the circumstances the duchess was hardly in a position to press for a more satisfactory settlement, but she was by no means inclined to abandon her efforts permanently. On the death of Count Aymon she brushed aside her renunciation of 1339 and once again put forth her claims, probably calculating that the difficulties of a regency would increase her chances of success.

While the regents of Savoy were considering how best to cope with this problem, Jeanne's health began to fail. By June 1344 she was clearly dying, but her death would prove of little solace to the Savoyards. Embittered by the whole affair, the duchess had resolved that her cause should not die with her. A week before her death on 29 June, she dictated a will by which she made Philippe, duke of Orléans, a younger son of the king of France, her universal heir, and ceded to him all of her rights to the county of Savoy.[55] With the obstinacy of her race, the vindictive duchess was counting upon the French king's well-known hunger for Rhône valley territories to ensure her revenge upon the dynasty which had refused to satisfy her claims.

This turn of events was cause for serious concern. The count of Geneva and Louis of Vaud sent ambassadors to Avignon to enlist the aid of Clement VI, a longtime friend of the house of Savoy who had lent his good offices in this same matter some years before. Throughout 1344-1345 the succession question was the constant preoccupation of the regents and the council of Savoy. Fortunately for the Savoyards, Philippe's other concerns made him anxious to avoid difficulties on his eastern frontier at this time. Civil war was raging in Brittany, and the English candidate, Jean de Montfort, was generally successful. Edward III had made it obvious that if he did not really want the crown of France, he did indeed want the duchy of Guienne with widened boundaries and without French suzerainty. And he was ready to back his demands with force. Under the circumstances the king of France could not afford to antagonize his Savoyard allies by insisting upon the claims of his son. The young duke of Orléans, in a treaty drawn up in the winter of 1345, agreed to abandon his claims to Savoy in return for an annual 5,000 *livres tour-*

[55] *Ibid.*, p. 70.

*nois.*[56] The treaty was concluded at Paris and ratified at Chambéry on 25 February 1346 by the count, the regents, and the council after "grant deliberacion."

## SAVOY AND THE DAUPHINÉ, 1342–1348

These years, so agitated by the pretensions of the duchess of Brittany, also witnessed the culmination of French efforts to acquire the Dauphiné. On 23 February 1343 the French plenipotentiaries at Avignon had concluded the first treaty of sale by which Dauphin Humbert II was to deliver his inheritance to the duke of Orléans, the same prince to whom Jeanne de Savoie had bequeathed her claims. The apprehension which reigned at the court of Savoy is indicated by the orders which the regents issued immediately following the death of Count Aymon. The castellans of frontier strongholds at Bâgé-le-Châtel, Châtillon-les-Dombes, and St-Germain-d'Ambérieux were commanded to strengthen their garrisons and watch for any hostile moves on the part of their neighbors.[57] The immediate danger stemmed apparently from the activities of Hugues de Genève, sire of Anthon and of Varey, and uncle of Amadeus III, who had long been on bad terms with his Savoyard neighbors.[58] Nor were the fears of the regents groundless. In 1343–1344, Pierre de la Baume, *bailli* of Bugey, made a raid near Varey and destroyed a mill there in reprisal for the recent destruction of one by the "gentes de Varey." Humbert de Corgenon, castellan of Lompnes, at the same moment gathered extra men at his castle to head off an expected raid by Hugues de Genève in the vicinity of St-Germain.[59] Perhaps the raid actually

---

[56] *Ibid.*, pp. 72–73. A subsidy was levied in some castellanies during the 1340's "pro facto duchissa Bretaignie." The royal treasury at Paris certified having received the full amount due on 19 November 1346. *AST, Principi del Sangue*, mazzo V, doc. 11.

[57] *ADCO*, B 9596, B 6766, B 7575.

[58] In July 1332 an open war between Hugues de Genève-Anthon and the count of Savoy culminated in a great Savoyard victory near Monthoux. Cf. anonymous *Fasciculum Temporis* (fourteenth century), published by Mallet in *MDG*, IX (1855), doc. 52ff. for details of this war. In 1339 the dauphin gave Hugues a number of castles and towns in Faucigny in exchange for Anthon and Hugues's holdings in Bresse and Revermont, which opened the way for further disputes with Savoy. Cf. Valbonnais, *Histoire de Dauphiné* (Geneva, 1772), II, "Humbert II," *preuves*, 379.

[59] *ADCO*, B 8223 (Lompnes).

took place, for the castellan of St-Germain reported (1343–1346) that a melee between the count's men from St-Germain and Ordonnaz with some "delphini" had resulted in the death of four of the latter.[60]

Interviews took place between Louis of Vaud and the chancellor of France during the summer of 1343, but without evident results.[61] The French undoubtedly attempted to soothe the fears of the Savoyards by pointing out that Jean of Normandy was healthy and had a son, and that both would very probably succeed to the French throne. The Dauphiné would thus be nothing more than the appanage for Jean's younger brother, Philippe of Orléans, whose descendants would soon be as independent of the French monarchy as were the Angevins in Provence. Perhaps there were also promises that Savoyard claims in disputed border areas would be fully satisfied. Whatever the details of the discussions, the regents seem to have been appeased, for in January 1344 they replied favorably to Pierre, duke of Bourbon, concerning a proposed marriage alliance with Savoy. This may be taken as an indication of amiable relations with France, since Philippe VI was the uncle of the bride-to-be.

This marriage project had been drawn up first in October 1340, and was to unite Amadeus and the eldest daughter of the duke of Bourbon, Jeanne, whose mother was Isabelle de Valois, sister of Philippe VI. The proposed alliance had resulted from several months of negotiations following the abandonment of a still earlier betrothal of young Amadeus to Marguerite of Luxembourg, daughter of the future emperor, Charles IV.[62] The marriage alliance with the house of Bourbon was no doubt conceived as a complement to the military alliance between France and Savoy and as a partial guarantee of its continuance. Jeanne de Bourbon was to bring to her husband a dowry of 50,000 florins "of the legal weight and mintage of Florence." Count Aymon had agreed to provide her with an annual income of 4,000 florins, or 6,000 if Amadeus had become count by the time of the marriage. The contract had been signed and sealed when Aymon died, but the

[60] *Ibid.*, B 9596 (St-Germain).

[61] Cordey, *Les Comtes*, p. 89.

[62] *Ibid.*, pp. 74–75. This first betrothal took place in 1338. Why it was abandoned remains a mystery.

duke of Bourbon was anxious to have it confirmed by Amadeus himself.[63]

Pierre of Bourbon was given the assurance he sought, but the French then presumed too much on the docility of their Savoyard ally. Perhaps partly as a result of these assurances, Philippe VI now made an important change in the provisions governing the transferral of the Dauphiné to his dynasty. On 11 April 1344, in utmost secrecy, a second treaty of transfer was drawn up between the French and the dauphin. By the terms of the new arrangement, Humbert's inheritance was to go not to Philippe of Orléans, but rather to the heir to the crown of France, Jean of Normandy.[64]

However secret this treaty might have been at first, it was not kept from the Savoyards for very long. The immediate reaction of the regents was to threaten to break off the marriage alliance with the king's niece, Jeanne de Bourbon. This threat was given added weight when emissaries from Savoy were sent to the court of Edward III. On 30 June 1345, from Sandwich, King Edward sent a letter to the council and regents at Chambéry in reply to their embassy.[65] In this letter the king stated that a marriage alliance between England and Savoy "would please us much," but that at the moment he had no daughters available. Edward proposed, therefore, that Amadeus consent instead to allow his sister Blanche, now nine years of age, to be married to one of the king's sons. The Savoyard emissaries had apparently also requested payment of back revenues from English fiefs granted to the count's forebears. To this Edward replied that since Count Aymon had always refused to do homage for these fiefs and had joined the French in the war, he could not reasonably be expected to pay the arrears. The king added, however, that if Amadeus would do homage and accept the military responsibilities of such an act, Edward would be glad to reciprocate "according to the ancient covenants drawn up between our predecessors and yours."

There is no evidence that the negotiations accomplished anything more than this exchange, but the probable object of this move had been to create uneasiness at Paris and not actually to conclude an alliance with England. The French king had to be

---

[63] Pierre was concerned enough about the matter to visit Savoy in person. *Ibid.*, p. 76.

[64] The texts of these treaties are published in full in Guiffrey, *preuves*.

[65] Text of the letter published in Cordey, *Les Comtes*, p. 77.

reminded that the interests of Savoy in the Rhône valley could not be ignored, and that adequate compensation for them must accompany any treaty annexing the Dauphiné to France. Philippe VI remained unmoved, however, so the regents turned to other projects which might prove more effective. By 1346 at least, negotiations were under way with the court of Burgundy, which had long enjoyed close relations with Savoy.[66] In 1307, Blanche de Bourgogne, sister of the present duke, Eudes IV, had married Edward of Savoy, and Blanche may well have played a key role in 1346–1347 when the regents began to look toward Burgundy for an alliance to compensate for the dangerous shift in the balance of power to the south. It was important for the Savoyards to secure as strong a bargaining position as possible before the French had actually taken control of the Dauphiné, and an alliance with Burgundy seemed an excellent means to that end.

Events in 1346 favored the course of Savoyard policy. Philippe VI surely knew about the regents' tentatives at the court of Edward III and in Burgundy, but he was in no position to do anything about them, particularly since the Savoyards were still willing to honor their military commitments. In July 1346, Edward III landed in Normandy, took the city of Caen, and was marching in the direction of Paris. Louis of Vaud, who in 1345 had joined Jean of Normandy in the Limousin and Auvergne, raised another army in the spring of 1346 in response to summons from the king of France. The Savoyards were on their way to France by August, but the French moved against the English invaders without awaiting their arrival. The French and English armies encountered one another at Crécy on 26 August, and the ensuing battle resulted in the first great military disaster for France in the Hundred Years War. By the end of the day when Louis of Vaud and the Savoyard troops arrived, the battle was over, Philippe VI had left the field, and the French army had been utterly routed. Louis of Vaud, without waiting for instructions, gave orders to head for Montreuil in all haste, for the English were reported withdrawing in that direction. Thanks to this quick thinking, the Savoyards succeeded in outflanking the victorious English and reached the town some hours before the marshals of Edward III appeared be-

---

[66] Cf. Jean Richard, "L'Accession de la Maison de La Tour au Dauphiné de Viennois," *Bulletin philologique et historique* (1951–1952).

fore the gates to demand entrance. Seeing the walls strongly garrisoned and the town ready to resist assault, the English captains decided against an attack and continued their march to Boulogne, burning and laying waste the surrounding countryside.[67]

The defeat at Crécy stunned and depressed the French king, who seemed unable to take measures to retrieve the situation. Edward III, knowing the weakness of his own position, was anxious to return to England with the trophies of war while he still had them, and he chose Calais as his port of debarkation. The city was bravely defended and held out through the winter, but by the spring of 1347 supplies were running low. The citizens of Calais repeatedly appealed to Philippe to come to their rescue. As the months passed, however, nothing happened except the arrival of English reinforcements, and the desperate citizens of Calais finally agreed to surrender to Edward if they were not relieved before the beginning of August. In July, Philippe got together an army of sorts and moved toward Calais, but in the face of harassment by the English advance guard, he halted for a few days, then withdrew. With all hope of relief at an end, the citizens of Calais surrendered to the English on 4 August.

It was against this somber background of military calamity for the French that the new Savoyard diplomatic offensive to counter French annexation of the Dauphiné took place. In 1346, Philippe Monsieur, the only son of Eudes IV of Burgundy, died, leaving a pregnant wife, Jeanne de Boulogne, and a two-year-old daughter named for her mother. Some months later Jeanne de Boulogne gave birth to a son, Philippe de Rouvre, as he was called, heir to all of his grandfather's vast possessions: the duchy and county of Burgundy, the counties of Artois, Boulogne, and Auvergne, and the barony of Salins. In April 1347, after many conferences with the Burgundians, Amadeus announced that he would not marry Jeanne de Bourbon and publicly repudiated the treaties by which his betrothal had been arranged.[68] Scarcely two months later, on

---

[67] Cf. Perroy; Cordey, *Les Comtes*, pp. 146ff. Froissart frequently mistook Louis de Vaud for the count of Savoy in his account of this part of the war.

[68] *Ibid.*, p. 79, points out that neither of the regents are mentioned in the documents repudiating the Bourbon alliance, nor were they present, apparently, when the documents were drawn up. This may have been intentional so that if necessary the regents could claim that their ward had acted against their wishes and thus extricate Amadeus, if the consequences of this bold act later required such a move.

16 June, a new marriage contract was drawn up in the cathedral of Châlon-sur-Saône. The young count of Savoy, "qui est ja bien prouche de puberte," was to wed three-year-old Jeanne de Bourgogne, granddaughter of Eudes IV.[69] By the terms of the duke's will, drawn up the preceding year, Jeanne was to be heiress of all of the Burgundian dominions should her infant brother die without issue.[70] The little princess was to have as her marriage portion the castles and revenues then held by her great-aunt Blanche, under whose care she was to live hereafter in the dominions of her future husband.

The provisions for marriage were followed by others for war. Duke Eudes needed help in his struggle to subdue the barons of the county of Burgundy, and the Savoyards were looking for allies in the event of war with the dauphin. The count and the duke accordingly promised mutual assistance for the space of three months, with Amadeus agreeing to furnish 300 men-at-arms at once for the duke's service. The day after the agreement was signed, Humbert de Savoie departed from Bourg-en-Bresse with a company of knights to reinforce the ducal army.[71]

Meanwhile the papal court at Avignon was the scene of other important developments. With French influence temporarily weakened after the disaster at Crécy, the opposition to the French acquisition of the Dauphiné was beginning to gather strength. In the spring of 1347, Humbert II returned from his crusade a widower, his wife, Marie de Baux, having died a few months before. Clement VI, formerly so favorable to the designs of Philippe VI, seems to have thought better of them, and he now encouraged Humbert to take a second wife. Such news must have cheered the Savoyards, who may have influenced the papal change of heart. The treasury accounts for 1347 show that envoys from Louis of Vaud were dispatched to the papal curia on several occasions during the year, and that Amadeo de Savoie, younger brother of Giacomo of Savoy-Piedmont and bishop-elect of Maurienne, was

---

[69] The text of the treaty is given in Guichenon, IV, *preuves*, 220. Servion, II, 73–74, wrongly identified her as Marguerite de Boulogne et Auvergne.

[70] Eudes' sister, Blanche, was next in line for the succession after Jeanne.

[71] Cordey, *Les Comtes*, p. 81, note 3. *ADCO*, B 6697 (Ambronay, 1347–1348) records the expenses of the castellan's son, Jacquemet de Belmont, who spent twenty-seven days in Burgundy with Humbert, bastard of Savoy.

at Avignon "with the dauphin" in August and September.[72] The alliance with Burgundy was now an accomplished fact. If the dauphin could be induced to take a wife and provided his subjects with an heir, the expansionist dreams of the French monarchy would be thwarted along the whole Rhône-Saône frontier.

### PIEDMONT AFFAIRS, 1342–1348

It was at just this moment that events in another quarter diverted the attention of the regents. Peace never lasted long in Piedmont and Lombardy, where the Visconti of Milan vied with the rulers of Montferrat, and where belligerent marquises of Saluzzo cast covetous eyes upon the possessions of Savoy and of the Angevins of Naples. From crenellated strongholds each noble suspiciously kept watch over his own dominions, anticipating danger from within as well as from without; and each waited eagerly for signs of weakness among his neighbors. The Visconti had secured control of Milan and were beginning to move to the south and the east, already creating the state that would swallow up the greater part of northern Italy before the end of the century. Early in the century the wealthy cities of Asti, Alessandria, Alba, and several others along the banks of the Tanaro, partly out of fear of the Visconti and partly out of fear of Savoyards and marquises of Montferrat, had appealed to Charles II, king of Naples, to take them under his protection. Charles, who was also count of Provence and thus had important territorial interests in the region, accepted their petition and designated his second son, André, as ruler of a new "county of Piedmont" with Alba as its capital. As long as Angevin power was strong in Provence and Naples, as it was during the first half of the century, the county of Piedmont could be maintained in the face of hostile neighbors who considered themselves robbed by its creation. But the balance of power was precarious at best, and the slightest change in the status quo meant crisis and war.

Just such a change occurred in 1343 with the death of Robert of Naples, whose successor was his seventeen-year-old granddaughter. Giovanna's sex and inexperience were political disad-

---

[72] Cf. *AST*, inv. 16, doc. 14 (1346–1349), *librata* section. The accounts for 1347–1349 at Montmélian and Chambéry also reveal innumerable conferences "cum gentibus dalphini."

vantages, and she proved unable to cope with the disorders of her kingdom or the intrigues of her court. The time was obviously ripe for a stroke against the Angevin possessions in Piedmont, now deprived of the indispensable backing of a strong ruler at Naples.

Giovanni II of Montferrat was the first to move. He allied himself with the Visconti and together their armies advanced against Alessandria and Asti, the most important of the queen's cities. By 1344 both had fallen into the hands of the aggressors, who swept on against Tortona, Bra, and Alba, which were also forced to surrender. Giovanna ordered her seneschal in Provence, Réforce d'Agoult, to move into the Piedmont at once to expel the invaders. With the assistance of the citizens of Chieri and of Giacomo of Savoy-Achaea, who had chosen to stand with the Angevins because he feared Visconti and Montferrat more, Alba was recovered. This had taken place in the spring of 1345, and the two coalition armies soon found themselves facing one another near the castle of Gamenario not far from Chieri. A general engagement took place on 23 April, the "battle of Gamenario," resulting in the defeat of the Angevins and their allies, and the death of Réforce d'Agoult on the field of battle. The Visconti-Montferrat tide swept on, laying siege to Alba and seizing Chieri. Prince Giacomo was now thoroughly alarmed and began to seek allies.

The logical source of help was his cousin the count of Savoy, but the prince was reluctant to ask for Savoyard assistance. He had very much resented being omitted both from Aymon's will and from the regency council established for Amadeus VI's minority. Giacomo had not forgotten that his own father had had strong claims to the county of Savoy. The memory of what the prince regarded as the injustice done to his father made him the more unwilling to accept the suzerainty of his transalpine cousins, whom he considered all too disposed to meddle and interfere. This attitude had first been made clear to Amadeus VI and his regents in 1344, when they had crossed the Alps briefly to watch the course of Piedmont affairs. The marquis of Montferrat had fallen seriously ill, and since he was childless, his death would have made his nephew, the count of Savoy, the next marquis of Montferrat. The regents had therefore established themselves at Rivoli, where they would be within easy reach of the marquisate should their presence there be needed. While in the Piedmont, they had taken

RHÔNE — GENÈVE
Bonneville
ARVE
St-Maurice ☨
RHÔNE
Martigny
M
CER
(Matt

Annecy

MONT BLANC
Courmayeur
Morgex
GRAND-
ST-BERN
AOSTA ☨
Qu
Châtelarge
VAL D'AOS
Cog
△ GR
PARAD

PETIT-ST-
BERNARD
La Thuile

CHAMBÉRY
ISERE
Bourg
St-Maurice
Montmélian
Moûtiers ☨

S A V O I E
ISERE
St Jean de
Maurienne ☨
ARC
MONTCENIS
SUSA
VAL DI

GRENOBLE ☨
San
Michele
della
Chiusa
Av

Lautaret
DORA RIPARIA
Perosa
Sestriere
P
CHISONE

DAUPHINÉ
Briançon
MONTGENÈVRE
Villa
Cavou
St

PO Barge
MONTE
VISO △
Casteldelfino
VALLE VA

VALLE MAIRA
SALUZ

DEMONT

advantage of the opportunity to remind the prince of Achaea of his status as a vassal of Savoy by summoning him to do homage for his territories.

Giacomo thus had no desire whatever to provoke a second visit from the Savoyards, but by the spring of 1347 there was nothing else to do. The Visconti alone would have been more than a match for him, and allied with Montferrat their numerical superiority was overwhelming. Alba was still holding out, but for how long was not certain. Once the Angevin territories had been conquered, there was nothing to prevent the conquerors from seizing the prince's possessions as well, particularly in the Canavese. Louis of Vaud was preparing to leave for France to join the army of Philippe VI when he received the prince of Achaea's appeal for help. The marshal of Savoy, Antelme de Miolans, was sent to the Piedmont at once with another army.[73]

Once at Rivoli the host of Savoy was joined by the prince's army, and together they moved to Chieri, which had expelled its recent conquerors and placed itself under the joint lordship of the count of Savoy and the prince of Achaea.[74] At the communal palace in Chieri on 19 May 1347, Louis Rivoire of Domessin in Savoy was installed as the count's vicar. The commune agreed to furnish troops in time of war, to pay an annual tax to the count, and to allow him to select their *podestà* from a slate of candidates presented to him by them. In all other respects the citizens were allowed to govern themselves. They could coin money, and they were exempted from all tolls in the territories of the count of Savoy. This last concession was much contested by others who, besides the count, had the right to collect such tolls, and the merchants of Chieri were not always able to enjoy full immunity.

[73] It is often stated that Amadeus VI accompanied Miolans in May of 1347, but the *ADS* accounts for Montmélian (castellany, 1347–1348) expressly state that the count was at Chambéry and Le Bourget in May, and his presence at Châlon-sur-Saône on 16 June for the betrothal to Jeanne de Bourgogne has already been noted. The same rolls state that he was at Montmélian on 18 and 19 June, doubtless then en route for Italy, since he was "veniendo de Pedemonte" at Montmélian on 16 September.

[74] Chieri was one of the few Savoyard Piedmont towns with a population above 5,000. Cibrario, *Della Economia Politica del Medio Aevo* (Turin, 1861), II, 50ff., lists 1,333 *foci* for Chieri and 700 for Turin in 1377. For the dedication treaty of 1347, see Cibrario, *Storia*, III, 107ff.; Armando Tallone, *Patria Cismontana* (Bologna, 1928ff.), p. xcix.

But the act won the affection of the population for their new overlord, and encouraged the citizens to rely upon his protection against the enemies which their privileges created.

From Rivoli and Chieri the Savoyard army moved southward in the direction of Alba. The Visconti were obliged to raise the siege of Alba, but they declined to give battle and by 1 July the Savoyards were in Cuneo and Savigliano on the frontiers of the marquisate of Saluzzo. On 9 July, Savigliano placed itself under the condominion of the count of Savoy and the prince of Achaea, as Chieri had done.[75] Amadeus joined the host probably in late June and was present for the closing weeks of the campaign. Its swift success may have contributed to his growing fondness for military life and the joys of war.

Thus far all had gone well for the Savoyards, but the Visconti were not long in redressing the balance. A new alliance was formed, this time including Tommaso II of Saluzzo and even Dauphin Humbert II, who lent his support while passing through Lombardy on his return from the crusade.[76] In August this coalition opened a new military offensive and rapidly overran nearly all of the Angevin territories, almost to the borders of the county of Provence. In the north Montferrat surprised the city of Ivrea and captured it, a heavy blow for the Savoyards. Ivrea was the principal city of the Canavese and commanded the route from Lombardy to the Val d'Aosta and the commercially important passes of the Mont-Joux.

At this point Clement VI intervened in the troubles of Piedmont and Lombardy. Humbert II reached Avignon by the fall

[75] The formal charter of dedication for Savigliano was drawn up later, on 23 January 1349.

[76] Ulysse Chevalier, *Regeste Dauphinois*, VI (Valence, 1923), doc. 35326. However, Humbert specifically reserved his prior obligations to the count of Savoy and the prince of Achaea when he joined this alliance. The ruler of Milan at this time was Luchino Visconti, who governed jointly with his brother, Archbishop Giovanni. Luchino was much the more violent of the two, and in 1346 he had driven his three nephews, Matteo, Galeazzo, and Bernabò, into exile on charges of having conspired against him. Matteo had married a Gonzaga princess and had fled to the court of Mantua. His two younger brothers had taken refuge in the territories of Savoy. Cf. *AST*, inv. 16, doc. 14: "libravit domino Galeachio de Vicecomitibus de Medyolani in exhoneratione pensionis quam dominum Ludovicus de Sabaudie, cotutor tunc domini, percipere debebat pro anno [1347]," three hundred florins.

of 1347 and there encountered ambassadors from Savoy. Negotiations touching both the Piedmont and the Dauphiné took place during the winter of 1347–1348, and both Louis of Vaud and Amadeus of Geneva came to the papal court for lengthy stays.[77] A new plan was evolved by which the Savoyards and the pope might accomplish their ends simultaneously in one major diplomatic coup: the marriage of the dauphin to Blanche, sister of the count of Savoy. Talks with the dauphin on this subject began in December, and according to the memoirs of Humbert Pilat, the dauphin's secretary, negotiations were arduous and long.[78] The dauphin fell ill and the pope accorded an indulgence of forty days to all who would pray for his recovery.[79] In January 1348 things had reached such a pass that conferences with the Savoyards were broken off, and the dauphin began to treat for the hand of a daughter of the duke of Bourbon. But this tentative seems also to have failed, and the Savoyards revived their project. Things went more smoothly this time, and the marriage treaty was in fact signed by both parties in May. The Savoyards could congratulate themselves on a diplomatic masterstroke. They had already outmaneuvered the French king in securing the Burgundian heiress, and they now seemed on the way to blocking French annexation of the Dauphiné as well.

THE BLACK DEATH · FRENCH ANNEXATION OF THE DAUPHINÉ

The year 1348 was one of great calamity in European history, and the Savoyards bore their share of the misery which it brought. Already in 1344 the Black Death had struck at Châtillon-les-Dombes, and in 1348 it was gathering a terrible harvest throughout Bresse. In his account for 1349 the castellan of Treffort reported that he had no revenue for *introgio*, no real estate sales or transfers, and no one could even be found to take the custodianship of the vineyards, so completely had the Death interrupted the routine of life. Officers at Pont-de-Vaux were trying to secure the heritages of serfs at Boz who had died without heirs, and at St-André-en-Revermont, Jean de Felinz added a gloomy post-

[77] Cf. Cordey, *Les Comtes*, p. 91, note 5.
[78] *Memorabilia Humberti Pilati* in Valbonnais, II, doc. CCLXXIX, 624–625.
[79] Chevalier, *Regeste*, VI, doc. 35527.

script to his account: already thirty-five *mansi* were vacant owing to the plague.[80]

Bresse was not the only province to suffer the ravages of the Death, which seems to have been presaged everywhere by unusually bad weather, heavy rains, and floods.[81] At Lompnes in Bugey by 1351–1352 the castellan reported that instead of the usual fifty-one men who owed annual payments for *garda* at Brenod and Corcelles, only twenty-five were still alive. At St-Rambert in Bugey there was no revenue from the fairs of the St-Michel and St-André because of the plague. In the castellany of Chambéry there were sixty-five vacant hearths in the immediate area "propter mortalitatem," fifty-five more vacant in the parish of St-Sulpice, and over a hundred in the *mistralie* of St-Jean-d'Arvey and Les Déserts.[82] In the parish of Lémenc on the hillside above Chambéry the depopulation was so great that the curé was forced to address himself to the syndics of Chambéry for candle wax, explaining that the priory was no longer able to meet its obligations in this respect owing to the high price of wax and the great multitude of people who had died.[83]

Everywhere the terrified population laid the blame upon the Jews, who were accused of having poisoned the wells and fountains in a diabolical anti-Christian plot. The count's officers tried to protect the accused, but all too often it was impossible to hold out against the infuriated populace. Bowing to the public demand (and not unaware of the financial advantages of doing so), the judges and procurators of the count held trials to hear the charges against the Jews, who were imprisoned pending the investigation, and whose property was confiscated. At Conflans the castellan

[80] *ADCO*, B 10156 (Treffort), B 9164 (Pont-de-Vaux), B 9531 (St-André).

[81] *Ibid.*, B 9028 (Pont d'Ain), B 9165 (Pont-de-Vaux), B 9531 (St-André), B 10311 (Versoix).

[82] *ADS* (castellany), Chambéry, doc. 25, 1348–1349. The barony of Faucigny lost between 25 per cent and 79 per cent of its population, with the average loss per village estimated at 50 per cent between 1339 and 1411, according to the calculations of Louis Binz, "La population du diocèse de Genève à la fin du Moyen Age," *Mélanges d'histoire, économique et sociale* (offered to Antony Babel, Geneva, 1963).

[83] Ménabréa, MS, Book V, Chapter VI. At Avignon the cemetery was not large enough for the "centum et centum" who died. Cf. *Memorabilia Humberti Pilati* in Valbonnais, II, 624.

placed fifty-four Jews under guard in the hospital and seized their possessions, while Bernard de Murbel at Aiguebelle drew up an enormous list of the property of Jews in his castellany who were killed in 1348 "propter rumorem populi occasione sumpta propter mortalitatem."[84] On 5 June 1348, however the council of Savoy ordered the castellan of Côte-St-André not to trouble the Jews of his area because of the poisoning charge.[85]

While the trial of the Jews went on at Chambéry, the Jews of the town were placed under arrest and taken to Montmélian in the hope that their lives would be safer there. When the trial was over, they were brought back to Chambéry with an escort of forty men-at-arms and were imprisoned in the castle. Despite these precautions the people charged the castle, overpowered the garrison, broke into the prison, and butchered several of the prisoners. Many of the assailants were in turn arrested, three were condemned to be beheaded, one to be hanged, and several others to be fined—but the deed had been done.[86] Under the circumstances the outcome of the trial was a foregone conclusion. The Jews were found guilty, eleven of them were condemned to be burned alive and the rest subjected to an enormous fine.[87] The count thus avoided the necessity of expelling such useful subjects from his dominions, as was demanded by the population—but he did not scruple to profit from their plight.

Several members of the count's own family were not to survive the fatal year. The Death was no respecter of birth or station. By the end of July, Dowager-Countess Blanche de Bourgogne was dead and her dower lands had returned to the comital fisc.[88] Two years earlier, in May 1346, little "Amadeus bastardus" had died; and now in August 1348, Jean la Mitre, bastard of Savoy and seigneur of Cuine, also died and was buried in the Dominican convent at Montmélian.[89] In September came a still more cruel

[84] *ADS* (subsidy), Conflans, 1347–1348; inv. 43, SA 1198. Murbel's report was received by the *chambre des comptes* on 20 August 1349.

[85] Chevalier, *Regeste*, VI, doc. 35904.

[86] Ménabréa, MS, Book V, Chapter VI.

[87] *AST*, inv. 16, doc. 14. The Jews were condemned to a monthly tax of 160 florins for the next six years, in return for permission to remain in Savoyard territories.

[88] The date is given in the heading of the Treffort account, *ADCO*, B 10156.

[89] Cf. *ibid.*, p. 12, note 16; *ADS* (castellany), Montmélian, 26 March 1348–26 March 1349, payment in wax "pro luminario . . . domini Mitre de Sabaudie

blow. Amadeus' younger brother, Jean, now just ten years old, fell ill at Montgelat in the summer of 1348 and died within a few months. Jean had been married just the year before to the daughter of Guillaume de Grandson, sire of Sainte-Croix. The most serious loss of all for the welfare of the state, however, was the death of Louis of Vaud, after some sixty years of active and adventurous life.[90]

Family calamities were accompanied by political misfortunes. On 13 December 1348 the Piedmont peace talks at Avignon came to an end, and neither branch of the house of Savoy secured the advantages it had hoped for. The marquis of Montferrat was to share the city of Ivrea with the count of Savoy, which annoyed the marquis, who wanted it all, and infuriated Giacomo, who lost his share entirely.[91] Montferrat expressed his dissatisfaction by hostilities in the Canavese, while the prince meditated future revenge. Chieri and Savigliano were confirmed to Savoy, but only on the condition that the Savoyards abandon their Angevin ally in the Piedmont. The Visconti retained Vercelli and Biella on the eastern frontier of the Canavese, thus threatening Savoyard interests in that region. Tommaso II of Saluzzo did homage to the lord of Milan, in spite of homage owed to Savoy and in addition to homage done to Humbert II during Tommaso's Dauphiné exile in 1342.[92] A worse peace could hardly have been made, for all parties were dissatisfied and prepared to violate it at the first opportunity.

---

quondam, sepulti apud Montemelianum in domo fratrum predicatorum in mense Augusti," 1348. Bernard, *Montmélian*, p. 136, seems in error in placing the death of the bastard Amadeus in 1348.

[90] *AST*, inv. 38, folio 43, doc. 2 (1345–1353), expenses in wax "pro luminario sepulturie Johannis de Sabaudie, fratris domini, die xi Sept.," 1348. Cf. *ADCO*, B 9028 (Pont d'Ain) on his marriage. The exact date of Louis of Vaud's death is not known, but in a document dated 29 January 1349 he is referred to as "quondam." Grenus-Saladin, *Documents rélatifs à l'histoire du Pays de Vaud* (Geneva, 1817), doc. 7, pp. 8–10. While all of these people no doubt did not die of the plague, the coincidence of so many deaths with its appearance justifies the suspicion that it did cause some of them.

[91] The arrangement at Ivrea was the subject of a second arbitration, that of Archbishop Giovanni Visconti on 25 September 1349. (Cf. Tallone, *Patria Cismontana*, p. xcix.) The city remained half under Montferrat and half under Savoy, but Giacomo got Cirié in return for his share of Ivrea.

[92] Cibrario, *Storia*, III, 114–116.

Finally, before the summer had hardly begun, the marriage alliance between the dauphin and the house of Savoy was broken off. The reasons were political as well as personal. The ceaseless rivalries between vassals of the count and the dauphin along the Rhône valley frontier were simply beyond the power of either prince to control. In spite of repeated affirmations of amity exchanged between the two, the castellany records abound in references to raids and threatened attacks in 1346–1348.[93] Moreover, while relations with the Dauphinois worsened, so did those with the French. The royal *bailli* of Mâcon reopened his quarrels with the count's castellans in Bresse, perhaps reflecting ill-feeling in Paris over recent Savoyard diplomatic policy. In 1346–1347 officers of the count sent to Mâcon were seized and imprisoned. The following year the *bailli* of Bresse ordered the castellans and nobles of the region to appear in arms before Mâcon on the eve of the feast of St-Laurent to protect the lands of the count "against the men of the king of France."[94]

The *cause célèbre*, however, was the war which erupted between Edward of Beaujeu, a vassal of Savoy, and three Dauphinois nobles—the lords of St-Trivier, Grolée, and Beauregard. Negotiations during the winter of 1347–1348 with a view to finding a peaceful solution to their differences were fruitless. In March 1348 the sire of Beaujeu captured Beauregard, a fief of the Dauphiné, and refused to surrender it when summoned to do so by the dauphin. Humbert became enraged, gathered an army of his own, and marched against Miribel on the Rhône, the most vulnerable of Edward's towns. The regents of Savoy protested against this act of war on the part of the dauphin in person, but without result. The siege of Miribel began on 6 April, according to the memoirs of Humbert Pilat, and sixteen days later the town surrendered.[95]

[93] *ADCO*, B 6774 (Bâgé), B 7101 (Bourg), B 9381 bis (Remens-en-Bugey). The report sent by Henri de Villars to Dauphin Humbert in June 1347 to bring him up-to-date on developments during his absence mentions continuous fighting between Savoyards and Dauphinois. Chevalier, *Regeste*, VI, doc. 35224.

[94] *ADCO*, B 7346 (Bresse, judicature, 1346–1347); B 6773 (Bâgé, 1348–1349); B 9164 (Pont-de-Vaux, 1348–1349).

[95] Thus Cordey, *Les Comtes*, pp. 96ff., has misdated this campaign. It could not have taken place in 1347 because Humbert had not yet returned from his crusade.

At this juncture it was apparently Amadeus' turn to become enraged, and he did so with all the recklessness of his fourteen years. He declared that if Humbert did not return Miribel to Beaujeu, the marriage alliance with Blanche de Savoie was off. Humbert's reply was as imaginative as it was insulting. Instead of marrying Blanche de Savoie, the dauphin announced that he would marry the town of Miribel. Before a great concourse of notables on 12 May 1348, Humbert declared that he would never allow Miribel to be separated from the Dauphiné in the future. Then, "as a sign of [his] great determination, he and the Dauphiné married [Miribel] with the ring of the lord bishop of [Grenoble]."[96] Amadeus must have mastered his indignation at this affront, however, because two weeks later, on 27 May 1348 at Avignon, the marriage treaty between his sister and the dauphin was drawn up despite the recent threats to call it off. Blanche de Savoie was to have the enormous dowry of 120,000 florins— precisely the price which Humbert had set some years earlier when he had offered to sell his inheritance to Robert of Naples. This fact suggests that nothing short of the annexation of the Dauphiné by Savoy was envisaged should the marriage prove childless.[97]

Unfortunately, there were too many forces working against this alliance, and the Miribel incident was a symptom, not a cause, of the fact. Too many Dauphinois nobles had been anti-Savoyard for generations, and too many of them still bore the scars of that proud enmity. In addition, too many of Humbert's associates had been won over by the king of France, and by now the French were willing to offer more for the Dauphiné than the Savoyards could match. There is no indication of a violent rupture, but by mid-June, Humbert had already forgotten his Savoyard fiancée and the treaty he had signed, and he was negotiating again for the hand of Jeanne de Bourbon, whom the count of Savoy had abandoned just a year before. Clement VI, who was only tem-porarily at cross-purposes with French royal policy, agreed as

[96] Humbert's words were "quod dictum castrum nunquam reddet, nec a Dalphinatu separabit, et in signum majoris firmitatis, ipsum sibi et Dalphinatu desponsavit per annulum domini episcopi." Cited in M-C. Guigue, *Topographie historique du département de l'Ain* (Trevoux, 1873), pp. 234-235.

[97] This is Cordey's opinion, *Les Comtes*, p. 91.

readily to this project as he had some months earlier to the Savoyard alliance.

The switch was a decisive triumph for French diplomacy. At first negotiations prospered, then Pierre of Bourbon began to hesitate. He seemed unwilling to bring the negotiations to a conclusion, then hesitated to fulfill his obligations.[98] Delays followed upon delays, and the dauphin grew angry. Finally he canceled negotiations and announced that he would not have the Bourbon princess at all. What Pierre of Bourbon's motives were in thus allowing so profitable an alliance to fail cannot be established beyond question, but subsequent events permit a fairly safe guess. For the king of France, Humbert's marriage to Jeanne de Bourbon would be better than a marriage to Blanche de Savoie, but no marriage at all was infinitely preferable to either match. Money and intimidation may have influenced the duke's change of heart, but the future of his daughter is eloquent in itself. Within two years Jeanne de Bourbon was married to the eldest son of Jean of Normandy, Charles, who had just become the first dauphin of the house of France. Bourbon thus had a daughter in the Dauphiné after all.

Certainly Humbert's efforts to find a wife had alarmed the king of France. No sooner had the Savoy and Bourbon matches been broken off than agents of Philippe VI descended upon the dauphin's court at Theyn during the winter of 1348–1349, no doubt hoping to put an end to the wife-seeking. This time they appealed to Humbert's religious inclinations. The dauphin's natural aversion for political responsibility was easily interpreted as a wholesome disdain for earthly things. It was pointed out how easily he might be rid of his creditors were he to allow the French king to make a cash settlement for the transfer of the Dauphiné.

At last a decade of ceaseless and skillful maneuvering bore fruit. Whatever voices might have been raised against the project, Humbert was once more resolved to abandon his inheritance as the price of financial and political security. On 30 March 1349 at Romans in the presence of French envoys and a host of prelates and nobles, the third and final treaty of "transport" was concluded. By its terms the Dauphiné was to go not to Jean of Normandy, but to his eldest son, Charles, then twelve years of age. Humbert was to

---

[98] Guiffrey, pp. 70–71; Chevalier, *Regeste*, VI, doc. 3600ff.

receive 200,000 florins and an annual pension of 24,000. He also would retain possession of the castle of Beauvoir-en-Royans, which he intended to convert into a monastery where he might withdraw from the world to live out his days in contemplation and spiritual solitude. On 16 July at Lyon, the last of the Tour-du-Pin to reign in the Dauphiné resigned his principality into the hands of young Charles de Valois. Scarcely more than a year later Philippe VI died, Jean of Normandy became king of France, and Charles became heir presumptive to the French throne. All that the Savoyards had been able to do had failed to prevent the annexation of the great province by the powerful neighbor to the west.[99]

As for Humbert's withdrawal from the world, a single year of contemplation and spiritual solitude at his palatial "monastery" of Beauvoir-en-Royans convinced him that this was not really the sort of religious life to which he had been called. By December 1350 he had left his solitude and had appeared at the papal court in Avignon, where the world was more to his liking. At Christmas the pope conferred upon him the first three holy orders simultaneously, and the new Father Humbert performed his first mass. Early in January 1351 he was honored with the title of patriarch of Alexandria and was soon after given the post of "administrateur perpetuel" of the archbishopric of Reims. Later in 1351 he went to Paris, and he was handsomely treated at the court of France during the remaining four years of his life. In January 1354, Jean II gave him the administration of the bishopric of Paris, and it was while on his way to Avignon to secure papal permission to substitute Paris for Reims that, on 4 May 1355, Dauphin Humbert left the world for good.

[99] The Savoyards may have earned some small reward by their obstinacy, if a treaty drawn up at Avignon in February or March 1349 can be so interpreted. The treaty itself has apparently disappeared; only a protocol remains which describes it, but does not stipulate the sum involved. Cordey, *Les Comtes*, p. 92.

# III

# $\mathcal{L}$or$\delta$ $\mathcal{C}$ount of $\mathcal{S}$avo$\gamma$

## 1348-1355

### INITIAL PROBLEMS · THE SAVOY-VISCONTI MARRIAGE

THE next seven years speedily introduced the teen-aged count to the burdens of statesmanship and war. His majority was declared on his fourteenth birthday, in January 1348, and the death of Louis of Vaud within the year underlined his need to grow up quickly. The council of regency, which was now known as the "council of Savoy" or simply as the "count's council," selected one of its own members, Guillaume de la Baume, "chivalier sans raproche," to fill the post held by the baron of Vaud, because some feared for the security of the state with Amadeus of Geneva as sole regent.[1] Both the regents and the council thus continued to guide their young master, and for the next few years the count's minority went on in practice, if not in theory. These were arduous years, and Amadeus' initiation was a baptism of fire. A long struggle with the new French masters of the Dauphiné created an undercurrent of apprehension, while actual fighting shattered the quiet of the mountains in Bugey, in Gex and Faucigny, in the Valais. In the midst of such tempests, young Amadeus VI made his debut upon the political scene in a style worthy of his illustrious forebears. At eighteen he was knighted on the field of battle; at nineteen he earned a permanent place in the annals of chivalry as the "Green Count of Savoy." The "Treaty of Paris" on his twenty-first birthday constitutes one of the most significant accomplishments in Savoyard history—the stabilization of the western frontier.

---

[1] At least so the chronicles affirm (Servion, II, 69; Cabaret, p. 135, *dorso*). Guillaume de la Baume was the sole legitimate son and heir of the famous Galois de la Baume who in 1348 was lieutenant-governor of Languedoc and Saintonge for the king of France.

76

At first the western frontier seemed more unstable than ever. The new French masters of the Dauphiné were even more aggressive in 1348–1349 than their predecessors had been. Young Dauphin Charles was under the tutelage of Henri de Villars, archbishop of Lyon, who promptly concluded an alliance with the count of Auxerre against the sire of Beaujeu and the count of Savoy. A few weeks later Alamand de Saint-Jeoire, bishop of Geneva and an ardent foe of Savoy, placed himself and two castles of his see under the protection of the dauphin. This act was mainly directed against the count of Geneva, but given the bad blood between the bishop and the count of Savoy, the move was also anti-Savoyard. Clement VI supported the bishop's action and threatened to excommunicate the officers of his "beloved sons," the counts of Geneva and Savoy, if they continued to molest the church of Geneva.[2]

Both counts reacted swiftly to protect their interests. Amadeus of Geneva protested to the dauphin, then seized the contested castles and replaced the delphinal banners with his own. Amadeus of Savoy sent to warn his Piedmont cousin, Giacomo of Achaea, that his services as a vassal of Savoy might be required in the near future. Then an embassy was dispatched to Milan, where the death of Luchino Visconti in the late summer of 1349 had created a situation more favorable to Savoyard interests. The new ruler of Milan was its archbishop, Giovanni Visconti, Luchino's brother; and his first act was to recall his exiled nephews to share in the government of the state. Matteo had taken refuge at the court of the Gonzagas, while the two younger brothers, Galeazzo and Bernabò, had found friendship and support in Savoy.[3]

The return of the brothers to participate in the government of the Visconti dominions provided an excellent opportunity for the count of Savoy to replace an enemy with allies. Galeazzo and Bernabò were grateful to the Savoyards for their hospitality and needed allies to strengthen their own return to power. The count and his advisers were quick to recognize the immense advantages

---

[2] Cordey, *Les Comtes*, p. 102; *AEG*, inv. A, item 254; *MDG*, XVIII, doc. 136 (27 October 1349). The sire of Beaujeu was still unreconciled to the loss of Miribel. Soon after Alamand de Saint-Jeoire's acceptance of the dauphin's protection, the bishop was officially named as one of Charles's counselors.

[3] *AST*, inv. 16, doc. 14 (1346–1349) records a pension of three hundred florins which Galeazzo received annually from the count's treasury.

which an alliance with Milan would give them in Piedmont affairs. The initiative seems to have come from Milan, but both parties were equally interested in the mutual assistance pact which was concluded in 1349.[4] The following year the Visconti alliance was made more permanent with the betrothal of Amadeus' sister, Blanche de Savoie, to Galeazzo Visconti. The first marriage treaty was drawn up at Chambéry on 26 May 1350, and the final contract was signed at Le Bourget on 10 September. "Nobilis, egregia, et excelsa" Lady Blanche, now fourteen, was to have a dowry of 50,000 florins, of which 10,000 were assigned on the revenues of the castellany of Yenne.[5] Twelve days later Blanche left Chambéry on the route of the Mont Cenis, escorted by her brother and her half brothers, Humbert and Ogier de Savoie. On 28 September the lords of Milan joined them at Rivoli and the marriage took place.

During the festivities which followed, young Amadeus decided to honor his sister and her husband by creating a new order of knighthood, somewhat grandly christened the "Order of the Black Swan." The fourteen members of the Order were to display on their shields, "or in another manner," the emblem of a black swan, with a red beak and feet, on a silver background.[6] No one was to be admitted to membership unless he had a "charger and a palfrey" and could serve for at least one week at his own expense whenever the need arose. The knights of the Black Swan vowed to assist one another at their own expense against all, even against relatives beyond the degree of cousins-german. Those in the Order were not to quarrel among themselves, and disputes were to be submitted to the arbitration of the others. Anyone who failed to observe this provision was to be expelled from the Order, and those remaining were to make common cause against him.

[4] The treaty, dated 8 October 1349 at Cirié, created a league among the Visconti, the counts of Savoy and Geneva, and the prince of Achaea. The last promised not to help any rebel subjects of the Visconti or to enter into any other alliance without the consent of the archbishop and his nephews. *AST*, *Trattati diversi*, mazzo I, doc. 17.

[5] Guichenon, IV, *preuves*, 181–182. The remaining 40,000 were to be deposited at Hautecombe until Amadeus had assigned to his sister properties that would yield this sum. If he had not done so by March 1351, the 40,000 florins went to Galeazzo, provided he agreed to use it only to purchase property in Savoyard territories west of the Alps.

[6] See the text of the Ordinances in Commentary, V.

In case of a dispute between a knight of the Order and someone outside its ranks, the knights were to summon him who was
not "of the oath" and make enquiry into the matter. Only if the
outsider was adjudged in the wrong and refused satisfaction could
the knight, aided by his comrades of the Order, make war upon
him. So that the Order might have funds at its disposal, each
knight-banneret was to pay eight gold *écus*; each "Chivallier simple," four *écus*; and each squire, one. The money was to be kept
at designated religious establishments and not to be spent, except
by command of the knights assembled on the Feast of Saint André, and then only for purposes "estreordinaire." Each new member of the Order, at least if he qualified as a "riche homme," was
required to pay these entrance fees according to his "puissance."
The final provision bound the "compaignons" to serve "les grans
seignours" of the Order (meaning the counts of Savoy and Geneva,
and Galeazzo Visconti) at the expense of said seigneurs "for their
persons."

This curious document reveals the extent to which young Amadeus was influenced by the chivalric ideas of the day, but it also
shows that he had more than tournaments on his mind. He was
inexperienced and unsure of himself, and on the eve of a confrontation with his western foes, he wanted moral as well as
financial and military support. It is only in the context of this
situation that the founding of the Order of the Black Swan can
be fully understood. Amadeus did not even participate in the en-
tertainments organized in honor of the newlyweds upon their arrival at Milan. At Turin the count bade his sister a fond farewell
and headed back to Savoy.

As it turned out, the winter of 1350–1351 passed more quietly
than expected, but there was considerable activity on diplomatic
fronts. The death of Blanche de Bourgogne had been followed by
that of her brother, Eudes IV, in 1349, and the Burgundian alliance was substantially weakened. The heir of the late duke was
only three years old, and the prospect of a long regency rendered
less certain the military assistance upon which the Savoyards had
counted. This development may have prompted the count to make
another move in the direction of an English alliance. The new
king of France, Jean II "le Bon," needed to be reminded that the
count of Savoy might well desert him for the English if he did not
put an end to harassments from the Dauphiné. While Jeanne de

Bourgogne was still being reared at the court of Savoy as the count's bride-to-be, envoys were sent to Edward III to broach the possibility of a marriage between Amadeus and the king's daughter Isabella.[7]

Nothing came of this move, but it reveals Savoyard maneuvering on the eve of a confrontation with the dauphin. It also provoked the first open breach with the count of Geneva. When the council of Savoy met at St-Genix on 9 July 1351 to hear the reply of the English ambassadors, Amadeus III declared his opposition to these anti-French negotiations and asked that his position be formally recorded. This is the earliest indication that the count of Geneva was no longer in accord with those controlling Savoyard policy.

### THE VAL D'AOSTA, 1351

In the summer of 1351 the relative quiet of the western front permitted Amadeus to make his first visit to a part of his inheritance which he had never seen—the duchy of Aosta, where the routes of the two St. Bernard passes descend into Italy. Once every seven years the counts of Savoy, as hereditary rulers of the Val d'Aosta, were authorized by custom to preside over the *Audiences générales* in the valley.[8] In mid-August preparations were complete, and the count set out for the Tarentaise with a large retinue of soldiers, jurists, and nobles, including the count of Geneva and most of the barons of Amadeus' council. Hugues Bernard, "professor of law and knight, judge of Savoy," headed a group of attorneys, clerks, and secretaries whose services would be as important as those of the soldiers to the success of the *Audiences*. At Bourg-St-Maurice the cavalcade began the zig-zagging 4,000-foot ascent to the summit of the Colonne-Joux, the medieval name for the Little St. Bernard pass, where a ruined column still stands as a reminder of the days when Roman legions had trod the same thin, rocky trail. Nearby on the summit of the pass stood the hospice founded in the tenth century by Saint Bernard de Menthon.

[7] Cordey, *Les Comtes*, p. 82; doc. 26, pp. 308–309.

[8] The earliest *Audiences* on record were held in 1233, the last 1466. Cf. Augusta Lange, *Le Udienze dei Conti e Duchi di Savoia nella Valle d'Aosta 1337–1351* (Paris and Turin, 1956).

Several hours ahead of the count rode his herald and 200 men-at-arms, for the customs of the Val d'Aosta provided that during the *Audiences* the count-duke had the right to garrison with his own men every stronghold in the duchy. The size of the garrison varied with the importance of the place, but few places were overlooked. The count's authority during the *Audiences* depended upon his effective, if temporary, control of the turbulent Valdostan nobility. The first stronghold to be garrisoned was the tower at Thuile, the first village on the Italian side of the pass. Farther down the wooded ravine, the valley of Courmayeur, in the shadow of the giant Mont Blanc, contained three more places to be occupied. At Morgex the count's outriders were met by the barons of Archet, who surrendered their three castles guarding the passage of the valley. Then the Savoyards rode on down the valley toward Aosta to occupy sixteen more strongholds in advance of their master's arrival.[9]

Some hours later the count and his nobles, with banners flying, filed through the slender valleys of the Dora to the plain of Morgex. A crowd of syndics, barons, and peasants had assembled to greet their "tres beau seigneur," the seventeen-year-old scion of the ancient Humbertines, who had ruled in these parts from time immemorial. The Archet were his hosts for his first night in the Val d'Aosta, for to them belonged the expensive honor of lodging the princes of Savoy whenever they crossed the mountains for the *Audiences*.

The next morning was Sunday, 14 August. The procession toward Aosta began to assume monumental proportions as hundreds turned out to view the spectacle and join the procession for at least a few miles. At La Salle the bishop of Aosta, Nicholas III Bersatori, in full ecclesiastical regalia and surrounded by his clergy, was waiting to escort the count the rest of the way. The warrior clans of Les Cours, of Sarriod-Bard, of Villa de la Tour de Gressan, now swelled the festive ranks; and as the company approached

[9] They were the castles at Châtelard, Rochefort, Introd, St. Pierre, Sarre, and Aymavilles; the "domos fortes" at Les Cours, La Salle, Avise, Allian, Ville-sur-Gressan, Planta, and Gressan; and the towers of Sarriod-La Tour, Gontard at Villeneuve, and Allian. A total of 199 Savoyard *clientes* garrisoned the twenty-two strongholds occupied above Aosta. Lange, doc. 44, p. 132.

Aosta, the church bells of the valley began to ring out "as a sign of honor and joy."[10]

At St-Pierre another host of Valdostan nobles joined the procession, which entered the town of Aosta through the gate of Pont-St-Genis. The bells of the cathedral now joined those of the priory of St-Ours in announcing the count's arrival. The streets were decked with rich hangings, and windows and balconies, particularly along the route to the cathedral, were laden with green bows and garlands of flowers.[11] Bishop Nicholas, who had ridden on ahead, now awaited the count on foot at the town gates. Amadeus dismounted, knelt before the bishop, and kissed the cross presented to him. Then the bishop raised him up and amid the cheers of the townsfolk led him through the streets to the cathedral. Before the high altar the count knelt again and prayed briefly, then Pierre de Challant, canon of Aosta, stepped toward to address him. "You have come to render justice to your people. You must swear to observe the good customs of our country and its charters, and to defend the rights of widows and orphans."[12] Amadeus knelt once more and solemnly swore to maintain the customs of the valley, the rights and property of the church, and the franchises and liberties granted by his predecessors.

The next day on the throne in the great hall of the episcopal palace, Amadeus VI, *dux Augustae*, received the homages of the Valdostan nobility. It was proclaimed that the count had come to Aosta to hold the *Audiences générales*, and that all peers and non-peers,[13] and all nobles or non-nobles who owed fidelity, homage, *plaits, gîtes*, services, or any other obligations on the occasion of the count's presence would have the space of one week in which to fulfill them. Anyone failing to do so would be prosecuted according to the customs of the valley. All lawsuits involving the count's interests which were already in progress in lesser courts were evoked before judges of the *Audiences*. On 16 August, Mas-

---

[10] *Ibid.*, doc. 46, p. 139: ". . . campane pulsate fuerunt ad boudetam in signum gaudii et reverencie donec tota comitiva domini transivit."

[11] *Ibid.*, p. 140: ". . . in qua civitate fuit cum gaudio et honore maximo recepto, cum carreriis paratis."

[12] *Ibid.* "Domine, vos venistis pro justicia tenenda et debetis hic jurare bonas patrie consuetudines servare, viduas, orfanos et eorum jura deffendere et chertras servare."

[13] *Ibid.*, pp. xxxivff. on peers and non-peers.

ter Hugues Bernard and Lancelot de Châtillon, the count's *bailli* of the Val d'Aosta, left with heralds and another company of *clientes* to garrison the remaining strongholds of the duchy—one man of the law, two hundred men of the sword.[14]

The *Audiences générales* consisted of three separate tribunals sitting simultaneously. The judges were chosen by the count from among the barons, bourgeois, clergy, and jurists of the valley. Each judge solemnly swore on the Holy Bible to render judgment according to the precepts of justice and the dictates of his conscience, and under no circumstances to accept gifts or favors from interested parties. A panel of eight judges would hear civil cases, and a second panel of five was named for criminal suits. The supreme feudal tribunal would be presided over by Amadeus himself, assisted by his council, in the great hall of the bishop's palace.[15]

The proceedings of the *Audiences* furnish much information on the nature of the count's authority in the Val d'Aosta. Probably nowhere else in his territories was the nobility more warlike and less submissive to the rule of law. Comital officers in the duchy were barely able to hold their own against the great baronial families whose gray rock fortresses lined the routes of the Mont-Joux and grimly guarded the entrance to every lateral valley. If the Valdostans fought for the count when he summoned them outside the duchy, they fought for their own account once they had returned. The only reckoning they ever needed to fear were the *Audiences*, few and far between.

On the first day of the feudal sessions the baron of Sarriod demanded that Henri of Quart surrender Pierre de Sarriod, for the customs of the valley required that all prisoners be delivered into the custody of the count's officers during the *Audiences*. The next day the count's prosecutor summoned the baron of Quart to com-

[14] *Ibid.*, doc. 46, pp. 134–135, 140–141. The strongholds were the castles of Quart, Brissogne, Fenis, Montjovet, Challant, Pont-St-Martin, Arnaz, Ussel, Châtillon, Cly, and Nus, and the tower of Nus.

[15] The feudal court consisted of the bishop, the prior of St-Ours, canon Pierre de Challant; the count of Geneva and the council of Savoy; the *bailli* of Aosta; and the peers of the Val d'Aosta: Aymon II de Challant, Jacquemet de Challant-Montjovet, Jacquemin and Pierre d'Avise, Alexandre de Nus, Jacquemet de l'Archet, Vionin Gontard, Jean de la Cour de Courmayeur, Henri Doczan, Jean de Gignod, Jacquemet de la Tour de Villa en Gressan.

ply and ordered Arducion de Valleise to surrender Dominique de Valleise, whom he was accused of having imprisoned. When Arducion finally confessed that Dominique had died in his dungeons, the count's officers charged him with homicide and imprisoned him in the tower of Châtelard near Morgex.[16] Henri of Quart, on the other hand, contended that Pierre de Sarriod had taken holy orders and was thus beyond the count's jurisdiction. This protest was ignored, and Quart was eventually forced to give up his prisoner and pay a fine of 2,000 florins for this and other misdeeds.[17]

Disputes among the barons were endless. Henri of Quart and Alexandre of Nus disputed criminal jurisdiction on the common boundary of their seigneuries. Quart, Sarre, and Challant were quarrelling over wardship of the child heirs to the barony of Verrès. Arducion, Jean, and Amadeus de Valleise were conjointly convicted of obstructing the *via publica*, of building a gallows on ducal territory, and of hanging a man on it. For such flagrant violations of the count's sovereignty, "vituperosa et nefanda crimina et delicta," all three were placed under detention.[18]

On 20 September at the request of the bourgeois of Aosta, Amadeus granted the privilege of new fairs to be held for three days in November and again in May. The *bailli* was instructed to see that the inhabitants of the valley were free to take part in them, and comital officers were expressly forbidden to receive perquisites from those attending. Above all, the *bailli* was to see that the nobles, particularly Henri of Quart, did not interfere with subjects who wished to go to the new fairs. Judicial fees in the count's courts were fixed at a lower rate so as to facilitate recourse to the protection of the law.[19]

[16] *Ibid.*, doc. 46, pp. 143–145, 168–169. Dominique was posthumously accused of innumerable crimes, including the murder of another member of the family, Jean de Valleise. *Ibid.*, p. 157. Arducion was later taken all the way to Rossillon in Bugey. Cf. *ADS* (castellany), Montmélian, 1351–1352, librata. He was forced to abandon all claims to the property of Dominique and his son. Lange, doc. 82, pp. 274–277.

[17] *Ibid.*, docs. 46 and 47, pp. 148, 165–166, 211–213.

[18] *Ibid.*, doc. 46, pp. 167–169. All but Arducion were later released on promises of good behavior (doc. 70, pp. 253–254). But they too gave up their claims to the inheritance of Dominique, which escheated to the count (doc. 71, pp. 254–256).

[19] Cf. J. A. Duc, *Histoire de l'Eglise d'Aosta*, 10 vols. (Aosta, 1908), III, 452–453.

On the afternoon of 3 October the *Audiences* at Aosta came to an end, and the count was escorted by Aymon de Challant on a visit to the rest of the valley. The company spent the night at the castle of Châtillon, for its seigneurs by custom owed the count and his suite bed and board for one day and one night during the time of the *Audiences*. Two days later Amadeus was at lofty Montjovet, where he was also entitled to a day and a night of hospitality, and the Challant clan turned out in formidable array to do him honor.[20]

On 6 October the count reached Bard, and three days of *Audiences* were held at nearby Donnas for the benefit of the inhabitants of the eastern half of the duchy. Here, where the great Savoyard fortress of Bard guards the narrow entrance to the Val d'Aosta from Italy, the first visit of Amadeus VI to the valley came to an end. As the count must have perceived, his authority in the duchy rested very largely upon a kind of partnership with the house of Challant, who commanded greater resources than any other family in the region. The Challants had been hereditary viscounts of Aosta until 1295, when Amadeus V had induced Ibal de Challant to surrender that dignity in exchange for the barony of Montjovet. Ibal the Great, who died in 1323, had been baron of Graines, Ussel, St-Marcel, Fenis, Montjovet, and Andorno; and three of his brothers were bishops—at Aosta, Sion, and Geneva. Pierre de Challant, coseigneur of Montjovet and canon of Aosta, had been named in 1343 to the council of regency. On this visit young Amadeus made the acquaintance of the leader of the clan during his lifetime, Aymon II, lord of Fenis and Aymavilles, a cultivated grand seigneur and famous castle-builder.

The value of the alliance with the house of Challant in the Val d'Aosta depended, of course, upon their devotion to the interests of Savoy. Amadeus' forebears had secured the adherence of the family initially by generous grants of lands and revenues. To retain their allegiance other means were employed. One was to preserve the power of rival families like the Quarts and Valleises, despite their frequent insubordination.[21] So long as these rivals were

---

[20] *Ibid.*, III, 449. Aware of the count's fondness for wild animals, the lords of Challant-Montjovet presented him with a large bear for his menagerie at Chambéry.

[21] Thus the Valleises were always pardoned for their many offenses, and in

strongly entrenched in the valley, the Challants were not likely to forget how vital to their own interests was the protection of their Savoyard overlords.

Another means of attaching the Challants firmly to the interests of Savoy is revealed by the career of Aymon de Challant. Since 1331 he had been castellan of Lanzo, some distance from his home valleys. In 1350 he had been made castellan of Avigliana in the Val di Susa, still farther south. Over the next three decades he would serve as castellan at Susa, Chambéry, Tarentaise, Ivrea, and Sallanches successively.[22] Through these posts, and through innumerable military and diplomatic missions, the great Valdostan seigneur became a veritable minister of state, concerned with serving the interests of the count at least as often as his own. When Aymon's cousin Iblet de Challant, one of the great warriors of the age, returned to the Val d'Aosta after years of service under the kings of France, he too was often removed from his ancestral valleys as the count's *podestà* of Ivrea, castellan of Avigliana, and captain-general of Piedmont.

For the rest, the authority of the count of Savoy in the Val d'Aosta was maintained by the *bailli* and the castellans of the four strongholds in the valley under the count's direct control— Aosta, Châtelargent, Bard, and Donnas. Their administrative power was greatly strengthened by the *Audiences générales*, which remained the chief instrument of Savoyard sovereignty.[23] Only during these sessions was the count in full control of the duchy; only then could he exact a strict accounting of obligations forgotten or ignored. This was his one real opportunity to cast down the high and mighty, to punish the wicked, to render justice to the poor and oppressed. The *Audiences* were still too few and too brief, but they were a foundation for more adequate government in the future. It was to be the work of Amadeus VI to use the *Audiences* and his four Valdostan castellans to build up such a

---

1355, when the count acquired the barony of St-Pierre from the Gontards, he enfeoffed it to Henri of Quart. Cf. Duc, III, 468–469.

[22] See Commentary, IV.

[23] The financial importance of the *Audiences* was not overlooked, to be sure. Lancelot de Châtillon reported something in the vicinity of 1,500 florins in gifts, *banna concordata*, etc.; and fines collected by the various tribunals totalled 1,188 florins. Lange, docs. 85, 86, 87, 88.

concentration of land and power as to render the authority of the count of Savoy unchallengeable in future centuries.

## TREATY WITH FRANCE · FIRST VALAIS EXPEDITION

In the fall of 1351 it was the French who again absorbed the attention of the Savoyards. Paris had at last awakened to the implications of the Savoy-Burgundy alliance of 1347, now that Eudes IV was dead, and perhaps Jean le Bon had got wind of the latest Savoyard embassies to Edward III. On 27 October 1351 at Avignon, a treaty of peace and friendship was signed with the French.[24] The dispute over frontier jurisdictions and vassals in the Dauphiné was postponed by simply agreeing to abide by the terms of a treaty of 1337 which was already hopelessly out-of-date. The important provisions of the treaty of 1351 concerned other matters. Jean le Bon wanted above all to break up the Savoy-Burgundy marriage alliance, because as matters now stood, should the infant Philippe de Rouvres die, Jeanne de Bourgogne would inherit the vast Burgundian dominions. To prevent such a possibility, Jean le Bon was ready to give Amadeus 60,000 gold florins, in addition to a palace in Paris, and a lucrative fief in France to replace the viscounty of Maulevrier, which the Savoyards considered too far away.[25] In return, Amadeus was to send Jeanne de Bourgogne back to France, renounce any thought of an English marriage, and promise to remain the military ally of the French. In December the Savoyard negotiators brought the treaty back to Le Bourget, where the count and his council approved it.

The treaty of 1351 was hardly a triumph for Savoyard diplomacy. The outstanding issues with the dauphin remained, and to abandon the advantageous Burgundian alliance in exchange for 60,000 florins and a few fringe benefits cannot be regarded as enterprising statesmanship. The treaty did gain time for the Savoyards, however, and they now needed time. In October 1351 the bishop of Sion, a faithful friend of Amadeus VI and his father, arrived at the court of Savoy accompanied by a handful of followers and bearing a woeful tale: there was rebellion in the Valais. The rugged inhabitants of the Valais were of a very different

[24] Cordey, *Les Comtes*, p. 105.
[25] *Ibid.*, p. 106. The exchange of Maulevrier for a nearer fief had been promised to Amadeus V, but had never taken place.

stamp from those elsewhere in the dominions of Savoy. For centuries the counts of Savoy had been attempting to dominate the whole upper Rhône valley from Lake Geneva to the Furka pass in order to control this important route to Italy.[26] The height of Savoyard influence was reached under Pierre II, but vigorous bishops at Sion since then had managed to emancipate the see from Savoyard tutelage. By the end of the thirteenth century the greater part of the population was grouped around ten village communes, five of them between Martigny and Sierre, where French was spoken, and five upriver from Sierre to the Furka, where the inhabitants spoke German. Across the Furka lay the famous Forest Cantons of Uri, Schwyz, and Unterwalden, whose inhabitants were already at the forefront of the struggle for Swiss independence.[27] These hardy sons of William Tell, sharing the language and culture of the peasants of the High Valais, were more than ready to lend their support to their weaker neighbors, whose aspirations for the same kind of liberty found stubborn opponents in the bishop of Sion and the Valaisan nobility.

From the bridge over the Morge a few miles below Sion, to the elbow of the Rhône at Martigny, the Valais had remained under the control of the counts of Savoy, whose castellans surveyed the valley from rocky perches at Saxon, Saillon, and Conthey.[28] In 1323, however, Bishop Aymon III de la Tour refused to perform the customary homage to Count Edward. In a treaty of 3 December 1327 he consented to do so only for the *via publica* the length of the valley and for Mörel, guarding the entrance to the High Valais.[29] He would not do homage, however, for the *regalia* of his see, nor for the *chancellerie,* as his predecessors had done. Count Aymon had been obliged to accept the same terms when he and the bishop did mutual homage on the bridge of Morge in January 1330.[30]

[26] The valley of Saas and the Monte Moro, as well as the Simplon, were much used by Lombard merchants at this time. Cf. L. Blondel, "Le Bourg de Viège," *Valesia,* 1957, pp. 313–316.

[27] The defeat of Leopold of Habsburg (Amadeus' uncle by marriage) by the Swiss at Mortgarten had taken place in 1315 and was still a vivid memory in these parts.

[28] The bishop held the castle of Martigny until 1379.

[29] Van Berchem, p. 67.

[30] In a treaty dated 11 January 1337, Aymon agreed to renounce his right to

The appointment of Guichard Tavel to the see of Sion in September 1342 was a great victory for Savoyard policy. The Tavels were a prominent bourgeois family of Geneva whose devotion to the house of Savoy had been demonstrated as early as 1289, when they headed a movement backed by Savoy to wrest the municipal government from the bishop. From 1331 to 1343, Berthelet Tavel was castellan of Ugine for the count, and from 1336 at least, Guichard Tavel had been among Count Aymon's familiars.[31] He served the count as jurisconsult during the *Audiences* at Aosta in 1337, was chancellor of Savoy in 1336 or 1337, and in 1342 helped in preparing Countess Violante's last will and testament. He was a canon of Geneva in 1338, but he did not take holy orders until after his appointment to the see of Sion. It was to Guichard Tavel that the bishop of Geneva, Alamand de Saint-Jeoire, is supposed to have exclaimed, on hearing of the death of Count Aymon, "Your Mohammed is buried, and the Church is at last safe from your attacks against it!"[32] Guichard's "Mohammed" had already named him to a place on the Savoyard regency council.

The thirty-two-year episcopate of Guichard Tavel at Sion was to witness decisive events in the valley's history. The new bishop was intelligent and energetic, arrogant and tactless. He was received in the Valais with suspicion and did little to allay it. He battled the chapter over notarial rights, and in 1344 he provoked an uprising in Sion by a flagrant violation of the town liberties. The Savoyards were busy in Piedmont at the time and could not send help, and the concessions which the new shepherd had to make in calming his enraged flock taught him his first lesson about his new assignment.

The first visit of Amadeus VI to the Valais occurred in January 1348. On the bridge over the "aquam vocatam Morgiam . . . in medio cursus aque," the bishop and the count "osculo intervento," did homage mutually for their fiefs in the presence of a great concourse of barons.[33] But the visit had another object.

the *regalia* and *chancellerie* for 3,400 florins, but for some reason the treaty was never carried out. *Ibid.*, pp. 81–83.

[31] *ADS* (castellany), Ugine.

[32] Van Berchem, pp. 90–91. Another book, the *Histoire de Genève des Origines à 1789* (Société d'Histoire et d'Archéologie de Genève, 1951), p. 127, has the bishop address these words to Barthélémi Tavel.

[33] *Ibid.*, doc. VI, p. 334.

Savoy had been at war with Luchino Visconti since 1347, and the latter had sought an alliance with the Valaisans. The Savoyards had already seized all Milanese merchants in their territories and were holding them as hostages of war. This interruption of the transalpine trade hurt the Valaisans as well as their bishop. The count's appearance with his regents was to prevent the inhabitants and the bishop from allowing their economic grievances to lead them to accept the alliance offered by the Lord of Milan.

The establishment of peace with Milan in April 1348 led to renewed commercial activity on Valaisan routes, but interference from across the mountains was followed by troubles at home. By 1351 the bishop was engaged in a struggle with the powerful La Tour family, hereditary *majori* of Sion, who possessed a vast array of castles and fiefs in the Valais, the Chablais, the Bernese Oberland, and Fribourg.[34] Bishop Guichard had decided that if he were to be his own master in the Valais, he would have to reduce the power of this family. He accordingly bestowed the fiefs of his see upon relatives and supporters whom he had brought with him to the Valais, and married his nephew, Jacques Tavel, to Jeanette d'Anniviers, heiress of one of the most extensive baronies in the region. In 1350 the bishop demanded that Pierre V de la Tour return Zermatt and the valley of St-Nicholas as well as Leuk and its valley, as properties illegally alienated from the see of Sion.

This demand was tantamount to a declaration of war, and while La Tour sent for help to powerful friends in the Pays de Vaud, Bishop Guichard sent for aid to the court of Savoy. The prelate tried to raise an army from the communes of the Valais, now formed into a "General Council of the land of Valais," but his appeal was ignored. The peasants had no love for the lords of La Tour, but they had still less for the haughty "outsider" bishop who had tried to overthrow their communes and circumscribe their modest liberties. In August 1351 the bishop was surprised by a band of La Tour's friends, and in the scuffle which ensued, one of his clerks was killed and several were wounded. The bishop, with his support slipping away daily and the ranks of his foes increasing, had little choice but to flee.

This was the situation facing the Savoyards in the fall of 1351,

---

[34] Cf. L. Blondel, "Le Château des de la Tour-Châtillon à Bas-Châtillon," *Valesia*, 1951, pp. 44–45.

and things appeared to be worsening since the bishop's flight. In December the community of Martigny, fearing for its safety, placed itself under the protection of the count of Savoy. The count made an effort to win over the cathedral chapter at Sion by ordering the castellan of Conthey to pay certain sums left to the chapter by the wills of Counts Edward and Aymon.[35] On 7 January 1352, Clement VI excommunicated the rebels of the Valais and ordered them to receive their bishop back in his dominions. Ten days later a troop of some thirty Savoyard knights moved against Ardon and Chamoson to punish the inhabitants for their misdeeds.[36] This move provoked an immense uprising—8,000 infuriated Valaisans, according to the report of frightened Savoyard officers at Sion. The peasants rapidly overran the count's castellanies of Conthey and Saillon and tried to capture the castle of Conthey. In response to frantic appeals from the castellans, the count of Gruyère and Aymon de Pontverre, sire of Aigremont, hastened toward the Valais with a hundred knights, while Jean de la Chambre, *bailli* of Chablais, came with reinforcements from the Maurienne. The rebels were driven back, and by mid-February relative quiet had been restored.

Full-scale military intervention in the Valais was obviously necessary if Savoyard influence was to be maintained, and the treaty with France in 1351 gave the count a free hand. In March the papal excommunication was published at Valère, the battlemented episcopal residence on a rock three hundred feet above Sion. By the end of the month the count was already at St-Maurice awaiting the arrival of the remainder of the army. Aymon de Challant, *bailli* of the Val di Susa, and even the marquis of Montferrat, rode into town with soldiers from Italy; the counts of Geneva and Gruyère appeared with warriors from the Genevois and the Oberland. This was an important moment for the eighteen-year-old count, astride an impatient warhorse, preparing to lead his vassals into war for the first time. At last the time had come for Amadeus to display the results of those years of training in the arts of warfare. He had learned to sit in council chambers, to listen to advice, to receive ambassadors. Now he must prove that he could ride at the head of a cavalry charge and wield the

[35] J. Gremaud, *Documents rélatifs à l'histoire du Vallais* (published by Société de l'Histoire de la Suisse Romande, XXXIII, 1884), V, doc. 1988.

[36] Van Berchem, pp. 172.

sword in real battle, where rude experience alone could make him into the warrior he aspired to be.

For a youth eager to swing the battle-axe, the campaign of April 1352 must have been disappointingly brief. The Valaisans were intimidated by the host gathered to subdue them, and they fled before the Savoyard banners. An attempt on the part of the citizens to seize Tourbillon, the great fortress above Sion on the promontory across from Valère, failed, and in discouragement they chose to surrender at the first summons, rather than attempt to resist. Guichard Tavel was triumphantly restored to his see, and his subjects swore loyalty and obedience to him once more.

The treaty now drawn up at Sion was intended to perpetuate Savoyard power in the Valais under the cloak of episcopal authority. The bishop named Amadeus to the important office of episcopal *bailli*, and Savoyard garrisons promptly occupied the strongholds of the town and its environs in the name of the bishop. Sion was required to swear loyalty to the count, excepting prior allegiance to the bishop. A fine of 2,000 florins (the town had scarcely over 2,000 inhabitants)[37] and an annual tribute were to reimburse the count of Savoy for the cost of the campaign. By late April the Valais seemed entirely pacified, and the count, flushed with the pleasure of his first military success, stopped at Monthey on his way home and granted a charter of liberties to the commune.[38] It remained to be seen, however, whether the political problems of the Valais could really be solved by military coercion.

SECOND VALAIS EXPEDITION · THE TOURNAMENT OF
THE GREEN COUNT, 1352–1353

The campaign of April 1352 can be taken as the point after which Amadeus VI began to rule as well as reign. Thus far he had been an apprentice to those more experienced in the complicated business of governing his scattered Alpine dominions. But the summer of 1352 was to be marked by sharp reversals of

[37] Sion had 480 *foci* in 1323. Van Berchem, p. 55, note 2. Provision was also made in the treaty for compensation to Palmeron Turchi, a merchant who had been robbed in the Valais despite his being under the count's protection. Treaty in Gremaud, doc. 1993.

[38] The Monthey charter is in Gremaud, doc. 1994. Amadeus perhaps hoped to encourage settlement there. Monthey had been hard hit by the plague.

policy, upheavals in the count's entourage, and a more martial approach to foreign affairs—all strongly suggesting a less experienced but more vigorous personality in command. Perhaps it was the victory in the Valais which had given the youthful count the confidence to take up the direction of his affairs without further delay. In any case, from this time on the influence of a new personality is steadily more discernible in Savoyard policy.

Relations with the French now suddenly grew worse, owing in no small part to the activities of Hugues de Genève-Anthon. All of the traditional hates and fears entertained over the centuries by the house of Geneva for the house of Savoy had collected in the breast of this energetic individual. He had received the seigneurie of Varey in 1308 from his brother Count Guillaume III of Geneva, and it was under the walls of Varey in 1325 that he and his ally the dauphin had inflicted upon Count Edward the most humiliating defeat in Savoyard annals. Hugues' marriage to Isabelle d'Anthon brought him the seigneurie of Anthon in the Dauphiné, which only strengthened ties of loyalty to the dauphin.

Between 1320 and 1329, Hugues de Genève-Anthon was the heart and soul of the resistance to Savoyard expansion and a great champion of the baronial independence of an earlier era. The death of Dauphin Guigues VIII at Savoyard hands in 1333 no doubt only consecrated Hugues' enmity for Savoy, and the pro-Savoyard leanings of his nephew, Amadeus III, were a source of endless exasperation. Hugues was lord of Cruseilles and Hauteville in the Genevois, and in 1344 his second marriage, to Eléonore de Joinville, brought him the important barony of Gex, located north and west of Geneva. This event in itself was a blow to Savoyard ambitions, and Hugues made matters worse by placing Gex under the protection of the dauphin, to whom he did homage for it. This act, together with Hugues' refusal to renew the homage owed to the count of Savoy for the barony of Gex, flagrantly violated the status quo as defined by the treaty of 1351 between the French and the Savoyards.[39] In addition, the French had not yet

---

[39] The barons of Gex owed homage to Savoy since 1286, when Pierre de Joinville, sire de Gex, did liege-homage and fidelity to Amadeus V "pro nobis, heredibus, et successoribus in barona de Jayz," except for fidelity to Béatrice, daughter of Pierre de Savoie, dame of Faucigny and widow of the dauphin. Cf. *MDG*, VIII (1852), doc. 8. This act was repeated in 1289 by Guillaume, brother and successor of Pierre de Joinville, and by Hugard de Gex, brother-in-law of Hugues de Genève-Anthon, in 1343. *MDG*, XIV (1862), doc. 213.

paid the 60,000 florins which they owed for the surrender of Jeanne de Bourgogne, and the Savoyards would not give her up until they did.

In the summer of 1352, Hugues de Genève went to Avignon "to cause all the trouble he could for the count of Savoy and his country,"[40] and a band of Savoyards apparently attempted to capture him. This incident enraged the Dauphinois and convinced Amadeus that the French had been acting in bad faith all along. In May the count declared null and void the treaty of 1351, accused the dauphin and his advisers of duplicity, and cited numerous injuries suffered at their hands. Georges de Solerio, chancellor of Savoy, who shared with Amadeus of Geneva the responsibility for the treaty with France, was accused of having accepted bribes from French agents to betray the interests of Savoy. He was stripped of his office, imprisoned, and replaced as chancellor by Jean Ravais.

These were bold acts for an eighteen-year-old. The pope was distressed, the king of France annoyed, and the count of Geneva, who had served Amadeus faithfully for nine years, deeply offended. The honesty of the count of Geneva—and probably that of Solerio—is difficult to question seriously. Their real failure was not that the treaty of 1351 was unfair to Savoy, but that it was not victory. The new count of Savoy meant to show the world that he was a man who required victories.

Amadeus III withdrew from the council of Savoy in July 1352, and soon after he sent a formal challenge to the lords of La Baume, whom he identified as his archenemies.[41] The count of Savoy, as a result of his impetuous action, now found himself in an awkward position. He did not lack respect and affection for his cousin, nor appreciation for past services. Still less did he wish to drive so important a prince into the ranks of his enemies. Yet it was impossible to permit warfare between the count of Geneva and the lords of La Baume, Amadeus' closest friends and advisers. The result of this dilemma was the alienation of Amadeus III, who now drifted toward the side of the dauphin.

At the same time, Hugues de Genève became the dauphin's lieu-

[40] These were the words reported by Jean de Ravoire, who claimed to have heard them. Cf. Cordey, *Les Comtes*, pp. 107ff.
[41] *Ibid.*, p. 100.

tenant-general in the barony of Faucigny, an excellent base from which to launch an offensive against Savoy. The need for allies was now urgent. On 6 June 1352 a defensive-offensive alliance for ten years was concluded between the count of Savoy and Albert, duke of Austria.[42] Should the count need reinforcements, the duke agreed to send, at his own expense, 200 cavalry from his lands in northern Helvetia for four months in any one year. In September, Amadeus crossed the Mont Cenis to raise troops on the Italian side of the Alps. Galeazzo Visconti promised to honor the alliance of 1350 by sending men-at-arms from Milan and mercenaries from Genoa at his own expense. The prince of Achaea, however, was disposed to bargain for his support, and a treaty concluded at Rivoli on 20 September 1352 granted Giacomo the castellany of Pont-de-Beauvoisin in Savoy and an annual pension of 800 florins.[43]

Amadeus could hardly have returned from Italy when bad news came from an unexpected quarter: the Valaisans were in rebellion again, Sion was in arms, the bishop and his Savoyard allies had taken refuge on the twin peaks of Tourbillon and Valère. The army being raised to oppose the dauphin and Hugues de Genève was hurriedly led over the passes into the Valais instead. Late in October the Savoyards reached Sion, where the Swiss of the Valais had assembled their own army of sorts to battle for independence. Under the walls of Sion on 3 November the two armies clashed. The Savoyard knights dismounted as the enemy approached, and Guillaume de Grandson led the first charge. According to Cabaret and Servion, the Savoyards utterly routed the rebels, leaving "of the Valaisans dead four thousand or about, but rather more than less," and the rest fled high up into the mountains.[44]

That the Savoyards won the day is beyond dispute, but the fact that Sion refused to surrender when summoned to do so suggests that the victory was less overwhelming than the chroniclers assert. On the following day the siege of the town began, but be-

---

[42] *AST, Trattati diversi*, mazzo I, doc. 19–22. Albert II (d. 1358) of Habsburg was a younger brother of the Leopold who had married Catherine de Savoie in 1315. In 1351, Albert was besieging Zurich, which had recently joined the confederacy of the Forest Cantons. He ratified this treaty on 6 September 1352.

[43] Treaty in Pietro Datta, *Storia dei Principi di Savoia del Ramo d'Acaia* (Turin, 1832), II, 180–185.

[44] Cabaret, p. 137 *dorso*; Servion, II, 76.

fore the trumpets sounded the assault, Guillaume de la Baume asked for the privilege of knighting his master on the field where he had distinguished himself the day before. Amadeus graciously acquiesced, and before an audience of "over two hundred lords, barons, and gentlemen," the count was formally dubbed a knight.[45] Sion was then attacked with fury and enthusiasm, and it soon surrendered. Amadeus declared in a burst of bravado that "par son bon Dieu" he would neither enter over the walls nor through the gates, but ordered a whole section of the wall torn down so that he could ride into Sion without lowering his banners. The town was frightfully pillaged, those still holding out in La Majorie were frightened into surrendering, and the bishop was rescued from his perch on Valère.

As in the previous April, Amadeus thought only of punishment in his hour of triumph, not of magnanimity. The peace which followed his speedy victory reveals little grasp of the real issues at stake in the Valais. All males of fourteen years or more were to present themselves before the count's officers within one week to take an oath of loyalty. The Valaisans were hereafter bound to send 300 men for the count's armies for six weeks each year, and every Christmas they were to pay one *denarius gros tournois* per hearth.[46] To reimburse the count for the expense of having punished them, the rebels were subjected to an enormous indemnity of 28,000 florins. Such peace terms as these only ensured that the resentful population would rebel again as soon as they were able. Even the cathedral chapter at Sion wrote Clement VI to deplore the damage done to the Holy Church and to blame the bishop and the count of Savoy for it. The leaders of the German-speaking communities of the High Valais who had headed the uprising fled northward across the Furka to the Forest Cantons and the emperor.

In Savoy, by contrast, spirits were overflowing. The youthful lord count of Savoy was now a knight and had proven himself on the field of battle. When Amadeus returned to Le Bourget in December, the citizens of Chambéry presented him with 300 florins in honor of his new knighthood.[47] From Le Bourget the

---

[45] Cabaret, p. 138, says Guillaume de Grandson performed the act.

[46] Gremaud, doc. 2003.

[47] Ménabréa, *Chambéry*, p. 156.

count crossed the Revermont to spend Christmas at Bourg-en-Bresse, where he could assemble troops, watch his enemies, and enjoy the holiday season at the same time.

At Bourg-en-Bresse during and immediately following the Christmas season of 1352–1353, Amadeus decided to celebrate both his good fortune and his nineteenth birthday. A series of tournaments would provide amusements as well as exercise for the great concourse of knights still with him since the Valais campaign.[48] This was undoubtedly the occasion on which the count, "beau et gracieux adolescent," created the sensation that subsequently earned him a place among the chivalrous figures of his century. When the trumpets announced the entry of the combatants into the lists, the count appeared at their head resplendent in green silk and velvet vestments under his armor, an emerald plume on the crest of his silver helmet, and astride a magnificent charger richly caparisoned in silver and green.[49] Behind him rode eleven of his noblest knights, also in green, and all were led into the arena by lovely ladies, each holding her champion captive by means of a long green cord attached to the bridle of his charger. Then the damsels, also in green robes, released their knights, and the tournament began. When the jousting had ended for the day, the ladies descended once more into the arena to "recapture" their champions and lead them back into the castle. Then the banqueting began in the great hall, in the course of which gold rings or batons were awarded to those adjudged the most valorous in the day's contests of skill and strength.

According to the chroniclers, the winner of the first day was Antoine de Grammont; the winner on the second day, Pierre of Aarberg; and the champion on the third day, Thibaut of Neuchâtel. Naturally, everyone was really convinced that the young count had outshone all of the others, and that he was permitting his friends to be acclaimed the winners out of noble modesty. On the last day of the tournaments, therefore, the four ladies who bestowed the prizes hailed Amadeus as the winner and offered him the customary rewards, the gold rings and the privilege of a kiss from each of them. Amadeus is supposed to have accepted

[48] *ADCO*, B 7104 (Bourg) records the expenses of 919 horses there in December–January 1352–1353.

[49] See Commentary, VI, for a discussion of this tournament and related problems.

the kisses with pleasure, but gallantly requested that the gold rings be given to the lords of Villars, Entremont, and Corgenon. At this the three knights complained that they would far rather have had the kisses than the rings, which caused "moult grant risee," the signal for gargantuan revelries lasting all night.[50]

Some of these details about the "Tournament of the Green Count" are doubtless purely imaginary contributions by the chroniclers, who were writing about it at a much later date. But there is no doubt that the Christmas tournament of 1352–1353 did take place, and it is a fact that from 1353 onward the records of the count's household show purchases of articles in green far more frequently than before. Not only was this the favorite color for garments made for Amadeus himself, but also for the clothing of valets and pages, for relatives, and even for close companions. Green was not the only color worn by the count after this date, but he does betray an increasingly persistent preference for this color over the years. It was probably the gradual development of this preference, rather than Amadeus' wearing of the green on any one particular occasion, that won him his famous sobriquet, "The Green Count of Savoy."

It was not unusual for fourteenth-century princes to display a preference for a certain color occasionally, but Amadeus' lifelong attachment to one color and his choice of green were somewhat unusual. In some quarters green carried unflattering connotations and was deemed a color to be avoided.[51] But in the Alps, where the winters are long and gray, the green of springtime, suggestive of youth and regeneration, is especially vivid and especially welcome. It is also possible that Amadeus had been taught to associate the color green with the "preux" of Charlemagne.[52] Some of the exploits popularly attributed to Charlemagne and his peers in the literature of the time were supposed to have occurred in Savoy, and stories about them had very likely been a part of the count's upbringing. Amadeus' fondness for green might therefore have been part of a desire to emulate the Carolingian heroes whose mighty deeds he had admired since boyhood.

[50] Servion, II, 83; Cabaret, pp. 139ff.

[51] Cf. Huizinga, *The Waning of the Middle Ages* (Doubleday, 1954), p. 271.

[52] Ménabréa, *Chambéry*, Book IV, Chapter VII, says that green was the color of the *preux* of Charlemagne, but I have been unable to confirm this.

CONQUEST OF THE PAYS DE GEX · BATTLE OF LES ABRETS

The winter passed quietly enough, aside from the pleasant clamor of tournaments, but with the spring thaws of 1353 the armies began to move. In April the dauphin's spies reported that "the count of Savoy has assembled a great multitude of men-at-arms, on horseback and on foot, for entering and offending our land."[53] In May, Savoyard spies notified the count that Hugues de Genève was at the head of troops preparing an invasion, but at this point the king of France intervened. Jean le Bon needed both Savoyards and Dauphinois for his forthcoming campaign against the English in Gascony. In mid-July the royal *bailli* of Mâcon approached the Green Count at Belley. Amadeus was willing to accept a truce and dismissed some of his army, but Hugues de Genève was resolved to fight—with or without the help of his French overlords. Pierre de Genève, sire of Alby and Balaison and governor of the barony of Gex for his uncle, ambushed some Burgundian troops in the pay of the count of Savoy while they were returning home after the truce. They were attacked on the lakeshore road between Geneva and Nyon and were pursued as far as Nyon. Many were killed, while others were captured and imprisoned at Gex.[54] At the same time, Hugues de Genève led his army first against Châteaugaillard, which he took by storm, then against Vesaney near Gex, which he razed.

Under the circumstances the count of Savoy could hardly be expected to observe the truce any longer. Such actions had lost Hugues de Genève all French backing, and the Savoyards were quick to see their chance, for without his formidable allies Hugues was no match for them. The count and his men rode directly to Geneva, where the army was assembling. Over 160 horsemen and 2,500 infantry, pledged to serve for a minimum of twenty-two days, streamed into town from the Pays de Vaud, sent by the widow and daughter of the late Baron Louis II. The count of Gruyère, Jean of Neuchâtel, the vice-castellan of Chillon, and dozens of other captains converged from far and near upon the camp at Geneva. From Italy came Gabriele di Rivoli with a com-

---

[53] Cited in Cordey, *Les Comtes*, p. 114, note 2.

[54] The 1353 war of Gex has been carefully reconstructed by Cordey, *Les Comtes*, pp. 115ff., from *AST, Comptes de guerre*, and castellany accounts for Chambéry, Chillon, etc., which I also have used.

pany of *brigandi*, the constables of Ivrea, Rivarolo, and soldiers from the Canavese. Aymon de Challant, an expert on siege warfare, arrived with Valdostan troops, and so did the often recalcitrant Henri of Quart, with a company of forty-five horses. Giacomo of Achaea sent another company from the Piedmont.

In early October the campaign began with an attack on the "château-vieux" of Les Allinges, facing the Savoyard "château-neuf" some fifty yards across a ravine on a high ridge not far from Thonon. Once this enemy outpost, which threatened Savoyard lines of communication along the lakeshore, had been eliminated, the army was ferried across the lake to join the main host at Geneva. The siege of Gex began on 26 October. The Green Count directed operations in person and pitched his own tent on the slopes below the walls, along with the rest of the army. The castle of Florimont north of Gex was besieged simultaneously, and Amadeus now got his first real taste of siege warfare. It was not until 11 November that Gex was finally taken by assault and burned, whereupon Floriment also surrendered. Within a few weeks the entire country had submitted, and "at the humble supplication of the bourgeois and inhabitants of Gex," Amadeus ratified their liberties and granted new commercial privileges to help them recover from the injuries of the war. The Savoyards had done well to act speedily, for on 10 November, Hugues de Genève had persuaded the governor-general of the Dauphiné to convoke his host for an invasion of Savoy.

What Hugues de Genève and his allies realized too late was that the count of Savoy had embarked upon a campaign of conquest, not merely a punitive expedition. The Pays de Gex was small but strategically located. Occupying the hinterland of Geneva, it controlled access to that city as well as to the pass of La Faucille over the Juras. The possession of Gex by the count of Savoy substantially strengthened his influence in Geneva itself. In addition, a number of fiefs scattered through the Valromey and Bugey were dependencies of the barony of Gex and were now confiscated by the count of Savoy. In Amadeus' eyes, Hugues de Genève, by refusing homage and becoming a vassal of the dauphin for Gex, had forfeited his fiefs. What Hugues had not known, perhaps, was that the count meant to keep them.

Protests soon rained upon the Green Count. The new pope, Innocent VI, sent the bishop of Cavaillon to arrange a truce before matters went further, and numerous envoys from the French king worked to the same end, but without success. Amadeus was enjoying the fight and was not at all disposed to call a halt while he was winning. Between December 1353 and April 1354, peace negotiations never ceased, nor did hostilities. By early spring spies reported that Hugues de Genève was in the Dauphiné preparing an attack upon the count's vulnerable Viennois castellanies in revenge for the seizure of Gex. In mid-April long lines of Savoyard troops filed down from their mountain bastion and along the valley of the Rhône to St-Genix. To the southwest, across the Guiers, lay the Dauphiné, sweeping up to a ridge a few miles away, where the count's *bastie* of Les Abrets guarded the route to Lyon. Hugues de Genève and a sizeable army were reported near Dolomieu, a Savoyard castellany a few miles north along the same ridge.

Amadeus ordered the host to advance westward up the slope to the ridge between Les Abrets and Dolomieu, apparently intending to move on toward La Tour-du-Pin and cut off the enemy's line of retreat. Hugues and his men moved to intercept them, probably as the Savoyards hoped he would do. A few miles north of Les Abrets the one really decisive battle of the war took place. Hugues and his allies were ancient foes of Savoy and were hoping for nothing better than to leave this stripling count measuring his length on the field. It was an exceedingly dangerous encounter for Amadeus, and he was aware of the fact. He made a special appeal to Saint George, vowing to give him the two best horses and the two best suits of armor taken from the foe if the victory were his.[55]

By the time the sun had set over the Viennois hills that day, Hugues de Genève and a handful of followers were refugees, their army was gone, and more than two dozen Dauphinois nobles were prisoners. The victory at Les Abrets stands as one of the major military triumphs of the Green Count's career, sweet revenge for the humiliation of Count Edward at Varey thirty years before. Uldric, one of the count's minstrels, rode exultantly back to Chambéry bearing the glad tidings to the anxious inhabitants. Some time later the army returned to a triumphant welcome in the capital.

[55] He later founded daily masses in honor of Saint George instead, Guichenon, IV, *preuves*, 196.

The count and his counselors had the good sense to follow up their victory. Within a few weeks of the battle, Amadeus was again at the head of his troops marching southward from Chambéry into the Grésivaudan. The dauphin's frontier fortifications at Glandon (Bellemarche) and Chapareillan were destroyed, scarcely twenty-five miles from Grenoble.[56] Then the count returned to the scene of his victory and advanced unopposed into his bailliage of Viennois to camp at Côte-St-André. While the dauphin frantically gathered a new army, the Savoyards ravaged his castellany of La Tour-du-Pin.[57]

There were now signs that the French had had enough. In 1353 the anti-Savoyard archbishop of Lyon had been replaced as lieutenant-governor of the Dauphiné by Aymar de Poitiers, count of Valentinois, who was not unfriendly to Savoy. Pressure from both the king of France and the pope increased the tempo of peace negotiations. On 26 June the papal ambassador at last persuaded both sides to accept a truce. This time it was loyally observed. In July, as a gesture of conciliation, the Green Count decided to parole the nobles who had fallen into his hands at Les Abrets. Each one knelt and swore that "comme loyal gentilhomme" he would return to Chambéry without fail on the third day of Pentecoste next, that he would not leave the *pays* without the count's written permission, and that he would give no aid or comfort to enemies of the count in the meantime.[58] On 12 July at Chambéry, twenty-six of the captured nobles solemnly took the oath and were set at liberty temporarily to arrange their ransoms.

To celebrate the victory over Hugues de Genève, Amadeus decided upon a ceremonious visit to the barony of Gex. In April the count's lieutenants had received the preliminary homages of the local nobles, and Thibaut de Châtillon had been installed as the new *bailli* for the Pays de Gex. The young count was begin-

[56] Servion, II, 95–96, reports (and Bernard, *Montmélian*, pp. 137–138, confirms) that Amadeus, after destroying these outposts, destroyed as well his own *bastie* facing Bellemarche at Les Mortes. By this gesture he apparently wished to indicate a willingness to confirm the status quo ante, rather than to seek advantages for himself.

[57] Whether the citadel of Tour-du-Pin was attacked or not, and, if attacked, whether it was taken or not, has long been disputed by historians on both sides. The documents shed no light on the subject.

[58] Text cited in Cordey, *Les Comtes*, p. 123.

ning to appreciate the political importance of personal appearances, and he clearly thought it would be wise to impress his new subjects with the splendor of their new master. Such a display would hardly restore their uprooted vineyards or their slaughtered herds, but it might make them feel that at least they now had a prince sufficiently grand and powerful to keep the peace in the future. On 22 July, Amadeus arrived at the lakeside castle of Versoix in gorgeous array, and two days later he received personally the submission of his new vassals at Gex. Another jewel had been added to the Green Count's coronet and a ninth bailliage to the states of Savoy.

TREATY OF PARIS, 1355 · ANNEXATION OF THE<br>BARONY OF FAUCIGNY

The remainder of 1354 witnessed the diplomatic sequel to the Green Count's warlike activities over the previous two years. Jean le Bon was now ready to work out a settlement that would end once and for all the Savoyard-Dauphinois boundary disputes that had troubled the peace for nearly a century. In a preliminary treaty drawn up and sealed at La Bâtie-Divisin in the Dauphiné on 11 October, the count of Savoy bound himself to surrender to the dauphin all of his holdings in the Viennois, and to renounce once again his betrothal to young Jeanne de Bourgogne.[59] In return the dauphin was to give up the entire barony of Faucigny, the barony of Gex and its dependencies in the Valromey, the homage of the count of Geneva, suzerainty over all fiefs located in the Genevois, as well as the Valbonne, the fertile valley of the Rhône above Lyon.[60] In addition, everything belonging to the

[59] The signers of this first treaty for the king of France were Nicholas Oyn, *bailli* of Mâcon; Berenger de Montaut, the archdeacon of Lodève; and Aymar of Valentinois-Diois, governor of the Dauphiné. For Savoy, the signers were Guillaume de la Baume, Jean Ravais, chancellor of Savoy, and the sire of Grammont. The count's holdings in the Viennois were specified as: Tolvon, Voiron, Châbons, Côte-St-André, Septême, St-Georges-d'Esperanche, St-Symphorien-d'Ozon, Falavier, Dolomieu, Jonage, La Verpillière, La Bâtie-des-Abrets, and Les Avenières. Text of treaty in Cordey, *Les Comtes*, doc. 29.

[60] The dauphin's holdings in the Valbonne were listed as Miribel, Montluel, St-Christophe, Meximieux, St-Maurice-d'Anthon. Varey was also to be surrendered to Savoy. Excepted from the exchange were the dauphin's fiefs held by Jean de Châlon-Arlay and Henri de Vienne.

103

dauphin between the rivers Ain and Albarine on the approaches to Bresse and Bugey was to go to Savoy.

Hereafter, the boundaries between the two principalities were to be defined by more easily recognizable natural limits: the Rhône, the Guiers, and the Isère. It was further provided that Jean le Bon must ratify the treaty within certain time limits or pay 25,000 florins, for which Aymar de Poitiers, his lieutenant-general, would be the hostage. This precaution proved unnecessary, for in November the treaty was ratified by both the dauphin and the king at Paris, and good relations had so far advanced that the count of Savoy entered into a defensive-offensive alliance with Aymar de Poitiers.[61] On 20 November the rectification of boundaries continued with a treaty between the count and the bishop of Mâcon by which the prelate's holdings in Bresse were exchanged against those of the count in the Mâconnais.[62]

The final treaty, the "Treaty of Paris," was not completed until 5 January 1355. In this last agreement the count of Savoy received several additional places to round out his dominions—in the Valbonne: Perouges, Gourdans, and Sathonay with their dependencies; in Bugey: the towns and castles of St-Sorlin-de-Cuchet, Lagnieu, Lhuis, and St-André-de-Briord with their dependencies. For these the count was to do homage to the dauphin, although the treaty expressly stated that for the lands received by the dauphin from Savoy no homage or fidelity would be owed. Amadeus may have been reluctant to accept such an arrangement, and the concessions to him in the final treaty which were not included in the preliminary agreement may have been necessary inducements: seventeen[63] other towns in the Viennois were to remain his as a private proprietor. The French clearly hoped to place the count of Savoy under feudal obligations less easy to ignore in the future than they had been in the past.

[61] Cordey, *Les Comtes, preuves*, doc. 28, p. 311.

[62] *Ibid.*, p. 126.

[63] They were Ornacieux, Faramans, Eclose, St-Jean-de-Bournay, Maubec, Les Esparres, St-Alban, Cézeneuve, Châtonnay, Serpaize, Formont, Villeneuve-de-Marc, Chandieu, Heyrieux, part of Meyzieux, Faverges, and La Palud. The final listing of the dauphin's acquisitions were Voiron, Tolvon, Les Avenières, Ile de Ciers, Châbons, Bocsozel, La Côte-St-André, Azieu, La Verpillière, Dolomieu, La Bâtie-des-Abrets, Lieudieu, Jonage, Septême, St-Georges-d'Esperanche, Venissieux, and St-Symphorien-d'Ozon.

Jeanne de Bourgogne, now ten years old, was to be sent back to her homeland in return for the viscounty of Maulevrier, the palace of the late king of Bohemia in Paris, and 40,000 florins, which this time were punctually paid. Jean le Bon had to promise, however, that Jeanne de Bourgogne would not be married to the dauphin at any future time. The fate of this little princess, a victim of her high birth and political expediency, was now sealed. The French had wrested her from the Savoyards, and they meant to see that the rich inheritance which might be hers would not escape them. According to the Savoyards, she was unsuited by nature to bear children.[64] In April she was escorted across Bresse by Amadeo de Savoie, bishop of Maurienne, with a large company of dignitaries. The count could not himself be present, but he tried to cheer his former fiancée with gifts of fine cloth, green hangings for her *camera*, silver, and jewelry.[65] At Mâcon on 18 April, Jeanne was delivered over to Gautier de Châtillon, master of the queen's household, who would conduct the child to the queen. The Savoyards received their 40,000 florins and withdrew. Not long after, Jeanne de Bourgogne was placed in a convent at Poissy, there to end her days.

The French king, thus having broken up the Savoy-Burgundy marriage alliance, was eager to provide a substitute. In order to prevent the Savoyards from approaching the enemies of France again, Jean II included in the Treaty of Paris provision for a new alliance with the house of Bourbon. Since the duke's eldest daughter, Jeanne, was now married to Dauphin Charles, the king proposed her younger sister, Bonne. The count of Savoy was willing to take her "if she pleases us," and Bonne was guaranteed an annual revenue of 3,000 florins as her dowry. This time both sides were genuinely interested in carrying out the treaty provi-

---

[64] "Mais lasse elle ne se trouva femme utille ne abille ne consonante adroitte nature, ne a avoir enffans . . . tellement quelle mesme desira et desmanda destre embeguynage et en religion," Servion, II, 73. It is just possible that she really did have some physical handicap, which would explain Savoyard willingness to part with her and the fact that the French do not seem to have tried to marry her to one of their own.

[65] *AST*, inv. 38, folio 1, doc. 12 (1354–1356). In spite of many errors, useful documents on this question are furnished in A. Dufour and F. Rabut, "La Rénonciation du Comte Amédée VI de Savoie au mariage arrêté entre lui et Princesse Jeanne de Bourgogne," *MSI*, XVII (1878).

sions. The king of France had obtained his principal objectives, and the Savoyards were content with the price they had exacted for them. With the prince of Wales ravaging southern France almost unopposed, Jean le Bon was glad to have the Savoyards now firmly on his side.

For the count of Savoy the Treaty of Paris was something of a triumph. Within a century a Dauphinois writer would complain that the lands ceded to Savoy in this exchange were worth 25,000 florins per year, while those obtained by the dauphin yielded only 1,500 annually.[66] These figures are greatly exaggerated, but the charge is probably essentially correct. Faucigny was a fair exchange for the Viennois and half the bailliage of Novalaise, but the Valbonne, Pays de Gex, and scattered castellanies in Bugey probably did give the count several thousand florins per year beyond what the dauphin received. Politically and militarily the Savoyard state was now more compact and had tighter frontiers. Some of the new baronies, such as Gex and Faucigny, gave the count control of strategically located regions where he had had little or no authority before. Other acquisitions, notably those in Bugey, increased his power in areas where it had been predominant but incomplete. The Chablais was now connected with the Tarentaise; Bugey and Novalaise were more solid territorial bridges between Savoy and Bresse. Possession of the Valbonne meant that the commercial route of the Rhône Valley from Lake Geneva to Lyon was more firmly than ever under Savoyard domination. These annexations did more than add luster to the fame of the Green Count. It is no exaggeration to state that they laid the territorial foundations for large-scale centralized government in the western Alps for the first time since the death of Pierre II in 1268. The creation of an administrative apparatus capable of ensuring the supremacy of comital authority was now only a matter of time.

[66] See Commentary, VII, for a full discussion of this question, which has never been adequately investigated. Papal commissioners inspecting the barony of Faucigny in 1339 when Humbert II offered to sell it to Benedict XII, found that it contained 11,577 hearths (50,000 to 60,000 people), of which 7,547 belonged to the dauphin. The regular annual income was 7,276 florins, not counting tolls collected at Beaufort, Flumet, St-Michel, Bonneville, and Bonne. Cf. Claude Faure, "Contribution à l'histoire du Faucigny au XIVe siècle," *RS* (1909), pp. 21-31, 148-158.

The Treaty of Paris remained only to be executed. On 11 February 1355 the king of France and the dauphin ordered Humbert of Thoire-Villars to do homage to the count of Savoy for his innumerable fiefs in Dombes, Bugey, and the Revermont.[67] Through the winter and early spring of 1355, the Green Count was largely occupied with receiving the oaths of fidelity from his new vassals and granting them investiture of their fiefs. A great tournament was held at Chambéry during the Christmas season of 1354–1355, probably to celebrate the conclusion of the era of war with the dauphins of Viennois.[68]

Then difficulties began to arise. Amadeus of Geneva refused to do homage to Savoy for fiefs held of the dauphin, and the dauphin's castellans in Faucigny refused to surrender their castles. The Green Count seems to have suspected the good faith of the French at once; an accord of 18 March 1355 provided that five of the Viennois castellanies ceded to the dauphin would remain in Savoyard custody until at least half of the castellanies of Faucigny were in the count's hands.[69] A major reason for the resistance of some of the Faucigny castellans was that they held their offices as security for debts owed to them by the dauphin, and they were not prepared to give up their posts until they had been paid.[70] In addition, the castellanies of Châtillon and Sallanches were claimed by Jean de Châlon-Arlay, and the castellans there received confusing and contradictory orders which made it difficult to tell where their duty lay.[71]

Of course there were other reasons for the resistance as well. All of the officers of Faucigny stood to lose their posts by the exchange of suzerains provided in the Treaty of Paris, and the posts of *bailli* and castellan were prestigious and lucrative, particularly when the overlord lived far away. Some Faucignerans no doubt

[67] Others who did homage are listed in Cordey, *Les Comtes*, pp. 129–130. Cf. also Saint-Genix, *Histoire de Savoie*, III, 453, doc. 6.

[68] *AST*, inv. 38, folio 1, doc. 12 (1354–1356) records many expenses "pro asculidiis domini Natalis Domini" of 1355, for men preparing the "campus ad jostandum," and "pro arnesio domini de josta."

[69] The Savoyards would hold Voiron, Tournon, Les Avenières, La Bâtie des Abrets, and Dolomieu, *AST, Traités anciens*, paq. VI, doc. 7.

[70] Cibrario, *Storia*, III, 129, saw this, but subsequent writers have almost unanimously ignored this view, which indeed he did not document. Ample proof is to be found in *AST, Traités anciens*, paq. VI, doc. 9.

[71] See below, note 83.

had more personal reasons for their attitude; many were veterans of the wars with Hugues de Genève, men who had fought against Savoyards all their lives. There also seems to have existed a certain provincial patriotism on the part of the inhabitants which induced them to follow the lead of the castellans in opposing annexation by Savoy. During the papal inquest of 1339 the people interrogated had proudly asserted that the barony of Faucigny was an alod, not a fief even of the Empire. They had been willing to admit only that the western part, between the river Giffre and the Genevois, was held in fief from the counts of Savoy.[72]

By the spring of 1355 it had become clear that the Green Count would have to occupy the barony of Faucigny by force, and he meant to do so before the resistance there or the urgings of Hugues de Genève and Amadeus III induced the French to change their mind about ceding it. The conquest of the barony would be a major military operation, of which the first move was to set up a blockade to prevent reinforcements from outside. On the north the *bailli* of Chablais closed the lakeshore route at Les Allinges and sent troops into the mountains to close off the passes at Abondance and St-Jean d'Aulph. The "big galley" and a flotilla to accompany it were quickly outfitted at Chillon for use in patrolling the lake along the stretch of enemy coastline from Hermance to Geneva. Martigny was strengthened to block the passage from Chamonix over the Forclaz, and Courmayeur on the Aostan side of the Mont Blanc likewise received a detachment.[73] Savoyard troops were also thrown into the valleys of Flumet and Beaufort, which communicated with the Tarentaise.

Blockading the western frontier of Faucigny was more difficult because it bordered the territories of the count of Geneva. It was possible to isolate Faucigny and the Genevois together, however, by garrisoning the Rhône valley castles from the bridge of Arlod to Seyssel and the fortresses on the Savoy-Genevois frontiers from

---

[72] Faure, p. 23. There was ill-feeling about the Treaty elsewhere, too. At Perouges in the Valbonne, Pierre Ranas was fined eighteen *denarii* by the castellan for striking Jean Ranas on the ear and exclaiming "Merda!" when Jean cried "Savoia!" *ADCO*, B 8759 (1355-1356).

[73] There is no pass there now, but tradition has it that there once was a "Col Major" between the valleys of Chamonix and Courmayeur. As Cordey points out (*Les Comtes*, p. 140, note 3), the detailing of a Savoyard garrison for Courmayeur in 1355 tends to support that tradition.

Chanaz, Albens, Cusy, and Châtelard-en-Bauges to Conflans, Ugines, and Faverges. Now that the Pays de Gex was in the count's hands, access from the Burgundies could be prevented by barring the Jura routes at Châtillon-en-Michaille, St-Cergues, Gex, and St-Claude.

The preparations for this campaign reveal much about the count of Savoy's military resources and the composition of his armies.[74] The core of the army were the *gentes armorum,* vassals of noble birth, mounted and fully armed. Those of knightly rank with one or two armed companions were classified as *milites bachalarii,* knights-bachelor, while knights with a large following of armed men, often including other knights, were classified as *milites bannereti,* knights-banneret. Humbert of Thoire-Villars, for example, appeared with 127 men-at-arms, including 15 knights-bachelor; and the sire of Grandson had a troop of 80 men-at-arms under his banner, including one bachelor. The knight-banneret enjoyed the privilege of commanding his own company under his own square-cut banner during the campaign, and he was paid twenty florins per month. The bachelors received fifteen florins per month, and the men-at-arms seven. "Foreign" nobles from outside the dominions of the count of Savoy, such as the counts of Neuchâtel and Gruyère, received ten florins monthly.

Knights and squires not riding in the company of a banneret were grouped into regiments under the command of the *baillis.* Jean de Blonay, *bailli* of Vaud for Catherine and Isabelle de Vaud, arrived with 122 men-at-arms, while his lieutenant, Arnaud d'Aigrement, captained 17 more. François de la Sarra, *bailli* of Chablais, led a company of 118 cavalry raised in the Chablais, plus another company of a hundred more from nearby areas. The remaining 240 men in the cavalry were furnished at the expense of the towns, the largest single contingent, 30, coming from Chambéry.[75] Each man-at-arms had from 1 to 6 or 7 squires, valets, or

---

[74] Léon Ménabréa, "L'Occupation du Faucigny par le Comte Vert," *MARS* (2nd series, I, 1851), 193ff., provides much of the data used in this account, taken from the *bailli* and castellany records in *ADS.*

[75] The 240 were recruited as follows: Chambéry, 30: Montmélian, 12; Aiguebelle, 10; Conflans, 12; Ugine, 18; Châtelard, 11; Pont-de-Beauvoisin, 8; St-Genix, 10; Yenne, 8; Seyssel, 15; Thonon, 8; Evian, 15; St-Maurice d'Agaune, 15; Villeneuve-Chillon, 10; La Tour-de-Vevey, 10; Vaux-le-Ruz, 3; Roue, 10; Romont, 13; Mont and Rolle, 9; Morges, 6; and Nyon, 7.

servants, who must also be taken into account in forming an idea of the size of the host outside the walls of Geneva that March.

This was the cavalry, which constituted the elite of the army. The infantry was almost exclusively composed of communal levies marching under the banners of their municipalities, but for this campaign, only the count's towns in the Pays de Vaud, the Pays de Gex, and the Chablais were laid under contribution. Leaving untouched the towns in Bresse, Bugey, the Valbonne, and many even in Savoy proper, the count raised over 13,000 men on this occasion.[76] In addition, 9 companies of *brigandi*, mercenary infantry, were brought from across the Alps. In each of the 9 *banderie* were 25 men, and 4 of the *banderie* were made up of crossbowmen. The rest consisted of *pavisarii*, pikemen with especially large shields which they were trained to use as protection for themselves and for the crossbowmen.[77]

Thus the great bulk of the army was made up of men who had always owed military service to the counts of Savoy, men who were fighting in his wars not because they were paid, but because this was among their traditional obligations. In spite of the fact that everyone in the army drew pay, only the *brigandi* from Italy and special teams of siege engineers were really mercenary troops. Warfare was not so professional in Savoy as it had become on the plains of Italy, and Savoyard armies were still the feudal hosts, less efficient and less treacherous than the mercenary regiments which the Green Count would encounter later in his career.

As the soldiers flooded into camp during the early spring, the count's marshals presided over the "monstra." Each man had to present himself and his followers and show each piece of equipment. Men, horses, harness, armor, and weapons were examined and inventoried by the clerks accompanying the marshals through

---

[76] The total was 13,120 recruited as follows: Thonon, Aulphs, Abondance, 2,300; Evian and Feterne, 1,200; Villeneuve-Chillon, 150; St-Maurice d'Agaune, 420; Monthey, 500; Sembrancher, 1,200 (Chablais total: 5,770). Conthey and Saillon (Valais), 1,400. Gex and Florimont (Pays de Gex), 1,260. Tour-de-Vevey, 1,700; Châtel-St-Denis, 400; Nyon-Prangins, 300; Mont, 160; Morges, 300; Roue, 120; Romont, 300; Moudon, 120; Yverdon, 350; Les Clées, 240; Versoix, 350; Agié, 350 (Pays de Vaud total: 4,690). Each man received one *denarius gros tournois* per day.

[77] Crossbowmen got four and a half florins per month apiece; *pavisarii*, four.

the camp. Since the count was obliged to make good any major loss sustained by his vassals during the campaign, he intended to see that nothing could be claimed missing later which in fact never existed. He did not wish to risk defeat at the hands of the foe owing to defective or insufficient equipment. Repairs or replacements deemed necessary by the marshals were noted in the records.

While the army was getting ready, carpenters at Geneva and Versoix were laboring to put the great war engines into fighting condition. A company of quarrymen in the nearby hills prepared cartloads of large rocks, carefully rounded to fit neatly into the giant slings. The great movable towers, the *berfredi*, used for assaults against enemy walls and towers, were each provided with a captain and a crew expertly skilled in maneuvering such machines. As in 1353 for the campaign against Gex, miners were brought from the Chablais and Lombardy.

The campaign began sometime in March, but exactly what happened remains a mystery. While Savoyard envoys at Paris protested over the resistance of the castellans of Faucigny, the siege of Hermance began, and the count invaded the barony. Both the barony and Hermance were stoutly defended, and the latter did not finally surrender until early June. The attempt to conquer the barony was apparently a failure, for in June, Amadeus appealed for more troops. Nine hundred more men-at-arms were raised from the nobility of Savoy, while 220 cavalry and 10,000 more men were furnished by the towns.[78]

As this second effort was being prepared, the embassy which had been sent to Paris finally returned (on 5 June) to Geneva. At St-Germain-en-Laye on 15 May a delegation of castellans from Faucigny had been instructed by the dauphin in person, in the presence of the Savoyards, to turn over their castles to the count of Valentinois or to commissioners sent in his place.[79] Nevertheless, during the rest of June nothing was accomplished, and if Amadeus did make a second attempt to take the barony by force, it was unsuccessful. The resolution of the Faucignerans to maintain their independence led them now to declare that even the dauphin himself had no right to cede them to anyone, for he and his predecessors had solemnly sworn never to do so.[80] The in-

[78] Ménabréa, "Faucigny," pp. 201–202.
[79] Faure, p. 150.     [80] *Ibid.*, p. 151.

habitants seemed convinced that if they continued to resist, they would soon get outside assistance.

In this they were disappointed. The campaign against the English was the sole concern of the French during the summer of 1355, and Jean le Bon needed the Savoyards. The Green Count had made it clear that no Savoyard aid would be forthcoming until every article of the Treaty of Paris had been fulfilled. Jean was thus in no mood to sympathize with the recalcitrant Faucignerans nor to listen to pleas in their favor advanced by the count of Geneva and his cousin. On 2 July 1355, in the orchard of the Franciscan monastery at Moirans, Jean Mistral, *legum doctor* and counselor of Amadeus VI, met with Aymar de Poitiers and formally demanded the surrender of the barony. The count of Valentinois acceded to their demand and named Henri de Montagnieu and Artaud Cara as his commissioners. Formal letters were prepared investing the two with the authority to transfer Faucigny to the count of Savoy. Other letters were written to each castellan and each community in the entire barony, explaining the relevant clauses in the Treaty of Paris and ordering that they accept the count of Savoy as their new overlord.

Armed with these documents, the commissioners set out for Conflans in the Tarentaise, where members of the council of Savoy awaited them. The dauphin's men presented their documents to Aymon de Challant, Humbert de Savoie, Jean de la Chambre, Hugues de Grammont, and Guillaume de la Baume, deputed by the count to undertake this business.[81] On 7 July the company left Conflans and followed the valley of the Doron to Beaufort. With them traveled the commissioners, a troop of soldiers, and heralds bearing the banners of the dauphin. At the bridge over the Doron they encountered a large crowd of people, clergy, and nobles. The commissioners asked who the seigneur of the castle and *pays* of Beaufort was. All replied that it was the dauphin, and that they were ready to obey him and live or die for him. The dauphin's deputies then came forward and showed to the crowd the Treaty of Paris, and the letters signed with the royal seal of Le Châtelet and the seal of the dauphin. Then they brought forth the letters from the count of Valentinois instituting their com-

---

[81] The details of the following account are found in the secretarial record in *ADI*, B 3865, folio 8, critically examined in Faure, *op.cit.*

mission, and the letters addressed directly to the castellan of Beaufort. The representatives of the community of Beaufort were summoned to recognize the count of Savoy and his heirs as their new lord and to take the oath of homage and loyalty to the barons of his council there present.[82]

When the commissioners had finished speaking, the nobles, syndics, and clergy took the documents, examined them carefully, deliberated for some time among themselves, and at last agreed to obey the dauphin's instructions. A Bible was brought out and the whole company solemnly swore loyalty, homage, submission, and obedience to Amadeus VI of Savoy and his heirs, and agreed that henceforth they should enjoy all of the rights and privileges in the Pays de Beaufort that the dauphin had had. Then the Savoyards were conducted to St-Maxime where the rest of the people of the community were waiting. They also took the oath of allegiance.

The procedure followed at Beaufort was repeated at Sallanches, Samoëns, Montjoie, and Flumet without incident. On 12 July at Cluses, the principal town of the important castellany of Cluses-Châtillon, the inhabitants at first refused to accept the credentials of the commissioners, and for awhile appeared disposed to resist.[83] But on the following day, after a town meeting in the local church, the chief syndic came outside the walls and announced that the community was ready to receive them and to swear allegiance to the count of Savoy. There were no further difficulties.[84] By 17 July, Savoyard castellans and garrisons occupied all fifteen

---

[82] The absence of the count himself on this occasion is puzzling. Perhaps it was thought wiser to delegate so delicate a mission to others and reserve the count's own first visit for a later time when the barony was wholly submitted to his authority.

[83] The reason for the resistance here was undoubtedly the fact that Jean de Châlon-Arlay had claims on Châtillon (and on Sallanches). On 13 June 1355 the king of France had ordered the count of Valentinois to turn both of these places over to Châlon-Arlay, and an act of 15 July attests to the remission of the castle of Cluses to the latter's officers. In view of such orders, the reaction encountered by the Savoyard delegation is entirely understandable. *AST, Traités anciens*, paq. V, doc. 4.

[84] The question of the dauphin's debts to the castellans of Faucigny remained, however. Between 16 and 21 July at Bonne and Geneva, officers of the count loaned a total of 7,400 florins to Henri de Montagnieu to enable him to pay debts to the dauphin's castellans of Châtelet-de-Credoz, Bonneville, Montjoie, Bonne, Flumet, and Allinges-le-Vieux. *Ibid.*, paq. VI, doc. 9.

castles of the barony, and Pierre Dameyssin was installed at Cluses-Châtillon as the first *bailli* of Faucigny for the count of Savoy. Even Amadeus III was ready to acquiesce, and on 20 July, in the Franciscan monastery at Geneva, did reluctant homage to his former ward.[85] The annexation of Faucigny through peaceful means is an important illustration of the extent to which respect for the law had gradually come to prevail in a land where such had not often been the case in earlier generations. The power of the law had actually proved stronger than the power of the sword, and diplomacy had succeeded where armies had failed. The Green Count, fond though he was of noble feats of arms, had learned a costly lesson in military failure; the pride born of too easy battle-field triumphs had been humbled. His handsome army, at a cost of 216,095 florins, had been unable to accomplish what a few small letters with large wax seals had been able to do.[86]

[85] Duparc, p. 293. Hugues de Genève was beaten but unbowed. In disgust he abandoned the mountain country of his birth and took service with the king of France. The castellan of St-Sorlin reported in 1358–1360 the revenues of St-Barbe and Maxillieux, confiscated from Hugues de Genève for refusing homage to the count of Savoy. *Inventaire Sommaire, ADCO,* B 9851 (St-Sorlin).

[86] Ménabréa, "Faucigny," p. 202.

# Magna Baronia

## 1355-1360

THE five years which followed the Treaty of Paris are significant years in the history of Savoy for several reasons. The major territorial acquisitions of the Green Count's career were carried out during this period, creating the geographical basis for a politically unified state which, for the first time in almost a century, comprised nearly the whole of the western Alps. This achievement was also important because it led ultimately to the stabilization of the western boundaries of the medieval Savoyard state and diverted the expansionist energies of the dynasty toward its other frontier, the Italian frontier. Amadeus VI now became involved in Piedmont affairs for the first time in his life, and he was to find that political as well as economic interests increasingly obliged him to strengthen his position on the Italian side of the Alps. This involvement in Italy, which was to be so important to the future history of that country, did not really become inevitable for the senior line of the house of Savoy until after the reign of the Green Count, who did not really begin to take Piedmont problems seriously until after 1355.

The beginning of the shift toward Italy in Savoyard policy was accompanied by equally important developments in the personality of Amadeus VI. He had begun his personal reign with triumphs on the battlefield, victories at the conference table, tournaments full of emerald pageantry. His fondness for pomp, along with an obviously youthful taste for military glory, was swiftly earning him a reputation as "moult vaillant et chevaleureux" in his time. Yet for the Green Count war was really a "joyous thing" only if it ended in solid, material gains;[1] there was never that passionate devotion to war for the sheer love of fighting that characterized so many of his celebrated contemporaries, particularly in France. Amadeus VI never ceased to be a champion of the chivalric ideals of his age, but at the same time he grew into a political realist of great ability. He never abandoned the desire to be known far and wide as a knight without fear and without reproach, but he dreamt of land and power above all. The most illuminating and believable remark which has been attributed to him is to be found in a letter dated August 1373 from his brother-in-law, Galeazzo Visconti. "Brother," wrote Galeazzo, "do you remember when you were at our castle of Pavia, and you came up to us under the porch where we were sitting and you said to us: 'Friend, by the Holy God, there won't be a year of my life that I won't have greater lands than any of my ancestors ever had, or that I won't be more talked of than anyone else of our lineage, or I'll die in the effort'?"[2] By 1359 a new color had been added to the Green Count's equipage—a great black charger named "Lucifer."[3]

One of the most fascinating aspects of the life of Amadeus VI is the conflict within him between the ideals with which he was brought up and the realities of political life as he found them. For the Green Count this conflict was sharpened by the dual character of his background. His forebears were sometimes Italians, sometimes Franco-Burgundians; his lineage straddled the Alps in the same way as did his sprawling territories. The Italian princes whom the young count was soon to meet were far less devoted to chivalric ideals, either in theory or in practice, than were the princes among whom Amadeus had been reared. This fact would be the source of many a moral dilemma in the years ahead. So far Amadeus had not really been forced to choose

---

[1] "It is a joyous thing, is war. . . . When you see that your quarrel is just and your blood is fighting well, tears rise to your eye. A great sweet feeling of loyalty . . . fills your heart on seeing your friend so valiantly exposing his body to execute and accomplish the command of our Creator" (ca. 1465). Cited from *Le Jouvençel* in Huizinga, *Waning of the Middle Ages*, p. 76.

[2] François Mugnier, "Lettres des Visconti de Milan et divers autres personnages aux comtes de Savoie Amédée VI, Amédée VII, et Amédée VIII (1360–1415)," *MDSS* (2nd series, XXXV, 1896), p. 404. My translation.

[3] *AST*, inv. 16, doc. 22 (1359–1360), *librata* section.

between power and virtue. He was not to be so fortunate much longer.

For the moment Amadeus was confronted with a task which did not involve unpleasant moral conflicts—that of strengthening the organs of centralized administration now that peace had been achieved. In February 1351, while Amadeus was still under the tutelage of his council, he had issued an ordinance fixing the *chambre des comptes* at Chambéry and clarifying its authority. On 27 July 1355 at Pont-de-Veyle, a second ordinance was drawn up concerning the resident council. The count's experience at the *Audiences* of the Val d'Aosta may have had some part in prompting his action. Since his visit there in 1351 many petitions had reached him from Valdostans complaining that his orders were not obeyed and protesting the "tyranny" of his officers and of local nobles.[4] Too often the count simply could not give such petitions the attention they deserved.

Amadeus' concern for this problem is reflected in the new statutes.[5] The most striking features of the reorganized council were the high rank of its members and the geographical scope which they represented. The count was making an obvious effort to draw both lay and ecclesiastical magnates into more direct participation in his administration. The four bishops of Maurienne, Tarentaise, Aosta, and Ivrea were included, along with the abbot of San Michele della Chiusa (Val di Susa), the prior of St-Ours (Aosta), the prior of Belley (Bugey), and the preceptor of St-Antoine in Chambéry. The nobles included Galois and Guillaume de la Baume, Humbert de Corgenon, and Jean de Saint-Amour from Bresse; Jean de la Chambre and Humbert de Chevron from Maurienne and Tarentaise; Hugues de Grammont and Louis Rivoire from Savoy proper. Among the eight jurists named to the council were the chancellor of Savoy and Hugues Bernard, "juris professor."

The original resident council had had six members in 1329; now it numbered twenty-six. Since most of the notables were employed by the count in other capacities and had time-consuming preoccupations of their own, the statute provided that any two or three of them were empowered to take action in the absence of the others. This meant in effect that the group of eight jurists

---

[4] Examples in Duc, III, 457–460.     [5] Text in Chevailler, pp. 362–363.

did the bulk of the judging, but that whenever particularly weighty matters came up, the tribunal could be expanded to include magnates with sufficient prestige to ensure enforcement of their decisions. All civil, criminal, and feudal questions were within the competence of the council, and the count specified that it should enjoy the same authority as if he were present in person. The count and his entourage of nobles and jurists would of course continue to constitute an itinerant "supreme court," but the resident council was now able to begin the task of creating standards of jurisprudence applicable the length and breadth of the count's transalpine dominions.

During his stay in Bresse that summer, Amadeus had other matters on his mind besides the reorganization of the resident council. Jean le Bon was planning a major campaign against the English for the summer of 1355, and he counted upon the assistance of the Savoyards. The host which finally gathered on the banks of the Saône at the end of the month numbered about 1,100 warriors, hence a total of 4,000 or 5,000 men.[6] The Savoyards camped at Cluny on 1 August, and two weeks later the Green Count rode through the gates of Paris for the first time in his life. He took up residence in the Hôtel de Bohême, given to him in the Treaty of Paris, and a few days after his arrival, he received the homage there of some of his new Faucigny vassals who had been away in France at the time of the annexation. At the end of August the count was at Rouen, where he did homage in turn to the dauphin for the fiefs acquired in the treaty. Charles authorized Amadeus to retain possession of the castellanies of Voiron, Les Avenières, Dolomieu, Faverges, and La Palud as security for repayment of the sums loaned in the dauphin's name over the previous four months.[7] The Savoyard was wise to demand security for these loans, which subsequent tribulations made the dauphin all too prone to forget. Charles little suspected that it would require more than twenty years of litigation to get those castellanies back into his hands.

[6] Cf. the roster in Guichenon, IV, *preuves*, 197–199.

[7] Cordey, *Les Comtes*, p. 130, note 5. In addition to the 7,400 florins paid to the dauphin's castellans in Faucigny in July, there were some 14,800 florins already loaned by the Savoyards to the count of Valentinois, Charles's governor of the Dauphiné, in March and April, presumably also in order to facilitate execution of the territorial exchanges, *AST, Traités anciens*, paq. VI, doc. 9.

By September the royal court had returned to Paris and the count of Savoy undertook to fulfill the last article of the Treaty of Paris: his marriage to Bonne de Bourbon, first cousin to the king.[8] No reports regarding the ceremony have survived, but it took place at the royal palace of Saint-Pol sometime during the closing days of September. Almost immediately after the wedding, Amadeus was obliged to return to the armies, and the young bride set out for Savoy without him.[9] Her father, the duke of Bourbon, gave her a minstrel to relieve the fatigue of the long trip, and her husband furnished an escort of some eighty cavalry. She crossed into the border province of Bresse from Mâcon, into the mountains of Bugey at Pont d'Ain, and into the Novalaise at Yenne on the Rhône. About the middle of October the princess was escorted by dignitaries from Chambéry on the winding trail over the Mont du Chat, the last mountain barrier between her and Savoy proper. Spread out below her lay Lake Le Bourget, the valley of Chambéry, and in the far distance, the great peaks of the High Alps. Later in her life, Bonne de Bourbon's preference for her husband's lakeside castles would result in architectual innovations of considerable importance in Savoy. That preference for lakes in the shadow of mountains may have taken root during her first autumn, while she waited at Castle Le Bourget in the marshy edge of the lake for her husband to return from the wars in France.

In October the Green Count was at the head of his troops in the pay of Jean le Bon, no doubt hoping for a chance to vindicate his recent promotion to knightly rank with mighty feats performed before an audience of famous warriors. The two armies encountered each other in Artois, but Amadeus was given no opportunity to cover himself with martial glory. Edward offered to do battle, but was refused; a subsequent offer from the French was refused by Edward. By then November was upon them, and with winter coming on, it seemed unwise to undertake a major campaign. The king of France ordered the withdrawal of his army, and by the end of the month the troops were largely dismissed. The Savoyard army had thus not been put to use, which

[8] Bonne's sister, Jeanne de Bourbon, was now the wife of Dauphin Charles. The other sister, Blanche, was married to Pedro the Cruel, king of Castile.

[9] The fact that Amadeus and Bonne were married and not betrothed suggests that Bonne was at least twelve years old; since she was the third daughter of a mother married in January 1337, she could not have been over fifteen.

made the venture an expensive one for the king. The count of Savoy alone received 1,000 florins per month for his presence, and the total cost of the Savoyard army, for what had been an agreeable autumn riding out, came to more than 13,000 florins.[10] By December, Amadeus was already back in Savoy. Jean le Bon did not avail himself of Savoyard services the following year, and it was without the Green Count that he marched against the English in the fall of 1356. Amadeus thus missed the fateful encounter on 19 September at Poitiers, where the French were crushed and the king taken prisoner along with many of his nobles.[11] The Savoyards had missed a good fight, perhaps, but they had also missed sharing the calamity which had now befallen France. For the next few years the Green Count could attend to problems in other quarters.

DOMESTIC PROBLEMS · AMADEUS VI AND CHARLES IV

During the count's absence in France, Emperor Charles IV had taken steps to nullify the advantages won by the Savoyards in the Valais, the Pays de Gex, and Faucigny. Rebellion in the Valais was so constant a threat that Savoyard castellans from Conthey to St-Maurice worked out a system of fire signals so that in a matter of hours reinforcements could be called up from Chillon.[12] In April 1354 the peasants of the High Valais burned one of the bishop's castles and murdered his lieutenant at Visp. At the end of the month Johann von Attinghausen, landamman of the valley of Uri, crossed the Furka and was accepted as rector of the Valais upstream from Visp. In July, Charles IV sent one of his counselors, Burchard Munch, to Leuk with orders to administer the High Valais in the emperor's name.

[10] Cordey, *Les Comtes*, p. 152.

[11] Pierre, duke of Bourbon, father of Countess Bonne, was killed at Poitiers and his memory was honored in a ceremony at the Franciscans' in Chambéry. A chapel was shrouded in black cloth and ornamented with 108 shields bearing the duke's arms, painted by "magister Johannes, pictor." *AST*, inv. 38, folio 1, doc. 13 (1354–1356).

[12] The *bailli* reported that he ". . . castellanos Contegie, Sallionis, Saxonis, Martigniaci et Sancti Maurici informavit super signia ignis que per ipsos fieri debebant ad habendam succursum pro terra domini de Valesio contra Valesienses rebelles," quoted from Chillon rolls by Blondel, "L'Architecture militaire," *Genava*, XIII, 293.

On 31 August the emperor reprimanded the bishop of Sion for having failed to seek imperial investiture of his temporal possessions, and the count of Savoy for having seized the government of the Valais without imperial consent. Charles then confirmed the privileges of the Valaisan communes and placed them under the suzerainty and protection of the Empire.[13] The rights of the bishop alone were reserved, a stroke aimed at separating the bishop from his Savoyard protector. At almost the same time, the emperor responded to appeals from Hugues de Genève against the "aggressions" of the count of Savoy by notifying Amadeus, on 21 August 1355, that the inhabitants of Faucigny and the county of Geneva had been placed under his special protection. Five days later the Green Count was ordered to abstain from all action pending imperial examination of the questions at issue.[14]

There matters rested while Amadeus attended to domestic problems. The ideal prince was bound by the codes of chivalry to protect the weak from the strong, and the Green Count meant to do his share of justice to the poor and innocent. The syndics of Chambéry complained that the new castellan, Aymon de Challant, had issued ordinances contrary to the town franchises, had used a false measure to determine the annual "toisage," and had imprisoned a citizen without bail despite a 1353 charter forbidding such a practice.[15] The count sent his chancellor to investigate and to annul any acts which violated the town charters. Then he ordered the castellan to release the imprisoned citizen on bail and to satisfy the bourgeois in the matter of the toisage.

This episode may have awakened Amadeus to the need to oversee more carefully the welfare of the poor and innocent generally, for a veritable inquisition into the conduct of his officers took place in 1356–1357. Pierre de Pont, judge of Faucigny, Gex, Chablais, Valais, and Geneva, was convicted of embezzlement and condemned to a fine of 600 florins. Humbert Paravisi, mestral of

---

[13] Gremaud, doc. 2022. The letters were issued from Regensburg on 31 August 1354 and published at Leuk in the Valais by Pierre of Aarberg in February 1355.

[14] Cf. Duparc, p. 295. Text in *MDG*, XVIII, doc. 150. Dated 26 August 1355 at Prague.

[15] Ménabréa, *Chambéry*, pp. 128, 129, 145. Toisage was an annual tax assessed per *toisia* (about six feet) of house frontage. The bourgeois often had trouble with Aymon de Challant, the powerful Valdostan lord, castellan of Chambéry for nearly twenty years. In 1370–1372 they made him a present of eight fine trout during a quarrel over the town watch.

Lompnes, was fined sixty florins for "several extortions committed in the discharge of his office," after an enquiry by the count's procurator in Bugey and Novalaise. Similar punishments were meted out to the former mestral of Modane in the Maurienne, and to three mestrals in the Tarentaise, following an investigation by Gui Barbier, "clericus domini." One Guillemet de Nons was fined 500 florins for various misdeeds, and Raymond de Beaufort, "lord of the Val d'Isère," was fined for offenses against the prior and canons of the Colonne-Joux hospice.[16]

The canons of chivalry, while praising prodigal generosity on the part of a prince, have never made of money-raising a virtue. In this respect Amadeus VI was always much more the so-called "new monarch," typical of a later period, than the flamboyant spendthrift eulogized by the troubadours. To compete with princes as wealthy as his French in-laws required careful husbanding of comital resources, and the Green Count devoted a large share of his time and talent to the problems of raising the money needed to finance his essentially political ambitions. In 1356 money was very much needed for a military expedition in the Piedmont.

Most of the funds required were obtained through a subsidy "graciously conceded to the lord count" for three years, payable each Easter at the rate of four *denarii gros tournois* per year per hearth. The tax was granted by "bannerets, religious, and nobles," but hearths belonging to nobles in direct proprietorship were exempt.[17] The subsidy of 1356 was more widely collected than had been those of 1346–1347, to pay off the duchess of Brittany, and of 1353, on the occasion of the count's "new knighthood." The subsidies of 1346 and 1353 had been collected almost exclusively from tenants on the count's own estates, but not from those on the estates of others. The financial need in 1356 was greater than before, however, and led to an important innovation in fiscal policy during the reign of Amadeus VI. This innovation consisted of taxing all non-nobles in the count's dominions, whether or not they lived on the count's private properties and within his immediate jurisdiction. This was a rather bold step in expanding comital jurisdiction, and it was sometimes necessary to negotiate with particularly important barons in order to collect subsidies in their territories. In 1356, Jean de la Chambre, viscount of Maurienne,

---

[16] *AST*, inv. 38, folio 1, doc. 13 (1356–1357), receipts.
[17] See Commentary, VIII, on this subsidy.

granted to the count a subsidy from Jean's "homines" living within the county of Savoy and the *mandamentum* of Montmélian at Tournon and Châteauneuf, but the viscount supervised the collection of it himself.[18]

Other sources of revenue in 1356 were the castellans, whose offices were sometimes used as collateral for loans. The castellan remained obligated to report income and expenses, just as before, but he could petition the *chambre des comptes* for permission to appropriate the annual surplus until the amount of his loan had been recovered. Thus Pierre Bonet advanced 300 florins "on the castellany of St-André-de-Briord," and Bartolomeo Dro of Rivoli furnished 200 florins on the revenues of the castellany of Cusy. The inhabitants of the Valdigne near Aosta also paid 200 florins for the privilege of a fair at Morgex, and the Challant-Montjovet brothers offered 4,000 florins to obtain in fief the escheated properties of Dominique de Valleise.[19]

While Amadeus was raising money in the summer of 1356, he undertook to restore his credit at the imperial court. Hugues Bernard and Guillaume de la Baume were sent to Prague to present the Savoyard version of the Valais and Faucigny affairs. On 17 July the ambassadors secured confirmation of the count's hereditary rights and titles, including his status as a prince of the Empire, but the crowning success of the mission came a few days later. Letters-patent were issued which granted to the count of Savoy an imperial vicariate in all but name. Amadeus VI was made the emperor's representative in all Savoyard dominions, with the authority "de non appellando" to decide appeals emanating from the courts of lay and ecclesiastical magnates "absque contradictione."[20]

This important document nullified the effect of the emperor's previous anti-Savoyard acts. Amadeus was now in a legally unassailable position to pursue his object of reducing the jurisdictional immunities of the great vassals and prelates of his transalpine state; he had become the fount of justice even for those who had no desire whatever to grant him such a role. On 31 August from Evian the count notified his subjects by letter of the

[18] *ADS* (subsidy), Maurienne, 1356.

[19] *AST*, inv. 38, folio 1, docs. 12 (1354–1356) and 13 (1356–1357). These were fiefs confiscated during the *Audiences* of 1351.

[20] Cf. Tabacco, pp. 36ff.

# Magna Baronia

imperial grant. The news was received with alarm in Geneva, where Alamand de Saint-Jeoire redoubled his determination to resist Savoyard encroachments. At Lausanne, Aymon de Cossonay protested angrily against the judge of appeals which the count promptly installed in his episcopal city. Elsewhere the news was received calmly, if not with rejoicing—the sees of Turin and Maurienne were held by relatives, and the prelates of Sion, Aosta, Ivrea, and Tarentaise were loyal Savoyards.[21]

### PIEDMONT AFFAIRS, 1356–1357

In the meantime, couriers crossing the Mont Cenis brought disturbing news from Piedmont and Lombardy. Giacomo of Achaea, seeking to profit from imperial favors bestowed upon him during the emperor's sojourn in Italy in 1355, had in December of that year imposed a set of new taxes on all merchandise crossing his dominions.[22] The prince was being strongly influenced to show more independence of spirit at this time, but his financial needs alone were sufficient explanation for the act.[23] He must have known that such a move would provoke a sharp response from Savoy, for the counts were vitally concerned with the safety of merchants using the Alpine routes. At Chambéry it was quickly concluded that if the new tolls remained in effect the Mont Cenis traffic might be ruined. From Pont d'Ain on 7 May 1356, Amadeus sent a strong protest to his cousin, reminding him of his duties as a vassal of Savoy.[24] Because of the universal outcry

[21] *AST, Principi del Sangue*, mazzo VI, doc. 3. Tommaso de Savoie was bishop of Turin from 1351–1360, and Amadeo de Savoie occupied the see of Maurienne from 1349–1376. Both were younger brothers of Giacomo of Achaea. Amadeus had tried to get the see of Lausanne for Tommaso in 1355. The bishop of Ivrea from 1346 to 1358 was the former abbot of Hautecombe and a member of the new resident council of Savoy, as were the prelates of Tarentaise and Aosta.

[22] On 26 April 1355, Charles IV had granted Giacomo the rights of coining money, creating notaries, legitimizing bastards, and taxing merchandise in transit. Datta, *Storia*, II, doc. XVIII.

[23] Datta, *Storia*, Book II, p. 172, regards the imposition of the tax as having been done chiefly to annoy the count, an explanation which wholly ignores Giacomo's desperate financial situation. F. Gabotto, "Pinerolo ed il Pinerolese dal 1356 al 1363," *BSBS* (IV–VI, 1899), 387, insists that prior to 1357 there is no evidence of a real desire for independence from Savoy, even on the part of Sybille de Baux, Giacomo's proud wife.

[24] Text in Datta, *Storia*, II, doc. XIX. Later, on 25 September 1356, the council

against the "pernicious and damnable" new tolls, the count ordered them withdrawn within the next six days. Failure to comply would result in a summons to appear before the council of Savoy to answer for offending actions. Giacomo sent envoys to defend his position before members of the council at Rivoli, but he did not withdraw his tolls.[25]

At the same time, the political situation in Lombardy was taking on new aspects. In October 1354 the archbishop of Milan, the chief architect of the Visconti-Savoyard marriage, had died, leaving the territories of Milan divided among his three nephews—Matteo, Galeazzo, and Bernabò. By 1355, Matteo was dead (poisoned, it was said), and his younger brothers divided the family possessions between them. Galeazzo became ruler of Como, Novara, Vercelli, Alba, Piacenza, and Bobbio, while Bernabò's share included the eastern half of Visconti acquisitions: Bergamo, Brescia, Cremona, Parma, Lodi, and Bologna. The great city of Milan the brothers ruled jointly, and they also shared their recently acquired suzerainty over Genoa. The current objective of Visconti activity in western Lombardy was the acquisition of the city of Pavia. This meant war with the marquis of Montferrat, and that very prospect was agitating the political atmosphere of the Piedmont at the moment. In June 1355 a league against the Visconti had been organized by Pope Innocent VI, who disputed control of Bologna with Bernabò, and the marquis of Montferrat had joined it.[26]

The outbreak of hostilities between Galeazzo Visconti and Giovanni of Montferrat was embarrassing for the count of Savoy, brother-in-law of one and nephew of the other. Both had aided Amadeus in his own campaigns in the Valais and Faucigny, and he was loath to turn against either one in the conflict gathering on the horizon. Even his political interests could not decide for him, for while an overly powerful Visconti state would greatly en-

---

of Savoy specified the towns (mostly on the route of the Mont Cenis) which claimed to be hurt by Giacomo's tolls: Chambéry, Montmélian, Aiguebelle, La Chambre, the diocese of Maurienne, St-Michel, Modane, Termignon, Lanlebourg, Susa, Avigliana, Rivoli, Cirié, Lanzo, and Caselle. *AST, Principi del Sangue,* mazzo VI, doc. 4.

[25] *Ibid.,* doc. 2.

[26] Luigi Scarabelli, *Paralipomeni di Storia Piemontese dall'Anno 1285 et 1617* in *ASI,* XIII (1847). Amadeus' adherence to the league had also been sought.

danger his Piedmont possessions, his immediate rival in the areas of concern, Ivrea and the Canavese, was Giovanni of Montferrat. In addition, so long as the marquis remained childless, Amadeus, by virtue of his mother's marriage contract, was the heir to his uncle's small but important principality. In view of these factors, the count's wisest policy was one of the strictest neutrality.

Giacomo of Achaea was beset by no such hesitations. His immediate neighbor to the east and his constant rival on all fronts was the marquis of Montferrat, and no hopes for a rich succession prevented him from following the policy dictated by his political interests. In January 1356, Montferrat launched an offensive to wrest Asti and neighboring cities from Visconti domination, and in June, Giacomo concluded a military alliance with the Milanese.[27] While the prince of Achaea invaded the Canavese, where Montferrat's holdings were most vulnerable, the Angevins entered the fray, hoping that the mutual involvement of Visconti and Montferrat would enable them to reconstitute the county of Piedmont, of which they had been despoiled a dozen years earlier. The vicar of Provence, acting on orders from the queen of Naples, invaded the Piedmont; in August, Demonte was captured, then Mondovì, Cuneo, and Cherasco in rapid succession.

In October the Green Count crossed the Mont Cenis with an army and camped at Rivoli. Giacomo of Achaea had not only refused to revoke his new merchandise tax, but had compounded his insubordination by seizing the town of Ivrea despite embassies sent to demand his withdrawal.[28] In early November, when Giacomo ignored still another demand for the removal of the tax, the count and the barons of his council declared the prince contumacious and decreed the confiscation of his fiefs.[29] The sentence was published at once throughout the Piedmont, together with an injunction to the subjects of the "rebel" prince to transfer their allegiance to the count of Savoy.

---

[27] The alliance was between the prince and the Visconti against both Montferrat and Saluzzo. Text in Datta, *Storia*, II, doc. XX. The best account of Piedmont political history in this period remains F. Gabotto, *L'Età del Conte Verde in Piemonte* (*MSI*, XXXIII, 1895).

[28] Cf. Datta, *Storia*, II, docs. XX-XXIII.

[29] *Ibid.*, docs. XXIV, XXV. On 20 October 1356 the council of Savoy, "nunc in Avigliana residenti," condemned Giacomo to pay 100 gold marks for imprisoning Bonifacio Boneti of Chieri and refusing to release him when ordered to do so, *AST, Principi del Sangue*, mazzo VI, doc. 7.

As Giacomo still made no move, the Savoyard hosts took the field. One army marched southward to the prince's capital of Pinerolo and rapidly occupied Buriasco and Frossasco, while the main forces under the count moved northward into the Canavese. The one major military operation of the campaign took place on 27 November—the siege of Balangero on a steep hillside commanding the approaches to the Valle di Lanzo. The fortress was well-supplied and the siege lasted through the winter. Not until 21 January 1357 did Balangero finally surrender, but its fall meant the end of resistance elsewhere in the region. Barbania was occupied soon after, and finally Ivrea as well.[30] In early February the Green Count was back at Rivoli, where citizens from Ivrea and other communes, together with leading nobles of the Canavese, made their submission and received confirmation of their privileges.

Giacomo of Achaea was now ready to admit the futility of further resistance. On 2 February 1357 he and his son Filippo appeared at the castle of Cirié and tendered their submission. Filippo was only seventeen, and this humiliation seems to have been the beginning of a life-long rivalry between him and the Green Count—a rivalry destined to end in tragedy. The count of Savoy was not altogether in the right in this quarrel, so long as might does not make right. The merchandise tax after all had been authorized by imperial charter, and Ivrea, theoretically held in condominion by the two cousins of Savoy, had in reality been ruled by the count and the marquis of Montferrat since 1347. Amadeus, instead of defending the prince's rights, had intervened to deny them and to humiliate his cousin before an audience of enemies. Filippo and his proud mother, Sybille de Baux, could do nothing for the moment except submit—and wait.[31]

The Green Count, however, had accomplished his objectives. Chivalric considerations of magnanimity were put aside in favor of frankly political considerations. Amadeus now held the greater part of the Canavese, taken from Giacomo and from Montferrat. The merchandise tolls were revoked while a commission looked

---

[30] Good relations with Montferrat led to Giovanni II's cession of his half of Ivrea to the count of Savoy late in 1356. Gabotto, *Età*, p. 33.

[31] Marie-José, pp. 110–111, gives the date of Sybille's death as 1350, but she was obviously very much alive in 1356–1357, and did not die until ca. 1362. Cf. Gabotto, "Nuovi contributi alla storia del Conte Verde," *BSBS*, IV (1899).

into the matter.[32] In the *procés-verbal* the count's officers declared that the Lord Count of Savoy had "not only jurisdiction, but *imperium merum et mixtum* . . . over the entire county of Savoy" (which in their view apparently included the Piedmont) by virtue of ancient imperial privileges.[33] Thus the count was entitled to intervene in all questions arising "either between private persons, or between the count and private persons." Since the prince's new taxes resulted in protests from the "majori parte populi," the count "a jure regalie" had the right to arbitrate. To this argument the prince's jurists replied that *imperium merum et mixtum* and *ius regalie* in Piedmont belonged to the ancestors of Prince Giacomo by virtue of ancient imperial privileges which the recent grant from Charles IV had merely confirmed. They may have been right, but the Green Count had the larger army.[34]

Amadeus' campaign in the Canavese had violated the claims of the marquis of Montferrat as well as those of the prince of Achaea, and the count now sought a way of appeasing his uncle without returning any of his conquests. Amadeus apparently hoped to accomplish this by forcing Giacomo to abandon his alliance with the Visconti in favor of a campaign against the Angevins in the south. Marquis Giovanni might be willing to consider the Canavese question settled in return for peace on his Savoyard frontier, since he needed every man he could find for the supreme effort against his arch foes of Milan. To what extent Giovanni committed himself on the Canavese is not certain, but he was in no position to refuse. Giacomo was easily induced to direct his military energies against his enemies to the south,

[32] The commissioners were Galois and Guillaume de la Baume, Humbert of Thoire-Villars, and the abbot of San Michele della Chiusa. Cognasso, *Il Conte Verde* (Turin, 1926), p. 102, thinks that this was only a device for postponing a showdown with Giacomo, and that no decision was ever rendered. This presupposes that Amadeus already envisaged a showdown in 1357, which is uncertain.

[33] *AST, Principi del Sangue*, mazzo. VI, doc. 12. *Procés-verbal* dated 20 March 1357.

[34] The treaty of 10 December 1294 between Amadeus V and Filippo of Achaea had in fact awarded *imperium merum et mixtum* to Filippo within his lands; but a merchandise tax affected neighboring territories, and the prince did have to rely chiefly upon the concessions granted by Charles IV in 1356 to justify his action. Amadeus' reaction was not unjustified, although his recourse to military force might be so regarded.

the Angevins and the marquis of Saluzzo. By the early summer of 1357, the prince and his troops were already assailing the strong-holds of Saluzzo, Revello, and Cardè.

Amadeus returned to Savoy in the summer of 1357 and took measures to relieve the distress of subjects whose villages had been destroyed during the wars with Hugues de Genève. He also made another move toward administrative centralization by establishing a *Cour des Monnaies* at Chambéry to coordinate mint-ing operations in his dominions.[35] Then, in May 1358, the emperor issued another series of acts injurious to the ambitions, if not to the rights, of the count of Savoy.[36] The count of Geneva and his dominions were exempted from the jurisdiction conferred on the count of Savoy by the letters-patent of 21 July 1356, and Ama-deus III was specifically authorized to appeal to the imperial court against decisions promulgated in the courts of Savoy, Dauphiné, or France. The count of Geneva was placed under imperial pro-tection, his fiefs and privileges were confirmed, and he was given the right to coin money during his lifetime, to legitimize bastards, and to create notaries in his territories. These privileges were part of Charles IV's usual policy of giving with his right hand what the left hand took away.

The count of Savoy was not the only one displeased by these concessions. The bishop of Geneva protested against the minting privileges, and when Amadeus III began coining money at An-necy, the bishop appealed to the pope at Avignon. The Green Count seconded the bishop's action and summoned the count of Geneva to renew his homage for the fiefs he held of Savoy, ap-parently with the object of reminding his cousin of his feudal subordination to Savoy. Amadeus III showed no disposition to obey, but in July he agreed to accept the arbitration of Jean de Bertrand, archbishop of Tarentaise.

Before the archbishop's decision was reached, however, another convention of great importance was drawn up which affected the

[35] Cf. *Inventaire sommaire, ADCO*, B 9504, B 7972; see Commentary, IX, on the *Cour des Monnaies*.

[36] These acts are in *Archives nationales* in Paris, *Duché de Genevois,* paq. V. Cf. Duparc, pp. 296ff.

arbitration and its results. This was the treaty of 27 June 1358 between Amadeus VI and the archbishop concerning their respective jurisdiction in the diocese of Tarentaise. The initiative seems to have come from Jean de Bertrand, wearied as he was by the endless encroachments of Savoyard officers in his province. Already much had been lost since the twelfth century, when imperial charters had made the archbishop the direct representative of the emperor in the whole diocese in matters temporal and spiritual.[37] The treaty of 1358 confirmed those losses against the dubious assurance that there would be no more in the future.

The archbishop was to have full jurisdiction over all "men of whatever sex," including strangers and foreigners, except for subjects, vassals, or rear-vassals of the count; and the prelate could not require military service from any of the count's men.[38] The count's castellans at Salins were to have no judicial authority whatever over the inhabitants of Moûtiers, but the count was in effect given high justice over all other inhabitants of the Tarentaise.[39] The archbishop retained low justice only over those dwelling on his own estates. The effects of deceased notaries were to be collected by the prelate's officers, but anything of value was to be shared equally with the count. The count's right to the property of deceased usurers known to have been such was confirmed, but in cases of doubt, the enquiry was to be conducted jointly by the officers of the count and the archbishop.[40] Modest though the prelate's rights were in this treaty, compared with those accorded two centuries before, the charter of 1358 was apparently regarded by the count as a gracious concession, for he obliged the church of Tarentaise to pay him 3,000 florins for it.

[37] The valley of Beaufort and the castles of Briançon and Conflans had already passed to the count of Savoy, but they had once belonged to the archbishop. On the latter's holdings, see Roubert, p. 110.

[38] Treaty published in J. A. Besson, *Mémoires pour servir à l'histoire écclesiastique des diocèses de Genève, Tarentaise, Aoste, et Maurienne et du Décanat de Savoie* (Moûtiers, 1871), doc. 85.

[39] However, to the archbishop went all fines, even those collected for crimes committed by the count's men. In case of doubt as to whether the punishment should be corporal or financial, the archbishop's officers would decide. If corporal, the criminal would be turned over to the count's officers to execute the sentence.

[40] The illegitimate offspring of priests, chaplains, and other ecclesiastics of the see of Tarentaise were to follow the condition of the mother.

This treaty was an important milestone in the forward march of comital jurisdiction in this region, once almost independent of the counts of Savoy. Of the fourteenth-century archbishops to follow, only one, Rodolphe de Chissé (1381–1385) from Faucigny, showed any disposition to turn back the clock. When Rodolphe was murdered in a peasant uprising, he was succeeded by Eduardo de Savoie in February 1386, and the new prelate's loyalty to his dynasty ensured the continued supremacy of the count's temporal authority in the province of Tarentaise.[41]

The willingness of Jean de Bertrand to abandon to the count of Savoy rights guaranteed by imperial charters hardly enhanced his prestige as a trustworthy arbiter in the eyes of the count of Geneva. The archbishop's decisions soon confirmed his suspicions. On 2 August 1358 the prelate granted Amadeus III's right to coin money, but on the questions of homage and appellate jurisdiction the decisions were in favor of Savoy. Amadeus III wrote indignantly to the archbishop that his decisions were "unjust and iniquitous," and vowed to appeal to the emperor "viva voce" to get them reversed. The matter of the homage, however, was worked out peacefully after all. At Geneva on 31 December the count did liege-homage to Amadeus VI in a manner satisfactory to both.[42] In return, the count of Savoy agreed to consider the archbishop's decisions null and void. Had the Green Count only engineered those decisions in the first place in order to exchange them against a firm renewal of his cousin's homage? The Genevois as a whole still eluded the Savoyard's grasp, but part had been recognized once more as feudally subordinate to Savoy.

In the winter of 1358–1359, Amadeus VI was given the opportunity to grasp a province that was probably richer than the Genevois. The Pays de Vaud, a land of fertile farmlands stretching from Lake Geneva to Lake Neuchâtel and eastward almost

[41] On 31 October 1358 a similar treaty with the Mareschal family of Montmélian spelled out comital power in the territories of an ancient and powerful clan. The Mareschal retained full jurisdiction over those living on their lands, except for crimes involving death or mutilation penalties, which fell under the count's authority. Cf. Dullin, pp. 192–193.

[42] *MDG*, XXII (1886), docs. VI, VIII, X; Cordey, *Les Comtes*, p. 135, note 4. Amadeus III did homage for Clermont, Duingt, Annecy, Thones, Gruffy, La Roche, Arlod, Châtel, La Bâtie, Gaillard, and the fiefs of Thomas de Menthon, Guillaume de Compey, and Aymon de Pontverre.

to the gates of Bern, was a *magna baronia* to tempt a prince far less land-hungry than the Green Count. The merchant caravans moving between Italy and northern Europe by way of the Great St-Bernard and Simplon passes traveled its lakeside routes, westward over the Juras into France and the Burgundies, or northward to Bern, Basel, and the Germanies.

Since 1287 the Pays de Vaud had been ruled by a cadet branch of Savoy, but at the battle of Laupen in 1339 the only son of Louis II of Vaud had been killed.[43] Louis's only daughter, Catherine, lost her first husband, Azzo Visconti, the same year, and her second husband, Raoul de Brienne, constable of France, in 1350. For two years Catherine and her widowed mother, Isabelle de Châlon-Arlay, "Les Dames de Vaud," governed the barony together. Louis II, on the death of his son, had persuaded Count Aymon to grant him the exceptional privilege of allowing his daughter to inherit the barony of Vaud. Catherine's failure to bear children during the six years of her marriage to Azzo Visconti may have led the count to hope that she was incapable of motherhood and that at her death the barony would still revert to Savoy. This hope seemed likely to be realized when her second marriage was also childless; but within a year of her third match, to Guillaume I, "the Rich," count of Namur (1337–1391), Catherine had a son, then a second son, then a daughter.[44] It had begun to look as if the Pays de Vaud was lost to the house of Savoy forever.

Catherine had no particular attachment for the country of Vaud, however, and she much preferred her elegant existence at Namur and Paris. Her father had bequeathed sizeable debts to his heiress, who found both the financial and the political burdens more than she cared to undertake. Guillaume de Namur apparently had no desire to retain a principality so distant from his own, and a rumor supposedly reached Savoy that he was

---

[43] When Amadeus V's younger brother, Louis, received the Pays de Vaud in fief-liege from the count, many reservations were made. All who traditionally owed liege-homage to Savoy were to continue to do so, and the barons of Gruyère, Châtel, and Cossonay were to hold their fiefs directly from the count. Louis's appanage contained ten castellanies: Nyon, Rolle, Morges, Moudon, Estavayer, Romont, Rue, Yverdon, Les Clées, and Vaulruz.

[44] Catherine's daughter, Marie, became countess of Blois and a patroness of Froissart. Marie-José, p. 115.

thinking of selling the barony to the Habsburgs. Amadeus VI at once sent Guillaume de la Baume to Namur to argue that the Pays de Vaud was part of the "signorie" of the counts of Savoy and ought therefore to be sold only to them. Guillaume the Rich was assured that the count of Savoy would give him "as much and more than *nulz aultre*," and the sale was concluded. Servion adds the dubious assertion that the Green Count was able to make the acquisition the more cheaply because Guillaume de la Baume had taken the cash with him and because the count of Namur was ignorant of the barony's real worth, owing to officers "who gobbled up everything." The treaty of sale was drawn up on 30 January 1359 at the castle of Morges on Lake Geneva. The price was 160,000 florins, payable in three terms ending with Pentecoste 1360.[45]

Raising the money to purchase the Pays de Vaud was a great strain on the count's financial resources, and the task was complicated by an unexpected military threat on the western boundaries of Savoy. The French monarchy may have been too crippled with internal crises to endanger Savoyard security during these years, but a new menace was just beginning to make its appearance: roving bands of soldiers released from the service of the English king by the truce.[46] They were forming themselves into companies with the intention of living off the provinces, for they

[45] Servion, II, 108; Cabaret, p. 151. *AST*, inv. 16, doc. 22 (1359–1360) confirms that Guillaume de la Baume was the ambassador. Eighty thousand florins were due before the fifth week after Easter 1359, 40,000 the day after Christmas 1359, and 40,000 on Pentecoste 1360.

[46] During the seizure of Paris by Etienne Marcel in 1357 and the Jacquerie of 1358, both Charles the Bad, king of Navarre, and the dauphin wrote to Amadeus VI seeking his help. The dauphin, Amadeus' brother-in-law, was only eighteen in 1356, when the capture of his father at Poitiers made him regent of France. Charles the Bad, the dauphin's rival, begged the count of Savoy to attend the meeting of the Estates-General in December 1357, and in August 1358 the dauphin made a touching effort to win Amadeus over to his side. See details in Cordey, *Les Comtes*, pp. 154ff. (See also R. Delachenal in *Bibliothèque de l'Ecole des Chartes*, LXXII, 1911, pp. 271–273, who shows that the 1357 letters were written by Charles the Bad, and not by the dauphin, as Cordey had supposed.) These letters reveal the prestige which the count of Savoy enjoyed among princes of the French royal family, but Amadeus was unable to answer the appeals of either side. He was ill in the summer of 1358 and had to cancel a trip to the Val d'Aosta, *ADS* (*receptor vini*), Le Bourget, 1352–1361, 1358). He was also probably wary of involvement in internal French power struggles.

knew that in many regions the inhabitants were almost defenseless. Already in 1359 some of the notorious "Great Companies" had begun to appear in Normandy, Berry, and Champagne, creating havoc and terror wherever they went. At first they were largely groups of Navarrais and English, later joined by others, particularly Bretons and Gascons. Early in 1359, Robert Knolles marched past Orléans at the head of such a company to seize and ransome the city of Auxerre. The fifteen-year-old duke of Burgundy hastily gathered an army to oppose their further advance into his territories, and sent to the count of Savoy for help, invoking the mutual assistance pact of 1347.[47]

In April a Savoyard company was sent into Burgundy, and a second army was already being raised when the news came that companies of adventurers were in Auvergne and heading for the Beaujolais. Antoine de Beaujeu appealed for help from Savoy, and Galois de la Baume was dispatched with a company of Bressan nobles. Within three weeks the marauders were driven from the Beaujolais into the county of Forez, where they burned Monbrison. Savoyard territories were safe for the time being, but the era of the Great Companies had only just begun. After the Peace of Bretigny in 1360, their numbers would greatly increase and their activities would trouble the land for the next twenty years.

Amadeus spent most of the spring of 1359 in Bresse and Savoy gathering men and supplies and preparing Bressan castles in case the brigands tried to cross the Saône. In the summer, however, the count's principal concern was again the purchase of the Pays de Vaud. Most of the money came from a subsidy of one florin per hearth, and everyone contributed—bannerets, *religiosi*, nobles, "burgenses et communitates."[48] The subsidy did not suffice, and the remainder of the money had to be secured by other means. The Jews were required to pay for three years in advance their annual tax of 100 florins. About 20,000 florins were raised from nobles and bourgeois for enfeoffments. The market fees at Avig-

---

[47] *ADCO, Inventaire V.* The pact of 1347 had just been renewed.

[48] The total raised in the collection of 1359–1360 was something over 63,000 florins *boni ponderis, AST*, inv. 16, doc. 22. Some 445 subjects of the count at Geneva and environs contributed, as did 179 persons in the castellany of Versoix, *MDS*, XVIII, 403. On the connection between subsidies and "estates-general" in Savoy, see Commentary, X.

# Magna Baronia

liana and Montmélian were given in fief for 1,000 florins each; "omnimode jurisdictione" over their territories was enfeoffed to François de Longecombe and Gaspard de Montmayeur for a total of almost 4,000 florins. Another 10,000 came from more permanent alienations: comital revenues at various towns went to the highest bidder; the Valleise brothers paid almost 3,000 florins for fiefs in the Val d'Aosta; "rebus et jurisdictiones" at Pierre-Châtel and Belley were sold to Pierre Gerbais and to the bishop of Belley.[49]

These measures yielded more than enough to meet the first installment, but much of the balance had to be obtained through loans. The officers of the Savoyard state now found themselves saddled with a new obligation, that of advancing loans to their suzerain, the income of their posts serving as security for repayment.[50] This was not the first time that a count of Savoy borrowed from his officers, but the treasury accounts contain an unusually long list of lenders for the period from 1 August 1358 to 1 August 1359. No fewer than eighty-two officers, including castellans, *baillis*, and judges, advanced money in 1358, and seventy-eight, many of them the same people, did so again in 1359.[51] It was almost as if the feudal custom of requiring aid and counsel from the prince's vassals had been converted into the obligation to advance loans. The money for the first installment was delivered to Guillaume the Rich on 17 June 1359, and two days later the final contract of sale was drawn up and sealed. The count and countess of Namur ceded to the count of Savoy the "localities, *mandamenti*, and jurisdictions" of twelve castellanies in the Pays de Vaud and six others in or around the Valromey. At the same

---

[49] *AST*, inv. 16, doc. 22. The total income reported in 1359–1360, including loans, was about 165,000 florins.

[50] This is a more accurate way of putting it, I think, than to say (cf. Dullin, pp. 41–42) that the count "sold" or "mortgaged" the offices of state. The lender was nearly always an officer already, i.e. he did not receive the office in return for the loan; and often the officer was transferred to some other post before his loan was repaid, i.e. he enjoyed no proprietary rights over his office as a result of the loan.

[51] *AST*, inv. 16, doc. 21: "Mutua facta domino per eius officiares super exitibus suorum officiorum pro anno domini [1358]," followed by another list for 1359. Francesco de' Medici at Geneva loaned 1,000 florins, and large sums were advanced by the wealthy treasurer-general of Savoy, Pierre Gerbais.

135

time, they sent letters to all of their vassals and subjects notifying them of the transaction and commanding them to receive their new overlord.[52]

Now that the sale was final, the Green Count wished to take formal possession of his new barony. The situation clearly called for the gaudy pageantry of which he was so fond, a *Grande Chevauchée* with liveried heralds, flying banners, and an immense retinue in splendid array. The count's new subjects must be suitably impressed with him, and he meant to see that they were. He had a new scarlet jacket lined with one hundred squirrel skins and twenty-seven ermine skins for the occasion.[53] The gorgeous cavalcade first crossed the Mont du Chat to Belley, where the new vassals of Bugey and Valromey presented themselves. The count then moved on to Seyssel on the Rhône and the Bourg-de-l'Ile at Geneva. The tour of the Pays de Vaud began on 13 July with dinner at Nyon and supper at Morges. Like the barons of Vaud before him, Amadeus would make Morges his capital for the province. On 14 July in the great hall of the castle, the Green Count received the homage of the nobles and communes of the country. He then confirmed the franchises of Romont, Moudon, Vaulruz, Rue, and Les Clées, and extended those of Romont and Gruyère to match the privileges of Moudon, which were accounted the most generous in the barony.

In the following several days the Green Count visited Moudon, Rue, Romont, Estavayer on Lake Neuchâtel, and Les Clées, which commanded a strategic gateway through the Juras to the Burgundies. Everywhere he was received cordially by the inhabitants, who paid the expenses of his stay, except in the smaller towns, where the count himself undertook to spare the population a burden too great for its resources. Dozens of nobles appeared to do homage and receive investiture of their fiefs in the course of the *Grande Chevauchée*, which came to an end on 20 July at Lausanne. There, in the cathedral, Amadeus did homage to the bishop, "his hands between the hands of the lord bishop and with the kiss of fidelity," for the fiefs which he held from the church of Lausanne.

Thus ended the ceremonious annexation of the Pays de Vaud,

---

[52] Details in Jean Cordey, "L'Acquisition du Pays de Vaud par le Comte Vert, 1359," *MDR* (2nd series, VI, 1907).

[53] *AST*, inv. 38, folio 1, doc. 13.

together with a population that would serve the counts of Savoy loyally for many generations to come. The Green Count had acquired another *magna baronia,* and except for the Genevois, his dominion now extended almost without interruption from the frontiers of the Dauphiné to the gates of Morat and Bern.

## PIEDMONT AFFAIRS, 1359–1360

Late in July, Amadeus was back in Savoy, preparing for another cavalcade—one considerably less festive than that just ended in the Pays de Vaud. In 1359 relations with the prince of Achaea took a turn for the worse. Sybille de Baux seems to have persuaded her husband that subordination to the count of Savoy could be tolerated no longer.[54] Giacomo accordingly decided to take advantage of the count's illness in 1358, and of his subsequent involvement with the Great Companies in Burgundy. The merchandise tax was reinstated, and the prince's subjects were forbidden to appeal beyond his tribunals to those of Savoy. When the pro-Savoyard Provana brothers of Carignano did appeal to the count's judge at Moncalieri, Giacomo accused them of treason and seized their possessions. Later, two men sent by the lord of Truffarello to enter an appeal at the same court were captured by the prince's men and put to death. Citizens of Chieri and Carignano accused of doing homage to the count of Savoy found their property confiscated and their persons in danger.[55] According to Cabaret, the Provanas appealed to the count against the treatment they had received, and Amadeus summoned Giacomo to appear at Chambéry and answer the charges against him. At this the prince was "très dédaigné" and in "grand fureur," and he allegedly had the messenger who brought the summons thrown into the Po, where he drowned.[56]

Whatever the measure of truth in these allegations, the prince had done more than enough to provoke retaliation. By mid-September 1359, Amadeus was at La Chambre in the Maurienne with his army, and three days later he had crossed the Mont Cenis and was camped at Avigliana. Giacomo showed no disposition to submit when summoned to do so, and in late October the Savoyard

[54] On this subject see Gabotto, "Pinerolo ed il Pinerolese."

[55] Datta, *Storia,* Book II, pp. 181–182.

[56] Cabaret, p. 151 *dorso.*

offensive began with devastating effect.[57] Baratonia, Fiano, Bruino, Trana, and Cumiana fell into the count's hands in rapid succession. By mid-November, Giacomo was ready to agree to the arbitration of his differences with the count, but this was only an attempt to gain time in the face of a new foe. Some of the mercenary bands against which the Savoyards had already fought in France had made their way into the Dauphiné and were heading for Italy. By Christmas, Giacomo had word that the notorious Anichino Baumgarten, with 800 horses and 700 infantry, was approaching the Piedmont on the route to Pinerolo.[58]

The prince could hardly have expected justice from the four Savoyards who were appointed to arbitrate his quarrel.[59] His representatives countered Amadeus' demands for unconditional obedience from his cousin with a list of past agreements which the count had not honored. The prince's envoys declared that the count had not behaved toward the prince as a suzerain was bound to do toward a vassal, and that Giacomo's resistance to such injustice was therefore within his rights. The arbiters were not impressed, and their decision was harsh beyond anything the prince could have imagined: a fine of 200,000 florins and confiscation of his Piedmont heritage.[60] The Green Count meant to take cruel advantage of the prince's weakness.

Giacomo's position was truly desperate. On 19 January 1360 the prince was at Rivoli, where the arbiters' decision was to be given, and he had agreed not to leave without the count's permission. But as the day for the sentence approached, the prince decided that his only hope lay in flight. Sometime after 22 January he eluded his hosts and took refuge at the fortress of Pinerolo where Princess Sybille and a strong garrison welcomed him. This was a brave move, but the prince remained gravely in need of men and money. An attempt on his part to collect an emergency subsidy

[57] See letter of 28 October 1359 from Rivoli in Datta, *Storia* II, doc. XXVI. Amadeus styled himself "comes Sabaudie, dux Chablaisii et Auguste, et in Ytalia marchio et princeps."

[58] I have adopted this version of his name because it reflects both his German origin and his Italian career. Other versions are Anequin Bongard, Hennequin de Bongart, Anichino de Baumgarthen.

[59] Guillaume de la Baume, Louis Rivoire, Jean Ravais, and the abbot of San Michele della Chiusa.

[60] *AST, Principi del Sangue*, mazzo VI, doc. 17.

in Pinerolo was ill-received, the first indication that zeal for Giacomo's cause was waning even in his own capital.[61]

On 27 January 1360 the "arbiters" produced a revised and slightly less severe sentence, but the principal clause remained the same: Giacomo must forfeit his fiefs.[62] Two days later the Savoyard host set out from Rivoli en route for Pinerolo and that evening encountered Pietro Ferrari, apparently sent by the commune (which later paid his expenses). The pro-Savoyard faction in Pinerolo had gained the upper hand and had persuaded the majority of citizens there to abandon the prince in order to avoid the disasters of a siege, the prospect of which was rendered the more terrifying by the expected arrival of Baumgarten. Sybille fled to Fossano to organize the resistance there, Giacomo retreated toward the south, and young Filippo was sent to Alessandria for safety—possibly to seek assistance there. On 30 January, Amadeus and his men entered Pinerolo without opposition; but the fortress, entrenched on the steep hillside above the town, held out stubbornly. It was not until 9 February that the garrison obeyed Giacomo's orders to surrender and thereby to save the place from destruction. The defenders were allowed to withdraw in safety, and Giacomo di Lucerna was installed as the count's castellan. Among the townspeople, sentiment for the prince of Achaea was by no means extinct, and numerous fines were collected in the next few months from citizens who had uttered "verba injuriosa" against the Lord Count.[63]

About this time the dreaded Baumgarten and his company arrived on the scene. The Green Count had no love for these people and was well enough acquainted with them to know how destructive they could be. But he could not afford to allow Baumgarten to enter the service of his rebellious cousin. The only way he could prevent this was to hire the company himself, before Giacomo's agents could do so. Unfortunately for the inhabitants of the Piedmont, Amadeus succeeded. The village of Miradolo, still loyal to the prince, was pillaged mercilessly by these ravenous new allies, and while the count and his troops invested Vigone

---

[61] Gabotto, "Pinerolo ed il Pinerolese," p. 394.

[62] *AST, Principi del Sangue*, mazzo VII, doc. 1.

[63] One citizen exclaimed "quod non credebat tantum vivere quod videret quod dominus comes esset dominus Pinarolii," a sentiment which cost him six *livres*. Gabotto, "Pinerolo ed il Pinerolese," p. 396.

and Villafranca without a fight, Baumgarten captured and pillaged Perosa.

The prince of Achaea was now at the end of his resources. In mid-February 1360 he offered to submit to the confiscation of his Piedmont holdings if he were given territories of equal value in Savoy. This offer was more than reasonable and was accepted by the count, who sent officers at once to take over the prince's remaining towns and castles. By the end of the month the entire Pinerolese (Cavour, Bagnolo, Moretta, and the fiefs of the Piossaschi and the Lucerna) was under Savoyard control; other towns farther south, however, refused to submit. This resistance encouraged Giacomo to repudiate his agreement and to make one last desperate effort to retrieve the situation on the battlefield. An engagement took place near Scarnafigi in early March, but the Savoyards won and Giacomo was taken prisoner. At about the same time, a Savoyard army, assisted by the troops of Baumgarten and another mercenary company, under the "Conte Lando" (or Landau), assailed the walls of Savigliano, the most important of the towns still loyal to the prince in the south. Amadeus, resolved now to crush his cousin, had called upon all of his allies. The bishops of Asti and Alba, the Visconti, even Federigo of Saluzzo, joined the count of Savoy in this spring campaign.[64]

The results were tragic for the valiant citizens of Savigliano, who were attacked by overwhelming forces. The walls were breached and the besiegers poured into the town, which was delivered over to the brutal soldiery. Houses, churches, palaces were sacked and burned while men, women, and children were assaulted, or tortured, or killed—according to the whim of their conquerors. The wanton destruction of this flourishing little city of some 6,000 inhabitants remains a deplorable event in the annals of the Green Count, but it created its intended effect.[65] The terror it inspired undermined whatever disposition to resist still remained elsewhere in the Piedmont. On 16 March 1360 the citizens of Turin made their submission at Chieri. Amadeus graciously pardoned them for their "rebellion" in supporting their prince and confirmed and extended their communal liberties.

[64] Cf. Gabotto, *Età*, pp. 117–118.

[65] See the contemporary account of this event in the "Destructio Saviliani que facta fuit sub anno 1360" published in Scarabelli, pp. 65–70.

The principal towns of the prince's dominions were now falling rapidly into the power of the count. Of the five most populous —Chieri, Savigliano, Turin, Pinerolo, and Moncalieri—only the last-named was still unsubdued.[66] The Moncalierese now sent ambassadors, but sought to make the prince's release from captivity the condition of their submission. Amadeus replied that Giacomo had submitted freely and was not being detained. On 19 March at the castle of Rivalta in the presence of Tommaso de Savoie, bishop of Turin, and several Savoyard barons, the prince himself assured the envoys from Moncalieri that he was not being held a prisoner by the count or anyone else. Giacomo then instructed the envoys to pledge to the Green Count's representatives that loyalty which they had up until then given to him. The envoys hesitated, but when they were assured that the privileges of their city would be respected, they obeyed.

The conditions which the count agreed to accept in return for the submission of Moncalieri reveal the strength of the Piedmont communes. Amadeus promised that he would never turn the city over to any other lord except to Giacomo or his son, and he bound himself to pay the prince's debts not only to the commune, but to private citizens of the town as well.[67] The citizens were exempted from military service "beyond the mountains," and on the Italian side of the Alps their service could not exceed forty days. The requirement to serve was limited to one suitable male between twenty and thirty years of age from each hearth per year, without the right to increase the length of service in one year on the grounds that no service had been required during a previous year. The Moncalierese were to be exempt from all tolls, taxes, and imposts everywhere in the territories of the count or of his vassals. The commune retained the authority to make its own laws and to oblige its citizens to settle both civil and criminal disputes in its own courts. There were a number of lesser provisions, but Amadeus accepted them all on 20 March, and on the following day the community received his officers. Within a few weeks the example of Moncalieri was followed by Turin and Carignano.

[66] All of these towns had between 4,000 and 7,000 inhabitants at about this time. Cf. Cibrario, *Economia*, II, 50.

[67] Gabotto, *Età*, pp. 118–119.

In mid-April three of the most important Piedmont noble families, the Provana, the Piossaschi, and the Lucerna, came to do homage and to receive investiture of their fiefs from the count. They too obtained considerable privileges in return for their submission: they were allowed the right to engage in private warfare, except against anyone fighting under the name or arms of Savoy; they retained the exclusive right to pursue outlaws on their own lands, except for traitors, assassins, and thieves; and they enjoyed full civil and criminal jurisdiction over their own subjects. Any disputes between or among these nobles in which the intervention of the feudal suzerain was justified must be settled "on this side of the mountains." It was agreed that if the bourgeois of Carignano would not admit the enemies of the Provana to their town, the Provana would not receive enemies of the commune in their territories. None of the "homines" of these nobles could become bourgeois in any commune unless he had lived there unclaimed for a year and a day. The count was forbidden to acquire any fiefs belonging to these barons without their consent, and if any fiefs escheated to him, he must restore them to the family for a just price. Under no circumstances, saving outright rebellion, could the count occupy any of their fortresses or "rocche." Finally, Amadeus swore that he would never allow these nobles to pass again under the yoke of vassalage to the prince of Achaea or his heirs; hereafter, these barons were to hold their fiefs directly from the counts of Savoy.[68]

This treaty reveals as much about the Piedmont magnates as the pact with Moncalieri reveals about the communes. The Piedmontese subjects were more unruly than those in Savoy, and bitter antagonisms permeated relations among nobles, between nobles and communes, and between the nobles and the prince. The Green Count might eventually be strong enough to establish his supremacy over them, but for the moment he would have to confirm their privileges and rely upon rivalries to strengthen his hand. "Divide and rule" was not a requirement in governing his Alpine territories, but this was Amadeus' first acquaintance with Italian politics. He was already discovering that if his projects here were to succeed, other methods than those to which he was accustomed were required.

---

[68] Text (dated 12 April 1360) published in Datta, *Storia*, II, doc. XXVII.

On 8 May 1360 at Turin the prince of Achaea ceded his Piedmont heritage to the count of Savoy in return for sixteen castellanies widely dispersed in Chablais, Faucigny, and Bugey.[69] Amadeus was mistaken, however, if he thought that Giacomo was
reconciled to his fate and without resources. Fossano, where Sybille
remained defiant, was still in his power and fiercely loyal. So
were Cavallermaggiore and Sommariva del Bosco, since all three
towns were held by the prince in fief from the Visconti and therefore were not included in the land forfeited by his rebellion against
Savoy. Filippo was still at large in Alessandria and might return
at any moment with allies for his father's cause.

For the time being, however, the Green Count was in control
of the Savoyard Piedmont. The problem was how to remain in
control. In May, Amadeus left Turin for the Canavese. He paused
at Lanzo and Cuorgne on the way and arrived at Ivrea on the
twelfth. There he inspected the great red brick "Castle of the
Four Towers," which had been begun on his orders in 1358 to
strengthen his hold on this key town. That same afternoon, however, he left for Milan. A major shift in the count's "foreign
policy" was now in the making. Thus far Amadeus, while watching out for his own interests in the Canavese, had attempted to
remain aloof from the Visconti-Montferrat struggle. But there
were now compelling reasons to abandon this posture of interested neutrality. In 1358, Giovanni II married a second time, to
Isabella of Majorca, who had given the childless marquis a son
(the first of four). The count of Savoy was no longer the heir
presumptive to the marquisate and its dependencies, and acquisition of them by succession was now doubtful. In addition, the
marquis was by no means reconciled to the loss of places in the
Canavese which the count had seized in 1356–1357. Giovanni may
even have threatened to help the prince of Achaea to recover his
heritage, should Amadeus not give up the contested towns in the
Canavese. The death of the Dowager Marquessa Marguerite de
Savoie in 1359 and the return of her dowry lands of Lanzo, Cirié,

[69] The prince was condemned to an indemnity of 140,000 florins. As payment
the count took possession of Pianezza and Cumiana (valued at 40,000 florins),
Miradolo (valued at 20,000), La Perosa and Val San Martino (40,000), Bagnolo
(10,000), and Moretta (25,000). For the remaining 5,000 florins the count reserved the right to take "other possessions" of the prince in Piedmont. *AST,
Principi del Sangue,* mazzo VII, doc. 3.

and Caselle to Amadeus' control severed another bond which had
helped to prevent uncle and nephew from drifting apart.

Amadeus now decided that the surest means of maintaining his
Canavesan acquisitions and of ensuring the submission of his
cousin would be an alliance with the Visconti. His offers were
welcomed at Milan. In November 1359, Galeazzo had at last over-
thrown the partisans of Montferrat at Pavia and had gained entry
to the city after years of warfare and intrigue. In February 1360
he had contrived to bring the city of Asti under his control as
well, in spite of all that the marquis had done to prevent it.
Galeazzo knew that Giovanni would never rest until he had
recovered these losses, and that an alliance with Savoy would
expose the marquis to a very timely "second front" on the west.

Bernabò Visconti also had reasons for looking favorably upon
closer cooperation with the count of Savoy. If Galeazzo's chief preoccupation over these years had been with Pavia, that of Bernabò
was with Bologna, which had been acquired for the Visconti by
Archbishop Giovanni in 1354. On the death of the archbishop the
city had eluded Visconti control, thanks to the maneuvers of
Giovanni d'Oleggio, "Captain of the People," at Bologna in 1355.
When Oleggio later discovered that he could not hold out alone,
he offered the city to the papacy. The offer was speedily accepted
and by April 1360, Cardinal Albornoz, legate of Innocent VI,
was in command of the city's defenses. At the same time, His
Holiness tried to revive the anti-Visconti league which had temporarily curbed Milanese expansion some years earlier. On 26
April he sent a letter to the count of Savoy exhorting him as a
dutiful son of the Church to take up arms against her principal
enemy, Bernabò Visconti.[70] Bernabò doubtless learned of the papal
effort to draw Amadeus into the new league; thus he shared
Galeazzo's eagerness to form a solid military alliance with Savoy
before the pope could do so.

For Galeazzo there was still another reason for a rapproche-
ment with Savoy. At this time he was laying plans to counter papal
influence in northern Italy by marrying his son, Giangaleazzo,
now age nine, to Isabelle de Valois, daughter of the king of
France. Jean le Bon needed an immense ransom for his release

---

[70] Cipolla, "Innocenzo VI e Casa Savoia," *MST*, VII (3rd series, 1902), doc.
LXXIII, 185–186.

from captivity in England, and Galeazzo was prepared to furnish the gigantic sum of 600,000 gold écus for the privilege of marrying his son to a daughter of France and for the French support of Visconti political enterprises which such a marriage would imply. For the delicate negotiation of such an important marriage, a better intermediary than the count of Savoy could hardly be found, for in addition to his excellent standing at the court of France, Amadeus was the uncle of the prospective bridegroom and, through his wife, brother-in-law of the bride-to-be.

On 24 May the Green Count took leave of the Visconti in Milan and on 12 June reached Chambéry, having left Humbert de Corgenon behind as his lieutenant-general of Piedmont. Amadeus found a festive atmosphere reigning in Savoy on his return. During his absence Countess Bonne had given birth to a son, named Amadeus after his father. The child had been born in March in the same castle of Chambéry as the count himself twenty-six years before.[71] The baby, now a healthy three-and-a-half months old, was the answer to the fervent prayers of the countess, who had been childless for five years.[72]

From Chambéry, Amadeus probably sent envoys to Paris to complete the negotiations for the hand of Isabelle de Valois.[73] Jean le Bon, presented with so magnificent an offer, did not hesitate. The county of Vertus in Champagne was designated as the princess's dowry, and by August, Isabelle was on her way to Lombardy. The "camera a la marquisa" at the castle of Pont-de-Veyle was put in order for her, and the Green Count was on hand in person to greet her when she arrived there early in September. After appropriate festivities in her honor, she was escorted to Chambéry, where she was received by the court of Savoy and

[71] Cordey, *Les Comtes*, pp. 210–211, establishes beyond doubt that Amadeus VII was born at Chambéry and not at Avigliana, as asserted by Cibrario, Guichenon, and local Aviglianese enthusiasts to this day.

[72] In 1358, Bonne de Bourbon had given birth to a daughter, but the baby died within a few weeks of its birth.

[73] Both Cordey and Cognasso affirm the presence of the count himself in Paris in June 1360, but do not document the statement. If the chronology given on the basis of *chambre des comptes* documents in Gabotto, "Nuovi contributi," pp. 13–21, for the count's whereabouts between 1359 and 1363 is correct, then his presence in Chambéry on both 16 and 20 June makes a trip to Paris impossible. *ADCO*, B 9956 (1359–1361) shows him at Chambéry on 22 June 1360.

by dignitaries from Milan who came to greet her on behalf of their master. By mid-September the company had left Chambéry to cross the Mont Cenis before the snows of winter made the route too difficult, and on 21 September the princess reached Susa. Amadeus remained in Savoy, but he sent an escort bearing wedding gifts of silver plate and armor to accompany Isabelle from Susa to Ivrea and on to Milan. The two children, Isabelle de Valois and Giangaleazzo, who soon after were made man and wife, could hardly have realized their role in the web of international diplomacy being spun about them. On the gala occasion of their wedding, it was rather their parents who rejoiced.

# Enemies of God, of Pity, of Mercy

## 1360-1363

THE early 1360's were difficult years for the Savoyards. There was rebellion again in the Valais, and the Green Count sought to cope with it more constructively than he had done in the past. There was also an increasing involvement in Piedmont affairs, the settlement of the long conflict with the prince of Achaea, and the beginning of a new rivalry with the house of Saluzzo. Amadeus' chief problem during these years, however, was the intermittent threat of the Great Companies which had been loosed upon the land after the Peace of Bretigny was concluded between England and France in the spring of 1360.

After years of campaigning, many soldiers had neither homes nor jobs to return to, now that their services were no longer needed. Widespread economic depression, particularly in areas which had suffered occupation during the wars, had created such misery and hardship that the inhabitants already there could hardly sustain themselves. Men who enjoyed the soldier's trade, as well as others who had come to look upon it as their only means of existence, were easily recruited by enterprising captains and formed into powerful companies of cavalry and infantry. Most of these soldiers would have preferred regular service under some great prince; but until such an employer might appear, they were ready to follow any commander who promised them protection and pay. Soon the land was full of private armies of adventurers, some of whom pretended to be acting on behalf of the king of England or of Navarre, although in reality they were beyond the control of any king. Led by resourceful and cunning captains, these armies made their way into central and eastern France, where royal power was weakest and least able to hinder their activities. Urban V described them as a "multitude of villains of diverse nations, associated in arms by avidity in appropriating to themselves the fruit of the labours of innocent and defenseless people, unbridled in every kind of cruelty, extorting money, methodically devastating the country and the open towns, burning houses and barns, destroying trees and vines, obliging poor peasants to fly; assaulting, besieging, invading, spoiling, and ruining even fortresses and walled cities; torturing and maiming those from whom they expected to obtain ransom, without regard to ecclesiastical dignity or sex or age; violating wives, virgins, and nuns, and constraining even gentlewomen to follow their camp, to do their pleasure and carry arms and baggage."[1] Provinces were plundered, cities too strong to take were threatened and forced to pay ransom. Sometimes, as in Froissart's famous description of the "Archpriest" Arnaud de Cervole, a band would seize a fortress and use it as headquarters while systematically stripping the countryside of whatever the wars had left to take.

These were the "enemies of God, of pity, of mercy" who during the Hundred Years War made the intervals of peace more terrible than those of war.[2] The rich cities of the Rhône valley— Lyon, Vienne, and especially Avignon, where the papal court seemed the richest plum of all to pluck—very soon attracted the attention of the adventurers. These cities were relatively weak, having only their own resources and those of local nobles with which to defend themselves. Moreover, once they had been plundered or forced to pay ransom, the marauders could move on to Italy, where hundreds of wealthy cities in constant warfare with one another provided endless opportunities for riches and employment. Even before the Green Count's return to Italy, a fresh company of brigands had entered the Beaujolais; and at the end of May 1360 a band of English soldiers attacked and captured the town of Beaujeu and lay siege to the fortress. Antoine of Beaujeu appealed frantically for help, and a second time Galois de la Baume, the count's captain-general in Bresse, hurried to the scene

[1] Letter dated 17 February 1364, cited in J. Temple-Leader and G. Marcotti, *Sir John Hawkwood* (London, 1889), p. 51.

[2] One of the famous German mercenary captains in Italy during this period wore the following motto across his chest in silver letters: "Duke Werner, lord of the Great Company, enemy of God, of pity, of mercy." E. Ricotti, *Storia delle Compagnie di Ventura in Italia* (Turin, 1845), II, 53.

with Savoyards and Bressans. After three days of hard fighting, the marauders, described as "Navarrenses et Englicos," were driven away and the town was rescued.[3]

The danger, however, was only beginning. The count's return to Savoy in mid-June 1360 coincided with the arrival of disquieting news. A horde of mercenaries called the "Tard-Venus" had recently been collecting in Champagne and was beginning to move southward into Burgundy. The Tard-Venus were a loose confederation of soldiers, each very much on his own, with captains for each group having a vague sort of authority over their followers; but no one at all had authority, vague or otherwise, over the whole gigantic host. Young Philippe de Rouvre, duke of Burgundy, found his own resources inadequate in the face of this formidable invasion of "gens sans tête" and sent to Savoy for help. Amadeus sent what men he could spare and threw additional garrisons into the Saône river fortresses. A company under Humbert de Sachins, captain of Bâgé-le-Châtel, remained in Bresse for the next two months to strengthen the army already there under Galois de la Baume, and the castles of Miribel and Montluel on the Rhône were heavily reinforced.[4]

In view of these preparations, and upon receipt of heavy tributes from the duke of Burgundy, the dreaded Tard-Venus decided to move out of Burgundy. But as they passed southward along the Saône, every precaution had to be taken to protect the people of the Beaujolais and Lyonnais. The Savoyards were successful in guarding their territories from the marauders, thanks to the protection of the wide-flowing Saône, but their less fortunate neighbors across the river endured the hardships of the damned. The *pestiferae societates* continued their southward march, and by December were nearing Avignon, causing panic in the city and surrounding regions. On 10 January 1361, Innocent VI appealed to the count of Savoy to come to the aid of the Holy Church, and four days later Dauphin Charles ordered his vassals in the Dauphiné to assemble at Vienne without delay, for the invaders were threatening to cross the river there.

In January 1361, Petrarch was sent to Paris by Galeazzo Visconti to congratulate Jean le Bon on his recent release from im-

---

[3] Cordey, p. 160.

[4] *ADCO*, B 6787 (Bâgé), B 8367, B 8368 (Miribel), B 8458 (Montluel).

prisonment in England. The poet was to return to the king a ring which he had lost at the battle of Poitiers and which Galeazzo had redeemed. Petrarch's comments on the state of France give a graphic picture of the sufferings which war and plague had brought to that unhappy land: "Everywhere was solitude, devastation, and sadness; everywhere fields untilled and neglected; everywhere houses in ruins or abandoned, save as they were protected by the walls of cities or castles; everywhere the melancholy traces of the English and the fresh and horrible scars left by their swords."[5]

Innocent VI considered the situation so menacing that he resolved to turn to the ultimate resource of the Church. He called for a crusade against the Companies, which had thus far received his spiritual blows of excommunication with soldierly indifference. The Tard-Venus had seized Pont-St-Esprit, scarcely twenty miles from Avignon, and were preparing to use it as a base of operations. The pope sent out urgent letters to the count of Savoy, the duke of Burgundy, and the governor of the Dauphiné imploring them to prevent at all costs the passage of the "sons of Belial" across their territories. In Savoy defense preparations went on, but the burden was heavy, for another formidable foe had reappeared: the dreaded plague. It had already broken out in the mountains of Bugey late in 1359 and throughout 1360 raged unchecked, according to the castellan of St-Rambert, who was soon himself among its victims.[6] Twenty-three families of the village of Varey died from the plague in 1361.[7] The Green Count's infant son fell

---

[5] Cited in A. S. Cook, "The Last Months of Chaucer's Earliest Patron," *Transactions of Connecticut Academy of Arts and Sciences,* (Vol. 21, 1916), p. 23, note 1. Petrarch very probably used the Mont Cenis route to get from Milan to Paris and back, but his only comment on his trip through Savoy was to mention the unpleasant and uncomfortable inns, and the "glaciem hieme horrida" of the Alps in February. Cf. E. H. Wilkins, *Petrarch's Eight Years in Milan* (Cambridge, 1958), p. 225.

[6] *ADCO,* B 9756 (St-Rambert). Half the population of the village of Evoges perished in this reappearance of the Death. Later on, in 1364, the count was informed that his castellan of St-Sorlin was forcing the inhabitants of Souclin and Soudon to pay the *garda* of five persons who had died during this "mortality" leaving neither heirs nor property. The fact was attested by the curé of the place and five "prudhommes," and the count commanded his officers to cease and desist.

[7] *Ibid.,* B 10297 (Varey).

ill at Rochefort, to the consternation of the countess, who took him away immediately to the more healthful environs of Evian, where he was placed under the watchful eye of the court physician, Master Palmieri.[8]

Plague or not, military preparations had to go on. No sooner had the first wave of *pestiferae* passed than another appeared. By mid-December a new host had been formed, largely remnants of the armies which some months earlier had been ordered by King Edward to withdraw from Normandy, Picardy, Anjou, and neighboring provinces. The leaders of this band were attracted as the others had been, by the fruitful lands of Burgundy and by the weakness of its boy-duke. In late December the brigands were ravaging the environs of Dijon and Beaune, and early in January, while the first army of Tard-Venus was encamped at Pont-St-Esprit, the second was already entering the Mâconnais. On 1 February 1361, Pope Innocent began trying to organize a league of nobles and princes of the region for their mutual protection. Count Amadeus sent another contingent of knights to the aid of Antoine of Beaujeu, whose territories were once again directly in the line of march which the marauders were following. Galois de la Baume took up his positions at Bâgé-le-Châtel and St-Laurent-les-Mâcon, hoping that his 100 men-at-arms, added to the garrisons already there, would be able to hold the Mâcon bridge in case the brigands should attempt to cross over into Bresse.[9]

The frightened Bressan population waited anxiously from January on, as messengers rode into the towns daily to report the approach of the Companies, which by now were divided into three main groups.[10] Spies were sent out to follow their every movement, and at Pont-de-Vaux a wooden tower was added to the top of the donjon so that the guards there could see the whole of the Saône valley between Tournus and Mâcon. Castellans everywhere in Bresse began building wooden archery platforms and new galleries along the tops of the ramparts, repairing their drawbridges, heightening turrets, and amassing crossbow bolts and missiles for the war engines. No heartening news came to relieve the general anxiety during that fearful winter. Not until spring did help seem

---

[8] *Ibid.*, B 9399 (Rossillon).

[9] Cordey, *Les Comtes*, pp. 160–161.

[10] Guigue, *Récits de la Guerre de Cent Ans: Les Tard-Venus dans le Lyonnais, Forez et Beaujolais, 1356–1369* (Lyon, 1886), pp. 50–51.

to be on the way. Jean le Bon finally responded to the appeals of the pope and sent a strong force under Marshal Arnould d'Audrehem and the Constable de Fiennes to dislodge the Companies at Pont-St-Esprit. At the same time, Innocent's league against the unholy invaders began to take shape with the arrival at Avignon of a host of nobles from the surrounding region, reinforced by men-at-arms sent by the king of Aragon.

During all of February and most of March, the Green Count was on the shores of Lake Geneva and in the Pays de Vaud, raising men and money for the defense of his territories. He had other reasons for spending so much time there and in the Chablais— the lengthy negotiations with the Valaisans were reaching a conclusion. The treaty imposed upon the population of the Valais in 1352 after the count's two victorious campaigns had proved unenforceable, owing particularly to the obstinacy of the peasants of the High Valais and to the intervention of Charles IV in 1355. The emperor had taken the communities of the Rhône valley under his protection and had ordered the count of Savoy to retire from the region, despite the latter's contention that he was merely upholding the lawful rights of the bishop.

As usual, Charles' intervention had served to confuse the situation—as perhaps he had intended. The three-cornered struggle among the nobles, the bishop, and the Valaisan communes was in no way resolved, and numerous bloody incidents had marred the tranquility of the years which followed. Savoyard castellans and embattled garrisons clung to their fortified perches atop Tourbillon, Montorge, and Conthey, defending the rights of the count of Savoy, while Guichard Tavel transferred the episcopal household to the castle of La Soie, located high up on a ridge well out of the reach of his undutiful flock at Sion. Farther upstream the landamman of Uri, Johann von Attinghausen, acting partly as a representative of the emperor, but perhaps more as a representative of the aggressive Forest Cantons across the Furka, proclaimed himself "rector of the land of the Valais above Visp." In January 1355, Pierre, count of Aarberg and the emperor's captain-general in the Valais, having already captured the bishop's castles upstream from Sion, lay siege to La Tourbillon, which was defended successfully by a tenacious Savoyard garrison. Then an imperial order arrived from Milan commanding Pierre to raise the siege and conclude a truce with the count of Savoy. Amadeus' ambassadors had obviously gained the emperor's ear.[11] A few months later when the imperial representatives left the valley, the communes realized that they had been abandoned and turned to other means of defense. The German-speaking communities between Leuk and the Furka formed a military alliance in October 1355 and swore mutual aid in protecting their liberties. The principal villages reconstituted their municipal tribunals, which by now virtually replaced the temporal authority of the bishop.

The situation remained tense. The bishop was determined to recover his rights as a sovereign prince of the Empire and was disposed to rely upon the backing of the count of Savoy. The communes were equally determined to resist any attempt at Savoyard domination, and the bishop's alliance with the count forced even those inclined to submit to episcopal authority into the camp of his most embittered enemies in the High Valais—enemies who were eager to imitate the example of the Forest Cantons in throwing off all authority save their ultimate allegiance to the emperor.

A variety of considerations now convinced the Green Count that his present mailed-fist policy in the Valais was unwise. During the nine years since his crushing victories over the rebellious Valaisans, they had continued to resist his authority and had taken advantage of him each time his back was turned. The various indemnities to which they had been condemned for their misdeeds remained unpaid, and any attempt to collect these sums was certain to provoke a full-scale rebellion. Amadeus, with the Great Companies hovering about his western frontiers, could not withdraw men from Bresse for a campaign in the Valais. Furthermore, he had just received the news of war in the Piedmont, which would soon require his presence there with all the men he could spare. Many Valaisan communities were ready to support the bishop in opposition to the nobles, once they could be sure that in so doing they were not delivering themselves into the hands of the Savoyard, whose taxes were as much to be feared as his vengeance. Would it not be wiser for the count to withdraw in favor of the bishop, already a firm friend of Savoy, and let him try to reestablish his authority without the dubious assistance of the Savoyards? Bishop Guichard may well have argued along these lines himself, now that it was clear that Savoyard intervention was endangering rather than strengthening his position.

[11] Details in Van Berchem, pp. 222ff.

At Evian on 11 March 1361, Count Amadeus ratified a new treaty which had been drawn up after many months of arduous negotiations.[12] In it he agreed to surrender his post of episcopal *bailli* along with the military and financial rights attached to it, in return for the sum of 13,000 florins. Rights which the count had never been able to exercise fully were thus exchanged for money badly needed for the coming campaigns. By way of guaranteeing the execution of the treaty, the count and the bishop agreed to remove their castellans at Tourbillon and Montorge and to replace them for the next nine years with Pierre and Boniface de Challant, coseigneurs of Montjovet in the Val d'Aosta and canons of the cathedral of Sion. These and other "neutral" castellans installed at Conthey-Saillon and Sembrancher swore to maintain the peace and to supervise with perfect justice the execution of the treaty terms.

The peace of Evian was ratified by the bishop and the cathedral chapter, and most of the communities of the Valais followed their lead. But the Germanic villages in the high valley of Goms leading into the Furka refused to accept the indemnity. It was a jarring note of discord all too likely to have reverberations in the years to come.

PIEDMONT AFFAIRS, 1361–1362

The settlement in the Valais had come none too soon, for the Great Companies were now threatening the peace of the Piedmont. Giovanni II of Montferrat had sent envoys to Avignon and Pont-St-Esprit in March while the Tard-Venus were being fiercely besieged by a royal army. On 5 April 1361 the hard-pressed brigands asked for a parley and agreed to abandon the Rhône valley in favor of northern Italy, where they were engaged to serve the pope and his allies against the Visconti.[13] The conflicting claims of the pope and Bernabò Visconti to the city of Bologna had finally led to Bernabò's excommunication. Milanese chroniclers recount that the lord of Milan was sitting

---

[12] Text in Gremaud, doc. 2062.

[13] Temple-Leader and Marcotti, p. 11, say that the Green Count advised Giovanni to hire the English companies. They are probably following Servion here, but the story is certainly false. Amadeus was allied with the Visconti and would hardly be advising Montferrat to hire men who might soon be employed against himself.

with some of his men on a bridge over the Lambro when the papal envoys approached with the bull of excommunication. The terrible Bernabò is supposed to have seized the bull, perused it with darkening brow, then gazed for a moment down at the swift waters of the river. Glaring at the envoys, he asked them if they would rather eat or drink. The frightened ambassadors, knowing Bernabò's grotesque sense of humor and certain that if they expressed a preference for drinking they would soon find themselves in the river, chose to eat. They were accordingly seized by Visconti men-at-arms and forced to eat the papal bull itself, parchment, seals, and all, while their tormentor looked on in sadistic amusement.[14]

Such behavior toward the ambassadors of His Holiness (or such an attitude, for the attitude was genuine if the act was not) was hardly conducive to a reconciliation of differences, and papal indignation in the fourteenth century was more likely to find expression in armies than in Latin. Bernabò's joke was costly for the Visconti in the years to come, and the Green Count had reason to fear that as an ally of the Milanese, he might have to bear some share of that cost.

Events moved rapidly toward a crisis. The terrible Tard-Venus who had accepted the papal terms were crossing the Alps to join the armies of the pope's ally, the marquis of Montferrat. Then word came that the count of Valperga, a powerful lord of the Canavese who was hostile to the increase of Savoyard influence, had also allied himself with Montferrat. To further complicate the situation, early in March Gaspare Lercaro, seneschal in Piedmont for Queen Giovanna of Naples, despairing of his ability to protect Busca from the designs of the marquis of Saluzzo, surrendered the place to the count of Savoy and implored his immediate assistance.[15]

The passage of the second horde of Tard-Venus away from the frontiers of Bresse to join their compatriots near Avignon in the spring of 1361 gave the Green Count the opportunity he needed to turn to the situation in Piedmont. On 4 May he left Chambéry

---

[14] Cited in Cook, p. 18. To paraphrase Sir Winston Churchill, tiresome investigators have undermined this excellent tale, but it still should find its place in any history worthy of the name.

[15] Gabotto, *Età*, p. 121; E. G. Léonard, *Les Angevins de Naples* (Paris, 1953), p. 392.

to cross the Mont Cenis, where the glaciers were cracking and mountain crevices were beginning to roar with the torrents of the spring thaw. Six days later the Savoyards reached Susa, and the next day the count met his Piedmont lieutenants at Rivoli. A week or so later, Amadeus sent a strong force to Susa, then rode southward to Pinerolo, perhaps hoping to dispute the passage of the Mont Genèvre with the mercenary companies whose arrival seemed imminent. About this time, news came that the English captain (variously called "Robert Asperin" or "Robin du Pin") and his company had taken a more southerly route and were advancing upon Savigliano. Panic reigned. The inhabitants of the surrounding country gathered up everything that could be moved and fled within the town walls, abandoning all else to the marauders. On 29 May 1361 the count summoned the representatives of the Piedmont communes to confer on measures of defense. The village populations throughout the land were advised to take refuge within the walls of fortresses and larger towns with whatever possessions they could carry with them. The communes were to provide for their own protection, then send whatever men they could spare to join the Savoyard host in an effort to rescue Savigliano. Humbert de Corgenon was sent at once to the threatened city, and in early June he wrote to the count at Moncalieri to complain that he was short of funds and that the *clienti* defending the place were on the verge of deserting.[16] Despite this situation the town was able to appear strong enough to discourage an attack, and Robin du Pin and his men decided against the attempt. After devastating the surrounding region, they moved on toward Cumiana, which was hastily reinforced.

At this moment the prince of Achaea unexpectedly reentered the picture. Over the past year up to the spring of 1361, he seems to have remained at Fossano quietly biding his time. Now he chose to strike, while the English company was moving northward toward the Canavese and the attention of the Savoyards was concentrated on hurrying the marauders out of the country with the least possible damage to the inhabitants. The Sartori, a powerful family of Carignano and traditional enemies of the pro-Savoyard Provana, were plotting with the deposed prince to deliver the city to him if he would attack in force. On 23 June he did so, the

16 Gabotto, *Età*, p. 122.

Provana were driven out, and Giacomo and his troops entered in triumph. No attempt could be made at this point to dislodge him from the town, but the Savoyard castellans at Miradolo and Cumiana reinforced their garrisons, while Giacomo Provana hurried to Vigone with orders to hold the place in readiness against any similar tentative there on the part of factions favorable to the prince.

In July the Green Count made a rapid trip back across the mountains to Savoy and the Pays de Vaud. It is not entirely clear why he should have left the Piedmont at so crucial a moment, but the sources suggest that mercenaries were threatening his northern frontiers. On his arrival in Savoy, he seems to have ridden straight to Evian, and to have spent nearly the whole of his time between early July and early August at Evian or Geneva. The castellany accounts for Chillon mention that in October 1361 a certain "societas" called "de Cornes" had appeared "de novo" near Montagny, not far from Fribourg—which presumably means that this band had been there before.[17] It was perhaps in order to oversee the defense of his most recent and richest possession, the Pays de Vaud, that Amadeus felt obliged to leave the Piedmont in spite of the dangerous situation there.

The count was not gone for long, however. By 4 August he was on his way to Italy once more, and on 26 August he was before the walls of Carignano with an army reinforced by contingents of Vaudois nobles. The siege of Carignano appears to have lasted the whole month of September, but it was unsuccessful, a costly effort both in men and money. Guillaume de la Baume, companion and former *tutor* of the count, was killed in action; and Amadeus' subjects, who had just contributed to the *subsidium* to pay for the Pays de Vaud, were still contributing years later to another one "pro expensis per dominum sustinentis ante Carnianum et in Pedemontem."[18] Giacomo could not be driven from the town, and the activities of Robin du Pin in the Canavese required the count to make peace with his cousin. The "perfidi et scelleratissimi" English were ravaging the north country unmercifully, and late one September night, without warning, they scaled the walls of Rivarolo. The smoke from burning barns and villages could be seen for miles around, and refugees reaching the count's camp at Carignano told terrible stories of suffering and

17 *AST*, (castellany), Chillon, 17 March 1361–29 April 1362.
18 *ADS*, subsidy accounts for 1362ff.

hardship. The combined efforts of the Savoyard cousins would clearly be required for the defense of their territories. On 26 September 1361 the reconciliation took place. A new treaty restored to the prince nearly all of the territories taken from him following his rebellion sixteen months before.[19]

The treaty came none too soon. By early October, Robin du Pin and his band had captured the towns of San Martino and Pavone near Ivrea, and the bishop, Pierre de la Chambre, had fallen into their hands and was being held for ransom.[20] On 20 October the Green Count moved northward into the Canavese with his army and took up a position at Lanzo, high up on a lofty ridge commanding the narrow defile where the valley of the Stura closes in suddenly before opening out on the plain. Exactly what happened next is not clear. According to Savoyard chroniclers, when Amadeus heard of all of the "gastemens et meschiefs" being committed by the adventurers in his country, he moved to Lanzo, which at that time apparently had no walls save for the castle.[21] The count sent soldiers and supplies to the nearby castles and towns, then ordered Giacomo of Achaea, Antoine of Beaujeu, and other vassals to join him there, for he intended to give battle to the brigands and "throw them out of his country." While awaiting the arrival of his full army, the count, "who was young," made merry with his followers and the ladies of the town, singing and dancing and never thinking to post guard. He ordered a great banquet set out in the hall of the castle, and the company feasted joyously until well into the night. At last the party broke up, and the count started to leave the castle to lodge in the town along with his men; the castellan and his wife, however, persuaded Amadeus to accept their hospitality and remain in the fortress.

Spies of the villainous brigands, whose leaders the chroniclers identify as "Messire Albrecht, Messire Robin Canole, Messire Jehan Agut, Messire Hennequin de Bongart, and le maistre de La Nef, captaynes des compagnez des angloys,"[22] had reported that "petite

[19] *AST, protocolli ducali,* serie camerale, doc. 68, folios 52ff.

[20] Gabotto, *Età,* p. 123.

[21] Servion, II, 118ff.; Cabaret, pp. 155ff.

[22] *Ibid.* Canole was Knolles, Agut was Hawkwood, Hennequin de Bongart would be Anichino Baumgarten. Temple-Leader and Marcotti, p. 15, think that Knolles, a "German knight of lowly origins," was the captain who engineered this surprise attack. The only other captain definitely in the region at the time

garde" was being kept at Lanzo. In the middle of the night the "angloys" quit their headquarters at Rivarolo and fell suddenly upon the sleeping town of Lanzo. In the confusion which followed, the count and his host in the castle prevented the entrance of the brigands into the fortress, but were powerless to prevent the seizure of the nobles in the town, of whom only a few escaped. Among these apparently was Prince Giacomo, who let himself down from a window with a cord and fled to the fortress of Balangero a few miles away. Antoine of Beaujeu and some fifty or sixty of his followers managed to throw themselves hastily into a strong house in the town and defended themselves so well that their assailants let them go for the low ransom of "xii frans."

Among those captured, however, was Guillaume de Grandson, the count's close friend and comrade-in-arms. Grandson, say the chroniclers, had spent some years fighting in the service of the English king in Guienne and was thus recognized by some of the brigands, his erstwhile comrades-in-arms.[23] A joyous reunion is supposed to have followed in which Grandson, knowing that his lord was blockaded in the castle of Lanzo with "nulle artillerie ne pourvision," resolved to deliver him. After a festive dinner he began to "parlamentier" with the captains. "Messigneirs," he said, "I marvel that you, who all your lives have sought honor, should now, without cause, without quarrel, without right, and without reason, wage war on one of the [most] good, noble, valiant lords of the [whole] world. He is gentle, wise, and courteous, and had you asked anything of him, be it supplies or money, he would never have refused you. And may it please God that he remain hereabouts, for you would all be his companions and friends, for he loves fighting. I urge you to merit a gracious gift from him and return his lands to him and be friends with him, for otherwise you will dishonor yourselves."[24]

Naturally this eloquent speech made such an impression upon the brigands that for "a fairly small sum of money" they came to an agreement at once with Messire Guillaume. All went off to Lan-

---

was Robin du Pin, who is not mentioned by the chroniclers. Arnaud d'Albrecht, who was probably the "Messire Albrecht," was still in France at the time, as was John Hawkwood, and neither could thus have participated in the Lanzo incident. See below, p. 171.

[23] See Commentary, XI.

[24] Servion, II, 120–121.

zo where the count gave a great feast for them and presented them with so many gifts that they became fast friends. The captains offered him their services and returned all of his towns and castles. After the festivities were over and they took their leave, promising the count their "faith and service," they went off into the territories of the lords of Milan and Pavia, where they seized many "lands, castles, and fortresses" and caused "grans daumages." Thus was delivered the count of Savoy.

This charming account invites incredulity and suspicion, and its romantic pro-Savoyard flavoring has caused it to be generally ignored by historians who accept without question the assertion of Matteo Villani that the count, in order to secure the release of himself and his vassals, was obliged to furnish the enormous ransom of 180,000 florins.[25] The Savoyard version of what happened cannot be rejected entirely, however, simply because some of its details cannot be substantiated. The persons mentioned in the chronicles as present on this occasion can be shown to have been there, except for the mercenary captains. If Antoine de Beaujeu did not get off with a payment of a mere "xii frans," he did free himself for the relatively low price of one palfrey and one warhorse, at a total cost of 120 florins.[26] It is also clear that Aymon (the son of the count of Geneva), Girard d'Estrées (chancellor of Savoy), and Eduardo de Savoie (a younger brother of Prince Giacomo) were obliged to ransom themselves, and that Guillaume de Grandson was wounded in the fighting when the brigands attacked.[27] This much can be confirmed from treasury and castellany accounts. But nowhere in all of the numerous subsidy accounts for 1361 or the years following, nor in the records of the treasury-general, which exist in unbroken series from 1355 on, is there any mention whatever of ransom money paid to anyone for the count.[28] In view of this fact it is impossible to accept Vil-

[25] Matteo Villani, *Cronaca* (ed. Florence, 1825), libro X, ch. lxxxiv. Cf. Dullin, p. 41, Marie-José, p. 147, Temple-Leader and Marcotti, p. 15.

[26] Cf. letter dated 8 February 1362 from Antoine to Louis de Beaujeu asking him to send 120 florins "por un coursier et un roncin que il a baillie au Engloys por notres ranczon." G. Guigue, doc. XLII.

[27] Cibrario, *Storia*, III, 171–172; Gabotto, *Età*, p. 123.

[28] The subsidy of 1361–1362 was for the Piedmont campaign, as the preambles of the rolls state and the *librata* sections confirm. The count did contribute to the ransom of some of his vassals in this and other campaigns, but it is inconceivable that a ransom for himself, especially one large enough to strain

lani's report as anything but grossly exaggerated rumor at best. If the Green Count did not actually befriend the foe and thus recover his lands and castles,[29] he did nevertheless contrive somehow to extricate himself from the situation with far less damage to his treasury than to his self-esteem.[30]

This episode must have been a bitter blow for a prince so young and so avid for martial glory. To have been outmaneuvered by a band of outlaws, by mere mercenaries, rudely wounded his aristocratic pride. Amadeus' contempt for mercenary companies, revealed in the letter of 1373 from Galeazzo Visconti, probably first took root in the incident at Lanzo, which marked the beginning of decades of warring against them. As the count declared in 1373, these mercenaries were "ribaus" and "gens de riens," and if they must sometimes be hired, that did not make them the less despicable.[31] Here Amadeus was caught between the chivalric ideals with which he had been reared, and the unlovely realities of war in his century. He was the son of the feudal traditions of conservative Savoy, where men were still brought up to take pride in fighting for their "natural lord," where nobles rarely considered any career other than one in the service of the comital dynasty. As long as the count was fighting feudal barons in Savoy, his feudal host was adequate to his needs. In the Alps, the backbone of armies on both sides remained the cavalry, and the cavalry was still the feudal nobility, trained from childhood to the difficult art of fighting on horseback and taught to admire noble feats even on the part of adversaries.

The Savoyard nobles, including the count, fought for political and economic advantages to be sure. But like their chivalrous counterparts at the courts of England and France, they were also vitally interested in a good, fair fight. The enemy should be summoned to do battle, and only if he would not respond or offer an adequate explanation was he to be attacked. No real satisfaction

---

the resources of the state, such as Villani's figure would do, could fail to appear somewhere in the numerous treasury or administrative records for these years.

[29] Pavone, at least, was not redeemed until 1364.

[30] Cibrario, *Storia*, III, 172, reports the existence at a later date of an insulting Latin inscription on a gateway at Lanzo, ridiculing the Green Count for this humiliation.

[31] Mugnier, "Lettres," doc. VII, p. 405.

could be had from having employed deceit and subterfuge to defeat an adversary. Certainly there was something cheap and
ignoble in sneaking up on the foe and catching him wholly off
guard, for such behavior suggested that a fair fight dare not be
risked. War was the noblest of manly pursuits, the finest of life's
opportunities for a man to show his courage, his daring, his skill
and resourcefulness. It was a "joyous thing" because it was full of
color and excitement. Fields glittering with a thousand spears, pol-
ished helmets and armor shining in the sun, sweating warhorses
stamping impatiently for the trumpet call to charge—these were
all part of the setting for heroic deeds and acts of comradeship in
battle. But heroes are men of courage, not cunning; of honor, not
deceit. Otherwise the product of war is not glory but shame. And
it was not for shame, but for honor that knights took up the sword.

On the plains of Italy life was not as it was in the mountains
of Savoy. The humiliation of Lanzo was the first bitter reminder
that the young count was no longer among his ancient and honorable foes. It was a lesson he would not forget over the years, as
he came to know better the sort of men against whom he must
compete in Piedmont and Lombardy.

By the end of November the Green Count was out of Lanzo and
back at Rivoli, more determined than ever to throw in his lot
with the Visconti, despite peaceful tentatives from Montferrat.
The "Englicos," at whose hands he had just suffered the most
profound humiliation of his life, were now, if they had not been
before, in the pay of the marquis, who still hoped to recover lost
ground in the Canavese. Early in December, Humbert de Savoie
and Louis Rivoire were sent as ambassadors to Milan, instructed
to convert the entente of the previous year into a positive defensive-
offensive alliance. On 26 December 1361 the treaty was signed
and sealed. Galeazzo agreed to furnish the count with fifty "gentium armigerarum equestrarum" and twenty "peditum" (foot
lancers) for a period of two years, with the right to reduce the
size of these companies during the winter. Amadeus engaged himself to maintain a force of 1,000 *barbuta*,[32] but also reserved the
right to decrease this number during the winter season. It was
agreed that any conquests made by the allies between the Po and

---

[32] A *barbuta* consisted of two men and a lance of three (at the minimum).
Cf. Temple-Leader and Marcotti, p. 16, notes.

the Dora Baltea or in the Canavese were to go to the count of Savoy, while Galeazzo would keep everything else. The count's bitterness over his humiliation at Lanzo appears in the provision that "Primo et ante omnia," the allies would use their combined forces in the destruction and expulsion of the "Societatem Anglicorum" then in the Canavese. No other enterprise was to be undertaken until this had been done. Then the allies would turn to Galeazzo's principal objective, the city of Asti. A final clause reveals another motive for the count's action: Fossano, Cavallermaggiore, and Sommariva del Bosco with all their dependencies were transferred from Visconti suzerainty to that of the count of Savoy, who thereby became the overlord of all of Giacomo's Piedmont dominions.[33]

Upon receiving news of this alliance, Montferrat loosed his dogs of war without further delay, and the winter of 1361–1362 was filled with raids and skirmishes. In January, Amadeus purchased the services of the "parva societas" of Giacomo di San Giorgio, partly to strengthen his army and partly to prevent their taking service with his enemies. In February mercenaries in the pay of the marquis entered the Piedmont and in a pitched battle at Staffarda encountered German mercenaries sent by Galeazzo to reinforce the count of Savoy.[34] The count and his allies were victorious, and enemy soldiers unfortunate enough to fall into their hands were executed on the scaffold—which reflects the count's view that they were criminals, not soldiers. The chroniclers relate that soon not a tree limb in the region was without a corpse dangling from it. The Green Count was taking his first revenge for the night of Lanzo.

THE WESTERN FRONTIER, 1361-1362 · THE PIEDMONT MARRIAGES

The victory at Staffarda more or less stabilized the situation in the Piedmont for the winter of 1361–1362. By early spring it was necessary for the count to return to Savoy, as a result of disquieting reports which had reached him over the past months. In November 1361 the young duke of Burgundy, Philippe de Rouvre, died

---

[33] Treaty in *AST, Ducato Monferrato*, mazzo IV, doc. 15. It is dated 26 December 1362, since the chancery at Milan began the year with Christmas.

[34] Galeazzo sent Fritz Stofler, Arrigo da Scala, Giovanni Scalaber, and Eberhard Destein. Montferrat's captains at Staffarda were "David," and Floro and Bartolomeo of Verona. Gabotto, *Età*, p. 125.

suddenly of the plague, leaving the duchy without a leader at just the moment when it most needed one. Perhaps influenced by news of the duke's death, the Tard-Venus who had not chosen to take service with papal allies in Italy began to move back up the Rhône toward the Burgundies, threatening the Dauphiné and the western provinces of Savoy once again. The king of France was sufficiently alarmed to name the count of Tancarville as his lieutenant in Burgundy, Champagne, Mâconnais, Nivernais, Beaujolais, and Forez, with express orders to protect those regions from the advancing hordes. In February 1362 the king gave Arnould d'Audrehem an identical commission for the Languedoc. In the Dauphiné a frantic assembly of nobles took place at Romans on 29 January to decide on measures of defense. One of the decisions was to seek the assistance of the count of Savoy.[35]

Amadeus left Rivoli for Savoy sometime after 6 April 1362 and was at the castle of Le Bourget ten days later. No sooner had he arrived than he received envoys from neighbors who brought him up to date on all that had taken place during his absence. Only a few weeks earlier, bands of adventurers coming from the lower Rhône had moved into the Lyonnais and had seized the castles of Rive-de-Gier and Brignais, almost at the very gates of Lyon. On 6 April a large army composed of nobles from the surrounding region, including a company of Savoyards led by Amadeus' brother-in-law, Jacques de Bourbon, had been attacked by surprise while moving against the outlaws at Brignais and murderously defeated. Bourbon and his son were killed, along with the counts of Forez and Joigny, while hosts of others were taken prisoner.

The disaster at Brignais had spread consternation throughout the region. The count arrived in Savoy to find his wife in mourning for the death of her brother, while castellans in Bresse and the Valbonne stockpiled weapons and supplies. At Lyon, where Marshal Audrehem was trying to organize the citizens for a siege, a veritable panic reigned. Now it was not just in the castellanies bordering the Saône, but throughout the country of Bresse that villagers trembled, for the brigands, heartened by their recent success, appeared ready to cross the river this time.

[35] Cordey, *Les Comtes*, p. 164.

The Tard-Venus were unable to capture Lyon, however, and being too numerous to maintain themselves under the circumstances, they began to separate into smaller groups in search of greener pastures.[36] One band headed for the Auvergne, another marched toward Burgundy, and others moved into the Vivarais and Forez. Later in April, Amadeus decided to make a pilgrimage to the shrine of St-Antoine-de-Viennois. The incident at Lanzo had suggested that somewhat more substantial divine assistance was desirable before any further enterprises were attempted. The count was warmly greeted at the Dauphinois frontier by Raoul de Louppy, the dauphin's lieutenant-governor, who was accompanied by a large retinue. In the convivial atmosphere of a sumptuous banquet, with plenty of good wine and roast mutton, the Dauphinois renewed their earlier proposal of a military alliance against the Companies.[37] The Green Count did not commit himself at once, despite the wine and mutton; but within two weeks after his return to Savoy an alliance was signed, and the Savoyards joined their onetime foes to present a united front against the marauders across the river.

During the summer of 1362 the complexion of Piedmont affairs underwent important changes, briefly distracting the count's attention from the Great Companies. The fiery Sybille de Baux died sometime in the winter of 1361–1362, and the removal of Giacomo's evil genius opened the way for a new accommodation between the cousins. A treaty of 2 July 1362 restored to the prince all of the Piedmont territories taken from him in 1360, and added Busca, which the count had acquired in the meantime. In return, Giacomo was to renounce all claims to any part of the Canavese, the city of Ivrea, or the castellany of Pont-de-Beauvoisin, which he had been given in a previous treaty. The prince also recognized

[36] Froissart reported them 16,000 strong at Brignais. *Oeuvres de Froissart*, ed. Kervyn de Lettenhove (Brussels, 1868), VI, 335.

[37] The feast took place on 30 April at Montrigant. Louppy had been instructed to receive the count of Savoy, "le honorer et le heberger en un des chasteaux du dit seigneur [Louppy], pour cause des gens de compaigne qui estoient a Brignay, en Piemont, et en Provence en plusieurs lieux, et mesmement pour parler a lui, avoir conseil et faire avec lui alliances sur le fait de la garde et deffense du dit pais du Dauphine, qui estoit en tres grand doubte." Cited in Cordey, *Les Comtes*, p. 164.

the right of the count to intervene in any disputes which might arise between him and his son or among their subjects. Giacomo promised to maintain the privileges which had been granted to nobles and communes by the count during his possession of the Piedmont. In the future all fiefs granted by the prince were to be recognized as rear-fiefs of Savoy, and the count reserved appellate jurisdiction over them. All officers of the prince must promise to obey the count of Savoy, rather than the prince, should the two come into conflict at some future time. Both the prince and his son did liege-homage to the count for all of their holdings, including the three towns formerly held of the Visconti, and for the reinvestiture agreed to pay an indemnity of 160,000 florins.[38]

Had Sybille still been alive, this treaty would probably have been no more effectively executed than the others had been. But she was now dead, and Amadeus resolved to take full advantage of the fact. An unmarried prince of Achaea was cause for concern; the count was determined that another Sybille should not appear to comfort the prince's later years and to trouble his own. Amadeus had no sisters or daughters with whom to fill the vacancy, but he had cousins. Marguerite de Beaujeu, sister of Antoine of Beaujeu, was sixteen, beautiful, and a Savoyard.[39] She was as devoted to the count as her brother was, and she could be counted upon to strengthen in Giacomo that proper sense of duty to the interests of the dynasty which had been so lacking in the past.

Fortunately, Marguerite pleased the prince, now fifty-one, and the marriage took place without further delay on 16 July in the cathedral of Belley. The Green Count would have many future occasions to congratulate himself upon this marriage, for Cousin Marguerite played to perfection her role in his well-laid plans for securing control of the Piedmont. After seven years of intermittent warfare, Amadeus was now on the threshold of a permanent peace with his Piedmont relatives. Giacomo's new attitude was illustrated by the systematic way he went about raising the immense indemnity required by the recent treaty. Nearly half the sum was

[38] *AST, Principi del Sangue,* mazzo VII, doc. 6.

[39] Marguerite was born in 1346 at the castle of Montmerle in Bresse. Her great-grandmother was Eléonore de Savoie, sister of Amadeus V, whose brother, Thomas, was Prince Giacomo's grandfather. The pope obligingly furnished the necessary dispensation for this marriage, which joined two persons within the prohibited degrees of kinship.

lent him by the Gerbais brothers of Belley, and 50,000 florins came from Antoine of Beaujeu, who thus acquitted himself of his sister's dowry and became Giacomo's creditor for 35,000 florins. The remainder was obtained by selling or pledging certain of the prince's Piedmont castellanies to bankers of Asti and Rivalta.[40]

But Giacomo's marriage was only half of the count's project for his cousins. Filippo, the recalcitrant son of Sybille de Baux, was still without a wife. The Green Count, while arranging a "safe" marriage for the prince, decided to do as much for twenty-year-old Filippo before he made any marital decisions of his own. The count's choice this time fell upon Alix de Villars, daughter of Humbert VI of Thoire-Villars, second cousin of Antoine of Beaujeu. Ties between Savoy-Achaea and Thoire-Villars were already close; Humbert's first wife had been Béatrice de Savoie, sister of Prince Giacomo.[41] Thoire-Villars was a close friend and vassal of the count, and his lands were so situated as to make cooperation with Savoy a virtual necessity for him. Like Marguerite de Beaujeu, Alix might be expected to remind her husband of his obligations to the house of Savoy, and at least the marriage would prevent Filippo from choosing a wife from among the enemies of the count in Italy. Alix was provided with a dowry of 15,000 florins, and the marriage took place on 19 September 1362.[42]

Meanwhile the Green Count was looking forward to a meeting with the king of France. Since July, Jean le Bon, who was on his way to Avignon, had been expected to pass through southern Burgundy and Bresse. Amadeus had ordered his Bressan castellans to lay up stores of poultry, hogs, and beeves, along with crossbow bolts and war machines—the latter in case bands of adventurers

---

[40] Guidetto Malabaila, citizen of Asti and banker at Avignon, purchased the fief of Sommariva del Bosco for 20,000 florins, and Andreone Solari of Asti lent 10,000 on the security of another castle. Nicolo de Rivalta bought the castle of Cumiana for 12,000. Cf. Cognasso, *Il Conte Verde*, p. 110.

[41] Alix de Villars was the daughter of Humbert's second wife, Béatrice de Châlon-Tonnerre.

[42] The dowry money was being paid directly into the count's treasury by Thoire-Villars as late as 1366–1368, the fourth and fifth payments coming on the feast of St. Michael 1368. *AST*, inv. 16, doc. 28, p. xiii, *grosse recepte*. Either Amadeus had advanced the dowry money, perhaps to induce Filippo to accept the marriage, and was being repaid, or else the count had appropriated this money—as he had Giacomo's dowry money—as contributions toward the 160,000 florin indemnity.

arrived first. The king did not actually set out from Paris until 29 August, however, and he did not reach the frontiers of Bresse at Châlon-sur-Saône until mid-October. The count of Savoy met him at Tournus and accompanied him as far as Mâcon, where the presence of Tard-Venus in the vicinity induced them to cross the Saône and continue the journey to Lyon along the left bank of the river. The French king was going to Avignon with the object of securing the creation of some French cardinals and the marriage of his son to the queen of Naples; the count of Savoy had intercepted the royal progress in order to discuss problems related to the execution of the 1355 Treaty of Paris.[43]

The company reached Lyon early in November, and Amadeus placed his hotel near the Porte du Temple at the disposal of his royal guest. A few days later Bonne de Bourbon, apparently desirous of seeing her French kinsmen again, arrived with her ladies by boat from Seyssel. Her arrival was not inopportune, for one of the matters which the count wished to discuss on this occasion was his claim that several thousand florins were still due on his wife's dowry. Amadeus also demanded back pay owed for his services in the armies of France seven years before. On the other hand, the French king wanted the count to surrender the Viennois-Novalaise castellanies which Amadeus was still holding as security for the debts incurred by the dauphin in 1355. In the end the king gave way to his persistent Savoyard cousins. Before continuing his journey to Avignon a week later, Jean promised to satisfy their demands.[44]

The count returned to Savoy, but remained there only long enough to make preparations for a trip to Avignon himself.[45] On 25 November he left Lake Le Bourget on a boat manned by twelve rivermen, passed through the marshy channel which flows into the Rhône at the northern end of the lake, then floated down the

[43] The king's marriage project was thwarted: on 7 November 1362, before his arrival at Avignon, the pope gave his consent for the queen of Naples' marriage to James, king of Majorca.

[44] In January at Avignon the count received 8,000 florins from the king "pro remanencia stipendiorum suorum temporis preteriti, quo servivit ei et gentes sue in guerris suis." *AST*, inv. 16, doc. 23 (1360–1363).

[45] It was probably while they were at Lyon that the king and count learned of the election of the new pope, Urban V, which had taken place on 31 October. Innocent VI had died on 12 September 1362.

river all the way to Avignon.[46] The thrifty Savoyards intended to
avoid the notorious scarcities and high prices of food in the pon-
tifical capital by providing their own. From his own estates the
count brought a motley herd of sheep, hogs, and cattle which
followed along the river bank a few days behind his boat, and
a barge with a built-in tank full of live fish was sent down later
from Bresse.[47] On the way Amadeus stopped to visit several religious establishments, notably St-Antoine-de-Vienne and the
Franciscan monasteries at Vienne and Valence.[48] The bourgeois
of Valence, probably hoping for the count's assistance against the
Companies, made him a present of six beeves and twenty-four
sheep, which he added to his herd.[49] On 2–3 December the Green
Count entered Avignon and took up residence, appropriately
enough, in the hostelry of Saint George. Antoine of Beaujeu,
Aymon de Genève, and others in his suite lodged in nearby inns
of the city or its faubourgs.

The principal reason for the trip was the problem of the Great
Companies. The new pope was resolved to carry out his predecessor's projected league against them, but Urban V envisaged a still
greater enterprise. He was dedicated to the idea of a great crusade
of Christendom against the heathens of the East, and he regarded
such an expedition as an ideal outlet for the warlike energies of
the mercenary companies ravaging France. To carry out this
project required the adherence of princes more trustworthy than
the mercenary captains; it required men whose dedication to the
cause of the True Faith could be counted upon. Urban knew
the bellicose and chivalric temperament of the king of France,
and had not forgotten that his father, Philippe VI, had taken
crusading vows which he had never fulfilled.[50] The Green Count,

---

[46] *AST*, inv. 38, folio 21, doc. 63 (1361–1365).

[47] *Ibid*. There was a troop of horses, 34 hogs, 108 sheep, 31 cows, and an ox.
The ox and five sheep died upon arrival.

[48] *Ibid*. He left alms and prayers at the hospice of Vienne and the Dominicans
of Romans also.

[49] *Ibid*.

[50] M. Prou, *Etude sur les relations politiques du pape Urbain V avec les rois
de France Jean II et Charles V* (Paris, 1888), pp. 24–25, shows that the arrival
of Pierre of Cyprus at Avignon in March 1363 led to the formal declaration of
the crusade; but Urban's earlier letters make it clear that he was already planning the expedition at this time. Cf. N. Jorga, *Philippe de Mézières et la
croisade au XIVe siècle* (Paris, 1896), pp. 157–158.

169

whose reputation as a warrior and a captain had been firmly established by the success of his campaigns of 1352–1355, was also approached by His Holiness. Apparently, Amadeus committed himself at least tentatively to participate in the project.[51]

Amadeus did not remain in Avignon more than ten days or so, for his presence in Savoy is clearly established by 20 December. The project for a crusade to the East had to be put aside for the time being in view of the rapidly deteriorating situation in the Piedmont. The notorious "White Company" in the pay of Giovanni of Montferrat was ravaging the lands of the Visconti around Novara. Galeazzo was demanding immediate assistance from Savoy in accordance with the terms of their alliance. Amadeus would have to return to Italy as soon as possible, not only to protect the Canavese, which would probably be the next objective of the White Company, but also to prevent his Visconti allies from reaching any private accommodation with Montferrat without his knowledge and consent.[52] Then, to complicate matters, Federigo of Saluzzo had begun a campaign to recover Angevin-held Cuneo and neighboring towns. Late in 1362 he captured the fortress of Castelletto, preparatory to an assault upon Cuneo itself. The Cunese began seeking allies on all sides, and made overtures to the count of Savoy.

Before he had even left Avignon, Amadeus had begun recruiting mercenaries for the coming Piedmont campaign. Some of these companies he intended to use in his own armies; others he meant to send to Galeazzo Visconti as a means of discharging his treaty obligations and of diminishing the threat on his western

---

[51] The usual assertion that Amadeus took the cross along with Jean II and others in March 1363 at Avignon is false, since his presence in Savoy can be documented almost day by day between January and June 1363. Cf. Gabotto, who has done so in "Nuovi contributi," pp. 13–21. But a letter to Amadeus dated 26 March 1364 from Philippe de Mézières in Milan (cited in Jorga, p. 241) proves that the count was committed to the crusade at least by the time Philippe passed through Savoy in December 1363, and suggests that the commitment was made at Avignon. If so, Amadeus must have made the commitment on this visit.

[52] Amadeus had got wind of parleys between the two in December 1362 at Valenza and had protested vigorously to Galeazzo. Late in January, Galeazzo replied that in response to the count's protests he had broken off negotiations with Montferrat, and he thanked his brother-in-law for his promise to send 200 *barbutes* to his aid. Mugnier, "Lettres," doc. 1, p. 393.

frontiers at the same time. On 12 December 1362, Amadeus engaged the services of Guillaume d'Etamenat and Pons Richard of Genouillac with twenty "gentilshommes" for a period of six months beginning with their arrival on the banks of the Saône on 1 April 1363.[53] During the winter of 1362–1363, messengers were sent to the "Captal de Buch," to Arnaud d'Albrecht, and to Thomas Chandoz to see if they could be induced to enter the service of the count in Italy as soon as the Mont Cenis was passable. Albrecht agreed to come, and while Aymon Bonivard went to Sainte-Marie-du-Puy in the Auvergne with cash in hand to close the deal, Humbert de Savoie and Guigues de Soumont began inspecting the equipment of the army already recruited.[54] Letters from Galeazzo Visconti in February and March reveal that both he and the count were having difficulty getting the men they needed, perhaps partly owing to the ravages of the plague. Galeazzo reported that he was sending his recruiters to Germany because the Germans were cheaper, and he complained that by 1 March the 200 *barbutes* Amadeus had promised had not yet arrived.[55]

The Savoyard army raised for the campaign of 1363 was noticeably different in character from those which the count and his forebears had commanded in the past. Clearly, the Green Count had decided that if he were to compete on equal terms with his Piedmont enemies, he would have to utilize mercenary companies in spite of his prejudices against them. He still considered them, man for man, greatly inferior to his Savoyards. There remained, however, the question of numbers. If he did not take the mercenary companies into his own service, they would be hired by his enemies—as he had already learned to his regret. In the present case there were compelling reasons for overcoming his private resentment against commercial soldiers. At one and the same

[53] Cibrario, *Economia*, I, 406.

[54] Cordey, *Les Comtes*, p. 170. Gabotto, "La Guerra del Conte Verde contro i Marchesi di Saluzzo e di Monferrato nel 1363," *Piccolo Archivio Storico da Saluzzo* (1901), p. 12–13, notes. This account has been reconstructed from *AST, Tesoreria Guerra*, doc. 17, and inv. 16, doc. 23.

[55] Mugnier, "Lettres," docs. 2 and 3, dated 1 February and 1 March. In both letters Galeazzo reminds Amadeus of his obligation to appear at the head of 1,000 lances by the Kalends of April, and he approves the count's intention to seek men in Burgundy and the Dauphiné.

time, the count could solve his own recruiting problem, relieve the pressure on his western frontiers, and deprive his adversaries of a dangerous source of manpower.

It would be a mistake, however, to exaggerate the extent of the change. Many of the mercenary companies now hired were in fact sent as the count's contribution to the armies of his Visconti allies. The army which he led in person against the marquis of Saluzzo was still primarily composed of his Alpine vassals. Etienne de la Baume, Aymon de Genève, Gaspard de Mont-mayeur, the Clermonts, the Bonivards, the Corgenons, and about eighty other nobles from Aosta, Bresse, the Valbonne, and the Pays de Vaud were among them; and each noble had from two or three to several dozen men-at-arms and knights. In such a host even Aimonone de Pomiers with his "magna quantitate gentium armorum" was probably in the minority.[56]

### THE SALUZZO CAMPAIGN, 1363

The Savoyard army left Montmélian in the middle of June, and by the end of the month the campaign against the marquis of Saluzzo had begun. At Villafranca the Green Count was re-inforced by the prince of Achaea and companies sent by the Pied-mont communes. In early July the town of Barge, which was defended by Azzo di Saluzzo, brother of the marquis, was cap-tured, and the castellan was induced to surrender both the fortress and his master for the sum of 1,000 florins.[57] Amadeus forced Azzo to surrender his appanage of Paesana, Castellar, and Sanfront, but restored it to him when he agreed to hold it thereafter as a fief of the county of Savoy.

Revello fell without resistance and the Savoyard army swung down to besiege Costigliole, as the prelude to a siege of Saluzzo itself. Costigliole surrendered in mid-July, and two weeks later Galeazzo di Saluzzo, another of Federigo's brothers, appeared before the count to make his submission. In this case the count reaped the advantages of a bitter rivalry within the house of Saluzzo. Galeazzo, whose appanage comprised the Valmaira, had

---

[56] Several of the largest mercenary companies then in Northern Italy, notably those of Hawkwood and Sterz, were now fighting for Pisa in the war against Florence, thus removing them from the Piedmont scene at least temporarily. Cf. Temple-Leader and Marcotti, pp. 17ff.

[57] Gabotto, *Età*, p. 131.

earlier that spring quarreled with the governor of the Dauphiné over border towns near Casteldelfino. Federigo, who needed the backing of the Dauphinois for his anti-Savoyard policies, disavowed his brother's actions and participated in the campaign to crush him. A treaty in March 1363 had obliged Galeazzo to give up several towns of his appanage and to hold the rest—even that part within the boundaries of the marquisate of Saluzzo—in fief from the dauphin. To spite his brother and the dauphin, Galeazzo now deserted Federigo and recognized his possessions as fiefs of the count of Savoy.[58]

If the marquis' brothers had deserted him, however, his own courage had not. While the Savoyard host was strengthened by a company of miners from Perosa and by Angevin troops under Francesco Bollero, Federigo and his men captured the castle of Busca by surprise. This annoying reversal merely hastened the siege of Saluzzo, which began in late July with a massive bombardment. Early in August, Federigo asked for a parley. A commission designated by the count to draw up terms of surrender accused the marquis of mistreating his subjects, an accusation obviously intended to justify the count's intervention in public opinion. The principal charge, however, was that Federigo had refused to do homage and swear fidelity to the count of Savoy and thus deserved to lose all of his possessions. The marquis was conducted in semi-captivity to Turin and then to Avigliana, where a final treaty was signed in mid-August. The marquis did homage to the count for his marquisate and its dependencies and agreed to pay a war indemnity of 16,000 florins, for which various of his wealthiest subjects were required as hostages. In return Federigo recovered possession of most of the twenty-seven towns and castles taken from him in a preliminary treaty.[59]

[58] In Savoyard eyes, this had been an act of aggression on the dauphin's part. The counts of Savoy claimed suzerainty over the entire marquisate, and this extension of delphinal overlordship was regarded as an unwarranted violation of Savoyard rights. Galeazzo's act of homage to Savoy is dated 23 July 1363. *AST, Saluzzo Marchesato*, 4th category, mazzo II, docs. 15, 16.

[59] *Ibid.*, doc. 17; Gabotto, *Età*, pp. 133–134. About this time Amadeus received a letter from Galeazzo Visconti, dated 21 July 1363. He had heard of the count's parleys with Montferrat and wrote to protest against a separate peace; but he concluded by authorizing Amadeus to go ahead and negotiate for both of them if mutually advantageous terms were to be had. Mugnier, "Lettres," doc. 4.

Federigo di Saluzzo was the kind of man who never gives up, and the Green Count soon repented of having set him free to resume control of his dominions. On 4 September 1363 the marquis did homage once more to the dauphin, this time for all of his possessions, thus opening the gates of Italy to the most dangerous of all the western powers. These were gates which the count of Savoy had hoped to close with the Treaty of Paris and the pacification of the Piedmont. The Savoyard victory over Saluzzo a month earlier had been turned into defeat almost overnight.

War with Saluzzo would probably have broken out at once but for the arrival of messengers from the pope, the Visconti, and the marquis of Montferrat with tidings of peace. The crusade upon which Urban V had set his heart could not be undertaken until peace had been restored in Italy. After months of negotiations, a truce had been achieved between Bernabò Visconti and Cardinal Albornoz, commander of the papal armies, and a real peace now seemed possible. Accordingly, a papal envoy now arrived at Casale with orders to bring to an end the wars of Montferrat, Savoy, and Visconti in western Lombardy and Piedmont. Giovanni II of Montferrat was ready to listen to peace terms, and so was the count of Savoy, if only to free his hands for a new campaign against Saluzzo. On 17 September a truce was concluded which pretended to be based upon an arbitral settlement handed down by the archbishop of Milan some ten years before. The towns and castles which Amadeus had taken from his uncle since then were to be placed in the hands of neutral papal officers until agreement could be reached concerning the final disposition of these places. Each side bound itself to refrain from further hostilities on pain of an enormous fine.[60]

Amadeus was now free to deal with the faithless marquis of Saluzzo, and Federigo was justifiably alarmed. He appealed to the governor of the Dauphiné, who had already ordered his officers at Briançon to stand ready to provide protection for the marquis should the count of Savoy attack him. What happened next is not entirely clear. The count must have received a strong warn-

---

[60] *AST, Ducato Monferrato*, mazzo IV, doc. 16. Amadeus had just concluded an alliance with Galeazzo Visconti specifically against the marquis of Montferrat on 27 August 1363.

ing from the dauphin's officers that any attack upon the marquis would constitute an act of war against the dauphin, and papal representatives in the Piedmont probably exercised all possible influence to prevent the outbreak of another war. Perhaps it was at this point that the dauphin undertook to pay the marquis' indemnity of 16,000 florins, which were certainly beyond Federigo's immediate resources.[61] Whatever the reasons, the count decided to postpone military action until he had had an opportunity to see the dauphin in person.

The Green Count remained in the Piedmont through September and most of October, and he was present at Pinerolo when Marguerite de Beaujeu gave birth to a son. The count acted as godfather at the baptism, and the child was named after him. When Amadeus headed back into the mountains in late October, he took with him the Savoyard castellan of Pinerolo, the last reminder of his distrust of the prince and of the wars of the past decade. Accounts between the count and his cousin were settled now, and the past could be buried. Marguerite would soon be unrivaled in her husband's affections. The future lay not with the lonely son of Sybille de Baux, but with the sons of the Savoyard wife.

The time had come to cross the mountains, before the snows of winter filled the valleys and passes again. The count's subjects in Bresse and the Valbonne needed his help. The "Sons of Belial" were on the frontiers again, this time more menacing than ever. In mid-September, Seguin de Badefol, one of the victors at Brignais the year before, suddenly came down out of the hills of the Auvergne with his great band and headed for Lyon. This time the rivers provided no effective barrier. The brigands swarmed into Dombes and the Valbonne for the first time. The Savoyard castellans at Miribel, Gourdans, Perouges, and Meximieux barricaded the portals of their walled towns. Terrified inhabitants and refugees from the countryside huddled within and prepared for the worst, while the plundering horde followed the river all the way to the gates of Montluel. While Simon de Saint-Amour,

---

[61] *AST*, inv. 16, doc. 28, 1366–1368, records that 4,000 florins were received from Raoul de Louppy, governor of the Dauphiné, on behalf of the marquis of Saluzzo, but the payment is not dated. The next account, doc. 29, 1368–1369, notes that half of 8,000 florins were still due from the marquis, which suggests that all but the last installment was now paid.

the count's special "captain of fortifications" for Bresse, hastened to reinforce Bourg, the *bailli* gathered men and supplies and held a council of war on 24 October, just as the count was crossing the Mont Cenis.

Perhaps news of the Green Count's imminent arrival reached the marauders. In any case, they chose to abandon whatever plans they may have had for pushing farther into the country, and withdrew rather precipitously. After an unsuccessful attempt to take Lyon by assault, Badefol and his men crossed back into France, seized Anse on the Saône, and by All Saints had made that unhappy town, a few miles north of Lyon, their headquarters. There they settled in for the winter—a winter which the miserable population of the Beaujolais would never forget. On the Savoyard side of the river, all available troops were concentrated in the towns and castles, patrols were organized, and a vast network of spies and lookouts were established. Amadeus visited the region long enough to inspect the defenses, then rode northward to the Pays de Vaud to raise more troops. Meanwhile the peasants of Bresse built higher walls and deeper moats and prayed for deliverance from these enemies of God, of pity, of mercy.

The departure of barons on a crusade. Under the knight on the left appears the legend "C di Savoi." Late 14th century fresco

Bonne de Bourbon
countess of Savoy

Amadeus' charter of 1287, founding a mass in honor of the Virgin

# *Imperatorie Majestatis Vicarius*

## 1363-1365

THE Great Companies were to darken the western horizon for many years to come, shifting like storm clouds, so that no one knew when or where the tempest would break. The threat of invasion was an almost continuous source of concern, but it did not prevent the Green Count from advancing both his power and his prestige during these years. The influence of fourteenth-century chivalric ideals now reached their height in Savoy, probably owing to the frequency of Amadeus' contacts in the ten years of his personal rule with such centers of knightly culture as the courts of France and Burgundy. Jean le Bon had founded a knightly order, and so had his chivalrous rival, Edward III. Amadeus was impressed by these men, and he shared their belief that princes had a special responsibility to set an example for others to follow. Tournaments, magnificent hospitality, and the founding of knightly orders based on codes of honorable behavior were means of discharging that responsibility. In addition, the idea of a great Christian crusade to the Holy Land was gaining ground once more in the West, owing to papal propaganda ceaselessly emanating from nearby Avignon, and this was also an idea which appealed to the Green Count's finer instincts. Amadeus was never a man to neglect practical matters, but these years were remarkable for the pageantry with which he clothed them.

For the Green Count, the strongest current of the times was the movement, spearheaded by the pope and the king of Cyprus, to launch a general European crusade against the Turks in the Near East. In December 1363 two ambassadors of the king of Cyprus, the archbishop of Crete and Philippe de Mézières, indefatigable laborers in the cause of the crusade, passed through Savoy on their way to Italy. Both men were impressed by the military preparations everywhere in evidence, and the count told them that the army being raised was for the crusade.[1] The ambassadors no doubt sought to strengthen the count's resolution with glowing descriptions of the ceremonies at Avignon on Holy Friday 1363, when Pope Urban had made his appeal for a crusade before a vast concourse of nobles and prelates. The king of Cyprus, Pierre de Lusignan, had been the first to commit himself, followed by the king of France and a great host of famous French barons.

The pope and his fellow enthusiasts had not failed to draw attention to the practical as well as the spiritual advantages of a crusade. Here was a means of winning worldly glory and eternal salvation, and at the same time, of ridding France of the scourging hordes of mercenaries, who might thus be induced to fight for their souls instead of merely for their skins. Blows dealt for the True Faith and the "Sainte Eglise" were certain to redeem the sins of even the worst of men and win them an opportunity for glory everlasting. The Green Count had already given signs of the weight which he attached to these considerations, and Mézières later claimed that he had received the most explicit assurances from the count. In January 1364 he wrote from Cremona to the doge of Venice, relaying the news of the count's commitment and urging the doge to work for the crusade with equal dedication. Pierre de Lusignan, who was now touring the courts of Europe in search of men and money, was expected to arrive in Venice soon. Mézières was hoping that the count of Savoy would be on hand and that a Venetian fleet would be waiting to carry the crusading army on its way.[2]

"The glory of princes is in their pride and in undertaking great peril."[3] It would be difficult to express more succinctly the non-religious considerations which induced the Green Count to think of a crusade to the East. Amadeus must have been greatly impressed by the reputation of the king of Cyprus, a celebrated "athleta Christi" around whose name glamorous legends were

[1] Jorga, pp. 220–221.

[2] *Ibid.* Pierre de Lusignan did not in fact reach Venice until November 1364.

[3] Cited from Chastellain, a writer at the court of Charles the Bold of Burgundy, in Huizinga, *Waning of the Middle Ages*, p. 70.

already gathering. Pierre de Lusignan had been received all over Europe with magnificent hospitality, owing to the admiration excited by stories of his knightly valor in the cause of the True Faith.[4] A count of Savoy might also add cubits to his stature by battling in a cause more glorious than conquering Valaisan peasants or subduing marquises of Saluzzo. Even the otherwise undistinguished Dauphin Humbert II had won at least temporary renown as a champion of the Faith by undertaking a crusade in 1345-1347.[5] The Green Count certainly did not intend to take second place to a dauphin of Viennois. As Amadeus grew older, he was beginning to understand more clearly what he wanted from life and how to achieve it. He was convinced that no deed was more likely to win him immortality than leading a crusade, and he was right. Two hundred years later this deed alone would be the theme of the *Amédéide* of Alphonse Delbène, a friend of Ronsard and abbot of Hautecombe: "I sing of the labors, the deeds, and the valor of the generous Amadeus, who from the mountains of Savoy went away to the East. . . ."[6] Five hundred years later a bronze statue of the Green Count dramatically slaying a Turk would stand in the piazza of the Palazzo di Città at Turin.[7]

In January 1364 the count decided to go to Avignon to reaffirm his adherence to the crusade and to confer on more immediate measures to be taken against the mercenary companies. On 19 January an assembly of princes from the region met with the pope, and a few days later a league was formed consisting prin-

[4] The famous poet-musician Guillaume de Machaut celebrated Pierre's capture of Alexandria in 1365 in a long poem. Cf. Aziz Atiya, *The Crusade in the Later Middle Ages* (London, 1928), pp. 319-320. Cf. also the fame won by Gaston Fébus for his "crusade" to Prussia in 1357-1358. Pierre Tucoo-Chala, *Gaston Fébus et La Vicomté de Béarn* (Bordeaux, 1960), p. 79.

[5] Details of this crusade are in Atiya, pp. 301-318.

[6] The poem was written between 1580 and 1588. Extracts have recently been published in Marie-José, pp. 199-200.

[7] The monument was commissioned by King Carlo Alberto and was unveiled on 7 May 1853. Jean-Jacques Bouquet, "Remarques sur l'idée de croisade dans l'expédition d'Amédée VI de Savoie à Constantinople," *Bulletin annuel de la Fondation Suisse* (University of Paris, VII, 1958), p. 32, has also noted the Green Count's "grande disponibilité de croisade." Amadeus knew that any expedition against the infidel would serve his purposes, whatever its geographical destination.

cipally of the rector of the Comtat-Venaissin, the count of Valentinois, the seneschal of Provence, the governor of the Dauphiné, and the count of Savoy.[8] The immediate objective was the protection of their common territories against the Great Companies, but Urban hoped to combine this project with the greater one of sending everyone, friend and foe alike, off to the Eastern Mediterranean to battle the heathen Turks.

It was probably on this occasion that the Green Count formally took the crusading vow, if he had not done so earlier. The consequences of this move, however, may well have weighed upon his mind. He was now irrevocably bound to take part in an expedition to the remote and dangerous East, with all of its uncertainties. His army would be only partly made up of his trusted Savoyards; bands of mercenaries, perhaps thousands of them, were also expected to participate. These were men he did not know, men he did not trust, men who had already shown too clearly the mischief of which they were capable. They would be bound to him, as to the cause of the crusade itself, only by tenuous financial ties and not by any sense of loyalty or duty, should things go badly. In view of this situation, the count naturally felt the need for some dramatic reinforcement of the traditional bonds which existed between himself and those of his vassals who had indicated their intentions of accompanying him on this perilous adventure. A greater sense of dedication between man and man on the eve of such an undertaking was necessary, along with a renewed spiritual dedication which would strengthen the conviction that these dangers would be confronted under the special protection of the Almighty and his saints.

These were undoubtedly the principal considerations which led to the formation of the Order of the Collar (which replaced the apparently defunct Order of the Black Swan), probably at Avignon in January 1364.[9] Pope Urban V, in grateful recognition of

---

[8] Prou, pp. 34–35.

[9] It is surely to misunderstand the significance of the event to attribute it merely to Amadeus' taste for feasts and tournaments, as does Cognasso, *Il Conte Verde*, pp. 140–141. He places the event at Chambéry in April 1364, although the fact that fifteen collars were made for the count by Italian jewelers at Avignon in January (*AST*, inv. 38, folio 21, doc. 63, 1361–1365) rather suggests the latter time and place. See Commentary, XII, for a discussion of these questions.

the count's willingness to join the crusade, bestowed upon him
at this time the coveted "Golden Rose," an honor reserved only
for those regarded as the most zealous sons of the Church. In
such an atmosphere it would have been natural enough for the
count's heart to "swell with honor" at the sight of "sy belle
compagnye" of men-at-arms and "sy belle noblesse," and for him
to carry out his decision to create an "order of xv chivallierz in
honor of the xv joys of Nostre Dame."[10] The insignia of the
Order as it first appears (on a manuscript of the cathedral of
Lausanne dated 1382) consists of a plain band of gilded silver
meant to fit around the shoulders near the neck, with a gold
clasp in front to which was appended three *lacs d'amour*, or love-
knots, forming a circle.[11] The knots were symbolic of the bonds
of faith and loyalty, of indissoluble union among the brother
knights of the Order. The much more elaborate collar of green
holly leaves on a gold chain was a later form, as was the name
"Annunciade" by which the Order was known after 1518. The
earlier collar was more functional and less decorative, and the
same might be said of the Order of which it was the symbol.

Since the original statutes of the Order have been lost, the
identity of the original fifteen members is not entirely certain.[12]
According to Servion, Count Amadeus was himself the first
knight, Amadeus III of Geneva the second, Antoine of Beaujeu
and Hugues de Châlon-Arlay the third and fourth respectively.
The fifth was Aymon de Genève-Anthon and the sixth was Jean
de Vienne, future admiral of France. The others were, in order,
Guillaume de Grandson, Guillaume de Chalamont, Roland de
Veissy "de Bourbonnoys," Etienne "bastart de La Baume & mareschal de Savoye," Gaspard de Montmayeur, Berloin de Foras,
"Chennart de Monthou," Aymon Bonivard, and Richard Musard.[13]

This list is interesting for what it suggests about the character
of the count's armies in general and of his crusading army in
particular. Most of those in the list can be definitely identified as
comrades-in-arms of the count for many years, and probably all
of them had served with him on at least one campaign. The

[10] Servion, II, 113.
[11] The form of the insignia described by Servion is a later version.
[12] See Commentary, XIII, on the founding knights of the Order.
[13] Servion, II, 115.

dynastic character of the group is also evident. The count of Geneva was Amadeus' first cousin, and Aymon de Genève-Anthon was first cousin to the count of Geneva.[14] Antoine of Beaujeu and Guillaume de Grandson were both second cousins to the count of Savoy.[15] In 1363, Hugues de Châlon-Arlay, whose family had contracted alliances with the dynasty of Savoy before,[16] had married Blanche, daughter of the count of Geneva, and thus was also a member of the immediate dynastic circle.

Of the remaining nine knights of the Order of the Collar, five had distinguished themselves for years in the count's service. Aymon Bonivard of Chambéry had served Amadeus in various military and diplomatic capacities over the years, had participated in the Saluzzo campaign, had been castellan of Seyssel since 1357, and was castellan of Thonon-Allinges from 1363 to 1380.[17] Guillaume de Chalamont belonged to a noble family which had long held fiefs of the counts of Savoy along the banks of the Ain and in the Valbonne. Since 1362, Guillaume had been castellan of Perouges in the Valbonne, and he held that post until 1375. He had accompanied Amadeus to France in 1355 and was at Saluzzo in 1363, to mention but two of the campaigns in which he participated. Etienne de la Baume had been a companion of the count since boyhood, and Gaspard de Montmayeur had been a comrade-in-arms at least since 1355, as well as an officer in comital administration since 1353.[18] Berlion de Foras, sire of Bourgneuf

---

[14] He was the son of Hugues de Genève-Anthon (d. 20 November 1363) from whom Amadeus had taken the barony of Gex in 1353. They had made peace by this time, and Aymon was frequently in the count's service. Amadeus gave him a warhorse on 16 February 1361 at Evian. *AST*, inv. 16, doc. 23.

[15] Guillaume de Grandson, lord of Sainte-Croix, was the son of Guillaume, sire of Grandson, and Blanche de Savoie, daughter of Louis I of Vaud. He had been made chancellor of Savoy in 1363, and had been with the count at Lanzo in 1361 and Saluzzo in 1363. As early as 1347 he had done homage for an annual pension from the count. (*AST*, inv. 16, doc. 14, 1346–1349). From then on Grandson and the count were practically inseparable. They even dressed alike, and frequently when Amadeus ordered new clothes for himself, he ordered an identical outfit for his comrade, who thus became a sort of "Green Knight."

[16] Isabelle de Châlon-Arlay was the wife of Louis II of Vaud, and one of Amadeus' aunts had married into the Châlon-Tonnerre branch of the family.

[17] He was also *courrier* of St-Jean-de-Maurienne 1351–1357 and 1374–1393.

[18] Gaspard de Montmayeur led Savoyard troops in the Piedmont, 1355–1360; was castellan of Chatelard-en-Bauges in 1355–1358; of La Rochette, 1358–1360 and 1364–1369; and of Tarentaise, 1369–1383, when he died.

and Ballaison, was a vassal of the count of Geneva primarily, but he had entered the service of Savoy along with his master.[19] He had been one of the knights of the short-lived Order of the Black Swan, had been at the jousts of Bourg-en-Bresse in 1353, had gone with Amadeus and the army to France in 1355, and had served as castellan of Yvoire and La Ravorée in 1357-1358.

Two-thirds of the knights of the new Order were thus relatives or longtime vassals of Savoy, or both, and they had given repeated proof of their loyalty. Beyond question also was the loyalty of Richard Musard, an English knight who probably landed in Italy about the time of the peace of Bretigny, when many English mercenaries went to Lombardy in search of fame and fortune, and had entered the service of the count during the campaign against Giacomo in 1361. When the count was besieging his cousin at Carignano, Musard took a solemn oath of loyalty to him "against everyone in the world," excepting only the king of England in person.[20] By 1362 he had become known as the "Black Squire" and was Amadeus' inseparable companion, a sort of personal bodyguard. In March 1364 he was made castellan of Aiguebelle, and Servion calls him a noble warrior, "valliant, bon & hardy."

The remaining three knights of the Order appear less frequently in the documents. François "Chivard" de Monthoux belonged to a family with possessions around Duingt and Talloires on Lake Annecy, so he was probably a familiar of the count of Geneva. He was in the service of the count of Savoy as early as the 1351 visit to the Val d'Aosta, and he proved himself a loyal companion during and after the crusade.[21] Roland de Veissy (also Vessy, Vaissy, or Veyssy) "from the Bourbonnais" may

[19] *AST*, inv. 16, doc. 14, 1346–1349: "libravit domino Berlioni de Foras, militi, cui dominus donavit annis singulis xxv florenos auri boni ponderis pro homagio per ipsum nuper facto domino." Letter ordering payment is dated Christmas 1349. The act of homage was probably in connection with Foras' participation in the Piedmont campaign of 1347–1348.

[20] Cf. Mugnier, "Lettres," pp. 389ff. In 1373 he was captain-general of Piedmont for the count, and in 1380 became castellan of Romont in the Pays de Vaud.

[21] Lange, p. 293: "libravit domino Chinardo de Monthou tramisso per dominum apud Arnaudum in Valle Augusta in garnisione," dated 1 September 1351. Cf. items 82, 85, 951, 952 in the crusade expense accounts published by Bollati de Saint-Pierre in *BSI* (1900).

possibly have been known to Countess Bonne, and may have been among those in the company of the king of France who had taken the cross in March 1363, since his previous record was chiefly of service to the king. Veissy fought for Jean le Bon at Poitiers and had been taken prisoner by the English. Charles V in 1363 rewarded him for his services with an annual rent, and Philippe de Mézières, to whom he had been sent as a messenger in 1364, referred to him as "egregium militem."[22] Jean de Vienne, sire of Rollans and Bonencontre in Burgundy, was also notable chiefly in the service of the king of France, but he was in the service of the Green Count at least as early as 1360 when he was referred to as "consanguineo domini comitis."[23] He was with Amadeus at Lanzo, and by 1364 was receiving an annual pension from the comital treasury.[24] His participation in the crusade of 1366-1367 and his nomination to the Order of the Collar, as in the case of Roland de Veissy, are more readily explained if these events did take place at Avignon. By January 1364 the count of Savoy seemed far more likely to actually lead a crusade than did Jean le Bon, who had decided to return to captivity in England because he was unable to raise the money for his ransom. If these men really wanted to fight the heathen and keep their crusading vows, as they clearly did, their wisest course of action would have been to attach themselves to the count of Savoy.[25]

That the Order was principally founded in preparation for the crusade seems clear in the light of subsequent events. Of the fifteen members of the original Order, only two—the count of Geneva and Antoine of Beaujeu—did not take part in the expedition, but they had probably intended to do so. Amadeus III discharged his obligation by sending his eldest son, Aymon; and since the count of Geneva died only a few months after the crusaders had departed, his withdrawal was probably owing to poor health. Antoine of Beaujeu was wholly preoccupied with the defense of his dominions against the Great Companies, particularly

[22] Jorga, p. 241. He was frequently an envoy for Amadeus in 1364-1365. Cf. Cordey, *Les Comtes*, p. 175, note 1; p. 180, note 3. By 1364 he was receiving an annual pension from the count. *AST*, inv. 16, doc. 26.

[23] *AST*, inv. 16, doc. 23 (1360-1363).

[24] *Ibid.*, doc. 26 (1364-1365).

[25] Jean de Vienne in fact became a famous crusader and was among the leaders of the crusade of 1395, which ended in the disaster of Nicopolis.

after many of them had refused to participate in the crusade as originally planned. It is possible that he was replaced on the roster of the knights of the Collar by Simon de Saint-Amour, who did participate in the crusade and was a member by 1366, when it had become clear that Beaujeu could not go.[26]

Naturally, the creation of a new knightly order required appropriate festivities, and the chronicles describe them with gusto. The count had ordered the fifteen collars made all alike and "moult secrettement," then ordered a great banquet. There were minstrels and "clerons & trompettes," and in the course of the feast a herald came forth to announce the creation of the new order and to read its ordinances. These contained many "bons & nottables chapitres," including the obligation to care for orphans and widows, to appease "false quarrels," and to uphold loyalty. Each knight was to be "sans raprouche" and to swear never to abandon one of his fellow knights "par vie ne par mort." Should any dissension arise among the knights concerning inheritances or lands or "aultres choses," the dispute was to be submitted to the judgment of four other brothers of the Order, who would act in such a way as to "procure the well-being, the honor, and the advancement of each."[27] Considering the close bonds of kinship and vassalage among so many of the company, this was not an idle provision. Each knight was bound to recite fifteen *Ave Marias* each day in honor of the Holy Mother of God, the Queen of Heaven, to whose service the brotherhood had dedicated itself, in the hope of securing her powerful protection on the dangerous enterprise ahead.[28]

When the ordinances of the Order had been proclaimed, the trumpets sounded and the herald cried out "cilence & paix," and the Green Count spoke: "Messignieurs, know that I swear and promise to uphold these ordinances, and if I take the first Collar, it is not as lord, but as brother and comrade of those who belong, for this is an order of brothers." Then the remaining fourteen charter members of the Order were named. Each took the oath

[26] See Commentary, XIII.

[27] Cf. the provisions for the Order of the Black Swan, Commentary, VI.

[28] Servion says that the count then founded a Carthusian monastery within the fortress of Pierre-Châtel, as the special burial place and headquarters of the Order; but there is no proof that this was done before 1383, when such provisions were made in his will.

to uphold the ordinances, and received his gold and silver collar. "And all took the oath according to the ordinances and kissed each other on the mouth and considered themselves brothers." Then the festivities really began. "The ceremony was over, there was joy abundant, ladies and demoiselles, liberality, honor, rejoicing and pleasure, *a comble mesure de tous instrumens*; and thus it lasted for three days with jousts, tournaments, games, masquerades, through the night until daylight. It would be impossible to describe the delights and amusements of the occasion, or how fine it was to see the fifteen knights with their fifteen collars all dressed alike. And thus was begun the Order of the Noble Collar of Savoy."[29]

Crusades were costly enterprises, and the count would need financial assistance to enable him to accomplish his vows. On 1 April, Urban V issued no fewer than seven bulls granting to the count of Savoy the right to collect various revenues from religious establishments in the twelve dioceses in his dominions.[30] The money raised was to help defray the cost of the expedition against the Turks. That Amadeus lost no time in collecting the money may be inferred from a papal letter of 5 May 1364 to the bishop of Mâcon, reminding him of the privileges granted to the count and ordering him to permit without hindrance the collection of the designated revenues in his diocese.[31]

### THE GREAT COMPANIES, 1363–1364

In the meantime, other developments rapidly altered the complexion of affairs. In April 1364, Jean le Bon died in England and with him died the hope of French leadership in the crusade. The new king of France, Charles V, had neither the desire nor the opportunity to undertake such an expedition. Moreover, the mercenary companies now appeared more intractable than ever. In February they seized Saint-Aubin and Charité-sur-Loire, and in March, Guillampot captured La Ferté, while the Bastard of Albrecht made himself master of Saint-Gengoux. When Jean

[29] Servion, II, 115–116.

[30] *AST, Il Viaggio di Levante*, mazzo III. These bulls have been published in Datta, *Spedizione in Oriente di Amadeo VI* (Turin, 1826), *documenti*, but they are incorrectly dated 1 April 1363 instead of 1364.

[31] Cordey, *Les Comtes*, pp. 195–196; *AST, Saluzzo Marchesato*, mazzo III, doc. 1.

d'Arguelle captured Romenay on the eastern side of the Saône a few miles north of the Savoyard castellany of St-Trivier in Bresse, the terror among the count's subjects reached its height.[32]

In addition to these difficulties, relations with the governor of the Dauphiné were worsening. Amadeus still held the castellanies awarded to the dauphin in the Treaty of Paris, and he was not minded to give them up. The count was well within his rights, for the sums of money owed him by the king of France since 1355 were still owing. To the king's complaints Amadeus replied that he was merely holding the castellanies as security for payment of these debts. He may also have hoped to force the French to withdraw their support of the marquis of Saluzzo by taking a firm stand in this matter. On 8 April 1364, Raoul de Louppy addressed a strong protest to the count demanding full compliance with the terms of the Treaty of Paris without further delay.[33] From the mountains there was no response—in June the count left for the Val d'Aosta.

The visit was not lengthy. The Green Count wished to reaffirm his right to hold the *Audiences* at least every seven years, and illness had prevented his doing so in 1358. On this occasion there were the usual appeals to be heard and the usual sentences to be handed down and fines collected. On 27 June the *bailli* was expressly instructed to provide the inhabitants of the Valsavarenche with legal counsel and defense, and to look into their complaints against comital officers there. At Aosta, Amadeus was unexpectedly reminded of his earlier visit by the appearance of one Catherine de Dovia and her son, Antoine, a lad of twelve.[34] The count received the lady with honor and recognized the boy as his own. Young Antoine was taken into the count's household as a page, there to begin his apprenticeship for the honorable career of a Bastard of Savoy.

The trip to the Val d'Aosta brought Amadeus both men and money, but by mid-July he had recrossed the Colonne-Joux and was back in Savoy. During July and August several of the Great Companies devastated the country between the Loire and the

---

[32] Cf. *Inventaire sommaire, ADCO,* Treffort, B 10164.

[33] Cordey, *Les Comtes,* p. 201.

[34] Lange, doc. 87, p. 295. Sometime between 14 July and mid-December 1364, Countess Bonne had a baby boy, christened Louis, but the child died within the year. Cf. Cordey, *Les Comtes,* p. 211.

Allier in the Bourbonnais.[35] In October the count joined the duke of Burgundy in an effort to eject the mercenaries from Charité-sur-Loire, but the brigands did not finally surrender until December. The Savoyards then hastened back to their own territories, for Seguin de Badefol was preparing aggressive enterprises from his headquarters at Anse. Aymon de Rougemont, *bailli* of the Valbonne, was sufficiently concerned to post guards around the clock in every fortress and town in the region, and to establish a roving force of thirty-three fully armed knights to patrol the river bank from Lyon to Neuville-sur-Saône.[36] Inhabitants of Lyon living near the gate of La Lanterne begged the *bailli* to place them also under his protection.

The count of Savoy now began to negotiate with some of the captains. Roland de Veissy was sent to the companies "en Bergoigne," and early in 1365, Etienne de la Baume was on mission to Seguin at Anse.[37] Envoys also sought out Arnaud de Cervole in the hope of persuading him to exchange the prospect of further plunder in "Sweet France" for that of riches in the fabled East. While the pope seconded these efforts and struggled to establish peace between the kings of France and Navarre over the Burgundian succession, the patriarch of Jerusalem as papal legate did what he could to induce the bishops and abbots of the count's dominions to contribute financially to the forthcoming crusade.

But Seguin de Badefol proved a stubborn man. He resisted all attempts to dislodge him from Anse, and spies from his camp who were caught by vigilant Bressans in their territories confessed that he was planning another attempt at crossing the river. The Savoyards expanded their own network of spies and counterspies. "Wife Ancelise," who lived in Anse in the very midst of the band of thieves, was the chief inside informer. She contrived to find out what news Seguin's agents had brought back from their reconnoitering expeditions, then relayed that information to the count's spies across the river.[38] Then, in the midst of this atmosphere of suspicion and fear, came heartening news: Holy Roman Emperor Charles IV was on his way to Savoy en route for Avignon.

[35] Cf. G. Guigue, pp. 98–101.
[36] *ADCO*, B 8550, B 8551 (Montluel, 1364–1365).
[37] Cordey, *Les Comtes*, p. 175.
[38] G. Guigue, *preuves*, p. 332.

# Imperatorie Majestatis Vicarius

Charles of Luxembourg had been hitherto known to the count of Savoy only as a somewhat difficult overlord. The two men had never met, but the activities of each had provoked repeated embassies between them over the preceding decade. The yoke of imperial authority upon the great vassals of the Empire was light enough in the fourteenth century, and certainly the count of Savoy could not pretend to have found it otherwise. But if imperial suzerainty no longer involved the burdens of actual service, it was still a force to be reckoned with, as Amadeus had already discovered. The conquest of Gex and Faucigny, the attempts to subdue the Valaisans, the disputes with the dauphin and the count of Geneva, the rebellion of the prince of Achaea—all had been substantially affected by the actions of the emperor.

"From what I have heard from those who speak of the emperor," wrote Villani, "he was of medium height, small by German standards; a little hunchbacked, which shifted his neck and face somewhat forward, but without encumbering him; his hair was black, his face somewhat flat, his eyes large, and his cheeks full; his beard was black and his hairline receding in front. He wore suitable clothing, always close-fitting, without ornamentation, but short, reaching only to his knees. He was not openhanded, took care to hoard his gold, and recompensed but sparingly those who served him in arms. He also had the habit, during audiences, of holding in his hands willow branches and a small knife; he would amuse himself by whittling at them attentively. While occupied thus with his hands and while petitioners knelt before him presenting their petitions, he would glance around at the assemblage in such a way that those speaking to him had the impression that he was paying no attention whatever to what they said; yet he followed them and understood them perfectly. In a few words full of good sense and suited to the requests presented, following his own wishes alone and without need of further deliberation or counsel, he would make a reply full of wisdom. And this in spite of the three activities in which he was simultaneously engaged and which in no way interfered with or troubled his judgment: the movement of his eyes, the labor of his hands, his full comprehension of the audience and his thoughtful replies. An admirable quality, and something remarkable indeed in a ruler."[39]

This was the emperor "semper augustus" whom the Green Count was at last to meet in person. He knew that Charles' journey to Avignon through his territories was not merely a pleasure excursion. The expansion of the French monarchy into the border regions of the Empire had continued through the century, and while Charles was powerless to prevent it, he did intend to maintain at least the legal unity of his imperial inheritance. He had just permitted the new duke of Burgundy to succeed to the lands of his predecessor in the Empire, but he had insisted upon full recognition of imperial suzerainty over those lands. He had been unable to prevent the acquisition of the Dauphiné by the French, but he had exempted the dominions of the count of Savoy from the jurisdiction of the kingdom of Arles, lest the French obtain that title and attempt to use it for further aggrandisement.[40] Now that the dauphin had become king of France (thus accomplishing in his person the annexation of the Dauphiné to France), the emperor decided that the time had come for a dramatic stroke to remind the French that the Dauphiné was still part of the Empire. It was mainly for this reason that Charles chose to go in person to Arles in the spring of 1365 and take up the crown of that kingdom himself. He was the first emperor to do so in two centuries.[41]

The count of Savoy was quick to see how profitable to himself the imperial visit might be. Success in Amadeus' efforts to extend his authority over the lay and ecclesiastical magnates of his mountains required a firm legal foundation and imperial backing. The emperor's concessions in July 1356 had been an excellent beginning,[42] but the resistance of some prelates, notably the bishops of Geneva and Lausanne, encouraged by contradictory policies

[39] Matteo Villani, *Cronaca*, libro IV, ch. lxxiv. My translation.

[40] The imperial act removing the territories of the count of Savoy from the kingdom of Arles is dated 17 May 1361. Cf. Dino Muratore, "L'Imperatore Carlo IV nelle Terre Sabaude nel 1365 e il Vicariato Imperiale del Conte Verde," *MAS* (2nd series, XVI, Turin, 1906), 166.

[41] Other reasons for the trip were the pope's desire for imperial assistance both in launching the crusade and in preparing for the return of the papacy to Rome.

[42] See above, pp. 123–124.

of the emperor himself, tended to undermine the count's position. If Charles really wished to contain the French, he would surely see that the authority of the count of Savoy must be strengthened, not diminished—for among the princes of the threatened region, who had more successfully resisted the pressure of French expansion than the Savoyards? With the Burgundies in the hands of the French king's brother and the Dauphiné in those of the king himself, only the territories of Savoy prevented French control of the entire Saône-Rhône watershed.

Amadeus' difficulties with Saluzzo, the Valaisans, and the Great Companies made him particularly anxious for the emperor's favor, and he decided to welcome his imperial suzerain in person. On his way northward in mid-April, Amadeus notified the citizens of Geneva of the emperor's visit, and the city fathers decided to offer a procession and a feast in his honor. In early May the count and a company of nearly sixty nobles with their retainers reached Morat on the northern edge of the Pays de Vaud, where Charles would first enter Savoyard territory. The town was alive with excited villagers and bursting at the seams with the horde of notables that had suddenly descended upon it. The festive moment called for festive colors, and the Green Count rose to the occasion with enthusiasm. Amadeus and his retinue were a riot of red, white, and green. The Savoyard company was dwarfed into insignificance on 4 May, however, when the emperor arrived. Charles was accompanied by six bishops, five dukes, a host of counts, marshals, imperial household officers, and a retinue of more than 2,000 persons—a display no doubt unsurpassed in the experience of the local mountaineers.[43]

Emperor Charles IV was about fifty now, a diplomat, a cultivated patron of the arts, a founder of universities, the writer of an autobiography. He had a taste for luxury and display, although he preferred to dress modestly himself, and he probably enjoyed the spectacle of the Savoyards in green. Amadeus could probably not win the emperor's friendship as a fellow connoisseur of arts and letters, but he could hope to accomplish the same end by

[43] *AST*, inv. 16, doc. 26, abounds with references to purchases of garments and banners for the occasion: "xiii ulnis persiti et rubei pro cuperata magni equi domini," "iiii ulnis panni viridis de Brucellis pro domino," "panno sirici viridis pro oppelanda longa pro domino," etc. For the emperor's retinue, see Muratore, "Carlo IV," p. 170.

being the perfect host. It was extremely important to make a friend of the emperor, for the count knew that his enemies were also hoping to profit from the imperial visit. Their efforts to cancel Amadeus' privileges must be thwarted, and the count of Savoy meant to see that they were. Everything possible would be done to place Charles under obligation to his Savoyard host.

The task was not an easy one. The very next day the bishop of Sion and his archenemy, Antoine de la Tour, appeared at Morat, and each gave his version of what had been going on in the Valais over the past ten years. Their narratives made amply clear how ineffective the Peace of Evian in 1361 had been. On that occasion the count of Savoy had agreed to abandon his post as episcopal *bailli* in return for 13,000 florins, but the bishop had been unable to collect that sum. The communes downstream from Sion had contributed their share, but those of the High Valais had refused. The bishop and representative of the other Valaisan towns had gone up to Ernen in October 1361 to enforce payment, but they had been attacked by the population. The bishop's retinue had been manhandled, several persons had been killed, and the bishop himself had been taken prisoner. He had obtained his release eight weeks later only by promising to pardon all of the rebels, to raise the interdict laid upon the three recalcitrant parishes, and to abandon all taxes in arrears, as well as the present subsidy. This humiliating treaty Bishop Guichard had been obliged to sign at Münster on 4 January 1362.

The bishop had chosen to accept his defeat at the hands of the peasants for the time being, and sought thereafter rather to win their support against his major foe, the lords of La Tour-Châtillon. The La Tour had never forgiven the bishop for having deprived them of their hereditary charge as episcopal *bailli*, and they bitterly resisted his efforts to recover properties which belonged to his see, but which for generations had been in the possession of their family. The bishop had bestowed the castle of Granges upon his nephew, who refused to do homage for it to Antoine de la Tour when summoned to do so. War had already begun when tidings of the imperial visit reached the valley, and both sides had hurried to Morat to solicit the emperor's support.

This was the first test of Amadeus' influence over his dangerous guest. Charles had acted against Savoyard interests in the Valais before; would he do so again? The Green Count must have talked hard and well, for the emperor refused to listen to the complaints of either side. He contented himself with ordering the bishop to release one of the peasant agitators whom he still held in prison at La Soie. Charles' refusal to take action clearly implied his willingness to leave the count of Savoy a free hand in the Valais, at least for the time being. The initial trial of strength was thus won by Savoy.

With appropriate pomp and splendor the imperial cortege now crossed the Pays de Vaud, the emperor riding under a canopy of cloth-of-gold born by four knights of Savoy,[44] while the Green Count rode ahead with sword unsheathed as a mark of especial honor. The vast host paused at Payerne, spent the night of 5 May at Moudon, and finally reached Lausanne, where the bishop took the opportunity to secure confirmation of the rights and privileges of his church. If he also protested again the presence of Amadeus' appellate judge in his city, as is likely, his protest fell on deaf ears. While at Lausanne, Charles granted privileges to the cities of Bern and Fribourg, however, and the count of Savoy sent his *bailli* of Vaud to request those two communities to contribute troops to the defense effort against the Companies.[45]

By 9 May the procession had reached Geneva, where the bourgeois turned out in vast numbers, hoping to receive favors and privileges in their turn. The emperor's stay was brief and unfruitful, thanks no doubt to the vigilance of the count. Passing southward through Rumilly, the bright column of nobles reached Chambéry two days later. At noon on 11 May 1365 the emperor entered the main gate of the Savoyard capital, where hundreds of dignitaries and nobles from the surrounding Alpine valleys were on hand to greet him. Countess Bonne de Bourbon and her court were accompanied by the countess of Geneva and her ladies, Marie and Blanche de Châlon, and the dames and baronesses of Châtillon, Ravoire, Loes, Grésy, Saint-Amour, Varax, La Palud, Montmayeur, Chalamont, and D'Estrées.[46] The archbishop of Taren-

---

[44] Cabaret, p. 195; Servion, II, 186–187. *AST*, inv. 16, doc. 26, mentioned "iii peciis panni aurei pro v giponis" for the count, Guillaume de Grandson, Etienne de la Baume, Gaspard de Montmayeur, and François de Montgelat, so the latter were perhaps the four knights. The cloth-of-gold is also mentioned in the treasury accounts.

[45] The archbishop of Besançon also came to Lausanne to receive investiture of the *regalia* of his church at the emperor's hands. Cf. Fournier, p. 486, note.

[46] For weeks in advance, splendid new garments had been purchased for the

taise was also present, and the chronicles report that several Savoyard prelates, surrounded by their clergy, came forth to greet the emperor carrying their most precious relics and chanting the *Te Deum*. Amid great popular enthusiasm, Charles IV was conducted through the town to the castle, while his suite overflowed the inns of the town and nearby villages.

That evening may have been full of gay festivities, but it was also full of hard negotiations on political matters. Charles may have whittled willow branches and uttered only trenchant replies full of wisdom while the count argued, but he later claimed to have been overwhelmed by his host's persuasive speech. Certainly the documents issued under the imperial seal on the following day were not to be had merely for the asking. Letters-patent fully confirmed the claims of Savoy to full suzerainty over the marquisate of Saluzzo, thus sweeping away with one blow the legal basis for Federigo's indiscriminate acts of homage to the dauphin and Bernabò Visconti.[47]

The real triumph, however, was the grant of an imperial vicariate. This act confirmed the privileges of 1356 by which the count was authorized to exercise in the name of the emperor full appellate jurisdiction over lay and ecclesiastical tribunals located within his dominions. This document went further, however, and gave Amadeus the right to receive in the emperor's place acts of homage and oaths of fidelity from those who held imperial fiefs in his territories, and these were clearly specified. The preamble addressed itself "to each and every vassal of the Holy Empire, archbishops, bishops, abbots, *religiosi* and prelates, and other men and persons, noble and non-noble, of the cities and dioceses of Sion, Lausanne, Geneva, Aosta, Ivrea, Turin, Maurienne, Tarentaise, Belley, and the county of Savoy; and lands, places, and

---

countess, her ladies, young Amadeus, his bastard brother Antoine, and their households: hundreds of ermine skins and vair, cloth-of-gold, red velvet, silver ribbons, and, of course, many yards of green cloth. The sixteen members of the resident council of Chambéry were given fine new robes for the occasion. Cf. *AST*, inv. 16, doc. 26; inv. 38, folio 21, doc. 64; inv. 39, folio 1, doc. 21.

[47] Cf. Fournier, p. 487, note 2. At Le Bourget on 13 April 1365, Amadeus had concluded an eight months' truce between Saluzzo and Giacomo of Achaea in the presence of an envoy from Bernabò Visconti. Muratore, "Carlo IV," p. 168.

districts of said county in the dioceses of Lyon, Mâcon, and Grenoble."[48] The bishops of Sion and Ivrea and the count of Geneva were specifically required to do homage to the count of Savoy for their imperial fiefs. The act further stated that this vicarial authority was to be hereditary in the house of Savoy until such time as it should be specifically revoked. Amadeus VI, count of Savoy and prince of the Holy Empire, was now a vicar of His Imperial Majesty, "Imperatorie Majestatis Vicarius."

The following day, 12 May 1365, was perhaps the proudest one in the career of the Green Count, one never to be forgotten in the annals of the Alpine dynasty. The customs of the age required that a moment of such importance be clothed in brilliant color; it must be a feast for the eyes, from which even the humblest imagination might draw nourishment for years to come.[49] An enormous dais had been erected in the square before the castle, surmounted by a canopy of cloth-of-gold. The sides were curtained in red and white, and large square banners with the arms of the Empire upon them were hung in the pavilion. Upon the platform sat the emperor, surrounded by the dukes, barons, and prelates who had accompanied him. Then into the square, "so filled with people that it could scarcely contain them all," rode six heralds, each holding aloft a standard representing the hereditary possessions of Amadeus VI. The first banner bore the emblem of Saint Maurice, patron saint of the house of Savoy. The second had a bright gold field with the red-clawed black eagle of the ancient Humbertines flapping in the mountain wind. The third banner was that of the marquisate of Susa, half white and half red with a castle in the center. The fourth and fifth banners bore the ducal arms of Aosta and Chablais, the former a silver rampant lion on a black field, the latter identical with the colors reversed. The bright procession of colored banners was

---

[48] G. Tabacco, pp. 38ff. Marie-José, p. 174, repeats the assertion that the vicariate cost the count some 100,000 florins, but a thorough search through treasury and subsidy accounts reveals no basis whatever for this contention, which must at least tentatively be classed among myths like that of the ransom at Lanzo.

[49] The description which follows is based wherever possible upon household and treasury accounts. The ceremonies are described in the chronicles with suitable embellishments; but details of clothing, food, persons present, etc., are mostly from sources cited above in note 46.

climaxed by the appearance of the herald of Savoy holding high the scarlet standard with the silver cross, the "vrayes armes" of Amadeus VI.

When the heralds had entered the square and had taken their places on either side before the imperial dais, the count himself appeared, mounted upon a magnificent charger richly caparisoned with embroidered hangings and silver harness, "richement vestu et bien a cheval, arme de belles et riches armes," with a velvet surcoat of emerald green trimmed in silver. Following him two by two came the nobles of Savoy, knights and squires in their finest armor and vestments, each mounted as handsomely as his purse could afford, and carrying a small red pennon with the white cross of Savoy upon it.

The count dismounted and knelt before the emperor to do homage for his lands and jurisdiction. Charles formally invested him with his titles and dignities and proclaimed his new status as imperial vicar. Then, to dramatize the majesty of the emperor and the subjection of all before his throne, imperial knights stepped forward, took the six banners from the heralds, and cast them upon the ground.[50] But as a knight approached the herald holding the banner of Savoy, the count interceded. "Sire," he is supposed to have said to the emperor, "with the other banners do as you will; but this one with the white cross has never touched the ground, nor ever shall, God willing."[51] The chroniclers affirm that Charles took this rebuff in the proper chivalric spirit by generously ordering that both the banner of Savoy and that of Saint Maurice be spared the indignity to which the other four were subjected.

When the homage and investiture ceremonies were over, the emperor and his host left the town square and rode with their companions into the courtyard of the castle. In the parade hall a sumptuous banquet was served to the guests, who were seated at tables on raised platforms along three of the four walls. The emperor's table was covered by eight yards of dark red silk, the others with checkered cloths. Charles first washed his hands, then he and the company took their seats at the tables. They were

---

[50] Cabaret, p. 195, and Servion, II, 188, have the same account, but Servion says that it was the custom not only to cast the banners on the ground, but to tear them as well.

[51] *Ibid.*

served by the count of Savoy and his nobles, who, mounted upon "great chargers and war horses,"[52] carried the platters into the hall on the end of lances adapted for that purpose. There were so many splendidly prepared dishes and vast platters of food that the chroniclers confess their powers of description utterly inadequate, but all found it necessary to remark upon the fact that "pour plus haulte excellence," there was a fountain in the hall which continually gushed forth red and white wine, "night and day," for the duration of the banqueting. Between courses a crowd of minstrels and jugglers provided music and acrobatics for the amusement of the diners.

The next morning the imperial cortege left Chambéry, the Green Count and his nobles providing the emperor's escort all the way to Avignon and Arles. Amadeus had no intention of allowing Charles an opportunity to alter any of his recent decisions. It was a wise precaution, for at Grenoble, Raoul de Louppy and a large group of Dauphinois nobles greeted the emperor and solicited on behalf of the king of France the title of imperial vicar over Savoy, the Dauphiné, Provence, Geneva, and Saluzzo.[53] Clearly the Green Count had lost no time in gaining the imperial ear; only his presence at this moment made it impossible for Charles to betray him. Louppy's request was refused, and the company, now several thousand strong, passed on to St-Marcellin, Romans, and Valence. At Valence the duke of Anjou paid his respects, and the bishop, Louis de Villars, reiterated his pleas for imperial assistance against the Great Companies.

From Valence the imperial party moved southward along the Rhône. On 22 May at the bridge of Sorgues, the Sacred College of Cardinals received them in the name of the Church and escorted them the rest of the way to Avignon. Charles remained with the pope until 2 June, discussing the Companies, the crusade, and Urban's plans to move the papal seat back to Rome. From these discussions emerged a new scheme: the mercenary companies were to be induced to go to Hungary, where King Louis "the Great" needed men for his wars against the Turks

[52] Details on food and table cloths come from the treasury accounts already cited; Charles' washing of hands and the table service on horseback are the versions in Cabaret and Servion.

[53] Cordey, *Les Comtes*, pp. 196–197.

and Bulgarians. Marshal d'Audrehem was to be dispatched at once to Hungary to obtain the king's agreement to this scheme, and Charles offered to provide for the transportation and maintenance of the Companies during the trip across the Empire to the king's dominions.[54] In the event that the king of Hungary should refuse to accept the aid of the Companies, which was considered unlikely, the emperor agreed to provide the means to send them by sea to the East to fight against the infidel.

That the count of Savoy participated in these discussions cannot be doubted, but his presence there is clearly demonstrated only by a document which concerns a different subject. This was the imperial act of 2 June 1365, the result of the "prayers and instances" of the count of Savoy, founding a university in Geneva.[55] "The charms of our said city of Geneva," declared the preamble, "the natural wealth of the site and its surroundings in all of the necessities for human life, the mildness of the climate, the ebbing and flowing waters, clear and swift, filled with innumerable fish of every variety, constitute an abundance most suitable for the reformation of human nature, for the stimulation of the mind, for the provocation and direction of the inner man toward the exercise of virtuous works, by which the well-being of the community is increased and the glory of the Empire enhanced."

The seven liberal arts were to be taught at the new university, where the students were permitted publicly to "read, teach, dispute, resolve doubts, define and decide questions." The honors and privileges of "magistri" and "doctores" could be awarded to those who "per rigorem publici et generalis examinis" were found worthy of such dignities. The "rectors, masters, teachers, students, and *auditores*" at the university were declared exempt from all taxes, tolls, and imposts during their course of study, and no one was to interfere with their coming and going. The university was to be placed under the patronage and high protection of the "illustrious count of Savoy." Amadeus and his successors were to have full power to correct and punish any who violated the liberties of the "generalis studii Gebennarum."

It would be ungracious to attribute the Green Count's action in securing this foundation to political rather than to intellectual

[54] Prou, p. 52.     [55] Text in *MDG*, XVIII, doc. 165.

motives, but it is difficult not to do so. Amadeus was a warrior and a statesman, but thus far he had shown little inclination to be a Maecenas. He doubtless had no objection to "inner men" devoted to virtuous works—provided that they were also devoted to the house of Savoy.

On 4 June 1365 in the church of St-Trophîme in the city of Arles, Emperor Charles IV was crowned king of Arles by Cardinal-Archbishop Guillaume de la Garde, in the presence of a large audience which included the seneschal of Provence, the duke of Bourbon,[56] the governor of the Dauphiné, and the count of Savoy. A few days later the emperor was on his way back to Germany. On 14 June at Vienne, Charles granted permission to Philippe le Hardi to marry Elisabeth of Hungary, niece of King Louis. From Vienne the imperial cavalcade crossed the Dauphiné, passed at Grenoble, and spent the night of 17 June at Les Marches, just inside the Savoyard frontier. On the return trip through Savoy, Chambéry was bypassed in favor of Le Bourget, where the emperor stayed the following evening.

Charles' reception at Geneva a few days later was chilly, owing to the disappointment of both the bishop and the citizens after his passage in May. Bishop Alamand was bitter about both the vicariate and the university charter, in which he saw only too clearly the hand of his dangerous Savoyard neighbor.[57] While Charles was at Geneva, perhaps partly to escape so uncongenial an atmosphere, he asked his host where the abbey of St-Maurice was located. When he discovered that it was not far away, he expressed a fervent desire to visit it, for, as he explained, it contained the remains of his "ancestors," Saint Sigismond and two of his sons.[58] While most of the imperial retinue continued along

[56] Louis II, brother of the countess of Savoy.

[57] The bishop carried his displeasure to the point of refusing obedience to the emperor and of sending him copies of the ancient privileges granted to his church to prove that Amadeus' vicarial powers were in direct violation of them. His protests fell on deaf ears.

[58] Charles IV was known in some quarters as the "Priest's king" for having been the papal candidate to oppose Louis IV in 1346–1347. But he is known as well to have been devout to the point of superstition in his religious observances. Cf. examples in his autobiography given in Bede Jarrett, *Emperor Charles IV* (London, 1935), pp. 33–62, especially p. 45. The accounts of Charles' piety in the chronicles of Savoy accord perfectly with other information concerning his personality.

the northern shore of the lake to Lausanne, Charles and the Green Count with a smaller company followed the southern shore to Thonon and Evian. After dining at Evian, they followed the narrow trail up into the mountains of the Chablais, with its forests "extremely thick and gloomy" and its "huge precipices of naked rocks rising up in a thousand odd figures, and cleft in some places, so as to discover high mountains of Snow that lye several leagues behind them."[59] From the pass at Morgins the trail led down into the valley of Illiez. At Monthey on the Rhône the count's castellan greeted the party. From the castle of Monthey it was just a few miles to the fortress-abbey of St-Maurice, sheltered under the edge of soaring cliffs on the sunny side of a rocky crevice formed by the sudden invasion of the valley by otherwise amiably distant mountains.

The abbot and monks of St-Maurice received their visitor with pleasure, but declared themselves quite confounded when he asked to see the tomb of the holy Sigismond. "Seigneurs," replied the abbot, "the church we know well [i.e. the chapel dedicated to Saint Sigismond], but we are ignorant of the location of the sepulchre."[60] Undaunted, Charles asked to see the chapel in which the tomb was supposed to have been, and was led into the abbey enclosure where it still stood. Then the emperor "brought out an ancient chronicle which contained the life of Saint Sigismond and the story of how he had been buried and walled up in an underground chapel." Having read the account aloud, he ordered the monks to bring torches and picks and led them down into the vault under the chapel. Charles told them where to dig, and they had hardly begun when part of the wall fell away, revealing a cave containing the remains of Saint Sigismond "and his two children next to him." The monks were astonished and delighted and began to sing hymns and praises to God with "moult grant devocion." The emperor, equally pleased, claimed as his reward the venerable skull for his relic collection. The remains of the saint were placed in a splendid gilt coffer with a handsomely sculptured exterior, which was installed under the altar of the chapel of Saint John. On the site of this chapel a new parish church was subsequently built and dedicated to Saint Sigismond.[61]

[59] Addison's description in 1701, *op.cit.*, II, 201–202.

[60] Servion, II, 189–190.

[61] Sigismond and his two sons were killed near Orléans by the sons of Clovis

While Charles was at the abbey, he wished also to see the body of Saint Maurice. His veneration for this saint was so great that only with difficulty could the Green Count prevent the emperor from dismembering this skeleton also in order to carry more relics back to Prague with him. Amadeus finally permitted his illustrious guest to take away the saint's battle-axe, in place of his bones.[62]

On 22 June the Green Count escorted the emperor along the Rhône to the lake, past Chillon to Vevey, where the bishop of Geneva was on hand to protest against the count's imperial vicariate once more. Amadeus had the satisfaction of seeing his enemy's appeals go unanswered again; and the following day, joining the rest of the imperial cortege, he set out to accompany the emperor as far as Bern. There the count persuaded Charles to issue separate letters to each of the eleven prelates concerned, expressly commanding them to recognize the new imperial vicar. To the lords of La Tour–Châtillon, to the counts of Aarberg, Strambino, and Masino (in the Canavese), and to the nobles of Dombes also went letters reminding them of Amadeus' recent appointment, and ordering them to do homage to him for their imperial fiefs.[63] When the Green Count headed back to Savoy a few days later, he had every reason for satisfaction. Fortune was shining upon his ambitions like the sun upon his Alps.

THE GREAT COMPANIES AND THE CRUSADE

The presence of the emperor had temporarily restrained the "pestiferous Societies" infesting the Beaujolais, the Lyonnais, and southern Burgundy, but it had not altered their intentions. No sooner had Charles vanished over the mountains into Germany than Amadeus received appeals for help from his lieutenants in

---

in 523. The reliquary containing the remains of the saint is still to be seen in in the parish church of Saint Sigismond at St-Maurice and it still bears the date 1365 upon it. Cf. Marie-José, p. 180, note 4.

[62] Muratore, "Carlo IV," p. 180, note 1, demonstrates that the chronicle account is correct in every particular that can be checked. It is worth noting that one of Charles' sons and a future emperor (1410–1437) was named Sigismond, which does suggest the emperor's interest in this rather obscure saint.

[63] *Ibid.*, p. 182. The total cost of the visit for Savoy was 18,350 florins "parvi ponderis." The subsidy collected in most of the count's territories brought in 19,017 florins "parvi ponderis." *AST*, inv. 16, doc. 27 (1365).

Bresse and the Valbonne, where the brigands seemed planning to strike next. Simon de Saint-Amour, with a company of sixty men-at-arms from the Dauphiné, hurried toward Neuville-sur-Saône to reinforce a company of about a hundred men under *bailli* Humbert de Corgenon, who was closely watching the ports of the Saône. By mid-July the count received word that the marauders, 120 lances strong, had actually crossed the Saône on a raiding expedition into Dombes.[64] Exactly what happened is not clear, but it is certain that they were promptly driven back across the river, and that some of them were taken prisoner.[65]

By now the position of Seguin de Badefol at Anse was becoming uncomfortable. The plans laid by Urban V and Charles IV at Avignon during the preceding weeks were being put into effect, and around the commanding figure of the Archpriest Arnaud de Cervole were being grouped not only the royal troops but also the companies of Lamy, Bertram, the Bour de Breteuil, Naudon de Bageran, and others. At St-Laurent in Bresse a conference took place between the representatives of the count of Savoy and the king of France. On 19 July 1365, Pope Urban announced that he had conceded the tithes of the French church for the next two years to the king in order to enable him to pay the expenses of the expedition to Hungary, and a legate was sent to Mâcon to absolve brigands who joined the enterprise from the sentences of excommunication incurred by their previous activities. Seguin, fearing that the great army being assembled for Hungary might well be used against him first, now consented to negotiate the conditions of his retreat from Anse.

By early August the army destined for Hungary under Arnaud de Cervole moved off through the Burgundies for Alsace and the Empire. Then a wholly unexpected reversal took place. The terrible reputation of the Companies had so far preceded them that their peaceful attempt to pass through Alsace provoked the most desperate resistance on the part of the inhabitants. As a result, these thousands of mercenaries were hurled back into the Burgundies near the northern frontiers of the Pays de Vaud. Amadeus sent Guillaume de Grandson to inspect the defenses

---

[64] G. Guigue, p. 117.

[65] The castellany accounts in Bresse record the expenses of having them executed at Bourg and Pont-de-Veyle by hangmen brought from Mâcon. *ADCO*, B 7116, B 9291.

of the region, and ordered the castellan of Gex to organize a spy system similar to that functioning in Bresse. The citizens of Bern and Fribourg also joined the effort to protect the whole of western Helvetia.

The situation remained unchanged through the summer, but in September, Seguin de Badefol, handsomely paid off by the inhabitants of Lyon and the duke of Anjou, relinquished Anse and moved off toward southwestern France. In October the constable of France, Bertrand du Guesclin, acting on orders from the king of France, persuaded some twenty-five mercenary captains to follow him with their men into Spain.[66] A civil war was raging there, and when the news came that Pedro the Cruel, king of Castile, had strangled his wife, who was the sister of the queen of France and of the countess of Savoy, Charles V seized upon this pretext for armed intervention south of the Pyrenees.[67]

It was now the turn of the count of Savoy to try to do something about the brigands still abroad in eastern France. To this end Amadeus addressed himself once more to Arnaud de Cervole, the "Archpriest," whose attempt to lead his men across Alsace had so dismally failed. The Green Count had a new proposal. If the Germans would not let the Companies pass, the count would undertake to provide the Archpriest and his men with safe passage across the Alps into Italy, if they would in turn agree to fight under his banner in the East. The response was favorable. It remained only to make the final arrangements and the crusade would be under way.[68]

[66] Cordey, *Les Comtes*, p. 179; G. Guigue, pp. 129–131; Perroud, "Les Grandes Compagnies en Bresse et en Dombes," *Annales de la Société d'Émulation de l'Ain* (Bourg, 1874), p. 277.

[67] The Savoyard chronicles recount that Amadeus at first decided to go on this expedition in order to avenge the alleged murder of his sister-in-law, but they give the episode an anti-Jewish character. Cf. Servion, II, 121–123; Cabaret, p. 156 *dorso*.

[68] On 4 November 1365 at Angoulême, Edward, the Black Prince, issued a letter, probably in response to a plea from the Green Count, addressed to 'touz capitains et autres gens de compaigne," ordering them to refrain from all destruction or harm to "nostre tres chier cousin, le comte de Savoie" or to his lands or subjects. The captains were to prevent anyone else from troubling the count as well, because he "a souvent fait et fait de jour en autre grandes courteoisies a touz noz genz qui passent parmy sa seigniorie, et autres bonnteez et naturesses que nous ont monstre nostre dit cousin." Text in Cordey, *Les Comtes*, doc. 33.

# VII

# Athleta Christi

## 1365-1367

### CRUSADE PLANS

THE death of Cardinal Talleyrand de Périgord, Apostolic Legate for the Holy War, in January 1364, and that of Jean le Bon the following April brought preparations for the crusade to a halt in France. In Savoy the Green Count seemed to be absorbed by other matters, but he had not in fact forgotten his vow to undertake the "voyage beyond the seas." Throughout 1364, Amadeus was in correspondence with Philippe de Mézières respecting the formation of a crusading army, and by the fall of 1365 the count was also in contact with Louis of Hungary, undoubtedly regarding the same subject.[1]

Amadeus had not changed his mind about making an expedition to the East, but he does seem to have been in doubt as to its exact destination. His first thought had been to join forces with the king of Cyprus, sail to Crete with him and reduce that island to obedience after its recent rebellion (in 1363), then to undertake a full-scale invasion of the Holy Land.[2] Crete at this time belonged to Venice, which was expected to furnish transportation and naval support for the crusaders in return for their assistance in restoring Venetian authority on the island. By the summer of 1364, however, the Venetians had put down the rebellion on Crete and were reluctant to endanger their commercial interests in the Near East by supporting an all-out attack upon the Muslim princes there. Moreover, the count of Savoy could not leave his dominions while the mercenary companies were roaming unchecked on his western frontiers, as they continued to do through-

[1] Jorga, pp. 234–241, 332, note 3.
[2] *Ibid.*, p. 237, note 5. This was apparently Amadeus' plan as late as March 1364.

out 1365. As a result, Amadeus was not among the crusaders who sailed from Venice on 27 June 1365 with the king of Cyprus, whose destination now was Egypt.[3]

The capture and sack of the great city of Alexandria by Pierre of Cyprus and his army in October 1365 created a sensation in Europe and doubtlessly reinforced the Green Count's determination to participate in such glorious enterprises. Only the Venetians failed to rejoice at the wanton destruction of this flourishing city, for they knew that such an act would ultimately provoke disastrous retaliation from the Muslim powers.[4] While the West exulted in this triumph for the Faith, the Venetians hastened westward with the false news that a peace treaty had been concluded between the victorious king of Cyprus and the sultan of Egypt. The object of the false report was to deflect the count of Savoy and others from their intention to reinforce the crusaders at Alexandria, which would have enabled the latter to follow up their victory.

The Venetians might have spared themselves the trouble of spreading this misinformation, at least as far as the count of Savoy was concerned. As early as the fall of 1364, Amadeus was seriously considering the alternative project of an expedition by land across the Empire to Hungary, the Balkans, and Asia Minor. This plan was more acceptable than previous schemes had been in the eyes of the mercenary captains whose companies were expected to participate, and it was therefore adopted at Avignon in 1365, five months before the fall of Alexandria.[5] When Arnaud de Cervole and his men were prevented from crossing into the Germanies in the summer of 1365, another route had to be found for them, but the plan remained basically unchanged.[6]

The decision to launch the campaign against the infidel in the Balkans rather than in the Holy Land had much to commend it from a practical point of view. The Green Count, however, zealous for the liberation of the Holy Sepulcher or eager to do battle

[3] Atiya, pp. 341–342, claims that even the Venetians who provided most of the fleet were not told of its destination, lest they sabotage the enterprise.

[4] *Ibid.*, p. 386. Alexandria was speedily recaptured by the Muslims.

[5] Cf. Aime Chérest, *L'Archiprêtre*, Chapters XI and XII.

[6] Jorga, p. 272. The Grand Master of the Hospitalers had proposed that he, the Republic of Genoa, and the marquis of Montferrat undertake the responsibility for convoying the Companies across northern Italy to the Balkans.

beside the famous Pierre de Lusignan, was not a man to take unnecessary risks. An expedition to the Balkans must have seemed less perilous than an invasion of the Holy Land, and the prospects for success considerably greater. The king of Hungary, a French Angevin by descent and a famous warrior, could be expected to lend his powerful support; and further assistance might be found among princes of western descent ruling in Greece. Most important, the reigning emperor of Byzantium, John V Paleologus, was first cousin to the count of Savoy. Thus a crusade which at least began in the Balkans would happily combine dynastic interests with the greater interests of all Christendom, even if it never reached the Holy Land at all. The Green Count had no desire to return from the East broken in spirit, bankrupt, and without anything to show for his efforts, as Dauphin Humbert II had done in 1347. Glory required victory, and Amadeus always calculated his chances very soberly on that score.

### PREPARATIONS AND DEPARTURE FOR VENICE

On 3 January 1366 at the castle of Le Bourget, "in the chamber behind the chamber over the cellars and next to the hall," the count drew up the act establishing the regency for Savoy during his absence.[7] Bonne de Bourbon was to have full authority over all "counties, baronies, lands, cities, towns, castles, and other . . . jurisdictions of every sort," and a council was named to assist her: the chancellor, Girard d'Estrées; the treasurer-general, Pierre Gerbais; Aymon de Challant, castellan of Chambéry and Tarentaise; and Humbert de Savoie, *bailli* of Savoy and castellan of Montmélian.[8] The countess was authorized to name others to the council if she wished, but ordinances issued by her required the concurrence of at least two of the counselors in order to become effective.

Preparations were interrupted at this point while Amadeus made a quick trip to Avignon. On 6 January 1366, Urban V, ap-

---

[7] This and other documents on the crusade are published in Pietro Datta, *Spedizione*, and in Bolatti di Saint-Pierre, *Illustrazioni della Spedizione in Oriente di Amadeo VI* in *BSI*, V (1900).

[8] The others on the council were Louis Rivoire, lord of Domessin and Gerbaix, who had been the count's vicar of Piedmont in earlier years; Aymon de Châtillon, castellan of Montfalcon; and Jean de la Chambre, viscount of Maurienne and husband of Agnès de Savoie, sister of Giacomo of Achaea.

parently despairing of ever realizing his dream of a great European crusade, revoked the bulls of April 1364 by which the count was authorized to receive ecclesiastical tithes over a six-year period. The death of the king of France and "alias causas . . . peccatis exigentibus" were cited by the pope as having prevented the crusade from taking place. At Avignon the Green Count no doubt protested this action by enumerating the preparations already completed and reaffirming his intention to make the trip. If Urban replied that he must conserve the resources of the church for a crusading effort of greater dimensions destined for the Holy Land, Amadeus could answer that an expedition to Byzantium might accomplish a dream almost as dear as that of liberating Jerusalem: the submission of the Eastern Orthodox Church to the Church of Rome. The pope's subsequent actions prove that he gave his blessings to the Savoyard undertaking, but his failure to reinstate the bulls of 1364 was the measure of his disappointment.[9]

The count returned to Savoy to assemble his army. As usual he took care to surround himself with relatives and close friends: his half brother Ogier; Humbert, bastard of Humbert de Savoie; Aimone de Savoie, younger brother of Giacomo of Achaea; and Amadeus' own son, Antoine, "bastardus de Sabaudie, junior" (to distinguish him from "Antonius, bastardus de Sabaudie, senior," who also participated in the crusade).[10] To these may be added such "adopted" brothers as Richard Musard, the Black Squire, who was the count's bodyguard, and Guillaume de Grandson, the count's cousin and "twin." Only two of the fifteen knights of the Collar failed to take part in the expedition, but each of them sent what may be considered a replacement. Amadeus of

[9] *AST, Viaggio di Levante,* mazzo I d'Addizione, doc. 13. I am indebted to M. Jean-Jacques Bouquet of Lausanne for bringing these facts to my attention. Although the pope's failure to lend his entire support to the count's expedition justifies reservations in classifying it as a crusade, I have chosen to do so because the Savoyards clearly thought it was.

[10] Bollati, items 168, 170, 171. This is Antoine Barbier's record of receipts and expenditures "racione passagii Domini ultramarini" from 12 June 1366 through 22 January 1368, published in full (the original no longer exists). All Bollati "items" hereafter cited are from this source. Aimone de Savoie had taken part in the Valais campaigns of 1352 and was the one for whom Amadeus bought the green outfit like his own before the tournaments of Bourg-en-Bresse. Cf. Commentary, VI.

Geneva was represented by his eldest son Aymon, and Antoine of Beaujeu was replaced by his uncle Louis de Beaujeu, sire of Alloignet.[11] At least half of the crusading army consisted of the hereditary vassals of the house of Savoy, and very few of the noble families of the count's dominions went unrepresented. These were men upon whom the count could rely when Arnaud de Cervole and his thousands of mercenaries arrived to fill out the ranks of the crusaders' host—mercenaries who were being taken to the East mainly in order to get them out of the West.[12]

Transportation by sea to the East remained a problem. The Venetians were proving unexpectedly difficult since the sack of Alexandria. Although the city had been rapidly recovered by the sultan of Egypt, the attack and the exceptionally destructive acts of the "crusaders" had seriously undermined relations with the Muslim powers. The Venetians were not disposed to assist any enterprise likely to antagonize the Muslims still further. Urban V was indignant at the Venetian attitude and wrote at the end of March in an effort to alter it. The letter had little effect, for envoys sent by the count to Venice returned in April to report that the Venetians would guarantee him only two galleys, and these only on the condition that he promise not to attack any part of the coast of Syria without their express permission.[13] Thanks largely to the influence of the pope, however, both Genoa and

[11] Duparc, p. 306. Muratore, "Les Origines de l'Ordre du Collier," *AHS*, XXIII and XXIV (1909–1910), concludes from the presence of Aymon of Geneva that the chroniclers were mistaken in listing his father in the first place. Hugues de Châlon-Arlay came with his brother Louis de Châlon-Arlay, and his cousin Tristan de Châlon-Auxerre.

[12] Atiya, pp. 383–384, thus misrepresents the character of the Savoyard army as "almost all . . . paid recruits" as opposed to "direct vassals" of the count. The extract of the treasury record of 1365–1366 (*AST*, inv. 16, doc. 27) published in Datta (*Spedizione*, pp. 257-259) lists 15 nobles accompanied by 73 *gentes armorum*, and a second group of 79 nobles with 10 *gentes armorum* each. This comes to 957 knights and vassals, and does not include such important people as Gaspard de Montmayeur, Etienne de la Baume, Berlion de Foras, Richard Musard, or Louis de Beaujeu—or the count himself and his *gentes domini*. If one accepts Delaville le Roulx's estimate that the total strength of the army was between 1,500 and 1,800 men, as Atiya does, then it was obviously not "almost all paid recruits."

[13] Jorga, p. 333. Amadeus had asked for five galleys and two "fustes," and offered in return to fight under the orders of the Republic after his expedition had been successfully concluded.

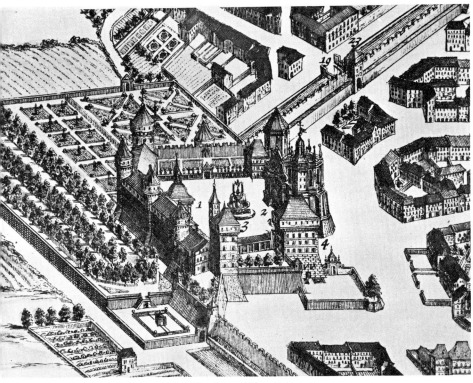

The Castle of Chambéry

The basin of Lake Geneva and the Alps of Chablais and Faucigny

The canyons of the Rhône, viewed from the southwest

The Abbey of Hautecombe on the shores of Lake Le Bourget

Marseilles offered to contribute ships for the expedition. In the original agreement at Avignon, Charles IV had promised to contribute to the transportation costs, but he in fact did not. The count of Savoy did not have sufficient funds on hand, and until the proceeds of a general subsidy could be collected for the "viagio ultramarino" (and it was not collected until 1368), he would have to resort to loans. Ten thousand florins were borrowed from bankers at Lyon, and the not uncommon recourse of pawning some of the family silver raised additional sums.[14]

In early February preliminary arrangements were completed. Amadeus took leave of his wife and his small son at Chambéry on 8 February and set out on the road to the East. Late in May the count was at Pavia, where he acted as godfather at the baptism of the infant son of his nephew, Giangaleazzo Visconti.[15] Blanche de Savoie, now a grandmother at thirty years of age, contributed more than prayers and good wishes to her brother on the eve of his departure. She assigned several of her *familiares* to the count's bodyguard and donated 4,000 florins to his needy warchest. Galeazzo could never be persuaded to take part in so unprofitable an adventure as a crusade, but he was willing to assist his brother-in-law with a variety of loans: 20,000 florins, 25 men-at-arms, some 600 *brigandi* under 16 *conestabiles,* and Cesare, one of his bastards.[16] Galeazzo agreed to pay the salaries of these mercenaries for the first six months, which he probably deemed ample time for so insane an expedition. Thereafter, the *brigandi* would be at the count's expense.

About half of the army under the command of Etienne de la Baume then left for Genoa, where they would board the gal-

---

[14] Cf. Datta, *Spedizione*, doc. VIII. Atiya, p. 383, seems to think that the count's resources amounted to no more than 778 Venetian ducats per year from his mints.

[15] Dino Muratore, "La nascita e il battesimo del primogenito di Gian Galeazzo Visconti e la politica viscontea nella primavera del 1366," *ASL*, XXXII (1905), pp. 265–272. The infant had been born on 4 March to Isabelle de Valois and Giangaleazzo, who was only fifteen. Amadeus had apparently reached Rivoli by 15 February and Pavia by mid-March, but had been obliged, for reasons unknown, to retrace his steps to St-Jean-de-Maurienne before returning to Pavia in May.

[16] Bollati, item 238. The count made a gift of 100 florins to "domino Cesari bastardo domini Galeaz" at Constantinople.

leys hired and waiting for them there.[17] On 1 June the rest of the army under the count left Pavia for Venice. At Padua, Amadeus was wined and dined by the Carrara, who offered him the use of their palace in Venice during his stay. On the count's approach to that city, envoys from the doge met him and requested that he not enter the city with more than fifty horsemen, for the sake of preserving peace and order. On 8 June the Green Count and his barons were honorably received in Venice by the doge and his council.[18] Now that the expedition was known to be heading for the Balkans rather than the Holy Land, the Venetians were more friendly to the idea.[19]

At Venice several more mercenary companies, Aymon de Genève, and a large contingent of Burgundians joined the host. Bad news also arrived: on 25 May, Arnaud de Cervole, who had assembled a large mercenary army at Tournus and was already marching to join the count, was assassinated by his own men somewhere in the vicinity of Mâcon.[20] The mercenary companies considered themselves freed of all obligations toward the crusade now that Cervole was dead, and the army rapidly disintegrated as each band went its separate way. The crusading host was thus reduced to a fraction of its intended size, and the dream of ridding the Saône valley of the brigands was shattered. Upon receiving this news the count must have considered turning back. Practical considerations—the need to protect his territories and the reduced size of the crusader army—certainly argued for such a course. But more than practical considerations were at stake. Amadeus was committed to a crusade for the advancement of the True Faith and the reunion of the eastern and western Christian churches. To turn back now would dishonor him. He had

---

[17] On 27 May, Hugues and Louis de Châlon formally contracted to serve the count for one full year with forty "gentil hommes," and Florimont de Lesparre, a veteran crusader, signed a similar contract to serve with thirty men-at-arms. Thus the Châlon brothers, despite dynastic affiliations with the count, were serving as mercenaries in this venture. Bollati, doc. III; Datta, *Spedizione*, doc. VIII; Atiya, p. 370, on Lesparre.

[18] Various dates have been given for the count's arrival in Venice, but Bollati, item 191, is quite specific. Cf. also item 916.

[19] The Venetians now offered more ships and even men, if the count would stop at the island of Tenedos and help them take it away from the Genoese. Jorga, p. 333.

[20] G. Guigue, pp. 164–166.

vowed to be an athlete of Christ, and he intended to do what he could to fulfill that vow no matter what the odds against him.

The Venetians now provided six galleys, which, added to the galleys hired at Genoa and Marseilles, brought the fleet total to about fifteen.[21] Etienne de la Baume had been designated as admiral, but until he joined the fleet with the Genoese galleys, Antelme d'Urtières, captain of the count's galley, would lead the flotilla.[22] Gaspard de Montmayeur, marshal of Savoy, was to be marshal of the crusader army, which was organized into three "batailles." The first was commanded by the count, assisted by Montmayeur, Jean and Gautier de Vienne, and Aymard de Clermont; the second was to consist of companies under Etienne de la Baume, the sire de Basset, and the sire of Saint-Amour. Everyone else, including the lords "of the lineage of Monseigneur," were to make up the "grosse bataille" commanded by Grandson, Grolée, Urtières, and Lesparre.

For sailing purposes the army was divided somewhat differently, according to the provinces from which the men had come. There was a galley of "Breysse," another "des gens de Foucignie," and another "des gens de Savoye." Detailed instructions were drawn up concerning the procedure to be followed, and fines were decreed for failure to observe them. No galley was to pass that of Monseigneur, and all were to sail within sight of one another. A complicated system of flag signals by day, and lantern signals by night, was devised so that orders could be transmitted en route concerning the course, the stops, and the manner of coping with enemies. No attack on sea or land was to be undertaken without express orders from the count, or without signals from the count's trumpeters.

### THE VOYAGE TO CONSTANTINOPLE AND THE CAPTURE OF GALLIPOLI

Time for the departure was drawing near. On 19 June the count's war chest was moved to Borgo San Nicolo where it could be more easily loaded on shipboard. To ensure the support of

---

[21] The exact number is difficult to determine because there is no list, and additional galleys seem to have been hired later on.

[22] The ordinances are published in Bollati, docs. IV and V. Admirals of galleys included Guillaume de Grandson, Tristan de Châlon, "Monsieur de Genève," Aymard de Clermont, and Jean de Grolée.

influential saints for this dangerous enterprise, Amadeus made generous donations to all of the famous churches of the city— San Marco, San Luca, San Giorgio, San Antonio. Spiritual concerns did not, however, entirely overshadow the worldly attractions of the marketplace. Two waterclocks were purchased for the countess and sent off to Chambéry; two long green mantles with hoods were ordered for the count and Guillaume de Grandson.[23] On orders from the count, his physician Gui Albin bought a great quantity of "medicines, unguents, and confections" from an apothecary, along with roasting spits for the ship's kitchen, amber goblets, copper bowls, and a chest of candy.[24] Amadeus saw that his wardrobe was provided with a fur-lined jacket of chamois leather and his "camera" with woolen blankets, two nightshirts, and six chamber pots.[25]

When these matters had been attended to, the count gave orders for the debarkation. His retainers, like himself, were decked out in green and gold, and they marched through the city from the Carrara palace to Piazza San Marco with white and scarlet banners raised high. The Venetians were reportedly so full of "grande merveillie" at the sight that they flocked about in great numbers to watch while the bishop solemnly gave his benediction to the kneeling multitude. Then, as the crusaders boarded the galleys, the crowd on shore filled the air with cries of "Viva Savoia . . . so loudly and so proudly that the whole square resounded with them, which was a wonder and a joy to hear and see."[26]

The largest of the galleys, the count's flagship, was decorated with brightly colored banners, and atop the highest mast floated an enormous scarlet banner with the white cross of Savoy. Next to it was a large blue flag with golden stars framing the image of the Virgin Mary, patroness of the Order of the Collar, whose knights were ostensibly setting forth to do battle in her honor. A pavillion of green cloth ornamented with the red and white arms of Savoy stretched nearly the whole length of the galley.[27]

[23] Bollati, items 20, 192: " . . . precio unius caufri corei empti ibidem pro portandis duobus relaugiis vitri domine Comitisse apud Chamberiacum."

[24] *Ibid.*, items 38, 61, 49, 50.

[25] *Ibid.*, items 198, 201: "gipis in quibus dominus jacuit in galea"; "sex urinaliis."

[26] Servion, II, 129.

[27] These details are in Bollati, item 269.

Green and red for strength and courage, blue for the Queen
of Heaven, white for the one True Faith—thus was the enterprise clothed in appropriate symbolic colors.

The departure took place around 21 June 1366. The first stop
was Pola on the southern tip of Istria, where the crusaders arrived two days later. One of the galleys had not been ready to
leave with the rest from Venice, and the stop at Pola was apparently to allow it to overtake the others. The Green Count
spent the night in the Franciscan monastery and left a generous
offering when he departed. From Pola the fleet sailed southward
along the Dalmatian coast to Ragusa, where the count was presented with sheep, torches, and wax candles. On leaving Ragusa
the Savoyards sailed on to the island of Corfu, gambling to pass
the time on shipboard and collecting miscellaneous gifts in ports
of call.[28] On 19 July the fleet arrived at Coron (in the province
of Messenia not far from ancient Pylos), then under Venetian
control, where an unexpected event took place. According to the
Savoyard chronicles, while the count was awaiting the arrival
of the fleet from Genoa, a ship came into the port carrying a
Greek noble who informed him that the "Desposte des Inus,"
identified as the cousin of Bonne de Bourbon, was in need of his
help. The archbishop of Patras had seized her lands, would not
give them up, and was at that very moment besieging her in
the castle of "Jungs."

The Green Count is supposed to have uttered a loud oath in
which he swore to honor his wife by aiding her cousin. He
gathered his men together and marched to the castle. When he
got there, the archbishop sent an envoy to inform him that this
war was being waged "for Christianity and to maintain the rights
of the church."[29] The count was impressed by this explanation
and summoned both the "despote" and the archbishop to defend their positions before him. After hearing both, he decided
that his cousin was in the wrong and must do homage to the
archbishop for the lands which she held, so that they would
not be lost to the Church. The despote proved agreeable to this
solution, did homage, and received investiture of the lands which

[28] Such as goshawks for hunting and a barrel of barberry juice. Cf. Bollati,
items 78–80 and 94–95: "Libravit . . . cuidam valleto qui domino presentaverat
. . . unum barrile de ribiola."

[29] Servion, II, 130ff.

213

had been invaded by the archbishop. The latter was delighted with the role of the count, "cherished him and praised him greatly and gave him many fine relics," then returned to Patras where he gave the count of Savoy great "fame and praise."

Despite its romantic damsel-in-distress flavor, this story is substantially borne out by other evidence. It is true that the heiress of the principality of Achaea and Morea was at this time Marie de Bourbon, daughter of Louis II of Bourbon and niece of the countess of Savoy. Marie had been married to Robert of Tarentum (of the Angevin house of Naples) in September 1347, and she had remained a widow since his death in 1364. She was struggling to maintain the rights of her young son, Hugues of Galilee, against the pretensions of Philip of Tarentum, who had already assumed her late husband's titles and had refused to honor her claims.[30]

By early 1366, Princess Marie and her son had recruited an army of considerable size from mercenary companies in Cyprus and Provence, and, relying upon the loyalty of many officers of the Morea, she had begun to try to establish her authority there. The archbishop of Patras, Angelo Acciajuoli, had declared for Philip of Tarentum, and the incident to which the Savoyard chroniclers refer was an episode in the war then raging between them. The expense records of the count's expedition refer to a gratuity from the count to Guillaume de Talay, who was at the time castellan of the important fortress of Junke (or Zonklon) in the bay then known as the "Port de Junch" or "Junke," now known as Navarino Bay, a few miles north of Modon.[31] This

---

[30] Hugues of Galilee was the issue of her previous marriage with Gui de Lusignan, eldest son of King Hugues IV of Cyprus, whom he had predeceased. Marie also disputed Pierre de Lusignan's claim to Cyprus on her son's behalf. Cf. R. Rodd, *The Princes of Achaia and the Chronicles of Morea* (London, 1907), II, 192, 204, 209ff.

[31] *Ibid.*, (Appendix I), 293–294. The count's presence is revealed in Bollati, item 150: "libravit . . . mariqueriis galee domini, quos dominus eis donavit quia gentes armata domini posuerant in terra ante castrum de Jonc"; item 222 mentions "exercitu domini ante castrum de Jonc." Item 115: "libravit [at Coron, 21 July] . . . Guillelmo de Taley, capitaneo castri de Jonc, ex dono sibi facto per dominum." Bollati erroneously transcribes the name as "Jout" throughout, which explains why he was unable to locate it. Atiya, p. 387, says Acciajuoli was archbishop of Neopatras and that the quarrel with Marie de Bourbon was over "possessions at Zuchio and the castle of Manolada."

is undoubtedly the place called "Jungs" in the Savoyard chronicles, since it was a common stopping place for sea travelers bound for the East.

It is also well established that Guillaume de Talay, faithful to the widow of Robert of Tarentum, had declared for Marie and had seized Simone del Poggio, the *bailli* of her rival, sometime in 1365–1366 during a parley. Talay had declared the man a rebel to Marie de Bourbon and had imprisoned him in the dungeons of Junke. This act had precipitated the outbreak of hostilities between partisans on either side. In July 1366 the forces of Philip's chief supporter, the archbishop of Patras, had succeeded in driving the princess and her son out of Achaea and had forced them to take refuge at Junke, where a siege had begun. Amadeus did answer Marie's call for help and offer his services as arbiter, but the results of his mediation were somewhat different from those reported by the Savoyard chroniclers. Marie and her son were induced to renounce all claims to Patras and territories subject to Angelo Acciajuoli, who was practically an independent sovereign at Corinth. In return the archbishop agreed to withdraw his forces from the Morea, pay an indemnity, and leave Marie and her son in peaceful possession of the southern part of the peninsula.[32]

Having rescued Marie and "defended Christianity," the Green Count could return to Coron and await the arrival of the fleet from Genoa. It was there by 27 July, and the eastward voyage was resumed. A day later the crusaders reached the small island of St-George of Albora at the entrance to the gulf of Aegina, where the count insisted upon stopping long enough for alms and prayers. On 2 August the fleet arrived at Negropont (ancient Chalcis) on the island of Euboea, now under Venetian rule, where an excellent harbor faced the mainland across the straits of Evripos. This would be the last stop before the crusaders encountered Turkish-held territories, so preparations for the coming campaign were completed.[33] Amadeus was probably hoping

[32] Rodd, pp. 210–211. Bollati, item 118, for 21 July at Coron, mentions a gratuity of two florins given by the count to Perrino, "fatuo domini Hugonis de Lusignian," which would seem additional proof that Amadeus was in contact with Marie and her son.

[33] The count seems to have been having some trouble keeping his turbulent crusaders under control. At Coron he had to pay both Micheleto Fosco and

for some word from the king of Hungary, who may have been expected to join him in Greece. Their combined forces would then begin the great military offensive to sweep the infidel from the continent of Europe.

The Savoyards awaited the arrival of their ally in vain. Louis had planned to lead an army against the Turks in conjunction with the count of Savoy, as had been carefully outlined in his correspondence with Urban V over preceding months. But the condition imposed by the pope upon the Greek emperor for military aid was that John promise to abjure the schism and to bring the Orthodox Church back to the Roman fold. By May 1366 no sufficient indication had yet been received at Avignon that the emperor was sincerely willing to accept this condition. Meanwhile, Louis of Hungary had many other uses for his army than to waste its time and his money awaiting favorable action from Constantinople or further word from the pope. During the spring of 1366 the king had opened a full-scale offensive against the Bulgarians, who were accused of having refused to pay the customary tribute and perform homage.

In reality this campaign was but thinly disguised aggression on the part of the warlike king of Hungary. The previous year, 1365, the Bulgarian Tsar Alexander had died, leaving his dominions divided among his three sons. To the eldest, John Sišman, went central and southern Bulgaria, stretching from the Danube to the Rhodope Mountains, with his capital at Tirnovo; to the second son, Stracimir, went western Bulgaria, of which the capital was Vidin; and the youngest son, Dobrotich, inherited the Dobrudja, bordering the Black Sea. This sudden weakening of the Bulgarian kingdom seemed to offer unhoped-for opportunities to the king of Hungary, who had long competed with his Bulgarian neighbors for control of western Macedonia and the valley of the Vardar.[34] Moreover, Stracimir was far from satisfied

---

Johannino Amoyrons for damage done to their vineyards by his men, and twenty-five florins to the Franciscans "tam ex dono . . . quam pro emenda quorundam dampnorum factorum in domo ipsorum in qua Dominus fuerat hospitatus" (Bollati, item 112). Cf. also Bollati, items 108 and 114. The count may have obtained two more galleys also: libravit . . . cuidam valleto qui per terram iverat oviam duabus galeis Domini que venire debebant" (item 133).

[34] Cf. H. A. Gibbons, *The Foundations of The Ottoman Empire 1300-1403* (Oxford, 1916), pp. 140ff.

with his share of the paternal heritage and had offered to divide his elder brother's portion of the kingdom with Sultan Murad in return for Turkish aid in conquering it. The king of Hungary may have got wind of these negotiations, and his swift invasion was perhaps an attempt to prevent any further Turkish advance in the Balkans.

Louis moved against Stracimir in the spring of 1366. The campaign lasted only a few weeks and ended with the defeat and capture of the Bulgarian prince, the seizure of Vidin, and the annexation of the principality. Louis at once announced that his principal motive for the attack had been the cause of the True Faith, and Stracimir's dominions were inundated by Franciscan missionaries charged with the task of converting the Bulgarians to the proper form of Christianity—Roman Catholicism.

Louis' involvement with the Bulgarians, however, meant that he was hardly in a position to move against the Turks as planned; and the count of Savoy found neither the king nor Hungarian troops awaiting him in Greece. Moreover, other serious developments had occurred since Amadeus' departure from Venice. John V, in despair over the advancing Turkish tide, had decided upon the final humiliation of going in person as a suppliant to Louis' court at Buda on the Danube. The emperor seems to have hoped that a dramatic personal appeal to the famous warrior king of Hungary might induce him to come to the assistance of the Empire before it was too late. Pope Urban, however, had been informed in advance of this plan, for on 22 June 1366 he wrote to the king expressing his surprise that Louis should contemplate assistance to a schismatic and a heretic, and warning him not to provide military aid to the emperor until he had proven his determination to convert to Roman Catholicism. This letter, added to Louis' growing appetite for Bulgarian provinces, had the desired effect: John's appeal was made in vain.

The worst was yet to come for the emperor. Having left Louis at Vidin, he was obliged to cross the territories of Sišman in order to regain his own dominions, but the Bulgarian tsar prevented his passage.[35] The failure of John's eldest son Andronicus to

[35] It is often stated that John was imprisoned by the Bulgarians, but there is no real proof of this. The count's expense records simply refer to efforts "pro expedicione domini Imperatoris Costantinopolis qui reverti non poterat propter impedimentum quod sibi faciebat Imperator Burgarie." Bollati, item III.

make conspicuous efforts to secure his father's safe return has given rise to the suspicion that Andronicus may have betrayed John to the tsar, whose daughter he had married.[36] The Green Count had probably learned of his cousin's misfortune by the time he reached Negropont.[37] He was now obliged to adjust his plans to the exigencies of war with the Bulgarians as well as the Turks.

With the depressing news that Louis of Hungary was not coming to his aid and that the emperor was practically a prisoner came more exact information on the strength and whereabouts of the Turks. This news may not have been much more encouraging than the rest. The great city of Gallipoli on the northern shore of the Dardanelles had for centuries commanded the passage of the straits into the Sea of Marmora. In the sixth century Emperor Justinian had undertaken important reparations of the ancient citadel there and had utilized it as a major depot for military supplies and as a troop base for the Persian campaigns. At the time of the Fourth Crusade (1202–1204), the fortress city of Gallipoli had fallen to the Venetians as their share of the spoils. From Venetian control it had passed to the Genoese in the course of a disastrous civil war among claimants to the Byzantine throne, and in 1354 it had fallen to the Ottoman Turks under Suleiman, a younger son of Sultan Orkhan I. Suleiman had been invited across the straits by John Cantacuzenus, rival of the Dowager Empress Anne de Savoie, then acting as regent for her son John V. The Turks had captured Gallipoli in the name of their ally John Cantacuzenus, but they were not ready to surrender to any ally so valuable a foothold on the European continent. The sons of the Prophet already ruled Asia Minor, and the internal strife in the remainder of the shrunken Byzantine Empire made it a tempting prize.

Thus 1354 was the initial date for the systematic movement of

---

[36] Gibbons, pp. 128–129; Ostrogorsky, pp. 479–480. It has too often been affirmed that Amadeus undertook the crusade of 1366–1367 in order to liberate his imprisoned imperial cousin. But John could not have encountered his "impedimentum" earlier than July 1366, by which time Amadeus was already under sail. Datta saw this, but others using his account, e.g. Jorga, p. 335, did not.

[37] Bollati, item 128, reveals a payment on 15 August at Negropont to a "truchimando domine Imperatrice Grecorum," suggesting contact with Constantinople by then at least.

the Turks across the Dardanelles and into the Balkans: first Gallipoli, then the thin peninsula forming the northern shore of the straits, and finally the mainland of Thrace to the banks of the Maritsa. In 1359 the Ottoman armies were seen for the first time under the walls of the imperial city of Constantinople. Its inhabitants were terrified and exhausted, but the great city still presented a sufficiently formidable exterior to discourage a serious attempt against it. The Turks moved instead against the hinterland. In 1361, Didymotichus on the Maritsa fell into the hands of Orkhan, and the next year Adrianople, capital of Thrace, was captured. Sultan Orkhan died in 1362, but his successor Murad I proved to be an even greater general than his father had been. In 1363 one of his generals, Lala Šahin, overran Macedonia and took possession of Philippopolis, which thereafter became the Ottoman capital for the province of Rumelia. As if to dramatize the fact that the Turks were in Europe to stay, Sultan Murad moved his court from Brusa in Asia Minor to Didymotichus, and then (probably in 1365) to Adrianople. This was the situation facing the count of Savoy on his arrival in Aegean waters in August 1366. The Savoyard chroniclers portray him as optimistic, despite the recent disappointments. Gaspard de Montmayeur was sent to the environs of Gallipoli, probably to reconnoiter, and his report must have convinced the count that operations could be carried through even without support from his Hungarian allies.

In the count's entourage precautions were taken against illness and contamination of food and water. A supply of water was bought at Negropont, and the Savoyards baked many of their own biscuit rations. The count's physician bought four "saculi pro stomaco," which may have been intended as some sort of internal disinfectant.[38] New banners bearing the image of the Virgin were made, and when everything was ready, the Savoyard fleet set sail once more. The chroniclers assert that it encountered the patriarch of Constantinople and Byzantine troops as it approached the Dardanelles. There is no verification of this in the expense records, but it does appear that the fleet was strengthened by the arrival of galleys from Francesco Gattilusio, a famous Genoese

---

[38] This is Bollati's suggestion, p. 47, note 1. Cf. items 130, 222, 265, 270.

corsair whose assistance to John V during the civil wars of the 1350's had won him the hand of the emperor's sister and the island of Lesbos.[39]

The army arrived before the walls of Gallipoli on 22 August, and an attack was launched. The results are clear enough, but the reasons for them are not. The chroniclers report that in the middle of the night the Turks decamped, and the following morning the Savoyards found the gates thrown wide by the inhabitants, who received them as deliverers.[40] Why the Turks should abandon so strategic a location after so short a resistance remains a mystery.[41] The fact itself cannot be doubted, however, for by 26 August, four days after the arrival at Gallipoli, both the town and the fortress were in Savoyard hands. It was the Green Count's first and most famous victory against the heathen Turks. On 27 August a messenger was sent westward with tidings of victory for the Savoyards at home, while Giacomo di Luserna was named commandant of the city. The citadel was entrusted to Aimone Michaele, who was no doubt enjoined to guard this gateway to the Dardanelles more stubbornly than his predecessors had done.[42]

After providing for the security of Gallipoli, the count reassembled the army and in early September set sail across the Sea of Marmora. A terrible storm mentioned in the chronicles (and confirmed by the expense records) impeded their passage for some time, but at last they arrived before the walls of the ancient city of Constantine, which still had a very imposing exterior. Approaching the city from the Dardanelles would have

---

[39] Cognasso, *Il Conte Verde*, p. 166; Ostrogorsky, p. 473.

[40] Servion, II, 139; Bollati, item 161.

[41] Gibbons, p. 128, and Atiya, p. 388, think that the episode shows what could be accomplished by a resolute body of fighters against the supposedly formidable Ottoman Turks. The garrison may have been undermanned and simply taken by surprise, having had no reason to suspect attack from this quarter. The Savoyard army could not have exceeded 3,000 or 4,000 men at the most, but historians since the Middle Ages have tended to exaggerate the numerical strength of the Turks.

[42] Datta, *Spedizione*, documenti, pp. 187–188, 196–201, 204. To garrison the place Amadeus detached the eighty-eight *brigandi* lent him by Galeazzo, forty-three archers and men-at-arms, and a select group of Savoyard nobles whom the count considered more trustworthy than the mercenaries. Michaele was in command of Gallipoli from 23 August 1366 to 13 June 1367.

taken them past a series of walled harbors beneath the towers of the capital itself, with the vast dome of Santa Sophia rising against the horizon. The fleet rounded the point facing the Bosphorus and sailed into the celebrated Golden Horn, with Galata on the right shore and the ramparts of the imperial city on the left. The crusaders docked at the Genoese port of Pera, across the narrow harbor from the Blachernae Palace and gate on the northernmost angle of the city walls. While many of his nobles were lodged in the "borgo de Veneciis" (the Venetian colony in Galata), the count himself was apparently offered a house in Constantinople, which he at once provided with furniture and utensils.[43] The records show that by 4 September the fleet had arrived, for on that date the count made his first visit to the city and paid the three months' wages of Paulo, his interpreter.[44]

### THE BULGARIAN CAMPAIGN, 1366–1367

Constantinople, once the proud city of caesars and mistress of the Mediterranean, was now but a shadow of her former greatness. The mighty land walls built by Theodosius II at the base of the peninsula, stretching from the Golden Horn on the north to the Sea of Marmora on the south, were some five miles in length, and it was perhaps that far from the land walls to Santa Sophia on the point of the peninsula. By Savoyard standards this battlemented enclosure was unbelievably vast. It had been designed to protect the nearly one million inhabitants of which the city had boasted in its centuries of glory; and the great structure remained, although the population now could not have exceeded 100,000. The Black Death which had struck Europe so cruelly between 1348 and 1352 had done its lethal work even earlier in Constantinople.

Long wars and successive losses of territory at the hands of both westerners and orientals had reduced the revenues of the Byzantine state to such a point that the Green Count's imperial cousins were now hardly the equals of his Visconti in-laws in wealth and splendor. While the customs revenues of Constan-

---

[43] Bollati, items 270, 271. Amadeus bought tables, cabinets, doors, and roasting spits for the kitchen; material for making beds and a cupboard (*dreczorio*); and a new lock and key for the "first door of the tower." Cf. items 222, 239.

[44] Datta, *Spedizione*, doc. XVII, p. 188.

tinople brought some 30,000 *hyperpera* annually into the imperial treasury, the Italian customs officers across the harbor at Pera and Galata collected some 200,000 *hyperpera* each year.[45] Moreover, much commerce which had once passed between Europe and Asia by way of the Golden Horn was now diverted by Italian maritime powers, who made direct contact with the Muslims of Syria and Egypt and carried goods brought from the East straight to Italy. Empress Anne de Savoie, at the outset of the civil wars some forty years earlier, had been obliged to pawn the crown jewels at Venice to raise a loan of 30,000 ducats with which to maintain her position and the rights of her son. At the imperial coronation of 1347, the chronicler Nicephoras Gregoras noted the unhappy fact that the jewels in the splendid imperial crowns were only colored glass; the robes only tinseled, not cloth-of-gold as in former times; the rich brocades only painted leather; the goblets at the coronation banquet no longer gold and silver and crystal, but only lead or earthenware.[46]

The imperial family lived principally in the Blachernae Palace across the harbor from Pera, and shortly after his arrival, the Green Count went to confer with the empress, Helena Cantacuzenus. In the absence of Louis of Hungary and of a Byzantine army, the Savoyards had no choice but to postpone any campaign against the Turks until after "Black John" was safely back in his capital.[47] Accordingly, two Savoyard nobles were sent to the "emperor at Vidin" to open negotiations.[48] Their mission was delayed at least a week by bad weather which prevented their sailing against the current of the Bosphorus into the Black Sea. The empress contributed 12,000 *perperi* to assist in the equipping of a full-scale military expedition against the Bulgarians, should

[45] Ostrogorsky, p. 469.

[46] George Young, *Constantinople* (London and New York, 1926), p. 111; Ostrogorsky, pp. 469–470.

[47] Young, pp. 112–113, says this was a popular nickname for John V Paleologus. For his meeting with the empress, Amadeus had ordered a full-length mantle of heavy green silk with the scarlet and white arms of Savoy covering the back. He also had two silk surcoats made and two green mantles lined with four hundred squirrel skins for himself and Guillaume de Grandson. Bollati, items 207, 208, 273.

[48] *Ibid.*, doc. XXVI. This item suggests that John had returned to Vidin when he found his return passage blocked by the Bulgarians, and it tends to confirm the view that John was not captured, but simply blockaded.

this prove necessary. She and the Genoese each agreed to furnish the count with two armed galleys, and a fifth galley was offered by Domenico Veyroli of Pera.[49]

In the meantime, the count had unhappy obligations to discharge. The capture of Gallipoli had not been without casualties for the Savoyards. Several of the count's companions had fallen in the assault on the walls. Simon of Saint-Amour and Roland de Veissy, both knights of the Collar, had been killed, along with a Savoyard, Girard Mareschal, and a Vaudois, Jean d'Yverdon. The Green Count had them transported to Pera and undertook to have them honorably buried. On 12 September, Antoine Barbier, the count's bursar, paid for eighteen escutcheons bearing the "devisa collarium," the insignia of the Collar, for the funeral of Veissy and Saint-Amour, while eighty-one wax torches and generous alms were provided for the burial of the others.[50]

If the Savoyard embassy brought a reply back to Constantinople from Vidin, it must have been an appeal for armed intervention, for the count now decided upon a campaign against the Bulgarians, Christians or not. The most vulnerable part of the Bulgarian kingdom was the Dobrudja, Prince Dobrotich's share of the paternal inheritance, which bordered the Black Sea. With large Turkish forces located in eastern Thrace, the safest procedure for an attack on the Dobrudja was to move up the coast by sea. On 4 October when the southerly winds over the Black Sea had abated sufficiently to permit the passage of a fleet northward through the Bosphorus, the Savoyards set forth once more, reinforced with a large new banner of the Virgin. Gaspard de Montmayeur and a fairly strong company were left behind to guard Constantinople.

By 6 October the fleet had negotiated the dangerous currents and rocks of the Bosphorus and had reached the port of "Lorfenal" on the Black Sea. A few days later the crusaders reached Sozopolis at the entrance to the Gulf of Burgas. What happened next is not entirely clear. The absence in the sources of any

[49] *Ibid.*, doc XXXIX. The perperi of Pera (or Constantinople) were exchanged at the rate of two for one gold ducat. Cf. account totals, Bollati, p. 25.

[50] Bollati, item 202. Atiya, p. 389, says that at this point Amadeus received an envoy from the king of Cyprus asking him to join his army for an attack on Egypt, but the count refused on the grounds that his first duty was to secure his cousin's release.

indication that a battle took place led Datta to suppose that the city was at that time in the hands of the Byzantines, but more recent authorities show that it was then under Bulgarian domination.[51] Sozopolis either surrendered without a fight or the Savoyards elected not to attack it at this time, but merely stopped there briefly before moving on.[52] In any case, within four days of their arrival at Sozopolis, they crossed the Gulf of Burgas and attacked Mesembria. Here a battle did take place, probably on 20 October, and both the town and the citadel were captured. The chronicles relate that it was a hard-fought contest and that when the city was taken at last, it was turned over to the Savoyard soldiery to be pillaged, while its inhabitants were "put to the sword . . . for the reason that they had killed so many of the Christians in the assault and there were many knights and squires wounded."[53] Around the same time, the important city of Anchialus was also attacked and captured, strengthening the Savoyard position at Mesembria and guarding the mouth of the Gulf of Burgas.[54]

So far all had gone well, but with winter coming on, the count was not disposed to lose any time. By 25 October the army had sailed farther northward along the coast with the objective of seizing Varna, capital of eastern Bulgaria and headquarters of Prince Dobrotich. Varna was a formidable obstacle, however, and its inhabitants were determined to defend it. "Trefforte, bien muree, & grandement garnie," Varna could not be taken by assault, so the army settled down to a siege. An inspection of the enemy's fortifications convinced the older heads of the count's council of war that this was the wisest course of action, but Jean de Vienne and Guillaume de Grandson were sent to "parlamenter" with the citizens in the hope of persuading them to yield without a fight. They refused, but agreed to send an embassy to Tsar Sišman to beg him to permit the Byzantine emperor's re-

---

[51] Datta, *Spedizione*, p. 124; Gibbons, p. 129; Ostrogorsky, p. 480.

[52] The expense records do not actually prove that the count was in the city in October. He was "apud Tisopuli" on October 17, 18, and 19, but this could have been his camp outside the walls. He is not clearly in possession of the city before January 1367. Bollati, items 280–286. Gibbons, p. 129, says he captured Burgas, but the documents do not confirm this.

[53] Servion, II, 143–144.

[54] Anchialus is called "Lassillo" in the accounts. Atiya, p. 391, says that Manchopolis and Scafida were also seized by the Savoyards at this time.

turn to his capital and to remind him of their plight should he refuse. In the meantime, the citizens agreed that if the count would refrain from hostilities until the return of the ambassadors, they would furnish his army with supplies. On 30 October, Amadeus sent an embassy headed by Paulus, the Latin patriarch of Constantinople, to Tirnovo, Sišman's capital, and over succeeding weeks a number of messengers were exchanged.[55]

The count was willing enough to observe the truce with the men of Varna, but his own men were restless for a fight. To remind the Bulgarians that he was not to be trifled with and to strengthen his position, he led his warriors against the town of Lemona, some thirty miles south of Varna on the coast. Both the town and its fortress were captured without serious difficulty, and 1,100 gold *perperi* were extracted from the unfortunate inhabitants, who rose in rebellion, only to be crushed a second time. The senior Antoine de Savoie was put in command of the garrison.[56]

Apart from this adventure, there was nothing to do but await the return of the ambassadors and fill up the long hours as well as could be done. The count was fond of playing at dice, and gambling games helped to pass the time.[57] For physical fitness, mock battles were held; jousts, "ludendo cum armis," were other attempts to keep the warriors usefully occupied. If the Savoyard chronicles are to be believed, however, such sports did not suffice. Several "iouvenes gens" who had not participated in the capture of Lemona were extremely "mal contens," and decided to find another castle for themselves. Having chosen the fortress of "Calocastre," a small town not far from Varna, as their objective, they boarded a galley by night, collected some scaling ladders, approached the fortress about midnight, and quietly climbed over the walls.[58] Five knights and ten squires succeeded in getting inside the walls, but the noise of the ladders attracted the atten-

[55] Bollati, item 388. Other members of the embassy were the sire of Fromentes, Albrecht of Bohemia, Guiot Ferlay, and Gabriel Biblia.

[56] *Ibid.*, items 358 and XII. The town is called Limona in the accounts and Lymeur in the chronicles. Atiya, p. 392, note 2, thinks it must have been captured before the army had moved on to Varna, owing to the distance between the two.

[57] Bollati, items 302, 303, 304, 317, 318.

[58] Servion, II, 146–147.

tion of one of the guards and he gave the alarm. The castle garrison was at once awakened, fell upon the Savoyards "so cruelly" that all were killed and "sliced up into pieces," and the scaling ladders thrown down from the walls. When the rest of the group outside the walls saw what had happened, they were "so angry and ashamed" that they hardly dared to show themselves before their master the next day.

The Green Count learned of their misadventure and gave them to understand that he disapproved. "Comrades," he declared, "they say that in games of war and of love, for one joy there are a hundred sorrows." Having edified them with this timely aphorism, he then granted them the satisfaction of avenging their slain comrades. Gathering together a "belle compaignie," he launched a full-scale attack upon the fortress of Calocastre, which was taken by assault and all of its inhabitants "sliced up into pieces," the same fate that had befallen his men.[59]

October passed into November. The count dispatched a Greek messenger to Prince Dobrotich and on 10 November received a messenger with news of the emperor and the tsar.[60] The embassy which the count had sent to Tirnovo on 30 October also returned on 10 November, and Amadeus sent the patriarch of Constantinople and two others back to the tsar with new instructions. Sometime during the month of November one of the count's men, Gui de Pontailler, marshal of Burgundy, and two of his followers were captured by the enemy at "Galataz" near Varna and were imprisoned and held for ransom near "Provat."[61] The failure of the Savoyards to take Varna had already weakened their position, and this mishap weakened it further. Tsar Sišman may have told the count's envoys that his raising of the siege of Varna and withdrawal to Mesembria would be the *sine qua non* for the return of the emperor. The count sent Fromentes to "Provat" to see what could be done about Pontailler and his men, then raised the siege and withdrew to Mesembria, leaving only a garrison at Lemona.[62]

[59] This story is not confirmed by items in the accounts, but the event may well have occurred.

[60] Bollati, items 326, 327.

[61] *Ibid.*, items 395, 503. Provat could be Provadiya, about twenty miles upstream from Varna. Galataz is identified only as "versus Varnam."

[62] *Ibid.*, item 395.

The Savoyards were in winter quarters at Mesembria by 18 November, but they seemed no nearer than before to their objective of securing the return of John V.[63] There was a continuous stream of messengers between Mesembria and Varna, Tirnovo, Constantinople, Pera, and Cape Kaliakra, where Prince Dobrotich was apparently staying.[64] The count's position at Mesembria was far stronger than it had been at Varna, for he held both Anchialus to the west and Lemona to the east. It now remained to prepare for the coming winter. Carpenters and masons were hired to provide the count's quarters with furniture and a small fireplace, and Amadeus soon had occasion to make use of the tunic lined with deerhide and wolf fur which he had purchased in Constantinople.[65] And all the while, funds were getting shorter—100 florins here, 500 there, over 9,000 gold *perperi* to Domenico Veyroli for the Genoese galleys from Pera, and 1,400 *perperi* for those from Marseilles.[66] The mercenary companies had to be paid as well, and so did the garrisons thrown into the occupied towns and fortresses.

There was nothing to do but try to wring more money out of the conquered population. Considerable quantities of salt, money, wax, *ferramente*, and spoiled wine were found in the fortress of Mesembria, and these were sold, along with more than 800 *quarta* of millet and 16 of rye found in the storage bins.[67] Then a tax was levied on the community. The citizens were extremely reluctant to pay, and several had to be imprisoned in the process; but the resulting 17,000 *perperi* were well worth the effort.[68] Two of the count's experienced administrators, Etienne Mareschal of Pont-de-Veyle and François de Montgelat, were ordered to enquire into the rights and privileges to which the count, as the new lord of Mesembria, was entitled. The Jews of the city were taxed,

[63] These dates are made clear in item 345. Datta wrongly dated the raising of the siege as 21 December and the arrival in Mesembria on the 26th.

[64] Bollati, item 360. Kaliakra is given as "Calliatra" in the text.

[65] *Ibid.*, item 273: "pro forratura unius tunice domini pellium cervorum, forrata de pellibus vulpium."

[66] *Ibid.*, items 354, 355, 356, 384.

[67] *Ibid.*, items VIII, IX.

[68] *Ibid.*, items 370 and XIII. The exact amount was 17,568 *perperi* "ponderis Mesembrie." The perperi of Mesembria or "Romanie" was exchanged at the rate of seventeen *perperi* for eight gold florins *boni ponderis*. Cf. *Recepta* totals, Bollati, p. 25.

one citizen paid to prevent his house in Mesembria from being destroyed, a widow was fined for hiding items belonging to her late husband which "pertain to the Lord Count."[69] Both grain and money were exacted with ruthless thoroughness from every possible source. Already at Varna the count had been obliged to borrow 200 florins from one of his Valdostan nobles, and he now received 500 more as a loan from his physician, Gui Albin.[70] With Christmas coming on, Amadeus distributed another round of alms to the religious establishments in the area and passed the time practicing at the crossbow with Richard Musard. For good measure, he had a pair of hooded jackets in green and a pair of mailed gloves made for himself and Guillaume de Grandson.[71]

In December came the news that Antonio Visconti, nephew of Bernabò, had been seized and imprisoned in the castle of Aitos a few miles up the Tundzha river from Burgas. The Green Count spent the day before Christmas having appropriate letters written up in Greek so that John of Constantinople, another of his interpreters, could set out at once to seek terms for Visconti's release.[72] Two days earlier the ambassadors to Tirnovo had returned with somewhat cheering news: Sišman had apparently decided to permit the emperor to cross his dominions to Kaliakra, north of Varna. The count immediately sent his squire Treverneys and two crossbowmen to Kaliakra to await the emperor's arrival.[73]

In the meantime, icy winds off the Ukraine and Tartary crossed the Black Sea and chilled the bones of the uneasy crusaders at Mesembria. The count had coal stoves installed in several rooms of the seigneurial palace of the city and no doubt drew his wolf-fur cloak more closely about him. At Anchialus a tax was levied, and, as at Mesembria, some of the inhabitants had to be locked up in a local church until they were ready to pay.[74] They finally did pay 2,700 *perperi*, and Girard de Grammont, who was re-

[69] Bollati, items XXIV, XXV, XXVIII.

[70] *Ibid.*, items XXXVIII, XXXIX.

[71] *Ibid.*, items 69, 370, 372.

[72] *Ibid.*, item 386. Aitos is given as "castrum Aquile."

[73] *Ibid.*, items 387, 392. Why the emperor should take this route is not clear. Perhaps Sišman was allowing Dobrotich to escort him back so as to ensure the surrender of places still held by the Savoyards in the vicinity of Varna.

[74] *Ibid.*, items 405, XXIII.

lieved as captain of Anchialus by Pierre Vibod, brought the money up to Mesembria by boat on Christmas night, which may have cheered the count a little, if it did not cheer his men.

A few musicians from the court of Constantinople were present to make cheerful sounds, but it could not have been a very contented army that saw the New Year come in with the bitter winds across the *Mare Maior* that winter of 1366–1367. The weather was hostile and so was the population, the latter increasingly so as the count's financial needs required additional contributions. Far more ominous of things to come, however, were indications that pestilence had broken out in the army. Gui Albin had to purchase several medicines at Mesembria "for several sick men among the count's followers," and on 29 December one of the nobles, Baudicat, was buried.[75] Young Antoine de Savoie, the count's fourteen-year-old son, fell sick also, and Antelme d'Urtières contracted an illness that disabled him from Christmas until Easter.[76] Early in January, perhaps to get away from the contaminated area, the count decided to transfer his headquarters from Mesembria across the Gulf of Burgas to Sozopolis.[77]

This move may have been influenced also by the news that the emperor was coming at last, directly to Sozopolis rather than via Kaliakra and down the coast as had been anticipated. On 23 January 1367, Gaspard de Montmayeur came up from Constantinople, and five days later Black John himself arrived in the city, the blockade imposed by his Bulgarian neighbors breached at last. For the next three weeks, while the cousins were together at Sozopolis, Amadeus tried to get what he regarded as a fair monetary reward for the expenses he had incurred on John's behalf. The accounts say that the negotiations occupied eighteen days, which suggests difficulty in reaching agreement on what constituted appropriate compensation. If the count hoped to be richly rewarded for his efforts, he was to be sadly disappointed. John is commonly accused of perfidy and ingratitude on this score, but it might be recalled that he was practically penniless

---

[75] *Ibid.*, items 377, 407.

[76] *Ibid.*, items 605, 762.

[77] Probably on 9 January 1367, the date on which the secretary, Antoine Barbier, reimbursed the men who had transported the count's wardrobe. *Ibid.*, item 411.

himself and hemmed in on all sides by powerful foes who had already deprived him of most of the richest territories of his empire. His failure to fill the emptied Savoyard coffers doubtless owed more to his inability to do so than to his ingratitude.

The emperor and the count of Savoy remained at Sozopolis until about the middle of March. Amadeus had still not secured the release of Antonio Visconti or of Gui de Pontailler and his men, and he needed the emperor's help in these matters. The situation was not improved when it was learned, sometime in late January or early February, that the inhabitants of Lemona had rebelled and were holding prisoner one of the count's vassals who had been sent on a mission to the area.[78] Another problem was what to do with the cities and fortresses which the count had captured during the campaign. Amadeus was willing to turn them over to the emperor, but he refused to do so without compensation. John finally agreed to pay 15,000 florins to defray the cost of the galleys the count had hired for the Bulgarian expedition, and this was apparently considered satisfactory for the time being.[79]

The presence of the emperor at Sozopolis is attested as late as 15 March, but he probably left soon after for his capital. On that date Amadeus went back to Mesembria to make one more effort to secure the release of some of his men in Bulgarian prisons. Guillaume de Grandson was sent with a company of men-at-arms to the castle of Aitos, where Antonio Visconti was being held, and apparently managed to set him free.[80] Prince Dobrotich finally agreed to ransom Gui de Pontailler and his men, and the count furnished 2,400 *perperi* for this purpose.[81]

---

[78] Lemona had been left in the hands of a Savoyard garrison under Antoine senior, bastard of Savoy. The chronicles assert that the inhabitants put the Savoyards off guard by various acts of kindness, then led them into an ambush in which Antoine de Savoie was captured. Servion, II, 154; Cabaret, pp. 173ff. Antoine is supposed to have died later in a Bulgarian prison. This version cannot be confirmed fully, but Lemona was lost and Antoine de Savoie senior does disappear hereafter from the treasurer's accounts.

[79] Only about two-thirds of this sum was ever actually received. Cf. Bollati, items XL, XLI, XLVII, XLVIII, XLIX.

[80] If Bollati, p. 99, note 2, has correctly identified the man, then Antonio Visconti's release was secured later, if not on this occasion.

[81] *Ibid.*, item 503.

# Athleta Christi

By the end of March the expedition against the Bulgarians had accomplished its ends, and it was time to turn once more to the Turkish menace which had been the original objective of the crusade. The Savoyards turned over the fortresses and cities in their possession to Byzantine officers and set sail for the Bosphorus and Constantinople, where they arrived on 9 April. "When the emperor . . . and the barons of Greece knew of the arrival of the count at Constantinople, the emperor, in order to receive his cousin the count more highly and honorably, made ready the priests, colleges, and all orders of religion, gentlemen, citizens, merchants, people, women, and children, and [they all] went to the seaside to meet the count, crying 'Long live the count of Savoy, who has delivered Greece from the Turks and the Emperor, our lord, from the hands of the Emperor of Bulgaria!' "[82] The rejoicings naturally were such as to defy description.

No welcome, however warm, could obscure the magnitude of the problems awaiting the crusaders. The greater part of the count's resources had been consumed in securing the emperor's release, and except for the capture of Gallipoli, no action had been taken against the Turks at all. The Green Count's finances were utterly exhausted, and there seemed no possibility of adequate assistance from his equally impoverished imperial cousin.[83] The count's men were tired and dispirited, and the toll from disease was beginning to rise alarmingly. Several had been buried within a few weeks of the return to Constantinople, others were seriously ill, and the situation was likely to get worse before it got better.[84] The only assistance Amadeus ever received from the

---

[82] Servion, II, 148–149; Cabaret, pp. 171ff.

[83] Amadeus was never too poor to help those worse off than himself. The records abound in gifts, not just to churches and holy men, but to followers who fell sick, impoverished nobles, and certain "pauperibus Englicis" who had served him at Mesembria.

[84] Bollati, items 469, 492, 504, 505, 524. To help keep up the morale of his men, the count encouraged a few festive occasions. Young Antoine de Savoie presided over a sumptuous banquet for nobles of the army on the Feast of the Ascension (item 558), and the count organized races of some sort (*palii*) at Pentecost for which prizes were given to the winners (item 567). About the same time, a sailing regatta was held, probably in the Marmora, also with prizes to the most skillful mariners (item 593), and the court of the emperor apparently participated in the festivities (items 591, 592).

king of Hungary consisted of two squires who had served him "in partibus Burgarie," and without a Hungarian army, a campaign against the Turks was impossible. In mid-May the Savoyards did attack and capture the castle of Eneacossia (on the northern shore of the Marmora on the road to Constantinople), and one of the count's men was rewarded for conspicuous bravery in planting the banner of Savoy on the tower during the fight.[85] Somewhat later, a Savoyard expeditionary force set fire to the castle of "Caloneyro," presumably in the same region.[86] But despite these minor military accomplishments, the count decided that it would be folly to remain any longer. His thirst for glory and reputation did not extend to a taste for martyrdom, individual or collective, and neither the cause of the True Faith nor that of his imperial cousin would induce him to prolong the risk of both physical and financial ruin. Many of his mercenaries had contracted to serve with him for one year, and he had no money with which to hire them for a longer period. Through April and May he was almost wholly occupied with paying his most pressing debts to the shipowners and trying to raise funds for the return voyage.

The Green Count still had hopes of accomplishing something toward the reunion of eastern and western Christendom before he left. He was no fool and no fanatic, and it could not have taken him long to discover how deep-rooted was the opposition of the Greek clergy and laity alike to such a union. His willingness to substitute the possible for the ideal was perhaps already indicated when he established the Latin patriarch at Gallipoli with funds and men to maintain himself, rather than at Constantinople, of which he was the rightful head in papal eyes.[87] The Greek patriarch could not be expelled, however sincere Black John's professed willingness to abjure the schism, for neither the clergy nor the population of the city would countenance it.

For the Green Count it was probably now a matter of saving face. He had undertaken the expedition to the East to help in

---

[85] In May the count also apparently returned briefly to Sozopolis to protect that city from a Turkish attempt to capture it, according to the findings of M. Jean-Jacques Bouquet of Lausanne.

[86] *Ibid.*, items 515, 523.

[87] *Ibid.*, item 500. Amadeus later took the patriarch back to Italy with him.

expelling the Turks from Europe and Asia Minor, and to help in ending the schism in Christendom. Thus far he had only succeeded in restoring the emperor to his throne and in strengthening John's position rather modestly, more at the expense of the Christian Bulgarians than of the heathen Turks. But if the dream of a great crusade against the infidel had faded away, at least Amadeus was still strong enough to drive a hard bargain in the reunion question. At Constantinople he demanded that the emperor furnish financial compensation for services rendered, for he could not otherwise pay the expenses of the return trip; and if John did not wish to abandon any future chance of aid from the West, the count declared bluntly, he would have to abjure the schism. Promises would not suffice, for experience showed that they could not be trusted. Amadeus' plan was to combine the religious and financial debts in such a way as to make it more difficult for the emperor to avoid either. It is possible that the Savoyards did have to resort to some spirited sabre-rattling to win their points, even if they did not actually go to war with the Byzantines, as the chronicles affirm.[88]

The results were reasonably satisfactory under the circumstances. On 29 May, through the offices of Nicolao de Quarto and Francesco Nigrino, bankers of Pera, the emperor turned over to the count the sum of nearly 35,000 *perperi* in gold, of which 20,000 were to be considered a loan.[89] This loan the Green Count agreed to repay within one month of the arrival in Rome of either the emperor or his eldest son. There they were to renounce the schism in the presence of the pope himself and receive His Holiness's instructions as to the manner of carrying out the reunion. Black John agreed in addition to send an embassy back with the count to communicate to the pope in the count's presence the emperor's sincere intention of bringing his church into the Roman fold.

[88] Servion, II, 152–153, 155–156; Cabaret, pp. 173 *dorso* ff. Some of the count's men, more determined than he to fight infidels in the Holy Land, now left for Cyprus to join the crusading effort there. One "dominus de Marseillie" got his pay for this purpose, as did Alegret de la Palud, Archimand de Grolée, and Termon Argod de Morestel (all Dauphinois). Bollati, items 509, 535, 537, 540. All were given their wages and gifts of money, but the count was not about to join them.

[89] Bollati, item LXXIII. The exact amount was 34,862 *perperi boni ponderis*.

The 35,000 *perperi* meant that the Green Count could discharge many of his debts at Pera and Constantinople and establish sufficient credit to borrow the remainder needed for the homeward voyage.[90] During the first week of June at Pera, he borrowed some 28,000 *perperi* from Italian bankers, and dozen of vassals advanced lesser sums both prior to departure and during the return trip. At the same time, Amadeus made his final visits at Constantinople and Pera, giving small gifts of money to those who had served him during his stay, from mariners on the Golden Horn to porters, valets, minstrels, and "trumpets" of the emperor. His generosity was particularly directed toward those who had fallen ill and would have to be left behind, of which there was an ominously large number. Master Gui Albin busied himself with the purchase of additional *rebus medicinalibus* for the count and his household.[91]

The time to leave had come. Masses were provided for at the church of the Dominicans and pious offerings had been distributed to nearly every church and shrine in the city, in the hope of obtaining adequate heavenly protection. The bear which the count had obtained in Bulgaria was loaded on shipboard, and transportation was arranged for a camel, with which the count no doubt intended to stupefy his mountaineers at home.[92] At Mesembria, Amadeus had been given a white falcon, and now on his departure the emperor gave him several fine hawks. The Genoese community of Pera, of whom he had been so excellent a customer, presented him with four large vessels of wine and some precious drugs.[93] On 9 June 1367 the debarkation took place from the docks at Pera. As on his departure from Venice almost exactly one year before, the count's flagship was hung with green

[90] Bollati, items 526–532.

[91] Amadeus was apparently moved at the spectacle of children being bought and sold in the slave market of Constantinople. He bought two little girls for seventy-two *perperi*, and a tavern owner of Pera made him a present of a third. Amadeus had his tailor Aymonet purchase red cloth and make tunics for them, while he himself bought shoes, stockings, "chemises," and jackets for them. He took them home and gave them to his wife. *Ibid.*, items 494, 499, 511, 572, 713.

[92] *Ibid.*, item 919 (dated 10 September at Padua). Amadeus had sent the Bastard of Compeys back to Venice "pro recipiendo camelo," which was expected to arrive soon by ship.

[93] *Ibid.*, items 389, 587.

curtains and canopies, and from the masts flew new banners of red and white silk. Naturally, Amadeus himself wore a long green ermine-trimmed mantle for the occasion, and he was attended by Guillaume de Grandson and a company of valets arrayed in the same color.

The Byzantines may not for long have remembered the "Frank" from the West with robes and retainers in emerald green. They had seen too many armies come and go over the decades, they had witnessed so much strife and endured so many reversals at western hands. Yet there may well have been regret at the Savoyard departure, particularly at the imperial court. With all their shortcomings, these knights from the West still represented the last best hope of the sinking empire of the East. If the "crusade" of the Green Count is judged only by the standard of practical success, then it must be classed as a failure. Amadeus VI came to restore an empire, and he succeeded only in restoring an emperor. He came to battle heathen Turks, but he more often battled Christian Bulgarians, leaving them still less able to oppose the Turkish advance. John V did promise to bring about the submission of the Greek Church to the Church of Rome, but the reunion of eastern and western Christendom was also a lost cause, and Amadeus probably knew it. Yet despite his meager accomplishments, there remains an element of grandeur in the goals and great courage in the effort to realize them. That he came at all to champion such mighty dreams is perhaps a fairer measure of the man.

By 13 June the fleet had reached Gallipoli. On the following day the count paid the salaries of the garrison and turned the town and fortress over to the Byzantines. A week later the Savoyards arrived at Negropont, where a number of the count's men, including young Antoine de Savoie junior, left for Cyprus to join the army of Pierre de Lusignan.[94] There were also men too ill to continue the journey who had to be left behind. Unfortunately, this was only the beginning. For the rest of the trip the count was obliged to leave comrades in port after port as the pestilence spread relentlessly through the ranks. At Modon six more men had to be left behind because of illness: Hugonin de Viry,

[94] *Ibid.*, item 564 lists them all. Amadeus made sizeable cash gifts to all of them.

235

two sons of Varrucler de la Baume, another Chignin, Humbert de Thoire, and Jean, "Bastard of the Dauphiné." At Clarencia, Giacomo di Luserna, the count's captain of Gallipoli, died and was buried in the Franciscan monastery. By 10 July, when the fleet reached the island of Corfu, the infection was rampant among the Germans and the *brigandi*.[95]

On 14 July the fleet passed Durazzo and three days later landed at Ragusa. The count went at once to kiss the sacred relics of the Dominican monastery in gratitude for his own health thus far, and he left generous alms both there and with the Franciscans. Here also he encountered thirty mariners who were supposed to have been shipped East on one of the count's galleys and who had apparently got no further than Ragusa.[96] Now the dreaded plague struck closer to the count himself. His clerk and bursar, François de Montgelat, fell ill and had to be left, along with Richard Musard. The count gave them each 200 *perperi* before sailing on.[97]

Finally, on 29 July, the fleet sailed into the harbor of San Nicolo at Venice. The Green Count was warmly welcomed, for the news of his victories over Turks and Bulgarians had preceded him. He took up residence again in the Carrara palace, where he would remain for the next five weeks, making the rounds of churches to offer thanks for his survival, and trying to settle a seemingly endless number of debts. His funds proved insufficient again, and he had recourse to borrowing from wealthy Venetians.[98] Several more of his men died upon arrival, among them his physician, Gui Albin, and the count had to superintend and finance their burials.

At this point Filippo of Achaea appeared with the news that Prince Giacomo had died in May. Marguerite de Beaujeu, as guardian for her two small sons, Amadeo and Ludovico, had at

---

[95] Clarencia was a small town on the western coast of the Morea, opposite the island of Zákinthos. Amadeus also gave thirty-seven Venetian *solidi* "to a certain poor woman lying in childbirth" at Clarencia. *Ibid.*, item 662.

[96] The count chose to pay them anyway, over 200 *livres* Venetian. *Ibid.*, item 671.

[97] *Ibid.*, items 670–677. Musard later recovered and rejoined the count before he left Venice in early September.

[98] Amadeus received a total of 8,872 ducats from Bartholomeo Michaelis (items LXXXXV and LXXXXVI) and 10,346 from Federigo Cornaro (item LXXXXVII).

once disputed Filippo's claims as Giacomo's firstborn son and heir universal. Bonne de Bourbon had barely managed to keep the peace between them thus far, and Filippo had come to Venice to be sure that his rival did not reach the count before him. Amadeus had foreseen this development in Piedmont affairs when he had engineered the marriage of Marguerite de Beaujeu and Giacomo of Achaea five years earlier, but he was hardly prepared at this moment for the sudden confrontation with his angry cousin. To gain time he put Filippo off with fair words, but postponed action until after he had disposed of his remaining crusade obligations.

The latter required a journey to Rome to present the ambassadors from John V to the pope, but money was needed to finance the trip. Amadeus wrote to Savoy to instruct the countess to send the treasurer-general to Pavia with all the funds that could be spared, and the count set out from Venice to meet him after one last flurry of debt paying.[99] The Green Count's progress across Lombardy in mid-September was a veritable triumph. At Padua the Carrara presented him with two splendid warhorses, and a few days later at Ferrara he received two more and was treated to a sumptuous feast in his honor. The Gonzagas of Mantua also sent minstrels with gifts and their compliments, and at Cremona a squire from Bernabò Visconti offered his master's congratulations and "a great dog."

Being at Pavia, where the count arrived on 18 September, was almost as good as being home. While Amadeus awaited the arrival of his baggage by water from Venice, he was able to relax and enjoy the magnificent hospitality of his sister and brother-in-law. Galeazzo insisted that he reside with them in the castle, and board and room was provided within the palace enclosure for seventy-six members of the count's retinue at Galeazzo's expense. Amadeus was given two more hunting dogs, which he sent off to Savoy along with "a certain bird called a papaguey" (a parrot), a gift from the East for his wife. Most important, however, was the arrival of Boniface de la Motte and Pierre Gerbais with cash from Savoy, and another round of debt pay-

---

[99] Between 23 and 26 August, Amadeus visited Treviso (Bollati, items 787–793). What motivated the trip is not indicated, but it was a festive affair with minstrels, trumpeters, and gifts.

ing took place. The total cost of the crusade was just above 225,000 florins *boni ponderis*.[100]

The count had scarcely a week of relaxation at Pavia before he was on the road again, this time heading for Rome. Everywhere he was received with conspicuous honor and popular acclaim as a hero of Christendom, which was sweet reward for the expenses and hardships of the expedition.[101] Always one to dress for a new role, he had a miniver-trimmed mantle "in the style of Tartary" made for him at Pisa.[102] At Viterbo the count, presumably no longer dressed *ad modum tartariscum,* encountered Urban V and presented the ambassadors from the Byzantine emperor, who relayed their master's promises to bring the Eastern Church back into the bosom of the Church of Rome. "The Holy Father and the cardinals, hearing the submission of the emperor of Greece, were marvelously joyful and commanded that he should be received kindly when he came and should be placed among the catholic kings, true sons of the Holy Church."[103] If suspicions lingered concerning John's true intentions, none remained concerning the accomplishments of the count of Savoy, who was the hero of the moment.

The Green Count was in attendance upon the pope when he made his solemn entry into the Eternal City on 12 October 1367. Amadeus remained in Rome for about two weeks, then, his mission accomplished, headed back for Savoy. He was received at Perugia by fourteen minstrels and an enthusiastic citizenry, who made him a present of wax and spices in sufficient quantity to require an extra mule to carry them. Celebrations in his honor

[100] Bollati, pp. 277–278 (converting all moneys into florins at the indicated rate). At Pavia, Galeazzo nobly came across with a loan of 92,000 florins. *AST*, inv. 16, doc. 26 (1366–1368).

[101] Not far from Siena, possibly on the road which Amadeus followed to get to Rome, is the town of Colle Val d'Elsa, where a fourteenth-century fresco ("school of Lorenzetti") portraying the count of Savoy is to be found on the walls of a hall in the bishop's palace. It represents a crusading expedition against the Saracens, and while it is probably not a true portrait of Amadeus VI, its existence is further evidence of the fame which the crusade won for him.

[102] Bollati, item 1019: ". . . pro furnimento cuiusdam robe domini facte ad modum tartariscum."

[103] Servion, II, 157. Marie de Bourbon was at the papal court at the time and no doubt recounted Amadeus' services on her behalf—including a loan of 300 florins on this occasion. Bollati, item 503.

were also held on his arrival in Florence in early November. By the time he reached Pavia in mid-November, he had acquired not only wax and spices, but fine Florentine woolens, innumerable hawks and falcons, a lion, and eighty hunting hounds from Bernabò Visconti.[104] Far more important than the gifts, however, was the universal esteem. Something of the glorious reputation enjoyed by celebrated "athletes of Christ" like Pierre de Lusignan and Louis of Hungary would hereafter attach to the name of Amadeus VI of Savoy.

[104] The return route took him to Parma, Borgo San Donnino, and Castel San Giovanni near Piacenza. Bollati, item 1107: "Libravit dicto Gorret, portanti leonem domini, pro expensis suis et eius socii"; item 1117: "Libravit de mandato domini quatuor famulis domini Barnabonis qui domino aduxerunt de Marigniano quater viginti canes quo dictus dominus Bernabo domino donavit."

# A Marriage and a Murder

## 1367-1372

THE expedition to the East had given the Green Count a respite from the problems of his Alpine dominions only by substituting the problems of a crusade. No sooner had he set foot in Italy again than messengers with tidings of woe and alarm descended from the Valais, from Savoy, from the Piedmont. The Valaisans were fighting with their bishop again; Emperor Charles IV had been induced (in September 1366) by the bishops of Lausanne and Geneva, in particular, to revoke Amadeus' imperial vicariate. Amadeus IV, who had succeeded his brother Aymon as count of Geneva upon the death of the latter in August 1367, was not the devoted ally of Savoy that his brother had been; and his vigorous support of the bishops in their struggle against the Savoyard vicariate did not augur well for future relations. And to deepen the somber hue of winter in 1367, the mercenary companies were gathering again along the banks of the Saône.

The most serious question of all, however, remained the disputed Piedmont succession. Twenty-one-year-old Marguerite de Beaujeu had entered into the struggle against her twenty-seven-year-old step-son with a zeal which exceeded that of the count himself. Were Filippo, as the firstborn son and heir universal, to succeed his father, Marguerite and her sons would be left with almost nothing. It was not for this that the teenaged girl had in 1362 married a man thirty years her senior. She had employed with great skill the advantages of her youth and beauty during the five years of their marriage. Even if Giacomo's testament of 16 May 1366 is a forgery, which is possible, there can be little doubt that it accurately reflected the prince's wishes at the time of his death.[1] Relations between father and son had been easily envenomed once Filippo had sensed what his stepmother was about, and her task had been made easier by the friction that had always existed between the two men. By the terms of the secret will of 1366, drawn up at Rivoli in the presence of the count of Savoy, Filippo was to inherit only the towns of Vigone, Villafranca, Miradolo, Bricherasio, and Moretta in the whole of the Piedmont, and even these were to be held in fief from his younger brothers.[2] The heir universal was to be Amadeo, the elder of Marguerite's sons, and after him, his younger brother, Ludovico. Next in line was still not Filippo, but a younger brother of Prince Giacomo, Aimone de Savoie, the friend and companion of the Green Count. The only son of Sybille de Baux was thus to pay dearly for espousing the goals which she had championed so vigorously: he was to be disinherited. In this scheme the count of Savoy was clearly involved from the very first.[3]

Filippo may have known nothing of the secret testament, but he was not in doubt as to the ill will borne him by his step-mother. Marguerite had constantly encouraged Giacomo's tendency to misconstrue Filippo's every action. Thanks in large part to her efforts, father and son had more than once proceeded from hostile words to hostile actions. Filippo had found ready support among the traditional foes of his father—the Provana, the Falletti, the Panissera—upon whom the count of Savoy had often relied in his past wars with the prince. Moreover, just beyond the hills, there were the ever-present mercenary companies, ready to come at the first invitation. Filippo had contacted them very

---

[1] In 1364 and 1365, Giacomo had revoked his son's legal emancipation and the concessions made to him at that time. *AST, Principi del Sangue*, mazzo VII, docs. 9, 11.

[2] Gabotto, *Età*, p. 151.

[3] Amadeus may indeed have been the principal author of the scheme. An indication of his attitude toward Filippo as early as 3 January 1366 is found in his own will, drawn up prior to the departure for the East. Here Amadeus stipulated that after his own son and his issue, the succession to his dominions would go to Amadeo of Achaea, then to his brother Ludovico, and finally to Aymon of Geneva, on the condition that he bear the name and arms of Savoy. Thus Filippo was entirely excluded from his rights to the succession in Savoy. Guichenon, IV, *preuves*, 216.

early in the quarrel, and he had even sought an alliance with the marquis of Saluzzo, who readily accepted the opportunity to disturb his Savoyard neighbors.

At Pinerolo on 29 January 1367, Giacomo had summoned his host for a campaign to expel the mercenary companies brought into his territories by his son. In a fit of rage he had declared Filippo ungrateful and disobedient, undeserving of the name of son. Minor skirmishes between the partisans of father and son disrupted the tranquility of the Piedmont during the winter and spring of 1367, and in April, Giacomo went to Pavia for additional support from the Visconti.[4] Galeazzo, who preferred to conserve the strength of his Savoyard allies for enterprises against their common foes, used his influence to effect at least a temporary reconciliation between the prince and his son. Filippo was summoned to Pavia, and on 1 May he promised to be an obedient son in the future and was invested by his father with Casal d'Osasco. At Pinerolo, however, Marguerite was in the meantime ordering the Piedmont communes to stand ready to furnish men and supplies on short notice. Military action was clearly being contemplated, if not against Filippo, at least against his mercenary allies. But within a few days after his return from Pavia, Prince Giacomo fell ill, and at Pinerolo on 17 May 1367 he died.

The moment the news of Giacomo's death reached Savoyard ears at Rivoli, the count's officers notified all concerned that the Piedmont was now under the special protection of Savoy. The Savoyard captain-general in Piedmont, François de Longuecombe, together with Humbert de Savoie and a company of nobles, rode to Pinerolo almost at once to offer assistance to Marguerite. Countess Bonne sent word that everything possible must be done to keep the peace until the return of the count from the East. In June when Filippo ordered the Piedmont communes to send representatives to take the customary oaths of loyalty to

---

[4] On 25 April 1367 at Pavia, Giacomo issued a public instrument denouncing Filippo's "multas ingratitudines, demerita, et offensiones," and accusing him of "incendia, predationes, roberias, homicidia, et alia multa maleficia." The prince refused all forgiveness for such vile deeds and declared that whatever arbitration or treaties might be concluded between them in the future, Filippo must nevertheless furnish satisfactory reparation for these charges against him. Text in Datta, *Storia*, II, doc. XXIX.

him as heir universal, he received letters from Bonne de Bourbon requesting that he desist from such action until her husband had returned and the late prince's will was unsealed.[5] At Vigone, Filippo summoned an assembly of Piedmont nobles and town representatives in violation of the countess's instructions, and the communes deliberated over whom to obey. In view of imminent danger from mercenaries and neighbors, Filippo was finally persuaded to accept a truce. At Pinerolo on 28 June the prince was given Vigone and Fossano for the time being; Marguerite received Cavallermaggiore and Cavour. Each then promised to make no further moves until the return of the count.[6]

When the Green Count disembarked at Venice at the end of July, he found his cousin awaiting him, eager for assurances of support. With fair words Amadeus put his fears to rest, and Filippo returned to Vigone full of joy and confidence.[7] Both previous and subsequent events suggest that the count had no intention of keeping his word, despite promises he may have given on this occasion. He had participated in the secret testament, and he knew that Filippo would never accept it without a fight. Whether the will had been his idea or Marguerite's is not really important, for by now their interests were identical. Marguerite and her sons would be dependent upon Savoy, and effective power in the Piedmont would be in the count's hands until the boys came of age. For the count of Savoy, Filippo's succession to the Piedmont would mean a return to the days of Sybille de Baux; it would mean wars to maintain dynastic solidarity, wars that would cripple Savoyard efforts to compete successfully with dangerous neighbors. Such a diversion of resources now would be fatal to the Green Count's ambitions in northern Italy.

Amadeus, while still at Pavia in November 1367 after his return from Rome, had come to an understanding with his brother-in-law about the Piedmont succession. Galeazzo proved amenable because he wanted something very particular in return. After long and complicated negotiations begun in the summer of 1366, the ambitious lord of Pavia was on the brink of another diplomatic marriage to dazzle his friends and astonish his foes. Having married his son, Giangaleazzo, to a princess of France in 1360,

[5] Gabotto, *Età*, p. 159.
[6] Text in Datta, *Storia*, II (documents for libro III), doc. 1.
[7] Gabotto, *Età*, p. 161.

Galeazzo now proposed to marry his daughter, Violante, to a prince of England, Lionel, duke of Clarence and fourth son of King Edward III. The formal offer was drawn up at Pavia on 19 January 1367, and the final treaty was signed at Westminster on 15 May.[8] The marriage contract endowed the bride-to-be with a large sum in cash and the Visconti holdings in Piedmont: the city of Alba, the towns of Cherasco, Cuneo, and Mondovì, suzerainty over Centallo and Carru—all to be held in fief from Galeazzo and his heirs.[9] Galeazzo might thus hope to find in this vigorous young son of the English king an ally capable of rallying the English mercenaries in Italy behind his own projects against Montferrat and the Angevins. At the same time, French influence penetrating the region through the Dauphiné and Saluzzo might be counterbalanced by creating the barrier of an English state in the Piedmont. On the English side Edward III was only too happy to find a principality for another of his ambitious sons.

The count of Savoy could hardly have welcomed the scheme with unrestrained enthusiasm, for he had designs of his own upon Violante's dowry towns.[10] Whether in those parts an Englishman would be a less dangerous neighbor than a Visconti was a troublesome question, considering the reputation won by English mercenary captains in Italy over recent years. But the marriage contract had been signed, and there was nothing Amadeus could do but make the best of the situation. Galeazzo now had need of someone who was known and respected by both the English and the French, and who could be counted upon to carry through the execution of the treaty. The count of Savoy was the logical choice, and he was willing (it would be a good chance

---

[8] It is commonly asserted that Amadeus was a party to the initial negotiations for this marriage, but I can find no proof of this. Cook, p. 24, points out that on 30 July 1366 (hence while Amadeus was on a galley heading east) the formal commission to arrange the marriage was given by Edward III to the earl of Hereford, who then went to Lombardy to discuss terms. Hence the months during which the crucial talks took place were precisely those during which the count was absent on the crusade.

[9] Cf. Cook, pp. 27–30.

[10] Amadeus had been obliged to recognize Galeazzo's possession of them, however, on the eve of his departure for the East. Act dated 28 May 1366. Text in *ASL*, VI (1906), 255–259.

to meet on friendly grounds with this new English neighbor) if Galeazzo would meet demands of his own. Galeazzo did. On 22 November 1367 the lord of Pavia reaffirmed his earlier grant of suzerainty over Fossano, Cavallermaggiore, and Sommariva del Bosco;[11] and he very probably guaranteed the count a free hand in the Piedmont succession affair.

What the count most needed now was time—time to get back to his capital and to pick up the innumerable threads of Savoyard affairs where he had left them almost two years before; time to assemble men and to put his finances in order. From Ivrea in late November, after sending his lion on ahead to Aosta,[12] he dispatched Ogier de Savoie and Hugues de la Fléchère to the Valais. There they were to make peace among the perennial combatants, if only long enough to prevent further deterioration of the situation until the count could take matters personally in hand. For the moment, Amadeus chose to ignore the emperor's betrayal in revoking his vicariate. Savoyard officers at Geneva and Lausanne were instructed to enforce the count's vicarial rights there despite excommunications showered upon them. Finally, at Rivoli in early December, the count formally postponed a decision regarding the Piedmont succession. He left for the snows of Savoy soon after, accompanied by Marguerite de Beaujeu and her sons, without even publishing Giacomo's second will.

At this move Filippo was justifiably suspicious. In mid-December there were reports that the prince was in contact with mercenary captains, and by the end of the year, Filippo had renewed his alliance with Saluzzo.[13] Amadeus responded by ordering the prince to come to Chambéry during the first week of January for the opening of his father's will. Filippo's failure to come,

---

[11] The act is dated 1367, not 1366, as in Cordey, p. 183, note 1.

[12] Bollati, item 1157. Perhaps the count hoped to amuse the Valdostans, whose arms featured a rampant lion. It was later taken to Chambéry. *Ibid.*, item 1219.

[13] *AST* (castellany), Rivoli, mazzo 10, doc. 63, 1367–1369, records expenses of Castellan Barthélémi de Chignin at Christmas (1367), when he went to Filippo at Vigone upon hearing of the prince's "ligam cum marchion. Saluciarum." There was a rumor that Filippo was planning to deliver Carignano into the marquis' hands, so the castellan went there and had all the locks in the town gates changed. *Ibid.*

despite an earlier promise to do so, seemed to confirm the rumors that he was preparing to resist.[14] The count probably did not expect him to honor his promise, but the attempt to transfer the succession case from Rivoli to Chambéry still served his purposes. If Filippo had come, he would have fallen into the count's power entirely; the prince's refusal to come cast him in the posture of a rebellious vassal.

The Green Count spent Christmas at Chambéry and Le Bourget, visited Faucigny, Evian, and Geneva, then returned to spend Epiphany at his capital. Raoul de Louppy appeared with a company of twenty-nine Dauphinois to argue fruitlessly over the Viennois castellanies, which Amadeus refused to unhand, and the Guiers river boundary, which he refused to concede.[15] Then they rode together down to Vienne, where the count again expressed his appreciation at the shrine of Saint Anthony for his safe return from the East. At Vienne, Amadeus learned that the Great Companies had returned from the campaign of the previous year in Castile, had been hurried out of Aquitaine by the prince of Wales, and were now moving into the Auvergne. Here was a subject on which the count and Louppy could agree. Amadeus promised to take up the matter of the Viennois castellanies with the king when he got to Paris next; then he and Louppy agreed on mutual assistance in protecting the Rhône-Saône frontier from the Companies.

Back in Savoy later in January and February, Amadeus was largely concerned about measures of defense. Toward the end of January, word came that two mercenary companies, hiding their arms under their clothes and dressed up as artisans and laborers, had tried to surprise the port of Thoissey on the Bressan side of the Saône.[16] Fortunately, the attempt failed, and the count sent reinforcements at once to the garrison of Bezenins, his nearest castle to Thoissey, to help prevent any further attempts. In mid-February the inhabitants of Lyon were sufficiently terrified by the increasing numbers of marauders in the environs to send for help to the Savoyards. Amadeus ordered Janiard Provana, *bailli* of the Valbonne, to reinforce the garrison of the city with

---

[14] Act of 3 December 1367 at Vigone. Datta, *Storia*, II, doc. II, 230–231.

[15] Cordey, pp. 201–203.

[16] G. Guigue, p. 171. Thoissey belonged to Beaujeu.

a half-dozen nobles and a company of twenty-four infantry.[17] This proved to be the last great scare for the next five years. The Companies, thwarted again in their efforts to cross the Saône, moved away toward the west; one band was exterminated soon after near Semelay by the Burgundians.[18]

### THE VISCONTI-PLANTAGENET MARRIAGE, 1368

During the spring the Green Count's attention was devoted to his approaching trip to Paris to meet the duke of Clarence. By now the subsidies levied in Piedmont and Savoy had somewhat restored his finances, and he could afford to take a sizeable company with him.[19] He left Bresse early in April and upon arrival in Paris lodged in his Hôtel de Bohême near the Louvre and the St-Honoré gate.[20] The first item of business was not the arrival of Clarence, but another round in the tedious wrangle over the Viennois castellanies. Amadeus discussed the matter with Charles V, but continued to drive a hard bargain. The Treaty of Paris had expressly released the king of France from all pecuniary obligations attached to the properties and jurisdictions exchanged, but it did not release him from the debts incurred by the refusal of his officers to obey his orders. Amadeus had spent close to 10,000 florins to induce the Faucigny castellans to comply with the Treaty of Paris, not to mention the immense cost of the army with which the count had at first attempted to coerce them; and until he received just compensation for these expenses, Amadeus would not surrender the Viennois castellanies.

On 16 April at the Louvre an agreement on this matter was reached. Charles agreed to pay his tenacious brother-in-law 50,-000 florins in return for the Viennois castellanies; but he also agreed that until at least 45,000 had actually been paid, the castellanies would remain in Savoyard hands.[21] Savoyard accounts

---

[17] *ADCO*, B 8554 (Montluel).     [18] G. Guigue, p. 174.

[19] Cf. *ADS*, subsidy accounts for 1368; *AST*, inv. 38, folio 1, doc. 16 (1367–1368); *ibid.*, inv. 16, doc. 28.

[20] The Hôtel de Bohême had been given by Philippe de Valois to John of Luxembourg in 1327. It was approximately upon the same location that Catherine de Medici built the palace later known as the Hôtel de Soissons in the sixteenth century; and this building in turn was replaced in the late eighteenth century by the Halle au blé. Cf. Cordey, *Les Comtes*, p. 128, note 2.

[21] Treaty in Cordey, *Les Comtes, preuves*, doc. 34. Fifty thousand gold florins

show that important installments were received on this sum, but the whole was apparently not paid. The count was still holding these castles nearly ten years later in 1377.[22]

With this business disposed of, the count could relax and enjoy the receptions planned for the duke of Clarence. The youth of the participants doubtless heightened the festive tone of the occasion—the Green Count at thirty-four was the eldest of the princes assembled.[23] Lionel of Clarence was met at the Louvre by the king, the duke of Bourbon, the count of Savoy, and a great concourse of barons and prelates. He and his suite were lodged in the royal palace, and on the day of his arrival they dined there with the king. This was the first of a series of magnificent feasts at the various palaces of the royal family in Paris. The Savoyards were treated to examples of splendor on a scale well beyond anything then possible at home, where life, like the scenery, was more often austere than grand, and almost never luxurious. Even the count must have relied more upon the emerald hue of his vestments than upon their quality for whatever notice he attracted, although he did stretch his purse to make the king a princely gift—a hat adorned with a ruby and several large pearls, which cost him 1,000 gold florins.[24]

Some of the most celebrated literary personages of the age were on hand, among them Guillaume de Machaut, now seventy years old, dean of the writers and composers at the royal court. At one of the banquets, Machaut, possibly because he was impressed by the Savoyard in green, offered one of his novels to the count of Savoy. Machaut was rewarded with a princely gift of 300 florins, but the unliterary Savoyard clerk who recorded the expense did not see fit to note as well the title of the work.[25] In the suite of

---

were held to be the equivalent of 60,000 florins "pois delphinat." *Ibid.*, doc. 36.

[22] On 11 June 1369 the count certified having received 4,000 gold francs from the treasury of the Dauphiné, out of 15,000 due as the first installment on the previous Easter. *Ibid.*, doc. 36.

[23] The king and the duke of Bourbon were thirty-one, Clarence was thirty, Jean of Berry was twenty-eight, and Philippe le Hardi was twenty-six. Cook, pp. 32ff. Enguerrand de Coucy, age thirty, was also there, and in view of his subsequent services to Amadeus VI in Italy, it is likely that that subject was broached on this occasion.

[24] *AST*, inv. 16, doc. 30 (1369–1371).

[25] Cordey, *Les Comtes*, p. 185, suggests that it may have been the *Livre du Voir Dit*, written by Machaut a few years earlier for Peronnelle d'Armentières.

the duke of Clarence was another famous literary figure, the chronicler Jean Froissart, who left descriptions of the duke's journey and activities during that eventful spring and summer of 1368.[26]

On 19 April the Green Count bade farewell to his royal kinsmen and set out for home to prepare the duke's reception in his own dominions. Several trunks, mules, and packhorses were purchased to carry all that the count had acquired during his stay in the French capital: a mantle and a *jaquette* lined with some 1,200 squirrel skins, fine Reims cloth for the countess, shoes, hats, gold necklaces, clasps, gilded belts, spurs, even straw hats and table knives.[27] The duke of Clarence left Paris the following day with a company of some 450 persons and arrived in Bresse a few days later. Amadeus had invited all the nobles and ladies of the country to take part in the festivities, perhaps hoping to impress his future Piedmont neighbor with the number of his vassals, if he could not do so with the modest splendor of his court. On 8 May, the date of Lionel's arrival, the castellans of St-Trivier and Pont-de-Veyle sent off cartloads of cheeses and fat roasting hens for the banquet tables at Bourg, where the great hall was bright with banners and rich hangings.[28]

From Bourg-en-Bresse the company "en tres noble et poissant arroi," in the words of Froissart, passed through the dark forested valleys of the Revermont, crossed the pass of the Cat, and arrived at Chambéry on 11 or 12 May. Froissart was sufficiently impressed by the welcome which his patron received at the Savoyard capital to leave us one of the rare contemporary glimpses of a festive occasion in the castle of the "nobles et vaillans" count of Savoy. The feasting and dancing lasted two days, and most striking of all at the court, which was "moult pleniere," were "one hundred and twenty young and beautiful ladies and demoiselles," the wives and daughters of the Savoyard nobles gathered at the count's request. Froissart himself furnished words for the songs

More appropriate for the conqueror of Gallipoli would have been *La Prise d'Alexandrie*, composed more recently in honor of Pierre de Lusignan's capture of Alexandria in 1365.

[26] Since Lionel of Clarence was Geoffrey Chaucer's earliest patron, it is possible that Chaucer was also present on this trip.

[27] *AST*, inv. 16, doc. 30.

[28] *ADCO*, B 9293, B 9961; Froissart, *Oeuvres*, VII, 246–247.

and carols which the ladies sang after the guests had satiated their appetites at long tables magnificently spread with "wines, meats, and platters" of every description. And even when the minstrels ceased playing, the joyous ladies continued their roundelays, dancing hand in hand and singing merrily. The Savoyard ladies, he declared, were "the freshest" in the country, and were "most richly and beautifully arrayed, most nobly and well decked-out," and their garments were of silk and "canjan," ornamented with pearls and precious stones. Songs and dances, virelays and roundelays filled the castle of Chambéry with merriment throughout the duke's stay.[29]

For the Green Count the festivities were but the frivolous exterior of purposes more serious. The knights who rode into Chambéry for the banquets brought armor as well as embroidered surcoats, battle-axes as well as jousting lances. The Piedmont succession could be deferred no longer, and the count was combining business with pleasure in escorting the English prince to meet his bride. On the crisp May morning when the duke of Clarence set out on the route to the Mont Cenis, companies of Savoyard lancers followed behind him. Marguerite de Beaujeu and her partisans were also present, and there can be no doubt that the Savoyard point of view on Piedmont affairs was fully presented to the duke during the long days in the saddle. For the moment, however, the Green Count chose not to strike. He accompanied the duke all the way to Pavia, where they were joined by English mercenary companies which included those of John Hawkwood. As the duke, surrounded by some 2,000 English troops, approached Milan, a colorful procession with Galeazzo at its head came forth from the city to greet them. Galeazzo was accompanied by Blanche de Savoie and her daughter-in-law, Isabelle de France, elegantly attired and escorted by eighty ladies of the court in cote-hardies of red with sleeves of white, the colors of Savoy, embroidered in trefoil figures. Behind the ladies came a company of thirty knights and thirty squires, all dressed alike and mounted upon jousting steeds, led by Giangaleazzo, now seventeen.[30] The Green Count was not in green this time, but sported instead a jacket of cloth-of-gold with

[29] Jehan Froissart, *Poésies*, ed. Auguste Scheler, 3 vols. (Brussels, 1870–1872), I, 222–223.

[30] Cf. Cook, p. 50, note 60.

crowns on it. The sleeves and hood had green linings, however, and nine of his familiars were outfitted in striped green cloth.[31] Red and white *cendal* for 320 pennons ornamented the lances of the count's retinue.

The bride-to-be was but thirteen years of age, and when the marriage took place in the cathedral on 5 June 1368, she was assisted at the altar by her uncles, the count of Savoy and Lord Bernabò, who had arrived unexpectedly a few days earlier. When the ceremony was over, a magnificent banquet was held in the center of the public square next to the cathedral. Food and drink were said to have been provided in such abundance as to have easily satiated more than 10,000 people.[32] There were thirty courses, and after each one splendid gifts were presented to the guests of honor: silver vessels, seventy horses caparisoned in silk and silver, costly suits of mail, massive steel helmets and breastplates, jewels of every kind, and rich garments of precious cloth. Galeazzo was a very rich prince, and no price was too great if it would make a firm friend of this potentially dangerous son-in-law.

At the first table sat Duke Lionel, the Green Count, Edward Despencer, two sons of Bernabò, and the poet-laureate, Francesco Petrarca. The repast consisted of a series of double courses of meat and fish, beginning with suckling pigs, gilded, with fire in their mouths, accompanied by crabs, also gilded. Following the presentation of the platters came the gifts, this time two greyhounds with velvet collars and silken leashes, and twelve brace of hounds held by chains of gilded brass, collars of leather, and silk leashes. Next came roasted hares and pike followed by gifts of greyhounds, goshawks, and silver buttons; the third course was gilded calf and trout accompanied by gifts of more hounds.

[31] *AST*, inv. 38, folio 21, doc. 66. Lionel had made him a present of a "gipono pagni auri . . . incluso cotone mangiarum ad astuludiandum" and he bought a pair of green jousting shoes. Antoine de Savoie entered into the festive spirit by purchasing on his arrival red silk for shoes, hoods, and sleeves, and a gold ribbon. Galeazzo gave him a warhorse, for which he promptly bought a saddle —all at his father's expense.

[32] A detailed description of this famous banquet is given in Cook, pp. 60–74. reconstructed from chronicle accounts. Cf. also Bernardino Corio (b. 1459), *Storia di Milano*, eds. Butti and Ferrario (Milan, 1856), II, 226–228. None is contemporary, and all are probably somewhat exaggerated.

And so went the gargantuan spectacle: quails and partridges with roasted trout; ducks and herons, gilded, with gilded carp; beef and fat capons in garlic and vinegar sauce, sturgeons in water; capons and meat in lemon sauce, beef and eel pies; meat and fish-galantine, roast kids, venison, peacock, pickled ox-tongue, and finally, cheeses and fruits of every description. Throughout the banquet Galeazzo himself acted as steward, personally supervising not only the serving of the platters, but the presentation of the gifts as well. When the feasting had ended at last and the participants had washed, expensive robes were distributed to everyone present. Bernabò gave money to the crowds of minstrels, jugglers, and acrobats, and the wines and confections were served. Thus ended one of the great moments in medieval culinary history.

Politically, the moment had a less pleasant side. Federigo of Saluzzo and Filippo of Achaea had both come to Milan not ten days before, and their presence had marred the occasion for the Green Count. Federigo left without a scene, but the count's hostility toward Filippo had blazed forth in the presence of both the duke of Clarence and the Visconti. Amadeus had publicly accused the prince of bad faith and malice, denounced him as a "traitor and a felon," and demanded justice. Filippo had no chance for a fair hearing in this company; all had been won over in advance by the count of Savoy. The duke of Clarence answered Filippo's appeal to his arbitration only by ordering him to appear before a tribunal soon to be chosen to hear complaints of his conduct. Filippo wisely left Milan at once and took refuge in his own territories.[33]

### THE END OF FILIPPO OF ACHAEA

When the wedding feasts were over and the tournaments in honor of the newlyweds had run their course, the Green Count took leave of his friends. Before his departure he presented Duke Lionel with his faithful Black Squire, the Englishman Richard Musard. Musard knew Piedmont and Italian affairs extremely well, and he was entirely devoted to the count of Savoy.[34] He

---

[33] Cf. Gabotto, *Età*, p. 169.

[34] On Lionel's death Musard rejoined Amadeus and remained in his service until the count's death.

could be counted upon to give the kind of advice the duke ought to have.

At Rivoli on 19 June, Amadeus ordered the testament of 1366 read publicly before the assembled representatives of the Piedmont.[35] Filippo was declared disinherited except for the handful of towns reserved for him, and five-year-old Amadeo was proclaimed the heir universal of the late prince. The proclamation was well enough received, partly because Savoyard rule offered the hope of internal peace, partly because Filippo's willingness to call mercenaries into the Piedmont had greatly diminished his popularity. Savigliano hastened to offer homage to little Amadeo, and this example was quickly followed by Villar, Cavour, Bagnolo, Barge, and Envie.

A formidable problem remained in the form of the Monk of Hecz, one of the most famous mercenary adventurers in Lombardy, now in the pay of Filippo. The Green Count wrote Hecz sometime in mid-June requesting him to abandon Filippo as a traitorous scoundrel and offering to pay him well for his defection. The Monk wrote back on 20 June politely declining the offer.[36] Filippo was a good and loyal man, he said, and had paid him and his men every florin of their contract with him. They would therefore serve him loyally to the death until the expiration of their contract, at which time they would be happy to consider the count's offer. Amadeus wrote angrily from Pinerolo a week later repeating the charges against the prince and concluding that he would be obliged to treat Hecz as an enemy if he persisted in the prince's service. From Vigone the next day Hecz replied only that he was sending a messenger authorized to deliver an answer in keeping with the honor of his company. Hecz then showed the count's correspondence to Filippo,

[35] *AST*, inv. 38, folio 21, doc. 66: "libravit dicto Gay messagerio misso [14 June] cum litteris domini ad plura loca Pedemontis cum litteris directis communitatibus dictorum locorum pro publicatione testamenti domini principis quondam faciendo"; "libravit ibidem dicta die Anthonio Chevrot messagerio misso cum litteris domini ad plura alia loca Pedemontis pro eodem." Cf. Gioffredo Della Chiesa, *Cronaca di Saluzzo* in *MHP*, V (ca. 1430), col. 1014.

[36] The correspondence here summarized is in Datta, *Storia*, II, 231ff. Also in June 1368 the castellan of Rivoli went to Cuneo to see Anichino Baumgarten "pro faciendo pactum cum eodem" so he would not join Filippo against the count. *AST* (castellany), Rivoli, mazzo, 10, doc. 63.

who was greatly incensed. The prince denounced the count as a liar and challenged him to a duel in the presence of the emperor, with one hundred of his men against one hundred Savoyards;[37] or if the count preferred to choose some neutral spot in Piedmont, Filippo would fight him with fifty knights against fifty.

For the moment, the Green Count had been outmaneuvered. He had sufficient confidence in his strength and skill as a fighter not to fear a duel for personal reasons, but the politician in him struggled with the knight-errant. Without a duel Amadeus was assured of ultimate victory over his far weaker rival; in a duel even victory might harm his cause by provoking an anti-Savoyard reaction in the Piedmont, for Filippo was both his kinsman and a native son. The Green Count much preferred other means of attaining his ends. He already had Clarence, the Visconti, and Montferrat on his side; in time Filippo and his mercenaries were certain to destroy themselves far more effectively than the count could do. Filippo must be allowed to accomplish his own undoing.

Yet the Green Count's knightly honor forbade him to refuse the challenge. Accordingly, he publicly accepted the prince's defiance, released him from the bonds of vassalage which would prevent his doing battle against his feudal suzerain, and agreed to the choice of fifty against fifty somewhere in Piedmont.[38] Then he sent his castellan of Lanzo to Pavia, probably suggesting an appropriate line of action for his brother-in-law. With or without prompting, Galeazzo sent messengers to Vigone on 21 July forbidding Filippo to participate in any such duel and threatening military action in case of disobedience.[39]

In the meantime the count, pretending to know nothing of

[37] Charles IV was then in eastern Lombardy. Amadeus had been in contact with him since his arrival in Italy. From Susa in May he had sent Guillaume de Pasquier "apud Paduam et Trevisum ad dominum Imperatorem Romanorum cum litteras domini." *AST*, inv. 38, folio 21, doc. 66. Charles wrote on 28 July 1368 to forbid this duel. Guichenon, IV, *preuves*, misdated 1369.

[38] Cf. letter of the count dated 11 August 1368 (Datta, *Storia*, II, doc. IX) suggesting either Vigone or Fossano as the place. On 9 August a man was sent to Vercelli and Biella "pro habendis viginti quinque brigandis et totidem balisteriis ad stipendiam domini," and ten mule-loads of tents and "pavaillionos domini" arrived about this time from Ivrea. *AST*, inv. 38, folio 21, doc. 66.

[39] Letter dated from Pavia. *AST, Principi del Sangue*, mazzo VII, doc. 15.

all this, continued his preparations for the duel. He sent to Lyon for armorers to put his equipment in order and hired men to prepare a park and lists for the contest.[40] Gaspard de Montmayeur, Antelme de Miolans, Jean de Grolée, and Pierre de Murs were sent to Vigone to arrange the details.[41] The date was set for 15 August and the place was to be outside the walls of Fossano. Giovanni of Montferrat was to act as the field judge. On the stipulated date the count, accompanied by the count of Geneva and at least five knights of the Collar, arrived with his host before the walls of Fossano.[42] There he apparently encountered a large army under Lionel of Clarence, who had chosen that moment to take possession of his Piedmont towns nearby. It is difficult to believe that this was mere coincidence. Filippo was undoubtedly meant to take the duke's presence as proof that Galeazzo intended to enforce his prohibition.[43]

Prince Filippo of course did not dare to appear. The Savoyards at once proclaimed him a coward as well as a scoundrel, to undermine his chivalric reputation, just as the publication of Giacomo's secret will had undermined his legal position. Then the count undertook to force the citizens of Fossano to expel him and surrender their town. Hecz, who commanded the defenses, appeared to be wavering, and Filippo saw that his only chance was to feign submission. He asked Montferrat to convey his desire for a parley to the count, who had retired to Savigliano. Amadeus granted a safe-conduct to his cousin, and on 21 August 1368 in the great hall of the Palazzo Tapparelli at Savigliano a treaty

[40] *AST*, inv. 38, folio 21, doc. 66: ". . . duobus nunciis missis de Rippolis apud Lugdunum pro aducendo operariis ad armandum domini et eus gentes qui cum ipso pugnare debent contra dominum Philippum" (early August). On 8 August: "libravit . . . Johannis Bartholomei de Secusia pro expensis unius parci fuste et cordarum quem dominus sibi comisit fieri facere pro pugna facienda per dominum et suas gentes contra dominum Philippum et eius gentes."

[41] *AST, Principi del Sangue*, mazzo VII, doc. 16.

[42] Knights of the Collar present were Antoine de Beaujeu, Chivard de Monthoux, Jean de Vienne, Guillaume de Grandson, and Guillaume de Chalamont. The court's household accounts provide a slightly different dating: on 16 August the Savoyards left Pinerolo for Savigliano, on 17 August they marched to Fossano, then back the next day to Savigliano. *AST*, inv. 38, folio 21, doc. 66, p. xxxiii.

[43] When Filippo wrote Amadeus of this development, he replied (11 August) that if the prince wanted the fight, Amadeus would so arrange matters that no one could prevent it. *AST, Principi del Sangue*, mazzo VII, doc. 17.

was drawn up between them.[44] Mass was celebrated and the cousins solemnly swore upon the sacred host to keep the peace. The validity of the secret testament of the late prince would be determined by two "prudhommes" of the count's council, who were also to decide upon an equitable partition of the inheritance.[45] Filippo promised not to build fortifications or acquire other possessions in the meantime, nor to give assistance to enemies of the count or of the princess. He also agreed to surrender whatever towns or castles he now held which might be awarded to his half brothers. Amadeus promised that the whole matter would be settled by 15 September before he left for Savoy again, and that he would abandon "all malice and rancor which said count has and had against Lord Filippo."

The melancholy drama now moved swiftly toward its climax. Filippo was surely not so naïve as to have supposed that the "arbitral" commission of Savoyards would do justice to his claims. He must have known that the count was determined upon his ruin and was only using the arbitration for public appearances. Yet he did nothing in ensuing weeks to strengthen his position, to provide himself adequately with allies, or to plan a strategy of defense. Perhaps he had been lulled into a false sense of security by the great reputation for honor and probity which his cousin now enjoyed.

The final act of the drama began on 6 September 1368 when the captain-general of the Piedmont, Barthélémi de Chignin, presented himself at Vigone and requested the presence of Filippo at Rivoli, where deliberations concerning the succession were nearing a close. The prince accompanied Chignin back to Rivoli four days later and probably heard the arbitral decision at that time. No text of it seems to have survived, but it could hardly have been more than a repetition of the terms of Giacomo's second will. Filippo then returned to Vigone, only to be summoned once more to Rivoli to answer the various charges against him.[46] He was suspicious and demanded a safe-conduct. It was

---

[44] Text in Datta, *Storia*, II, doc. X, 240–243.

[45] Jean de Grolée, sire of Neyriat, Pierre de Murs, knight and *legum doctor*, and Pierre Gerbais (now styled as *domicellus* and lord of "castri rubei") were the three men who arranged the terms of the truce.

[46] *AST* (castellany), Rivoli, mazzo 10, doc. 63, makes it clear that Filippo made two trips to Rivoli in September. On 10 September the castellan escorted

granted to him on 24 September, guaranteeing his safety and that of fifty men-at-arms through the end of the month "et ultra per tres dies," and it was valid anywhere in the territories of Piedmont, Savoy, or Dauphiné.[47] During this time, Filippo was not to be restrained or molested in any way for misdeeds attributed to him by his enemies. Confidently armed with these assurances, Filippo left his strong fortress at Vigone and arrived at Rivoli a few days later.

The prince could not for long have remained confident, once he and his men had ridden into the cobblestone courtyard of the great citadel above the Susa road. Perhaps for a moment he suspected, as the great iron gates swung slowly closed behind him, that he was already a prisoner. As he entered the great hall he recognized but one friend—or former friend—in Giovanni of Montferrat. No justice could be expected from the others— Savoyards and Genevans from across the Alps, Visconti and Piedmontese enemies from nearer home.[48] No sooner had he appeared than his archenemy, Princess Marguerite, presented her long list of charges, blaming him for the burning of towns and villages, the massacres of men, women, and children—indeed, every calamity suffered by the population of the Piedmont over the past several years was laid to his charge.[49] He was denounced as a traitor for refusing to obey his natural suzerain and kinsman, the count of Savoy, just as he had disobeyed his late father and brought sorrow to his declining years. Marguerite concluded her performance by demanding that the perpetrator of such "nefandissima crimina" be brought to justice.

---

him to Rivoli, then back to Vigone; then on the last day of September, "post prysiam dicti domini Philippi," on orders from both the count and the prince, the castellan and his men seized control of Vigone.

[47] *AST, Principi del Sangue*, VII, doc. 21.

[48] Count Amadeus IV of Geneva was present, suggesting that after his act of homage to the count of Savoy on 13 May 1368 (Duparc, p. 310), he was on fairly good terms with Savoy. Yet it is entirely possible that he saw Charles IV on this trip to Italy and arranged then for the imperial acts of February 1369 so prejudicial to the claims of the count of Savoy. *Ibid.*, p. 311.

[49] Text in Datta, *Storia*, II, doc. XI, 244–248. Filippo "invasit, insultavit, invadi et insultari fecit illicite terram" and caused "homicidia, incendia, plagia, raptas, depredationes, rapine, latrocinia, falsitates hominum et mulierum captivationes, adulteria, incestus sacrilegia membrorum hominum mutilationes et quamplurima nefandissima alia crimina."

When Filippo saw to his horror that the court was prepared to act upon these accusations, he protested that his safe-conduct guaranteed him against prosecution on such charges. The count apparently denied that the safe-conduct contained such guarantees and ordered the prince to produce it. He could not. Either he had really been so careless as to leave it behind, or his enemies had contrived to steal it from him. Unable to find it among his effects, he demanded permission to send to Vigone for it. Antonio Galletti, one of his clerks, was ordered to go for it—and never returned. While awaiting Galletti's return, the count placed both Filippo and Marguerite under arrest, pending a full hearing of the charges involving them.

This public display of impartiality set the stage nicely for the turn which affairs had now taken. There was no longer any question of deciding between two wills; that decision had already been made in Marguerite's favor. The Green Count knew that Filippo would never accept such injustice, however, and the accusations subsequently introduced by the princess were designed to transform the hearing on the will into a treason trial. When Galletti did not come back, Amadeus and a six-member commission declared (28 September) that the safe-conduct issued by the count did not apply to the present situation.[50] The promise not to prosecute charges against the prince referred only to charges that he had violated the rights of the count of Savoy. Since Filippo had failed to perform homage to his half brother Amadeo, as required by the second will, he was being prosecuted not for violation of the count's rights, but for violation of Amadeo's, which the count of Savoy was duty-bound to defend.

Two days later the Savoyard judges handed down their decision.[51] Filippo was declared to have furnished no adequate proof of his right to properties not granted him in the second will, and his present occupation of some of them, notably Fossano, was declared treason. His persistent refusal to do homage to his half brother meant that he had violated his feudal obligations and merited the loss of all of his fiefs. His use of the title "prince of

---

[50] The commission included Montmayeur, Bonivard, D'Estrées, and the three original judges (Pugini, Solerio, and Lageret). Gabotto, *Età*, p. 174. Cf. Datta, *Storia*, II, docs. XII, XIII; and *AST, Principi del Sangue*, mazzo VII, doc. 21.

[51] Datta, *Storia*, II, doc. XIV, 253–256. *AST, Principi del Sangue*, mazzo VIII, doc. 1.

Achaea" was declared a usurpation, since it belonged only to the heir universal. The count, to ensure the condemnation of his opponent, sent to Savigliano (and perhaps elsewhere) to invite all enemies of the prince to come forward with their grievances against him, that these might also be laid upon the scales already so heavily weighted against him. This move itself suggests the weakness of the case against the prince and furnishes a chilling indication of what the future had in store.

For weeks the inquisition continued. Filippo was transferred from Rivoli to the great fortress of Avigliana, along with his judges and accusers. He was permitted to attempt a defense, but apparently refused, preferring to throw himself upon the mercy of the count.[52] Filippo's familiars were intensively questioned in the effort to assemble as much damaging evidence as possible. The tragic ending to this affair is still shrouded in mystery. When the sentence came, if it came at all, it meant only death for Filippo of Achaea. Once the heavy gates of Avigliana's dungeons had closed behind him in the fall of 1368, he must have known that all was lost.[53] Some have asserted that he was never seen again, others that he reappeared and was publicly executed. Giovanni della Chiesa, writing some sixty years later, reported that the prince was proclaimed a traitor and was publicly drowned in the small lake near the castle of Avigliana, in keeping with the penalty for treason prescribed by local custom.[54] The documents only show that on 20 December 1368 the Green Count was at Avigliana with "several others," and that he had instructed Pierre Gerbais to meet him there concerning "a certain matter." Whether public or private, the "certain matter" was very probably the death of the prince of Achaea.

The postscript to the Piedmont succession affair was a treaty

[52] Cibrario, *Storia*, III, 219.

[53] *AST* (castellany), Avigliana, mazzo VIII, doc. 59, 1366–1369, p. xxx: "Et pro expensis domini Philipi de Sabaud. quem tenuit undecim septimanis et duobus diebus . . ."; " . . . Johanne de Croso qui dictum dominum Philippum per certum temporem in dicto castro Avill. custodivit." If Filippo was transferred to Avigliana on or about 1 October, as indicated in other sources, this item would place what was no doubt his execution on about 18 December.

[54] Della Chiesa, col. 1015: "Nel mese dy decembre essendo stato iudicato sopra la causa dil signor philipo figlolo primo dil condam principe iacomo. El conte el fece anegare publicamente nel lago dy Aviglana." Neither Cabaret nor Servion mention this affair at all.

between Marguerite de Beaujeu and the count drawn up a year later at Le Bourget in Savoy. The princess signed over to Amadeus her rights to the Piedmont and to the guardianship of her sons and declared her "true and spontaneous" intention of withdrawing from the world into the order of Saint Clara.[55] The count agreed in return to give her a cash settlement of 4,000 florins and an annual pension of 600 for the duration of his regency in the Piedmont, but there is reason to think that the cash settlement was never fully paid.[56] If so, the fact may help to explain why Marguerite did not enter a convent as she had promised. Her brother, Antoine of Beaujeu, died childless in 1374 and made his sister the heiress to extensive family holdings in the Beaujolais, Mâconnais, and Bresse. Marguerite lived out the remaining decades of her life in the pleasant country of her childhood and died at Lyon in 1401.[57]

This unexpected denouement to the Piedmont succession affair strongly suggests that Marguerite had been merely a tool in the hands of the Green Count all along. Surely no woman of sufficiently forceful character to have conceived and executed the stratagems by which Filippo of Achaea was brought to ruin would so meekly have abandoned to another not only the fruits of victory, but even her own sons. The possibility that the count forced her into retirement against her will seems ruled out by the fact that she does appear from time to time at the court of Savoy under entirely amiable circumstances.[58] If she was not pleased with her fate after 1369, her dissatisfaction has left no trace in the

[55] Treaty dated 5 December 1369. *AST, protocolli ducali*, doc. 48, folio 15.

[56] *AST*, inv. 16, doc. 29; *protocolli ducali*, doc. 48, folios 26 and 27. The first installment of the 4,000 florins—2,500—was apparently paid at Easter 1370, but an extension of six weeks was granted on 14 May 1370 for the remainder. The pension was assigned on Les Clées in the Pays de Vaud.

[57] *ADCO*, B 572, *Seigneurie de Beaujeu*, paq. 8, doc. 10. Antoine's will is dated 14 August 1374 and left to Marguerite "all of [Antoine's] lands, jurisdictions, and properties in the duchy of Burgundy, the land of Beaujeu, and the castles of Berzé, Cenue, and Julienne." Marguerite made her own will in 1388.

[58] Her presence at the court of Savoy is clear from items in the countess's household accounts (*AST*, inv. 39, folio 1, doc. 25). In September 1380, Marguerite appeared at Duingt for the wedding of her son, and two months earlier Amadeus had granted an annual *rente* in wine to one of her ladies at her request. *ADCO*, B 9613.

sources. For the next ten years the governor of her sons and the ruler of her principality was the count of Savoy alone.

The long-coveted Piedmont was now in the power of the Green Count, whose officers had been taking over quietly ever since Filippo's imprisonment in September.[59] So long as the Green Count had sufficient pride to overawe his conscience, he might well glory in his accomplishment. Now indeed he had more territory than "nul mes ancesseurs." From the banks of the Tanaro to the shores of Lake Neuchâtel, his power was felt and feared.

### PIEDMONT AFFAIRS AND THE REVERSAL OF ALLIANCES

Miscellaneous concerns required Amadeus' presence in Savoy almost continuously between December 1369 and Christmas 1371, but Piedmont affairs must have remained uppermost in his mind. On 17 October 1368, scarcely five months after his marriage to Violante Visconti, Lionel of Clarence died suddenly at Alba. The English, under the leadership of Edward Despencer, professed to believe that their master had been poisoned, and they refused to return Violante's dowry towns to Galeazzo, as provided in the marriage contract. A letter from Edward III to Despencer in December reveals that the English were hoping for a child from Violante, in whose behalf they might continue to hold the Piedmont appanage.[60] By the spring of 1369 it was clear that Clarence had left no heir, but the English still refused to surrender the towns. Galeazzo at once undertook to recover his daughter's dowry lands by force, and Despencer turned to the marquis of Montferrat for help. Giovanni II had joined the new league of Italian powers which Urban V had organized against the Visconti in the summer of 1369, and he was quick to take advantage of the weakened position of the English.[61] In October he "loaned" 16,000 florins to the English captain, who agreed that security for

[59] Amadeus had been designated as regent for Marguerite's sons by Giacomo's will. Cf. act of council of Savoy on 5 September 1368, *AST, Principi del Sangue*, mazzo VII, doc. 19.

[60] Cook, p. 105, note 3. Edward ordered that the towns be returned to Galeazzo, however, once it was clear that Violante was not with child.

[61] The papal league against the Visconti was not formally signed by all parties until 31 August 1369.

repayment would be the Piedmont towns still in English hands, notably Alba and Mondovì. This was a thinly disguised sale, for repayment had to occur within eight months, and by the end of November both towns were under Montferrat control.

The Visconti reaction to this development and to the papal league against them was a league of their own with Can Grande II della Scala and a sweeping offensive against Montferrat which brought them to the walls of Alexandria. By the spring of 1370 armies under the serpent banners had overrun the Novarese and Montferrat territories on the left bank of the Po. The culmination of this victorious campaign was the capture of Casale, capital of the marquisate, in early May. In an attempt to protect his remaining possessions, the marquis appealed for help to Avignon, and Urban V responded by inducing new hordes of mercenaries to cross the Alps and take service with the anti-Visconti forces.

These developments were cause for considerable anxiety among Savoyard officers in the Piedmont. There was already a disturbing concentration of mercenary companies in the region, and by the spring of 1371 those of the Visconti, heady with the wine of victory, were becoming increasingly difficult to control. Iblet de Challant, Amadeus' captain-general of the Piedmont, kept the count constantly informed of events, and in February, Richard Musard was sent across the Alps to inspect defenses in Savoyard territories. A few months later the passage of several mercenary companies through the count's dominions created a situation so dangerous that recourse to the count's warrior cousin Enguerrand de Coucy was contemplated, and efforts were secretly made to draw Anichino Baumgarten and his company into the Savoyard camp.[62] To make matters worse, the marquis of Saluzzo took advantage of the prevailing confusion to muster his army at Carmagnola, an outpost of his marquisate particularly well-placed for launching an attack against the lands of the prince of Achaea.

Although the Green Count had many old scores to settle with Federigo of Saluzzo, the causes of the present conflict were a legacy from Giacomo of Achaea, whose responsibilities Amadeus now assumed. As early as the spring of 1369 the count had gathered an army of mercenaries for a campaign against Saluzzo —the first army he had yet commanded in which the chief

[62] Gabotto, *Età*, p. 196.

strength was clearly furnished by the commercial soldiers he so despised. The projected campaign was postponed, owing to out-side pressure which resulted in a truce; but the episode sheds light on the extent to which the Green Count had adapted to the conditions for military and political success on the Italian side of his Alps. The old feudal values were gradually giving way before materialistic considerations, and the count now resorted to purchasing the loyalty of men and even to subsidizing their baser instincts for his own political gain. Instead of driving the Monk of Hecz from Fossano in a victorious campaign, Amadeus bought his withdrawal in November 1368 for 19,000 florins, then proceeded to hire the greater part of Hecz's company for his own forthcoming campaign against Saluzzo. The following January, Amadeus attempted to bribe one of Federigo's mercenary cap-tains, Henriet, to betray his master, seize the castle of Saluzzo, and deliver the marquis and his family into Savoyard hands for 16,000 florins.[63] Nothing came of this unsavory deal, but it deepens the shadow cast upon the Green Count's chivalric reputation by the affair of Filippo of Achaea, and it reveals Amadeus' growing readiness to permit ends to justify means.

The Green Count crossed the Mont Cenis sometime in late November or early December 1371, and a few days before Christ-mas his envoys returned from Vercelli with a contract in which Anichino Baumgarten agreed to join the Savoyards with his com-pany for the next eight months.[64] On 8 January 1372 the power-ful Falletti clan of Racconigi were induced to abandon the mar-quis of Saluzzo and deliver their town into the count's hands in return for his promise to employ them as his representatives there.[65] The marquis of Saluzzo was naturally alarmed by these developments, and he appealed for aid to his most recently adopted suzerain, Bernabò Visconti. Bernabò did protest against the count's obviously hostile intentions, but his protests were ignored.

[63] *Ibid.*, pp. 177, 179.

[64] The treaty with Baumgarten dated 22 December 1371 provided that he would serve the count for eight full months at 5,000 florins per month, but specified that he was not bound to serve more than one month beyond the eight if he did not wish to do so. *AST, Trattati diversi*, I, doc. 26.

[65] Gabotto, *Età*, p. 198. Racconigi had been taken by Saluzzo from the prince of Achaea some years before.

The count's campaign against Saluzzo in the spring of 1369 had been halted by the intervention of the Visconti. Amadeus' refusal now to heed their protests points to a significant change in his views on Italian affairs since he came into control of the Piedmont. Visconti successes over the past two years were beginning to appear dangerous. Agents of both the pope and the marquis of Montferrat, with whom relations had steadily improved, urged upon Amadeus the view that the Visconti power was the real threat to his security. Still more important, old Giovanni of Montferrat was nearing his end. His four sons were all under eleven years of age. Visconti armies had already overrun the greater part of the marquisate, and they stood ready to seize what remained. On every side were mercenary captains with voracious appetites who would leap at the chance to seize a Piedmont principality. Amadeus might well be sought as a protector for Montferrat, and he did not want his earlier alliances with the Visconti to jeopardize such an opportunity.

For these reasons the Green Count ignored angry warnings from Bernabò Visconti on behalf of the marquis of Saluzzo and moved toward closer ties with Montferrat. Bernabò sent reinforcements to Federigo, despite the count's protests, and in early March, Amadeus' campaign against Saluzzo began. By the end of the month Revello, Rifreddo, and Caraglio had fallen, and in May the siege of Carmagnola began. The swift success of Savoyard arms owed much to the expert generalship of Baumgarten, ably seconded by Enguerrand de Coucy (whose status as a mercenary was mitigated by his kinship to the count) and Iblet de Challant—three of the most famous warriors of the day.[66]

In the midst of the war against Saluzzo the news came that on 11 March, Giovanni II of Montferrat had died, leaving his eldest son and successor, Secondotto, under the guardianship of Otto of Brunswick.[67] The count of Savoy had not been named regent for his cousin, but he knew that sooner or later Brunswick would have to seek Savoyard assistance if the marquisate was to be preserved from Visconti aggression. This fact was made equally clear

---

[66] Enguerrand de Coucy may have been in Amadeus' service as early as November 1371, as affirmed by Cognasso, *Il Conte Verde*, p. 197.

[67] Otto of Brunswick was a German cousin of the late marquis and a member of the family of the dukes of Brunswick. He had come to seek his fortune in Italy in 1363 and had served Giovanni II loyally ever since.

to Otto of Brunswick after his proposals for a peace settlement were scornfully rejected by Galeazzo at Pavia in May. Galeazzo knew that he had Montferrat at his mercy, and he was not inclined to be merciful. As Amadeus had foreseen, Otto had no choice but to turn to Savoy.

The Green Count so far had preserved the peace at least technically with Galeazzo, in spite of being at war indirectly with Bernabò. But the alliance which had benefited both sides for the past twelve years was being subjected to strains far more intense than ever before. As border incidents between Visconti and Savoyard subjects multiplied, particularly in the region north of the Po where Galeazzo's conquests had created a common frontier, relations between the brothers-in-law grew increasingly strained. The threat that Galeazzo would now annex or dismember the marquisate of Montferrat, added to a Visconti victory over the papal league forces in early June, convinced Amadeus that something must be done to stop further Visconti expansion in the Piedmont. The marquis of Saluzzo was only too ready to accept a truce, and on 17 June the Green Count signed a treaty of alliance with Otto of Brunswick, his wards, and his allies.[68] By the terms of the treaty the count agreed to aid in the defense not only of Montferrat lands, notably the city of Asti, but to help recover everything which had been lost since the outbreak of the war in 1369. Neither side was to make peace without the consent of the other, nor even to conclude a truce unilaterally. Two-thirds of the territory of Asti recovered from the Visconti was to go to the count of Savoy, and one-third to young Marquis Secondotto.[69] Except for the county of Biandrate, the other lands reconquered were to be divided equally between the two allies. Savoy was to furnish 200 lances to Montferrat at once, at an estimated cost of 200,000 florins. As security for reimbursement of that expense, the count was given the castle and lands of Chivasso, the whole of the Canavese (except for lands there belonging to

[68] The allies included the bishop of Asti, the marquises of Ceva and Incisa, Manfredo di Busca, and Tommaso Malaspina. Treaty in *AST, Ducato Monferrato*, mazzo IV, doc. 21.

[69] Cibrario, *Storia*, III, 224, says that this rather curious name derived from the fact that he was the second marquis to bear the name of Otto. Marie-José, p. 207, affirms that he was so named in honor of the patron saint of Asti, Saint Secondo.

Otto of Brunswick), Riva, Poirino, and the fief of Moncucco.[70] The result was to dismember the marquisate almost as effectively as the Visconti could have done.

A spirited correspondence now followed between Pavia and Savoyard headquarters at Rivoli.[71] Amadeus decided that if Galeazzo would guarantee the territorial integrity of what remained of the marquisate, war between them might still be avoided. But Galeazzo wanted the rich city of Asti and he made this the *sine qua non* of all negotiations. According to Savoyard chronicles, the count sent envoys to tell Galeazzo that if he would not raise the siege of Asti voluntarily, Amadeus would force him to do so. Galeazzo's response was to urge his brother-in-law to "do the worst and the best he can, because the siege will not be raised."[72] At these words the count was supposedly "merveilleusement mal contant," declaring that he would have expected more compassion from Messire Galeazzo for "widowed ladies and orphaned children, cousins-german of my sister, his wife;" but he added that he well knew the "tirannie" of the Visconti, for "when [Galeazzo] has destroyed the children of Montferrat, he will destroy my nephew and Amadeus, my son, and afterwards me."

The chronicle version of the count's reasons for his change of heart is substantially borne out by a letter to Amadeus dated 3 July 1372 in which Galeazzo reveals his point of view.[73] The count had apparently sent to ask if Galeazzo would accept the mediation of the pope or of some mutual friend in settling his differences with Montferrat, and he had notified his brother-in-law that the dominions of the late marquis were now under his protection. In his reply Galeazzo expressed his amazement and dismay that after so many years of friendship, Amadeus would now wish to join the ranks of his enemies. Galeazzo stated that he was sending his chancellor, Giorgio di Vercelli, to try to reason with him on this matter. As for the count's suggestions, Galeazzo replied rather sourly that he knew that Amadeus was

---

[70] The places in the Canavese were listed as Mazzé, Mercenasco, Castiglione, Candia, Orio, Settimo, Leyni, Rivara, Rocca, and Favria. On 20 December 1372, Brunswick ordered the nobles and towns of the region to take the oath of fidelity to the count of Savoy. *AST, Ducato Monferrato,* mazzo IV, doc. 22.

[71] Cf. Mugnier, "Lettres."

[72] Servion, II, 163.

[73] Text cited in Cognasso, *Il Conte Verde,* p. 198.

now coprotector of Montferrat, but that the count had previously promised not to accept such a position. Alluding to the count's present status as regent for the sons of Marguerite de Beaujeu, Galeazzo added that "you take more pleasure in being a [regent] than we." Then he repeated his demand that Asti, "which is ours,"[74] be returned to him before any peace with Montferrat could be considered. "When Bernabò offered to mediate in the affair with Saluzzo," he continued, "you refused, saying that you did not wish to abandon your rights. Nor do we. We want Asti, which is ours. Are you going to defend the marquisate? With the help of God and our rights, we will seek to recover that which belongs to us."

Despite the fine sentiments attributed to the Green Count by the chroniclers, his heartfelt compassion for a widow and her "orphaned children," the treaty of 17 June shows all too clearly that he would exact his pound of flesh in return for preserving them from the "tirannie" of the Visconti. Machiavelli would later declare that it is better for a prince to be feared than loved, if he cannot be both, and that every prince "must know how to play the beast as well as the man."[75] Amadeus VI had clearly already reached similar conclusions on his own. The ruthlessness which characterized his dealings with both Montferrat and Piedmont cousins after 1367 could be excused on the grounds that only by such methods could a strong and orderly state be created in the Piedmont, and that an orderly state was essential to the general welfare. Machiavelli later advanced this very argument; but it hardly conforms to the ideals of Christian chivalry with which the Green Count began his career. Otto of Brunswick might well have done better for his wards if he had simply given up Asti to Galeazzo and turned his arms against Savoy.

All that now remained for the count to do was to enter the pope's anti-Visconti league, and the reversal in Amadeus' Italian policy would be complete. Negotiations to that end were begun almost at once, and on 7 July the treaty was drawn up and sealed. Gregory XI had already secured the adherence of Niccolo d'Este, the Carrara of Padua, the queen of Naples, the king of

---

[74] Asti had been seized by the Visconti in 1345 and taken from them by the marquis of Montferrat in 1356.

[75] *The Prince*, Chapter XVIII.

Hungary, the republics of Genoa and Florence, the bishop of Vercelli, and now both Montferrat and Savoy. The final inducement to the count had been the pope's offer of supreme command of league forces in western Lombardy—an offer which attests to the Green Count's growing military reputation.

Amadeus accepted the prestigious command offered him and agreed to join the coalition—but at a price. While the count bound himself to furnish 1,000 lances at his own expense, Gregory XI was held responsible for 600 more and 10,000 florins per month to pay for a second company of 500.[76] The treaty also provided that by 15 October 1372 the count must be in the field between the Ticino and the Adda (hence in the midst of Visconti territories) with a minimum force of 2,000 lances. So that he might not fear a Visconti attack upon his own dominions in his absence, the pope promised to send 300 lances to the Piedmont at his own expense.

The Green Count was now to match wits and talents with the most formidable captains of fourteenth-century Italy, and Savoy was to figure as a major power among the Italian states for the first time in many a year. It remained to be seen what success the feudal lords from the Alps would have upon the plains of Lombardy, where the ravenous serpent on the Visconti banners was a far more appropriate symbol than the white cross on the banners of Savoy.

[76] *AST, Trattati diversi*, I, doc. 27. Published in Datta, *Storia*, II, doc. XIX.

# The Serpents of Milan

## 1372-1377

### SAVOY VERSUS VISCONTI: A CLASH OF TRADITIONS

THE highroads of the Green Count's ambition had led him irresistibly down from the mountains of Savoy to the spacious plains of Lombardy. The society which he found there was as different as the scenery he had temporarily left behind him. Nature was parsimonious in Savoy, but in Lombardy she distributed her favors with abundant generosity. Savoy was a land of shepherds, farmers, and huntsmen; small towns grew slowly along the caravan routes that crossed the cold massifs, and the castles that crowned the rocky hilltops were often as barren within as they appeared to be from without. By contrast, the fertile plains of Lombardy, which sometimes stretched as far as the eye could see, were dotted with populous towns and wealthy cities far greater than any in the dominions of the count of Savoy. Here learning and the arts flourished as princes and cities vied with one another for the most distinguished poets and scholars, the most skillful artists, and the most beautiful monuments which wealth and taste could supply. The tempo of economic development may not have been what it was a century before, and cultural achievements may not have been what they would be a century later; but northern Italy still held its place in the forefront of European cultural and economic progress.

The political climate surrounding these accomplishments was less edifying, if no less remarkable. Sismondi's declaration that this was a bad time for "humanity" is not without some justification. Cruelty, faithlessness, and crime among ruling groups are nothing new in the history of mankind, but the political fragmentation of Italy did serve to multiply examples of them to the point that criminal practices were more characteristic of political life there than elsewhere in Europe. Among greater and lesser ruling families alike, few if any had accomplished their rise to power without resorting to such practices. Preeminent in power, wealth, and unscrupulous ambition (at least in contemporary eyes) were the Visconti of Milan, who by 1370 had brought almost all of western and central Lombardy under their sway.

The famous brothers, Galeazzo II and Bernabò, grew up in a political environment very different from that which prevailed in the Alps. Amadeus had one very distinct advantage over his far wealthier Visconti neighbors. He was the direct descendant of the same family which had ruled in those ancestral Alpine valleys for some four hundred years—and by far the greater part of his dominions consisted of ancestral valleys. The vast majority of his subjects felt an hereditary allegiance to his dynasty, and while they might occasionally complain and resist, they never seriously thought to rebel.[1] Life was quiet in those upland meadows and in the towns and villages grouped along the mountain routes near bridges over chasms and torrents. Foreigners, with their strange ways and strange ideas, did not come to live there in sufficient numbers to disrupt seriously the tranquility of that existence. The inhabitants honored, even when they did not love, their princes. In their struggle against local oppressors, the count was often their protector and ally. On the whole, the count's power was not great enough to cause them fear nor weak enough to lead them to seek protection elsewhere.

The Visconti did not enjoy such advantages. The dynasty had come into power in Milan scarcely a century before, and its position in the rest of Lombardy dated largely from the conquests of the past thirty to forty years. Nowhere was their domination established upon a legal foundation so venerable, so certain, so unquestioned as that which supported the house of Savoy. The riches and power which the gifted brothers now enjoyed were themselves inducements to others of equally modest origins to emulate the Visconti example, perhaps at Visconti expense. As the great political structure which the Germanic emperors had sought in previous centuries to impose upon Italy gradually

---

[1] The only two rebellions in Savoy in the fourteenth century (excluding the Piedmont and the Valais) were by peasants in the Maurienne (1327) and Tarentaise (1386) against their bishops.

collapsed, initiative in political affairs passed to local magnates. Success was founded not upon legal right, for there was no clear-cut legal tradition, but upon skill and cunning in a highly competitive environment. Individual talent counted for more than valid claims, for talent determined success, and the claims of the strongest and cleverest would prove sufficiently valid once they had been made good. A prince less clever, less unscrupulous, or less cruel than his foes was likely to fall victim to them himself, as Machiavelli later pointed out.

Ceaseless internal and external dangers arising from the uncertainty of political tenure stimulated rulers to ceaseless activity. One reason for the successful establishment of Visconti power in Milan and Pavia was the ability of the brothers to combine vigilant internal security measures with a restless and energetic foreign policy which helped to absorb the attention of would-be rebels. At home the Visconti brothers inspired fear, awe, and admiration by the cruelty of their punishments, the rigor of their justice, and the splendor of their churches, palaces, and courts. Outside their native city they sought recognition among the powers of Europe with spectacular marriage alliances, military conquests, and ceaseless extensions of their dominion. No one knew how far their restless ambitions might lead them, for every success was needed to strengthen their position in the two great cities upon which their power was largely based. Both Milan and Pavia had been important capitals since Roman antiquity; their location on the fertile plains of the Po and their command of the routes to northern Europe had always provided their rulers with sizeable revenues. The great monetary wealth furnished by Milan alone suffices in large part to explain how the Visconti were able to extend their sway over so wide an area and to confront so successfully the various coalitions raised up against them.[2]

In states recently acquired by conquest from jealous neighbors, the ruler had to make himself feared as well as respected if he expected to be obeyed. The infamous "quaresima" provided for in an edict, probably issued by Galeazzo in 1359 (the year of his seizure of Pavia), outlined a hair-raising program of tortures for

---

[2] The chronicler Corio, II, 269, affirmed that Bernabò exacted from his subjects taxes amounting to 5,000 florins per month, in addition to his normal annual revenue, which was 100,000 florins.

traitors and their accomplices, whom Galeazzo tended to define as anyone who had opposed him in the recent war. The title derived from the forty-day duration of the program, which terminated in the prisoner's death on the forty-first day—if he had not already died.[3] Brother Bernabò's acts of cruelty, if less systematic in prescription, were more imaginative in execution— at least if there is any truth in the many stories about him. Bernabò's passion was purebred hunting hounds, some five thousand of them, and many of his most brutal punishments were inflicted upon those accused of mistreating them or of violating his monumentally severe game laws. If the Milanese chroniclers are to be believed, a man caught killing a boar, Bernabò's favorite game, was not infrequently blinded or hanged.[4] On one occasion Bernabò is said to have burned down the house of a man who had not paid the fine levied upon him for having transgressed the game laws.

Bernabò's long wars with the papacy led him to perpetrate many acts of cruelty against churchmen. He is accused of having once burned four nuns to death and of having his buffoons roast an Augustinian monk in an iron cage for his own amusement.[5] Such acts against the clergy were not conceived of as acts against God, however, for Bernabò chose to circumvent the Church and seek divine favor more directly through copious gifts to religious houses and charitable foundations. In one of his *Novelle*, Dati relates that the lord of Milan once came upon a dead body left unburied by a priest because no one could pay the burial fee. Bernabò at once had the corpse properly buried at his own expense, and the offending priest along with it.[6]

Galeazzo was much the more quiet of the two brothers. While

[3] Details in Cook, p. 16, note 7, from the original in *RIS*, ed. L. A. Muratori (Milan, 1730), XVI, 410. Galeazzo is thought to have actually inflicted this program of horrors upon prisoners in 1362–1363.

[4] Cf. Corio, II, 268–269.

[5] *RIS*, XVI, 795. Many of these tales were probably just horror stories deliberately circulated against him by the Church, his chief foe.

[6] Cited in Dorothy Muir, *A History of Milan under the Visconti* (London, 1924), p. 70. Galeazzo was reasonably faithful to Blanche de Savoie, but Bernabò reportedly had thirty-six children by eighteen different ladies. *RIS*, XVI, 799-800; Corio, II, 326–327.

Bernabò enjoyed leading his armies in person and overseeing the most trivial details of government, Galeazzo preferred to delegate these responsibilities to others, especially in his later years. Both brothers were well educated, but it was Galeazzo who refounded the university of Pavia and endowed its faculty, who brought to the Visconti court the poet-laureate of Italy, Francesco Petrarca. Galeazzo's pride and joy was the great castello of Pavia with its vast park, perhaps the most magnificent princely dwelling in Europe at the time. Petrarca, who spent his summers at Pavia between 1363 and 1367, wrote a description of the city and its castle in a letter to Boccaccio in 1365: "You would find the city beautifully situated . . . on the margin of gently sloping banks, where it raises its crown of towers into the clouds, and enjoys a wide and free prospect on all sides. . . . One can see in one direction the snowy crest of the Alps, and in the other the wooded Apennines. . . . Lastly, in order of time, though not of importance, you would see the huge palace, situated on the highest point of the city; an admirable building, which cost a vast amount. It was built by the princely Galeazzo, the younger of the Visconti, the rulers of Milan, Pavia, and many neighboring towns, a man who surpasses others in many ways, and in the magnificence of his buildings fairly excels himself. I am convinced, unless I be misled by my partiality for the founder, that, with your good taste in such matters, you would declare this to be the most noble production of modern art."[7]

The famous emblem of the Visconti, a serpent from whose open jaws emerges a human figure, was first found carved upon a stone in the palace of the archbishop of Milan at Legnano. Its origins remain somewhat obscure, but according to the chroniclers, it represented the brazen serpent of the Old Testament in the act of swallowing up a Saracen.[8] As the Visconti became the hereditary "vice conte" of the archbishopric of Milan, they came to adopt the traditional emblem of the community whose armies they commanded. By the fourteenth century the serpent banner meant Visconti more surely than it meant Milan.

[7] Cited from J. H. Robinson and H. W. Rolfe, *Petrarch* (N.Y., 1914), pp. 323–325.

[8] Additional details in Muir, pp. 6–7.

# The Serpents of Milan

These were the famous brothers with whom the Green Count, after many years of friendly intercourse, now found himself in conflict. The armies under the serpent banners were at that very moment encamped before the walls of Asti. The defense of the city was ably conducted by Otto of Brunswick, but the garrison was not large and reinforcements were desperately needed. Galeazzo, indisposed by temperament and by gout, was not with his troops at the siege, but Giangaleazzo was. The lord of Pavia had secretly instructed his captains to prevent the twenty-year-old prince from exposing himself at any time to the dangers of actual battle.[9] The real fighting was to be conducted by Galeazzo's professional commanders, among whom was the famous English captain, John Hawkwood, at the head of his "White Company."

The first objective for the Savoyards was to raise the siege of Asti, and this was accomplished during August 1372. On 25 August, Giangaleazzo, exasperated by the failure of the siege and by parental restrictions, sent a herald to challenge his uncle to a duel. Naturally, the challenge was accepted with pleasure, and naturally, the duel never took place. Each side blamed the other for this, but aside from the scandalous impropriety of an experienced warrior fighting a duel with his inexperienced nephew, the real reason was the unwillingness of either side to follow the rules of chivalry if they violated the rules of political good sense. The rescue of Asti resulted in letters of congratulation from the pope to the Green Count, and in the desertion of the Visconti by John Hawkwood, who blamed the failure of the siege upon the interference of "scribblers" at Pavia.[10] To recompense the count of Savoy for his expenses in coming to their aid, the citizens of Asti gave him the town of Poirino, south of Chieri.[11]

In October the pope's nephew and brother arrived from Avignon with men and money for the anti-Visconti offensive, and the Angevin seneschal of Provence also appeared with an army. Amadeus was obliged to surrender to the Angevins the town of

---

[9] Gabotto, *Età*, p. 208.     [10] Temple-Leader and Marcotti, p. 72.

[11] Gabotto, *Età*, p. 209. Poirino had already been given to the count as security for money owed him by Marquis Secondotto, but on 23 August 1372 the town went to Amadeus in full proprietorship. The act was confirmed a few weeks later by Secondotto and his regent Otto of Brunswick.

Cuneo, which he had captured in the meantime, but the arrival of allies enabled him to cross the Dora and drive the Visconti out of most of the Vercellese by early December.[12] The Visconti promptly mounted a counteroffensive to the south which soon forced Amadeus to withdraw from the Vercellese in order to protect his Piedmont interests, much to the indignation of Gregory XI. The treaty of July 1372 had specified that the count of Savoy, as captain-general of the league forces in western Lombardy, was to have invaded Visconti territories beyond the Ticino by 15 October. On that date Amadeus had not even left the Piedmont, and his subsequent campaign into the Vercellese, while it constituted a major offensive against the Visconti, still did not satisfy the geographical requirements of the treaty. To papal protests, however, the count replied that the men and money promised by His Holiness in the same treaty had not yet arrived, notably the men who were to protect the Piedmont from Visconti incursions during the count's absence.

Various difficulties forced the postponement of the campaign until February 1373, by which time the promised men and supplies had reached the Green Count's Piedmont headquarters. Anichino Baumgarten had recently deserted to the Visconti, but this setback was balanced by an important league victory over Bernabò at Crevalcuore near Bologna. This victory had opened the way for an advance from Bologna toward Milan, and Gregory XI was particularly anxious that Amadeus be ready to move against Milan from the opposite direction at the same time. The pope's wishes were fulfilled in mid-February, when the count advanced without resistance across the Vercellese to the banks of the Ticino. Amadeus' plan was to cross the Ticino and descend upon Milan from the west, while the other league army, under the Cardinal-legate Filippo Cabassole, moved up from the southeast.

Bernabò and Galeazzo had powerful armies at their disposal, and the success of the campaign depended upon the ability of the two league armies to engage the enemy forces at the same moment, without permitting the brothers to engage them separately. Accordingly, the Savoyards decided against an attack upon Novara and moved past the city to the north. On 22 Feb-

---

[12] *Ibid.*, pp. 211ff. The towns of Santhià, San Germano, Tronzano, Magnano, Verrone, and Castellazzo fell into the count's hands on this campaign.

ruary they crossed the Ticino, despite Visconti efforts to stop them, and marched past Milan, ravaging the villages and fields as they went. By early March they had taken up a strong position in the town of Vimercate, northeast of Milan. The Visconti were momentarily overwhelmed by the tide of invasion, and they hastily opened negotiations in order to gain time. Bernabò sent envoys to the camp of the cardinal-legate, while Galeazzo sent his son to arrange a truce with the count of Savoy.

The Savoyard chroniclers accuse Bernabò of poisoning the bread, wine, and victuals at Vimercate while the count was there in the early spring of 1373. But, "as God willed it," a certain man who had seen Bernabò's spies poisoning the supplies went to the count and warned him, so that few of his men actually died. Moreover, many of those ill with the poison were miraculously cured by a "vinage" made with the precious ring of Saint Maurice, which the counts of Savoy since the time of Pierre II always wore. A brew made with the assistance of this marvelous ring "expoisoned" those who drank it, and only those who did not drink of it died.[13]

Whether or not his supplies had really been tampered with, the Green Count decided that it would be wise to move farther away from Milan toward central Lombardy and the other league army. In early April the host abandoned Vimercate and took up a new position at Brivio on the Adda. This site had several advantages, for in addition to permitting the troops to forage on the rich plains around Bergamo, the river could be used for defense purposes. The count ordered the construction of a bridge, and the army immediately set to work building fortifications. From this position Amadeus could harass the Visconti and at the crucial moment move swiftly either southwest or southeast, whichever was required to join in a full-scale engagement with Visconti armies.

Unfortunately for the league, the moment was to come and go without the decisive results on which the pope had laid his hopes. Enguerrand de Coucy and John Hawkwood, at the head of the league armies, set out from Ferrara in April, moving west-

---

[13] Servion, II, 196ff; Cabaret, pp. 200ff. This story, whether true or not, reveals Bernabò's reputation only a generation later. Aside from faulty chronology, the narrative of this campaign given by these chroniclers is substantially borne out by other sources.

ward toward Brescia, presumably intending to join the Savoyards on the banks of the Adda. The Visconti had not been inactive, however, and the negotiations between Bernabò and the cardinal-legate had given the former time to assemble his forces. Galeazzo sent his brother all the men he could spare, including Anichino Baumgarten and Giangaleazzo, and Bernabò's son-in-law, Duke Stefan of Bavaria, was expected to send 1,000 lances southward over the Alps by the middle of May. In the meantime, Visconti captains made a concerted effort to break up the bridges which the Savoyards had just built on the Adda at Brivio.

Bernabò realized the necessity of preventing at all costs a juncture of the two league armies. Something had to be done without delay, even though all of his reinforcements had not yet arrived. According to Savoyard chroniclers, Bernabò's decision to march against Hawkwood and Coucy (who were now in command of the papal army) instead of against the Green Count was prompted by Giangaleazzo's promise not to fight against the count of Savoy—but Giangaleazzo had not promised not to fight against the other league captains. Why the Savoyards did not march eastward at once and force a juncture with their allies is not clear. Either they could not because of the strength of the forces sent to hold them at Brivio, or they were not informed of the movements of their allies and did not realize that the battle was at hand. In any case, the decisive moment came on 7 May 1373 at Montichiari on the banks of the Chiese south of Brescia. The battle was bloody, and on both sides the warriors "tangled so heartily against one another that it was a marvel to behold." In the fray Giangaleazzo was hurled from his horse and forced to flee, leaving both helmet and lance behind. In spite of the numerical superiority of the Visconti forces, the "saige gouvernement" of Coucy and Hawkwood won the day for the league. Along with serpent banners, Francesco d'Este, Ugolino and Galeazzo di Saluzzo, and many other important nobles fell into the hands of the victors.[14]

[14] Cibrario, *Storia*, III, 229. Temple-Leader and Marcotti, pp. 75–76, follow the chroniclers who stated that the league army was at first defeated, but that from his vantage point at Montichiari, Hawkwood, seeing the Visconti ranks break as the mercenaries went for the spoils of victory, regrouped as many men as he could and attacked, taking the enemy by surprise and turning defeat into victory.

So far all had gone well, although the battle had been premature according to league plans. It was after the victory, however, that the gravest mistakes were made, for the victors did not follow up their advantage by pressing westward to effect the juncture with the count of Savoy. How such experienced commanders could have committed so grave an error, despite papal letters warning them against just such a mistake, is difficult to understand. Possibly the victory was less overwhelming than the chronicles suggest, and the victors were too weakened by their own losses to dare to risk another encounter with enemy reinforcements. It is also possible that Visconti money had succeeded in lessening the ardor of the papal captains—or simply that no one but the pope himself really wished to see the brothers of Milan entirely crushed beneath the hand of a triumphant church. Whatever the reason, the league forces withdrew from the battlefield and slowly returned to Bologna. The Green Count was reportedly shocked by the news, as well he might have been. The situation was serious, and there was only one course of action—to get to Bologna before the Visconti recouped their forces and crushed him.

The chronicles describe in great detail the manner in which the Green Count contrived to extricate himself and his army from this predicament, since it traditionally ranks as one of his more remarkable feats as a military leader. Apparently the leaguers crossed the Adda as quickly as possible and marched past Bergamo, heading southeast. They were unhampered by the enemy until after they had crossed the Oglio, where they encountered a large army which Bernabò had sent down from Brescia to intercept them. The climactic moment came near the powerful enemy-held fortress of Montichiari, which blocked their line of march. Behind them the Visconti captains had opened the water gates on the Oglio so that they could not retreat. The only way to advance was through a narrow ravine south of the fortress, and this was blocked by a detachment from the garrison.

The Green Count decided that they would have to force a passage and make a run for it, affirming that he would rather "risk everything breaking through and die fighting," than to perish of hunger or tamely surrender to Bernabò.[15] At this the

---

[15] Servion, II, 201ff; Cabaret, p. 205.

banners were hoisted and the trumpets sounded, and the host advanced into the ravine. Otto of Brunswick and the Montferrat troops threw themselves against the barriers built in the ravine and managed to make an opening. This success caused the defenders to withdraw toward the fortress, and the vanguard of the army was able to pass through the opening. The Green Count and his whole "bataille" followed, and behind them came the rear guard, commanded by Raymond of Turenne, the pope's nephew. The enemy, seeing that the leaguers were forced to pass in single file through the opening, attacked the rear guard. Raymond of Turenne and his men dismounted, allowing their horses and valets to pass on. Then, turning to face the foe, they fought in slow retreat, backing their way through in perfect order. When the news of the escape of the count's army reached Bernabò at Brescia, he is supposed to have flown into one of his famous rages, denouncing all of his captains as traitors and threatening to decapitate them all. At this the captains were "courrouciez" and threatened in turn to leave his service, but Bernabò "gave them money and reconciled them."

The Savoyards could now move unimpeded southeastward past Mantua to Ferrara, and by the end of June they had reached Bologna. Coucy and Hawkwood were reported to have been suitably embarrassed at having abandoned their colleague at Brivio, and they were as relieved as the count that he had managed to extricate his men from so difficult a situation. From Bologna the combined league armies marched westward along the south bank of the Po, utilizing the river to protect their flank. The Visconti had concentrated their forces on the banks of the Nure at its confluence with the Po near Piacenza, however, thus blocking any further advance.

It was in August 1373 that Galeazzo sent the Green Count the famous letter making fun of him for having abandoned his camp, full of supplies, and for having retreated by a circuitous route, "twelve miles, when the distance was only two," clambering around through mountains by paths that even goats and wild animals would have found difficult and fatiguing.[16] "In truth, we can hardly believe that all this could come from a head as good as yours and from a heart as great as yours!" Galeazzo

[16] Letter of 11 August 1373. Mugnier, "Lettres," doc. VII, 403–405.

taunted his brother-in-law on his earlier remarks about mercenary troops. Amadeus was reminded of his last trip to Pavia, where he had denounced them all, with a few exceptions, as "truans." He had declared that all he needed was 1,000 good lances from the mountains of Savoy and one good captain who was not afraid to fight on foot when the enemy was on foot, and "by Holy God" he would put to rout all of the soldiers of "Messire Hanequin" (Baumgarten), of Galeazzo and Bernabò, and of all of the barons of Lombardy and Tuscany, because they were all "guarscon et touls ribaux et sont gens de rien." It was then that the Green Count had added the remark that "by Holy God, there won't be a year that passes that I won't have more lands than had any of my ancestors, and I will be more talked of than were ever any of my lineage, or I'll die in the effort." Galeazzo quipped that the count had certainly not won any lands, but he certainly was more talked of than anyone else, and he "might well die of it." If all the Visconti soldiers were "ribaus et guarscons," then why did the count refuse to come down and fight them, instead of remaining "always on the mountain tops, surrounded always by fortifications and trenches?"

But this letter sheds very little light upon the rather obscure activities of the Green Count during the remainder of 1373. Apparently the Savoyards had been forced to retreat by the Visconti, who were trying to shame them into doing battle. Letters in October to Richard Musard, captain-general of the Piedmont, and to Bonne de Bourbon reveal only the count's concern for the defense of his territories during his absence, and his intentions of going to Venice in search of more mercenaries for the league armies.[17] Early in January 1374, Amadeus crossed the Apennines at the head of 2,000 lances in an effort to protect Lucca and Pisa from Visconti designs. From Pisa the count shipped his men to Savona, since the Visconti controlled the land routes, and by 24 February he was back at Rivoli in the Val di Susa. After such a year of trouble and fear, it is easy to believe the chroniclers' assertion that his subjects were "right willing" to have him back.

Once back in his own territories, the Green Count prepared to reverse his Italian foreign policy as dramatically as he had done two years earlier. On 9 March 1374, Galeazzo opened negotia-

[17] *Ibid.*, doc. XLIII (misdated 1375); Cognasso, *Il Conte Verde*, p. 210.

tions, and Amadeus was ready to listen to proposals of peace. From Savoy he had disquieting news of more threats from the Great Companies beyond the Saône. At Montmélian, Humbert de Savoie was alarmed by the situation, and the count visited him in mid-March to confer on measures to be taken. At the same time, envoys were sent to Avignon to extricate the count from further obligations toward the league and probably to advise Gregory XI also to negotiate with the Visconti. On 30 April, Savoyard representatives secured letters from the pope certifying that the count's obligations under the treaty of 1372 had been entirely fulfilled, and that nothing more might be required of him by invoking its terms in the future.[18]

The Green Count's hands were now freed for other enterprises. On 6 June he attended a meeting with his nephew and his sister, whose despair over the wars pitting her husband and son against her brother had caused her to work ceaselessly for a reconciliation.[19] Galeazzo was badly afflicted with the gout now, and he increasingly delegated the conduct of affairs to his capable son. No one at Pavia had been in full sympathy with Bernabò's policies, and after the near-disaster of 1373, many feared that the elder Visconti would be the destruction of them all.

The outcome of the meeting was a renewal of the treaty of friendship and assistance concluded between Galeazzo and Amadeus back in 1360. The count agreed to furnish his brother-in-law with 200 lances for four months a year, while Galeazzo promised 400 to the count for the same term whenever he needed them. Each agreed to aid the other with all of his forces in case of a major campaign against "their enemies." What the Green Count had in mind is revealed by Galeazzo's promise to give no aid either to Bernabò or to the marquis of Saluzzo, in return for the count's promise not to join any papal enterprise against the Visconti. Thus the pope's captain-general had unceremoniously bowed out of the anti-Visconti league as soon as it suited his interests to do so.[20]

[18] Gabotto, *Età*, pp. 218–219.

[19] Bernabò is said to have been so angry at his brother's separate peace that he tried to assassinate Blanche de Savoie, whom he held responsible for it. Cf. *RIS*, XVI, 797.

[20] The count's commitments were not to take effect until after the expiration of his league pact, i.e. three years from 7 July 1372. Galeazzo's obligations and

# The Serpents of Milan

Saluzzo was thus to be the next military objective of the count of Savoy, as soon as a decent interval had elapsed to allow for the expiration of engagements which bound both sides not to do what they had just agreed to do. On 4 June 1374, Gregory XI concluded a truce for one year with the Visconti brothers, however, and Amadeus was induced to extend his truce with Saluzzo for another six months.[21] Another reason for the truce was the famine which the recent wars had caused in the Piedmont and which obliged the count to prohibit the export of foodstuffs from the region.[22] Moreover, family tragedies and new threats from the Great Companies on his western boundaries required the count's presence in Savoy. Ogier de Savoie had died at Bons-en-Bugey around Christmas 1373, and Humbert de Savoie died sometime the following March, leaving two sons and a considerable vacancy in family affections.[23] In September 1374, Antoine of Beaujeu, the count's cousin and frequent companion, was another victim of the year, dying childless and leaving his possessions to his sister Marguerite. The most tragic loss of all, however, was the death of Antoine de Savoie, the count's twenty-two-year-old illegitimate son.[24]

The winter of 1374–1375 was spent raising armies to protect the Rhône valley territories from the Great Companies. This time the situation was more serious than ever before because it was not merely a question of raids, but a real invasion threat. In the

---

other treaty provisions were to become effective on 1 October 1374. *AST, Trattati diversi*, I, docs. 29, 30.

[21] *Ibid.*, doc. 32.

[22] Gabotto, *Età*, pp. 220–221. Thirteen seventy-four was a hard year in Bresse and Savoy also. Cf. *ADCO*, Bressan rolls for 1373–1375, and *ADS, subside* rolls for 1373. During June–August 1374, Amadeus helped the Visconti to retake Galliate and aided the bishop of Vercelli in recapturing the castles of Sant'Andrea and Vercelli.

[23] *ADS* (castellany), Montmélian 1373–1375: Humbert de Savoie's expenses at Le Bourget "in festo epiphanie [1374] ubi fuit de mandato domini quia dominus ipsum misit apud castellanum Bonitiarum pro morte domini Ogerii bastardi de Sabaudie." Humbert's eldest son succeeded him as sire of Arvillars, and his second son became sire of Mollettes. Both married into Savoyard noble families and founded dynasties.

[24] Marie-José, pp. 60–61.

Dauphiné, Olivier du Guesclin was at that very moment forming
a large company which he reportedly intended to lead into Lombardy by way of Savoy. The bourgeois of Chambéry worked
frantically at their new fortifications,[25] and the whole population
around Montmélian was mobilized to block passage into Savoy
by fortifying the group of castles located in the Isère valley above
Grenoble. Antoine de Malaspina was sent to Genoa to hire crossbowmen, and relays of spies were sent into the Dauphiné to watch
the movements of the Companies. The count of Geneva also
joined in the defense effort, partly out of duty and partly because
his own properties in the Grésivaudan were even more exposed
than the frontiers of Savoy.

At the same time, mercenary bands were threatening the Pays
de Vaud. They had been reported in the vicinity of Morat, laying
waste to the countryside as they moved. While garrisons were
being doubled in the castles guarding the southern approaches
to Savoy, more men had to be hastily moved to Gex, Versoix, and
points north of Lake Geneva. The danger on the northern
boundaries, it turned out, was created by the Green Count's cousin, Enguerrand de Coucy, who had decided to claim a share of
his mother's Habsburg inheritance in northern Helvetia. In 1375
he assembled a great horde of mercenary companies and moved
from the Lyonnais into Alsace. When Leopold II of Habsburg
refused to admit Coucy's claims, war began and lasted through
most of 1375.[26] Peace was not restored until early 1376, when
Leopold was forced to cede the counties of Nidau and Büren to
his formidable cousin.

The situation remained tense for some time, but Savoyard defenses proved equal to the challenge. The Green Count's subjects everywhere remained beyond the reach of the marauders
who were ravaging the green fields of France and Italy. Although
the Savoyards could not know it, this was the last real threat
from the Great Companies. The frontiers of the Dauphiné were

[25] Amadeus had first ordered the construction of new walls to enclose the
faubourgs of Chambéry in an ordinance dated 18 March 1371.

[26] This was the Leopold of Habsburg who was killed by the Swiss in the
battle of Sempach on 9 July 1386. On 20 November 1375, Amadeus sent envoys
to conclude an alliance with the duke of Austria against "insurgentibus et
regnantibus" and "societatibus inimicis et congregationibus gentium nefandarum."
*AST, Trattati diversi,* I, doc. 31.

endangered again in 1377, but Savoy was not; and in spite of occasional scares, nothing would again create a reign of terror such as the Saône valley population had experienced over the past fifteen years.

While the menace of the Companies postponed the count's enterprise against Saluzzo, Federigo had not been inactive. It was clear that he could no longer rely upon the Visconti, for Galeazzo had joined his archenemy, and Bernabò was preoccupied elsewhere. The marquis could not face the might of Savoy alone, nor could he hope for a settlement which he could honestly accept. He had defied the count of Savoy too often to expect anything but demands for unconditional surrender. Another protector must be found, preferably one too distant to interfere in the internal affairs of the marquisate, but not too distant to furnish prompt military aid. From his embattled hilltop Federigo surveyed the horizon for a likely candidate for his next oath of undying loyalty, and his gaze rested again on the Dauphiné. As in 1363, Paris seemed very far away, and French domination, even if it came to that, was preferable to the domination of the count of Savoy.

Early in 1375 the marquis notified the representatives of the king of France of his desire. French envoys were sent to Saluzzo on 22 March 1375 to receive the marquis's homage to the dauphin. French overlordship was considerably more expensive this time than it had been twelve years before. That a man so tenacious of his independence from Savoy should have so tamely accepted the conditions now imposed upon him suggests that passion, rather than reason, swayed the marquis at this point. Federigo was forced to sign away permanently the upper valley of the Varaita, called the castellany of Sant'Eusebio.[27] Then to bind him more tightly to his new masters, he was obliged to purchase 10,000 florins' worth of fiefs elsewhere in the Dauphiné. Until he fulfilled this obligation, he was to surrender the town of Carmagnola and its fortress to the dauphin's lieutenants. Federigo's homage to the dauphin was understood to be liege-homage for the entire marquisate, not just a part of it, and the

---

[27] The castellany of Sant'Eusebio consisted of the towns of Chaudanes, Sant'-Eusebio, Bellion, Pont, and Chianale. The treaty was signed on 11 April 1375. Gabotto, *Età*, p. 224.

marquis was specifically required to recognize the ultimate jurisdiction of the royal courts of France. In return for all of this,
Federigo received the promise that he would be protected from
all his enemies.

On 20 April, Gui de Morgis and a company of Dauphinois arrived at Carmagnola and hoisted the lilies of France over the
towers of the town. The Green Count was at that time in the
Maurienne on his way to Italy, apparently unaware of these
latest developments. By early May he had reached Rivoli, where
he convoked the communes and nobles of Piedmont in preparation for the campaign. Envoys were at once sent to him by Charles
de Bouville, governor of the Dauphiné, to inform him of the new
state of affairs and to forbid him in the name of the king of
France to attack or in any way injure the marquis of Saluzzo.
The envoys were dismissed with a blast of rage which found
milder expression in protests sent at once to Paris. A considerable
correspondence developed between Charles V and his angry
brother-in-law over ensuing months. On 6 April, Charles wrote
from Paris to his "dear and very beloved brother" that he had
received the letters concerning the Saluzzo affair, and he thanked
Amadeus for the expressions of loyalty and goodwill with which
the count had wisely seasoned his anger. The king declared that
he had set the date of the hearing for All Saints and concluded
by asking for news of the "bon estat" of the count, of "our very
dear sister, the countess, and of your son, our nephew."[28] About
two weeks later Charles wrote again to say that although Federigo
had come to Paris in person to plead his case, the count need
have no fear that his rights might be neglected. Royal concern
for the count's feelings was heightened by the news of mercenary
companies advancing toward the Dauphiné. Charles concluded
his letter by begging Amadeus to come to the aid of "nostre pays
et nos subgez," just as he would aid the count were the situation
reversed.

The count continued to remind Charles of his views on this
affair, but he must soon have suspected that the French would
not surrender the advantages of suzerainty over the marquisate.
In a letter from Paris in June 1375 to his "esteemed brother,"

[28] This letter and the others concerning this matter are found in Cordey,
*Les Comtes, preuves,* docs. 37–40.

Charles summed up the controversy with admirable brevity, if not impartiality: ". . . a dispute over the homage of the said marquis, which you say belongs to you, the said marquis affirming the contrary, and which belongs to us and to no others because of our Dauphiné."[29] The king expressed his satisfaction that, instead of resorting to arms, both parties had submitted the dispute to arbitration, and he especially thanked the count for having halted the "enterprise begun by you against [the marquis]." Since it would inconvenience the count to come to Paris, the king delegated final jurisdiction in the matter to the duke of Anjou, who was on his way to Avignon. Charles asked the count to plead his case before so friendly a judge in the papal city.

Amadeus did go to Avignon, probably in June or July, and there was apparently a stormy interview with Federigo in the presence of the duke of Anjou. During the truce to which both parties had agreed, the marquis' troops had surprised the castle of Cervignasco and had captured some of the count's men. If this event was known to the count, as it may have been, this would account for his explosion of rage.[30] When Amadeus laid eyes upon the "rebel," he turned to Louis of Anjou and demanded justice: ". . . He is my man and in doing fidelity he swore and promised to be faithful and loyal to me and mine, which he has never held to, and has sought to do harm to me and my country, acting against his oath and promise."[31] The count worked himself into a fury and declared that if the marquis dared to deny the truth of what he said, he would "battle him in your [Anjou's] presence, and with the help of God and of the good knights Saint George and Saint Maurice, I'll leave him dead or vanquished!"

Federigo weathered this verbal tempest undaunted and replied that he was "good and loyal" and that he had never done anything he ought not to do. If the count wished to insist upon his charges, then he would defend himself, also with the aid of God and Saint George (Saint Maurice was known to be pro-Savoyard), and would prove the count a liar. He then proffered other "in-

[29] See Commentary, XIV, on this question.

[30] This event occurred on 4 June 1375. Cibrario, *Storia*, III, 234; Gabotto, *Età*, p. 226.

[31] Servion, II, 208ff. Della Chiesa, col. 1022, misdates the event 1374.

jurious words," especially "concerning the affair of Messire Philippe de Savoye," and he ended by flinging down his own challenge. This reference to ugly rumors about the Piedmont succession reveals what was still being said of the matter at least a generation after the event (when the chronicles were written), if not at the time.

Louis of Anjou was "mal contant" with both sides and refused to permit the duel. He decided that the question was too difficult for him to settle, and it was referred again to the king and council at Paris.[32] The Green Count's anger at this maneuver led him to make a legal countermove: an appeal to the imperial court at Prague. In the eyes of the emperor the case was clear. The marquis, a vassal whose territories lay entirely within the boundaries of the Empire, had appealed to the jurisdiction of a foreign monarch without the consent of the emperor, thus violating the feudal rights of his imperial suzerain. In decrees of 11 November 1375 the marquis was declared a felon, his marquisate was declared forfeit to the count of Savoy, and Federigo was expressly forbidden to bring this case in the future before any but an imperial tribunal.[33] The count's defeat at Paris was thus reversed by victory at Prague in his perennial struggle to dominate the indomitable marquis. But the victory was theoretical, while the defeat was real. It is to the credit of the Green Count that he recognized Saluzzo as a lost cause for the time being and wasted no further substance in pursuit of it.

### RIPAILLE, THE VALAIS, THE VAL D'AOSTA, 1375–1376

The remainder of 1375 and the early part of the following year were absorbed by events in Savoy, the Valais, and the Val d'Aosta. The Green Count spent some time with his family for a change, particularly at Ripaille, where, since the spring of 1371, Bonne de Bourbon had been supervising the construction of a great manor house. This was the chateau of Ripaille, later the scene of many dramatic events in Savoyard history. At this time it was rather modestly described as "the house of the Lord Count called

---

[32] A royal letter of 9 May 1376 confirmed Federigo in all of his possessions. Final action (in the marquis' favor) did not come until 1390.

[33] Gabotto, *Età*, p. 231; Cognasso, *Il Conte Verde*, p. 220.

Ripaille, situated next to the forest of Ripaille below Thonon near the lake," and it had none of the elegant gardens or spacious outbuildings with which subsequent centuries endowed it.[34]

The construction of this chateau, as well as its location, points to important developments in the Savoyard state of the second half of the fourteenth century. The possibilities for Savoyard expansion south and west were largely ended by the Treaty of Paris, and the acquisition of the Pays de Vaud placed Ripaille more nearly at the center of the count's dominions than was Chambéry. Ripaille in the Chablais was within easy reach of the Maurienne, the Val d'Aosta, the Valais, Faucigny, and the Pays de Vaud. It lay nearer the great transalpine crossroads of western Helvetia, which were more frequented now that war conditions in France had discouraged the use of more westerly routes. During the lifetime of the Green Count, Ripaille would never replace Chambéry as the administrative capital of the Savoyard state—as it was to do after his death—but it soon became his favorite spot for relaxation, and the countess devoted herself to making it the cultural capital of the Savoyard Alps.

Ripaille reflected both the expansion of Savoyard power northward and the advent of a quieter age—the end of the era in which the dominant notes of these wooded valleys were the call of the war trumpet, the clatter of armor, the tumult of local wars. The incessant campaigns of the Green Count helped to keep the nobility fully occupied elsewhere and took the edge off their martial ardor when they came back home. Ripaille was the first building ever constructed by the counts of Savoy for comfort, not for defense; it was their first residence located with an eye to the beauty of the site, rather than to its military importance.

The architect was Jean d'Orlyé, formerly one of Amadeus junior's tutors, who supervised the construction under the watchful eye of the countess. Bonne de Bourbon was determined to have at last a manor house large enough to contain an entourage which had grown considerably over the years, particularly since the arrival of the princes of Achaea. She shared her husband's fondness for comfort and entertainment, and her household swarmed with musicians. She was herself an accomplished performer on the harp, and is credited with having introduced some-

---

[34] Max Bruchet, *Le Château de Ripaille* (Paris, 1907), *preuves* V, VI.

thing of a vogue for that instrument in Savoy. At Ripaille, Lake Geneva was at hand for excursions, and the game-filled forests nearby had made the place a favorite hunting ground for the counts of Savoy long before anything but a simple wooden lodge existed to house them. The manor house now nearing completion was built for light and air, with large lattice windows to let in plenty of sunshine. The central part of the building was of stone, two stories high, and contained a vast banquet hall with a soaring *charpente* roof supported by over one hundred elegantly carved wooden columns. On either side of the main building were wings containing the apartments where guests and members of the court were accommodated.[35]

While Bonne de Bourbon pursued the construction of her palace in the summer of 1375, Amadeus was suddenly called away by news of violence again in the Valais. What had once been the peasants' struggle for liberty had for some years now become a battle to the death between the ancient Valaisan house of La Tour–Châtillon and the "foreign" house of Tavel, represented by Bishop Guichard and his nephews. In November 1365 allies of the bishop had envenomed the struggle beyond hope of remedy by murdering Isabelle de Biandrate, aunt of Antoine de la Tour, and her small son while they were crossing the Rhône at Naters. From then on, life in the Valais had been but one long nightmare of killing and destruction, arrested periodically by truces that barely enabled the combatants to catch their breath. Whichever side won the war, the peasants stood to lose, and it was they who suffered most. Villages were burned to the ground, vineyards uprooted, crops destroyed in the fields.

The Green Count had long since abandoned his youthful determination to crush the Valaisans by military force. He had discovered that it was wiser to divide and rule, and for the past fifteen years his role had been chiefly that of a peacemaker. In October 1368, while involved in the Piedmont succession affair, Amadeus had attempted to make peace between the La Tour and the Tavel, invoking his authority as suzerain of both and as "imperatorie majestatis vicarius," despite the emperor's revocation of that title two years before. The La Tour were ordered to do homage to the bishop for certain holdings, and the bishop's nephew was to do

---

[35] Further details in Bruchet, *Ripaille*.

homage to La Tour for possessions acquired through his wife, Jeannette d'Anniviers. The bishop and citizens of Sion were to pray for the souls of Isabelle de Biandrate and her son, whom they had so effectively helped to depart this life. In June 1370 at the abbey of St-Maurice, the count made still another attempt to keep the peace by reiterating the mutual obligations of the two sides and by threatening the troublemakers with "our perpetual indignation."[36] By September, Amadeus was gone again, however, and more than his indignation, perpetual or otherwise, was required to prevent war in the Valais.

In January 1373, Guichard Tavel secured another major advantage in the power struggle with La Tour when he acquired the office and castle of La Majorie at Sion. This dignity, with its numerous military and judicial prerogatives, had once been hereditary in the La Tour family, who bitterly resented its loss. The head of the family, Antoine de la Tour, had now come to look upon the seventy-three-year-old prelate as the one man responsible for the destruction of his family's position in the Valais. On the morning of 8 August 1375, Antoine and a select group of henchmen made their way up the steep hillside on the northern rim of the Rhône valley near Sion. Beyond the first line of hills on a precipitous ridge stood the castle of La Soie, where the old bishop lived. Somehow La Tour and his men got past the entrance fortifications and into the courtyard garden, where Tavel and his chaplain were strolling and reciting the canonical hours. The desperados fell upon the bishop and his clerk, dragged them to the edge of the walls, and hurled them down to instant death on the rocks of the chasm below.[37]

When the news of the crime reached the valley, the population was at first incredulous, then indignant. The bishop, once their enemy, had for some years past become their most effective ally in the ceaseless struggle against the depredations of the Valaisan nobles. The murder of the bishop was the signal for a stormy uprising directed principally toward the La Tour, but indirectly against the entire noble class. The inhabitants of the valley of Goms near the Furka, and the peasants of Brig, Leuk, Sierre,

---

[36] Gremaud, docs. 2135, 2137, 2146.

[37] I follow Van Berchem, p. 312, note 2, who refutes, I think successfully, the arguments of M. Charrière that Antoine himself did not participate in the assassination.

and Sion came together at once, resolved to turn the situation to their own advantage and avenge the bishop's death at the same time. They hastily distributed arms, then invaded the territories of the murderer. The castle of Granges was the first to fall, then the fortress of Ayent.

Antoine de la Tour called upon the nobles of the valley to join in putting down the rebellion, lest they all perish at the hands of their subjects. A considerable number of nobles answered the appeal and the baronial host encountered the rebels near the bridge over the Rhône at St-Léonard. There a fierce battle took place between the feudal host and the sturdy Swiss peasants. The baronial ranks were broken, knights and chargers went down before the murderous axes of the peasants, to be butchered with no more mercy than they would themselves have shown. Antoine succeeded in escaping, and some weeks later returned with his brother-in-law and nobles of the Emmenthal at the head of a new army. The Valaisans, who had already burned Conthey and torn down the walls of La Tour's ancestral castle of Châtillon, met this new enemy at Arbaz. Again the baronial army was crushingly defeated, La Tour's brother-in-law was captured and killed, and Antoine himself barely escaped with his life.

When news of these events reached the Green Count on the shores of Lake Geneva in the late summer of 1375, he at once ordered reinforcements for Chillon and increased the garrisons of his fortresses in the lower Valais. Then he came quickly to terms with the murderer of his friend, the late bishop of Sion. Antoine de la Tour could never again return to the Valais, but the Green Count was hoping to take his place. He bought out La Tour's properties and rights in the Valais, notably Châtillon and Conthey with their dependencies. Then he prevailed upon Gregory XI, who still needed his help in Italy and did not wish to offend him, to appoint as successor to Bishop Guichard the count's cousin, Eduardo de Savoie, who had been bishop of Belley since 1370. The pope complied with the request, and Amadeus, keeping Conthey for himself, bestowed the ruins of Châtillon upon the new bishop of Sion, along with the fortresses attached to his see.[38]

[38] On 3 January 1376, Amadeus granted both Conthey and Saillon to his cousin personally, not as bishop of Sion. Antoine de la Tour, whose only daughter had married Jean de la Baume-Montrevel in Bresse, received a few lands in

The Valaisans were to discover that they had got rid of La Tour only to make room for the far more formidable count of Savoy, who could congratulate himself on a very skillful manipulation of unexpected events.

In July of the following year, Amadeus went to the Val d'Aosta to hold the *Audiences*.[39] The peace of the valley had been shattered by a fresh outbreak of hostilities between the rival families of Challant and Quart, provoked this time by the installation of Boniface de Challant as bishop of Aosta on the death of Emeric II de Quart in October 1375. The Green Count was now sufficiently powerful to take strong measures against those who had broken the peace. If the Quart family had borne the brunt of his wrath some years back, it was now the turn of the Challants, hitherto his favorites. Pierre de Challant, lord of the great barony of Cly, was condemned before the feudal tribunal for repeated lawlessness, and his fiefs were confiscated. The seigneurie of Cly, one of the most extensive in the valley, passed into the hands of the count of Savoy and remained there.[40] The annexation of Cly to the comital domain is a striking illustration of the increase in the Green Count's power in the Val d'Aosta since his first visit in 1351. The powerful relatives of the condemned man—Iblet, Aymon, and Bishop Boniface—apparently did not dare to intervene on his behalf.

The barony of Cly was not the only one on which the Green Count had designs. On 2 August, Henri of Quart, who had no sons, was compelled to avow publicly before the feudal tribunal that the greater part of his possessions, carefully specified, were fiefs held directly of Savoy.[41] Amadeus obviously had his eye upon that great inheritance, which, if added to the barony of Cly and the count's other possessions, would make him the richest landowner in the duchy. This preliminary action seemed advisable

---

the canton of Fribourg and was taken into the count's service as castellan of Romont in the Pays de Vaud. He died at L'Albergement in Bresse in 1405.

[39] The *Audiences* had also been held in 1368, when Henri of Quart was fined for various misdeeds.

[40] Not until 1384 was Pierre de Challant restored to favor when Amadeus VII gave him the seigneurie of Châtel-St-Denis near Fribourg.

[41] They were the castles of Quart, Brissogne, Sarre, St-Pierre-en-Châtelargent; the maisons-fortes of Pollein and Porte-St-Ours; and jurisdiction over the Valpelline and Dove.

since the wife of the baron of Quart was the sister of Amadeus' archenemy, Federigo of Saluzzo. The count's timing was ideal. Late in 1377, Henri of Quart died without male heirs, and Amadeus immediately confiscated his vast dominions on the grounds that they could not pass to females. The lawsuits which this action provoked did not come to an end until 1385, but the count of Savoy was wholly victorious.[42] This acquisition was no doubt doubly welcome; while securing additional lands and castles, Amadeus was also avenging himself indirectly upon the marquis of Saluzzo.

This was not the Green Count's last visit to the Val d'Aosta, but it was the last time he would preside over the *Audiences générales*. In the quarter century that had elapsed since his visit of 1351, much had been accomplished. Slowly but surely Amadeus had managed to advance his control over the semi-independent barons of the valley by employing essentially the same techniques which had succeeded elsewhere in the Savoyard Alps. Local magnates had been kept busy on military campaigns and on various diplomatic and administrative assignments which frequently removed them from their home valleys for months or even years at a time. The count's relatively frequent visits to the Val d'Aosta had continually strengthened the hand of his officers there and had enabled them to execute sentences against even the high and mighty which were profitable for the count. In the Val d'Aosta as elsewhere, Amadeus VI deserves credit for having provided more effective government than most of his predecessors had done, and for having laid the territorial foundations for strong centralized government in the future.

AMADEUS "MONSEIGNEUR"

·

THE ANNEXATION OF BIELLA AND THE END
OF THE PIEDMONT REGENCY

One final matter required the Green Count's attention west of the Alps during the winter of 1376–1377. Young "Amadeus Monseigneur," the count's son, was approaching his seventeenth year,

[42] On 29 December 1378 the inhabitants of the seigneurie of Quart asked for and obtained from the count confirmation of their ancient privileges and liberties. Duc, IV, 81.

and it was time to introduce him to more serious responsibilities than hunting and hawking. He seems to have been a good-humored and popular young man, but he had thus far given evidence of more brawn than brains. What was needed was a wife and an independent establishment where he might begin his apprenticeship in the arts of government. In May 1372 the count had already chosen as his future daughter-in-law little Bonne de Berri, the fourth and youngest daughter of the elegant Duke Jean of Berry, brother of the king of France.[43] Whatever the child may have lacked in womanly charms was more than made up in a dowry of 100,000 gold francs and the explicit reservation of her rights as a future heiress or co-heiress to her father's vast possessions.

The time had come for the marriage to take place, and sometime after Christmas 1376 the count and his son left Savoy for Paris. To make certain that the wedding occurred under the most favorable auspices, Amadeus consulted the king's astrologer, Thomas of Bologna.[44] Thomas pronounced 18 January 1377 a suitable date, and the ceremony accordingly took place at the Hôtel de St-Pol in the presence of the king, the queen, and the royal court. The count of Savoy, not to be outshone by his magnificent in-laws, turned out in green taffeta with cloth-of-gold embroideries on the sleeves, an elegant waistband of gold in the form of lions and hounds intertwined with foliage and vines, and innumerable clasps ornamented with diamonds, pearls, sapphires, and rubies. His son emulated the paternal example and suggested his own future epithet in choosing bright red for his outfit.[45]

The Green Count remained in Paris after the wedding long enough to conclude at last the twenty years of litigation over the provisions of the treaty of 1355. The Viennois castles ceded to the dauphin had never been surrendered because Amadeus had never received the sums promised him at intervals over the years.

[43] The marriage contract was concluded at Valence on 7 May 1372. The bride-to-be was about four or five years old at the time. Cordey, *Les Comtes*, p. 213.

[44] Details in Cordey, pp. 214ff. Thomas of Bologna was the father of the celebrated biographer of Charles V, Christine de Pisan.

[45] Cibrario, *Economia*, II, 84; Ménabréa, *Chambéry*, MS, Book IV, Chapter VII. Perhaps because of her young age, Bonne de Berri returned to her home in Bourges after the marriage, instead of accompanying her husband to Savoy. She did not finally come to Savoy until 1381.

A quarrel over the Guiers River boundary between Savoy and the Dauphiné had never been settled even tentatively. On 24 February 1377, Charles V and the Green Count affixed their seals to a treaty which ended once and for all the controversies over these matters. The count agreed to cede Tournon and Voiron by 1 April and everything else which he had once owned south of the Guiers from St-Genix to the point where the Guiers flows into the Rhône. He also gave up the castles of Les Avenières and Jonage, provided that Charles satisfied certain claims upon them. It was stipulated this time that the *Guiers vif* (nearer Savoy), and not the *Guiers mort,* would henceforth constitute the boundary in that region between Savoy and the Dauphiné.[46]

In return for these concessions, Charles agreed to pay the count 16,000 gold francs, after which Amadeus must make no further demand for compensation for his expenses in acquiring Faucigny. Two days later the count acknowledged having received the full amount due.[47] In March the king sent letters to Charles de Bouville, governor of the Dauphiné, informing him of these arrangements and ordering him to take possession of the lands in question, which he appears to have done without hindrance. The proverbial tenacity of the Savoyard mountaineer in the Green Count had paid him well in the end. The total of sums received over the years from the French king, added to the revenues of the disputed territories, which had been flowing into Savoyard coffers these twenty years, were ample recompense for the count's obstinacy.

Back in Bresse in the spring of 1377, Amadeus bestowed the "barony of Bâgé and the seigneurie of Bresse" upon his son, in keeping with the custom of the dynasty since the land of Bresse had first come into the family a century before. Amadeus V, Edward, and Aymon had all been lords of Bresse as soon as they were heirs apparent to the county of Savoy, and only the minority of Amadeus VI at the time of his father's death had interrupted that tradition. Bresse was a good place for learning the arts of

---

[46] Amadeus thus ceded the part of Pont-de-Beauvoisin on the south bank, the part of St-Genix on the south bank, the *bastida* of Les Abrets, and the *castra* of Dolomieu, St-Laurent-du-Desert, Faverges, "Palude," Miribel-les-Echelles, and Pressins. Cf. treaty in Cordey, doc. 41.

[47] *Ibid.*, doc. 42.

government and war, for it combined a resourceful population with an infinity of troublesome neighbors.[48]

The mettle of the young man was tested at once. While at Paris in February, the new sire of Beaujeu, Edward, had done homage to the count of Savoy and had received investiture of all that he possessed on the imperial side of the Saône.[49] Edward therefore refused to repeat those acts of submission in favor of Amadeus junior, apparently because he had not yet received the money which the count owed him in return for his homage. According to the Savoyard chroniclers, young Amadeus sent to his father for advice before taking action. The count is supposed to have replied, "Go back to Amadeus and tell him that if he does not force the seigneur of Beaujeu to submit for the lands which he holds in the country of Bresse, he shall never have any part of my possessions."[50]

It is difficult to accept this version, for the Green Count had long since ceased to look upon warfare as the most effective means to his ends. It is highly unlikely that he would have provoked a conflict in this fashion between his son and a family with whom he had enjoyed such friendly relations for so long. The war that resulted from Edward's refusal to do homage to Amadeus junior looks much more like the work of a young man all too eager to show the world without any prompting that he was a worthy son of the Green Count. He responded to Edward's defiance with alarming vitality, and the six years of warfare that followed intermittently did much to injure the prosperity which years of peace had brought to the land of Bresse.

For the moment, Amadeus was obliged to leave his rambunctious son to his own devices. The count's personal attention was required by significant events in the Piedmont. In March 1377, Violante Visconti, who had been widowed so young by the unexpected death of Lionel of Clarence, was married to Secondotto of Montferrat. The entente between the marquis and Galeazzo Visconti thus became an open alliance between potential foes of

[48] In the documents young Amadeus is hereafter entitled "lord of Bâgé and Montluel," indicating that his dominion included not only Bresse, but his father's holdings in Dombes and the Valbonne as well.

[49] Thoissey, Lent, Chalamont, Montmerle, Villeneuve, and Beauregard.

[50] Servion, II, 218; Cabaret, p. 215.

Savoy.[51] At the same time, young Amadeo de Savoie was approaching his fifteenth year and his legal majority. The Green Count now had to prepare for the accession of the sons of Marguerite de Beaujeu to the government of their inheritance.

These questions were made more serious by a quarrel between the bishop of Vercelli and the commune of Biella which offered the count of Savoy an admirable opportunity to advance his designs in the northern Vercellese. Biella was a small town on the edge of the plains east of Ivrea. Amadeus VI had acquired most of the Montferrat holdings between the Alps and the Dora Baltea in the course of the past twenty years, and the campaign against the Visconti in 1373–1374 had left him with important footholds in the Vercellese.[52] The acquisition of Biella would not only help to consolidate previous territorial gains, but would also open the way to further Savoyard advances in the region between the Dora and the Sesia.

The count's first step had been to authorize his lieutenant at Ivrea, Iblet de Challant, to form a pro-Savoyard party in the town and to encourage the citizens to resist both the bishop of Vercelli and partisans of the Visconti. In the winter of 1376–1377 the exasperated bishop imprisoned a number of refractory citizens of Cavaglià and Crevacuore at Biella, which provoked the Biellese to undertake a surprise attack upon him during his sojourn in their midst in early May. Thirty citizens took a solemn oath to carry out the project, and in the middle of the night they fell upon the garrison of the castle, massacred the bishop's supporters, and captured the prelate in his bedchamber.[53] The bishop was imprisoned in the great tower of his own castle, and the excited citizens promptly released the men from Cavaglià and Crevacuore. News of the revolt spread far and wide through the Vercellese,

---

[51] Treaty in *AST, Ducato Monferrato*, mazzo IV, doc. 27, dated 7 July 1377. Secondotto received the castles of Quarto, Azano, and Malamorte near Asti. He was also to have Casale after Galeazzo's death.

[52] Notably Cavaglià, San Germano, and Santhià. On 19 July 1376 at Samoggia near Bologna, papal representatives succeeded in making peace between Montferrat and Galeazzo Visconti, thus isolating Bernabò on the eve of a new papal offensive against him. In that treaty Amadeus had been forced to agree to return these towns to the bishop of Vercelli, but he had so far failed to do so. *AST, Trattati diversi*, I, doc. 33.

[53] Gabotto, *Età*, p. 240.

and fear soon followed exultation. The citizens were happy to be rid of their bishop temporarily, but they did not wish to fall under the "Visconti tyranny." Instead of turning toward Pavia for protection against the bishop's allies, several towns of the Vercellese followed the lead of Biella and turned toward Savoy.[54]

The Savoyards needed no second invitation. Richard Musard, the count's lieutenant in Piedmont, gathered troops and hurried northward. At the same time, Iblet de Challant went to the town and endeavored to interpose his mediation between the bishop and his rebel subjects. The citizens would have nothing to do with their bishop, however, and merely repeated their demand for annexation to the dominions of the count of Savoy. While the commune sent letters attempting to justify their action to the pope, Iblet de Challant appointed one of his kinsmen as *podestà* of Biella. Then he transferred the bishop from his dangerous prison amid a hostile population to the relative security of the great Challant stronghold of Montjovet in the Val d'Aosta. The bishop remained imprisoned, despite the excommunication of his captors, for a full year. On 29 November 1377, Gregory XI wrote to demand that the count of Savoy release the bishop and return to the Church some fifteen towns and fortresses in the Vercellese which had been taken during the wars, or which had voluntarily placed themselves under Savoyard rule.[55] The pope's demands went unheard. The Green Count's power was now preponderant in the northern Vercellese, and he meant to keep it so.

The sequel to the Biella affair came in October 1379, when the citizens accepted the terms on which the count had agreed to become their lord and protector.[56] Amadeus then went to Biella in person, swore to uphold its traditional liberties, and promised to select his *podestà* from a list of four persons chosen by the

[54] The towns to do so were San Germano, Verrone, Santhià, Buronzo, Candelo, Carisio, and Villarboit.

[55] They were listed as Santhià, Borgo Alice, Tronzano, Carisio, Verrone, Candelo, Buronzo, Balocco, Castellengo, Mombello, Cascine di Roasenda, Villarboit, Greggio, Palazzo, and Magnano. Gabotto, *Età*, p. 242.

[56] At Rivoli in July a delegation from the commune had formally asked Amadeus to become their ruler for the next thirty years. In August an accord had been drawn up to be submitted to the citizens for their ratification. For details on the annexation of Biella, cf. *ibid.*, p. 253.

communal council from the population of his dominions. The territory included in the dedication treaty was understood to comprise, in addition to Biella itself, eleven other towns and several villages.[57] These towns quickly followed the lead of Biella in ratifying the treaty, and they were soon joined by five other towns not originally included.[58] The northern Vercellese was thus quietly annexed to the states of Savoy, and the destiny of the Alpine dynasty as an Italian power was consolidated. Upon the Green Count's acquisitions in the Vercellese, the Canavese, and the Piedmont, the princes of Savoy would one day found an Italian kingdom.

When Amadeus crossed into Italy in early September 1377, he had riding beside him the young princes of Savoy-Achaea. Together they descended the winding trail from the Mont Cenis into the green valley of Susa. For nearly ten years the sons of Marguerite de Beaujeu had been removed from their Piedmont hills and plains; during ten of the most impressionable years of their lives they were brought up among the family in Savoy. It remained to be seen if the future would reward the Green Count's cares and strategems. His control of the Piedmont had advanced his own interests, to be sure, but it is fair to say that both branches of the dynasty had profited. The ten years of Amadeus' government in the Piedmont had been relatively prosperous for a population to whom war was part of the normal routine of life. The harvests of 1377 were abundant, and the year itself was one of the most tranquil of the century—a fitting conclusion for the Green Count's regency, and certainly its principal justification.[59]

Prince Amadeo was formally invested with his principality on 21 November. Three years later the count of Savoy married him to Catherine de Genève, the youngest sister of the count of Geneva. Like Marguerite de Beaujeu before her, Catherine had

---

[57] The eleven included were Andorno, Bióglio, Mortigliengo, Zumáglia, Ronco, Chiavazza, Occhieppo Superiore, Sordévolo, Vernazza, Pollone, and Tollegno.

[58] The five were Gráglia, Camburzano, Mussano, Caresana, and Magliano. In these places, however, Amadeus reserved his right to the property of persons who died intestate without children. *Ibid.*, p. 254.

[59] *Ibid.*, p. 242. Amadeus reserved 1,000 florins of annual revenue as his half of some forty towns and fiefs when the prince was invested. *AST, Principi del Sangue*, mazzo VIII, doc. 4.

been raised among the vassals of feudal Savoy, and Amadeus was counting upon her to keep her husband mindful of his duties.[60] Again the Green Count was not disappointed, and his heirs ultimately reaped the benefits of his Piedmont policies. Prince Amadeo proved obedient and loyal throughout his life, and so was his younger brother, Ludovico. When Ludovico died without heirs in 1418, the Piedmont returned permanently to the senior line of the house of Savoy.

[60] The marriage took place on 22 September 1380 at Duingt on Lake Annecy in Savoy, and Marguerite de Beaujeu emerged from her retirement for the occasion.

# X

# The Later Years
## 1378-1382

THIRTEEN SEVENTY-EIGHT was a bad year for the high and mighty of the earth, and its victims included an unusually large number of friends and relatives of the count of Savoy: Pope Gregory XI; the queen of France, sister of the countess of Savoy; Emperor Charles IV; Galeazzo Visconti, the count's brother-in-law; Secondotto of Montferrat, the count's first cousin. Two of these fatalities seemed to mark the beginning of a new chapter in European as well as in Savoyard history. The first, the death of the pope and the election (or elections) which followed it, plunged the Church into a crisis from which it would never fully recover, a crisis which presaged the not-too-distant century when the unity of medieval Christendom would be shattered forever. The second, the disappearance of Charles IV, resulted over the next generation in an almost total eclipse of imperial influence in international affairs. This fact was in turn partly responsible for the long schism in the Church, as well as for the rapid rise of a French Burgundian state that would ultimately absorb even Charles' ancestral duchy of Luxembourg. The emperor no longer served as an obstacle, however feeble, to French expansion farther south into Provence and Italy, and this fact continued to affect the history of the house of Savoy. Like the French, and partly because of the French, the Green Count had become increasingly interested in Italian affairs over the past twenty years. Now he was to become involved in Italy as an ally of the French, perhaps for the first time in the history of his dynasty. This alliance between the French and the Savoyards would be repeated many times subsequently in the history of Italy, ultimately with more advantage for Savoy than for France.

In Savoy the year began with the strange affair of Pierre Gerbais, "citizen of Belley," as he was styled in the treasury records
of 1358 when he first took up the duties of treasurer-general of
Savoy. He was of bourgeois origin, "ex probis parentibus," but
his phenomenal rise to power and wealth belongs among the
great success stories of the century. Pierre Gerbais was in many
ways an earlier, though less spectacular, Savoyard version of the
famous Jacques Coeur of Bourges, banker of Charles VII. Pierre
and his brothers were bankers at Belley who had bought precious
silver vases from the court of Savoy as early as 1347, and who
soon were among the count's creditors.[1] For a full twenty years
Pierre Gerbais was treasurer-general for Amadeus VI, greatly to
their mutual benefit. The vast liquid assets of the Gerbais brothers
furnished the count with money whenever he needed it, and the
count in turn assisted the rise of the Gerbais into the ranks of the
Savoyard nobility. In 1364 when Pierre was serving as castellan
of Châteauneuf-en-Valromey, he was given the land and seigneurie of Songieu, together with the "villages, waters, fishing, forests, hunting, and dependencies" and justice "haute, moyenne, et
basse" in augmentation of fief, on condition of homage and fidelity
to the count.[2] This was in addition to many other holdings already
granted to him in 1357, 1359, and 1363, which included a large
part of the castellany of Rossillon and the *mandement* of Virieu-
le-Grand north of Belley.[3] In 1366, Pierre had been named to
the council of regency established prior to the count's departure
on the crusade. In February 1373 at Settimo, Amadeus rounded
out Pierre's holdings in Bugey by enfeoffing the "citizen of
Belley and seigneur of Châteauneuf-en-Valromey" with the castle

---

[1] *AST,* inv. 16, docs. 18 (1353–1354) and 14 (1346–1349). Amédée de Foras,
*Armorial et Nobiliaire de l'Ancien Duché de Savoie* (Grenoble, 1863–1900), III,
92, erroneously states that Gerbais sold these articles to the court of Savoy. In
fact the regents had pawned them to raise money for the Piedmont expedition
of 1347. Pierre furnished 28,064 florins for the purchase of the Pays de Vaud
in 1359–1360 (and he was repaid in full on 10 January 1369). *Ibid.,* docs. 22
(1359–1360) and 29 (1368–1369). In 1363, Pierre Gerbais loaned 77,000 florins
to Giacomo of Achaea to enable him to pay the indemnity imposed upon him
by his treaty with the count.

[2] *ADCO,* B 7445. In July 1365 he was enfeoffed with Sutrieu and other villages
in the area, including Fossias, St-Maurice, La Balme, Lalleyriat, Biolay, Belmont,
and La Condamine. *Ibid.,* B 7447.

[3] *Ibid.,* B 9398, B 9400, B 9403.

of Cordon and the parish of Colomieu. By now Pierre Gerbais was a territorial lord with dominion over dozens of villages and several thousand subjects.[4]

The peak of his career, however, had been reached. On 8 August 1377, André de Belletruche, Pierre's lieutenant at the Treasury, took over his master's responsibilities, which suggested that all was not well with the citizen of Belley. At the château of Ripaille in May 1378, the count called Pierre and his brother Amblard into his presence along with Lord Guillaume de Luyrieux and forced them to sign a treaty of peace. The Gerbais and the Luyrieux, neighbors in the Valromey, had gone to war, and the treaty stipulated heavy fines for any future violation of the peace.[5] The document does not indicate the cause of the conflict, but its tenor suggests that Luyrieux was the aggressive party, for it is particularly he who is ordered to secure ratification of the accord by his chief supporters in the war. In any case, the treasurer-general and his family were on bad terms with the nobles of the region over which their dominion had been extended so strikingly.

Soon after this event a multitude of enemies came forth to accuse Pierre of malversation, of betraying his trust, and of cheating the Lord Count of Savoy. He was arrested and imprisoned in the dungeons of Chillon sometime in the course of the year,[6] and his properties in the Valromey were confiscated by the count's officers. Aymon Rigaud was installed as temporary castellan of Bons-en-Bugey, "confiscated from Pierre Gerbais following his condemnation by the Conseil de Savoie."[7] But the investigations of the charges against him went on year after year, and when at last it seemed clear that he was not guilty, his enemies did not scruple to produce another accusation: that he had been the accomplice of one Jeanne de Grammont, accused of having poisoned her husband (just as Jacques Coeur was to be accused of poisoning Agnès Sorel). This charge was also eventually revealed as false, but it was not until six years after his imprisonment at Chillon, in 1385, that Gerbais was fully exonerated. He was

[4] *Ibid.*, B 7449 lists 974 hearths in the "terre de Valromey" alone, when these fiefs returned to the comital domains.

[5] Text in Cibrario, *Storia*, III, *documenti*, 341–344.

[6] A. Naef, *Château de Chillon*, 2 vols. (Lausanne, 1929, 1939), II, 25.

[7] *ADCO*, B 9406 (Rossillon), B 9765 (St-Rambert).

nominally restored to his properties, but in fact most of his wealth had already passed into the hands of the count and had been alienated beyond recall.[8] The only satisfaction of Pierre's declining years, besides the clearing of his name, was from the careers of his sons, Gaspard and Antoine, who were taken back into comital service and were able to restore the family fortune and reputation.[9] The true cause of the disgrace of Pierre Gerbais remains unknown. A treasurer-general is never popular, and the rapid rise of this bourgeois family probably antagonized many old noble families in the Valromey. The suspicion lingers, however, that the Green Count's willingness to listen to the charges against Gerbais was not unrelated to the fact that he was so prominent among the count's own creditors.

It was probably in early 1379 that Amadeus issued his famous "Capitula, Statuta, et Ordinamenta" which constitute his greatest contribution to Savoyard law and mark a major step toward administrative centralization.[10] The preamble states that the count wished to provide for the welfare of his subjects, particularly the "poor and miserable person" who was oppressed by long and costly lawsuits. In the first of some sixty-seven articles, Amadeus decreed the establishment of a "pauperum advocatus" in permanent residence at Chambéry. This was an attorney paid by the state whose sole task was to represent the poor in lawsuits at no cost to themselves.[11] All parties at law were to be provided with legal counsel if they so desired, and the resident council as well as *juges ordinaires* were empowered to force lawyers to take cases

---

[8] *AST, Comptes . . . des guerres*, doc. 21. For example, in 1383, Amadeus enfeofed Etienne de la Baume with the "jurisdicione, redditibus et pertinentiis castri Sancti Denysi prope Sanctum Germanum de Amberyriaco, quod castrum olim fuit Petri Gerbaisii."

[9] *Ibid.*, inv. 38, folio 21, doc. 69. Both were receivers in the count's household from 1376 to 1390. Cf. Gerbais article in Foras, *Armorial*, III.

[10] There is no date in the text of the document; that of 1379 appears on the authentic copy of the act in the *Chancellerie de Savoie* in *AST*. The text is published in full by C. Nani in *MSI* (2nd series, XXII, 1884), 249–296. This edition is based upon a second copy of the statutes found at Sallanches, correcting some of the errors of the Turin copy and adding a few new articles. Most of these statute articles have been recently published in L. Chevailler, pp. 363–374.

[11] Chevailler, p. 58, notes that while such provisions were later found in Italian legal codes, until 1610, France had no attorney for the poor comparable to that in the Savoyard statutes of 1379.

if they would not do so willingly. A lawyer who refused was subject to suspension from his profession and a fine. Thus the public responsibilities of the legal profession were recognized by comital statute, and the state took upon itself to ensure that they would not be neglected in the future. The resident council and the *juges ordinaires* were ordered to render decisions on all cases within one year, and appellate judges within six months, not counting the holidays of Christmas, Easter, and harvest time.[12]

The membership and competence of the resident council were defined with more care than in the statutes of 1355.[13] It would hereafter consist of a chancellor and two collaterals, an attorney, and "procuratores fiscales"; but its membership could at any time be increased by the addition of the chancellor-general of Savoy or of prelates and barons on the count's council.[14] Decisions were by majority rule in cases of disagreement, and in the absence of the rest, one judge alone sufficed to render valid decisions. Thus the course of justice could not be obstructed by absenteeism, as was perhaps the case with the twenty-seven-member council established in 1355. Magistrates of the council were forbidden to hold any other judicial offices, to hear cases they may have heard before, or to accept payments, pensions, or gifts from parties appearing before them, except for the "drulliis aut munusculo," the customary perquisites. The council was guaranteed almost universal competence in civil, criminal, and even feudal matters. It was empowered to transfer to itself any case pending before a lower court, particularly when "the magnitude of the cause or the importance of the plaintiff, or the *miserabilitas* of the defendant" seemed to require it.[15]

The count of Savoy was not yet in a position to establish a judicial monopoly throughout his dominions, and no effort was made to deny competence to seigneurial or ecclesiastical courts. But further steps were taken toward restricting their power. Knights-banneret (the lowest rank of nobility in the count's dominions after marquises, counts, and barons) were recognized to have the right to institute either temporary or permanent judges within their own lands, and they were granted the authority to hear

---

[12] Chevailler, *Droit romain*, Art. VIII. The articles hereafter cited are from this work.

[13] *Ibid.*, pp. 135–136.     [14] Art. IX.     [15] Art. XIV.

and settle civil cases. But in criminal matters the bannerets' courts could only hear the evidence; the sentencing remained the prerogative of the count's judges.[16] It was added that in bannerets' courts as well as in those of the count, the suit must be decided before the end of the assizes, with the judge subject to a fine of one florin for every day thereafter that the case was still pending.[17] As for ecclesiastical courts, laymen were forbidden to bring before an ecclesiastical tribunal any matter in which the count's courts were competent.[18]

Beneath the resident council in the judicial hierarchy was the *juge générale* of appeals, sitting at Chambéry to improve the efficiency of appellate jurisdiction. On the bailliage level the judges were obliged to hold assizes at least four times a year, one for each season.[19] Prisoners held on criminal charges were to be interrogated and charged within ten days of their arrest, or the captor was subject to a fine of five *solidi* for every additional day the man was detained. All judges, from the *judex major* of the bailliages to the castellans and mestrals on the local level, were forbidden to accept bribes or gifts of any sort (excepting of course the customary fees) in return for the discharge of their judicial duties. Although the common practice of arranging *concorda* was recognized (*concorda* permitted a guilty party to avoid the penalties prescribed for his crime by paying instead a sum of money agreed upon between him and the judge), judges were strictly required to keep a written record of all *concorda*, as well as of all condemnations, so that they might be subject to review. Certain crimes, notably those involving death, forgery, and false witness, could not be settled by *concorda* at all. Moreover, no *concorda* could be arranged except while the assizes were in session, and they were required to be concluded in the presence of both the castellan and the judge.[20]

---

[16] Art. XXIII.

[17] Art. XXIV. Exceptions were allowed if investigations relative to the case were still going on, or if some question remained as to the law which should apply. Otherwise no case could be deferred to a subsequent assize.

[18] Arts. LIV, LV. Any layman who ceded his interests in a case to a clergyman in order to get it heard in an ecclesiastical court, automatically lost the case and was fined.

[19] Art. XXII.

[20] Art. XLVII. The castellan was to receive one-fourth of the *concorda*,

Castellans were under supervision respecting their treatment of prisoners, for it was customary for those in charge of prisons to regard them as sources of profit. The statutes provided that no man could be incarcerated except on order of the count, the council, or a duly instituted judge, nor released without the authorization of whoever ordered the arrest. Any prisoner wishing to provide for his nourishment and comfort at his own expense had to be allowed to do so without paying any sort of compensation to the castellan, except for bedding and utensils, for which the fees were fixed.[21] A "simplice agricola" paid just two *denarii* per day; a "mediocri homine," whether farmer or bourgeois, paid four; a "person of quality" paid eight. The same class distinctions were made in the fines to be collected from persons failing to answer a court summons. Farmers and manual laborers owed five, ten, and fifteen *solidi viennois* for the first, second, and third offenses; nobles (except bannerets), bourgeois (except craftsmen or laborers), and notaries were assessed at twenty-five, fifty, and one hundred *solidi viennois* for the same offenses.[22]

A number of articles in the statutes dealt with the office of notary, defining its functions and setting the fees according to the nature of the service. There were two kinds of notaries in Savoy, besides those authorized to draw up acts for private persons, and the count claimed the sole right to license them. Those bearing the title of "secretarii domini" were in charge of preparing all official documents emanating from the count and his curia,[23] while the "clerici curiarum" attached to the resident council drew up and registered acts concerning the count's financial and proprietary rights. These were kept in a special register which could

---

while one-ninth of the remainder was divided between the judge and the procurator, two-thirds to one-third respectively.

[21] Art. XLIX. If the prisoner wished to be provided for at the castellan's expense, the fees were one *denarius gros tournois* per day for farmers and laborers, two for "burgensibus vera" and notaries, while nobles were to be charged three or four "according to the quality and power of the captive noble."

[22] Art. XVI. Bannerets were fined ten *livres* for the first offense, the fine doubling on each subsequent offense. All fines stated above were doubled if it was a criminal, rather than a civil, case.

[23] While the fee for a will depended upon its length, given equal length, that of an impoverished noble was to be less than that for a wealthy bourgeois. Economic, not social, status was the determining factor.

be consulted by castellans, judges, and *baillis* who, like the notaries themselves, had an obligation to oversee the interests of their master.[24]

In sum, the statutes of 1379 reveal the Green Count's concern for the rights of his weaker subjects against would-be oppressors, including his own officers. They also reveal a desire to provide a more coherent body of regulations coordinating the efforts of the ever-increasing judicial bureaucracy through which his own authority penetrated to the population. Although these statutes were not meant to apply to dominions on the Italian side of the Alps,[25] although they are often rather roughhewn and lack comprehensiveness, still they constitute an essential part of the foundation upon which the structure of Savoyard law was later built, notably in the *Statuta Sabaudie* promulgated by Amadeus VIII in 1430.

The Green Count's statutes reflect the growing Savoyard state, the problems it was encountering, and the desire of the count to cope with them in a constructive way. The statutes may also reflect the misery of the Black Death generation: vacant cottages on the mountainsides, depopulated villages, and beggars on the steps of the parish churches. The count may have been moved to include the provisions safeguarding the poor because they seemed more numerous than before. The subsidy accounts for 1379 contain unusually frequent references to rural poverty, to the number of hearths from which no contribution could be obtained. On the other hand, there are suggestions that in places the Savoyards were recovering from the ravages of the plagues of 1348–1352 and 1361–1362, no doubt in large part because they had been spared the plague of war. The number of hearths at Chambéry increased from 435 in 1331 to 677 in 1387, and a few other towns in the region also show increases during the second half of the century.[26] The city of Geneva also seems to have been recovering slowly, with a population increase comparable to that of Chambéry.[27]

[24] Provisions for this sort of register had been made as early as Pierre II and were reiterated in the statutes of Edward in 1325. Chevailler, p. 71, note 146.

[25] The preamble even to the statutes of 1430 states that its provisions would in no way derogate from the customs of the Val d'Aosta, the Pays de Vaud, the *terre* of Italy, Piedmont, and Provence.

[26] Cf. Cibrario, *Economia*, II, 50.

[27] M. Binz gives 491 *foci* for Geneva in 1356 and 653 for 1377. I am indebted

Certainly for members of the house of Savoy life was becoming more comfortable, even luxurious. The growing wealth of the family was reflected in the construction and furnishings of Ripaille, in the costly garments and rich fabrics purchased with increasing frequency for the princes and their households. Fortresses were becoming more pleasant as residences. The chambers in the castle of Chambéry contained more elegant hangings and frescoes now than when the Green Count was a boy. His own bedchamber was decorated with a tapestry of green silk embroidered with cloth-of-gold *lacs d'amour*. The countess's apartment was hung with a large tapestry of scarlet trimmed with gold and silver and depicting, among other things, a noble lady on horseback followed by her squire.[28] Another chamber became known as the "chamber of the eagles" because of another tapestry purchased in 1376 which was made of silk and ornamented with flying eagles interspersed with *lacs d'amour*. In 1376–1378, Chambéry obtained its first mechanical clock, installed by the Green Count on the great tower of the castle, where it created a sensation with its striking of the hours.[29] During these same years at Château Chillon, glass was installed for the first time in the roses and *quatre-feuilles* of the great windows of the hall of justice and in the apartments of the count and countess. By now there were handsomely decorated stoves permanently installed in all of the principal rooms of the castle, and the doors to the Green Count's chambers were studded with gilded nailheads.[30]

### PIEDMONT AND ITALIAN AFFAIRS, 1378–1379

Early in 1378, Amadeus also was drawn into Piedmont affairs. Shortly after the marriage between Secondotto of Montferrat and Violante Visconti, Giangaleazzo contrived to take advantage of his new brother-in-law. Hatred between the young marquis and his regent, Baldassare of Brunswick, had been building up for some time, partly owing to the control exercised by Brunswick over the city of Asti, the most important of the towns still in

---

to M. Binz for having allowed me to see the manuscript of his article prior to publication.

[28] Ménabréa, *Chambéry*, MS, Book IV, Chapter VII.
[29] *Ibid.*, Book V, Chapter IX.
[30] Naef, II, 57, 60, 73–74.

Montferrat's hands.[31] Things had reached such a pass that Baldassare had taken over full control of the city and had forbidden Secondotto entrance into his own capital. The marquis had flown into one of the passionate rages for which he was already notorious, and had turned at once to his brother-in-law. Giangaleazzo was quick to seize upon this unhoped-for opportunity to acquire dominion over a wealthy city which had always eluded even his father's grasp. In February 1378 the marquis forced a triumphal entry into the city at the head of a Visconti army, accompanied by Giangaleazzo, whose men immediately took possession of the fortifications.

In gratitude for this assistance, Secondotto made Giangaleazzo governor of Asti, reserving to himself only the right to appoint its judges and *podestà*. The lord of Pavia promised to exercise his new authority on the marquis' behalf, not on his own, and to surrender the city to him whenever the citizens and nobles of the *contado* should so decree. It was a great triumph for the Visconti and a bitter setback for the Green Count, who not many years before had gone to war to preserve Asti from just this fate. This time he had been outmaneuvered by his nephew, who would outmaneuver many another in his time. There was nothing for the count of Savoy to do now except to assemble his men and move to Chieri, where he might restrict the Visconti success to the city of Asti by taking up a position on the nearby frontier.

The death of Galeazzo at Pavia on 4 August 1378 offered an opportunity to attempt some kind of accord with Giangaleazzo, now ruler in name as well as in fact. Blanche de Savoie played her usual role of promoting family harmony and smoothed the way for conversations on the touchy subject of Montferrat. Nothing short of the partition of the marquisate was now envisaged by these two "protectors" of Secondotto. Here again the Green Count reveals the cold, calculating intelligence that had succeeded so well in the affair of Filippo of Achaea a decade before; and Giangaleazzo was a worthy counterpart in every way. The personality of the young marquis, although it in no way excuses his guardian's designs, doubtless contributed to their success. In

---

[31] Baldassare was the brother of the original regent, Otto of Brunswick, who had left Piedmont to become the fourth husband of the queen of Naples in 1376.

Servion's words, Secondotto was "tresmal morigine" (of evil manners or conduct), "and he was called the 'bad marquis.'" He would not obey the advice of the count of Savoy, his cousin-german, "of Messire Otto of Brunswick, his tutor, nor of his noblemen and communes of Montferrat, but instead chose to follow the counsel of Messire Bernabò and Messire Galeazzo, ancient enemies of his father, who had promised him one of their daughters."[32]

Secondotto was accused of having already killed a man (he was hardly more than sixteen at this time), and of having sliced off the leg of another with his own hand. He reputedly took by force any woman that pleased him, drove away all of the "gentlemen, counselors, and servants of his father," took to consorting with "gens de Malle vie," and gloried in living a "disorderly life." The Green Count tried to reason with him: "Fair cousin, I did my best to help you, to maintain and defend you, to preserve and guard your country, and I did it with my own person, with my men, and with large sums of gold which I spent; but when I see that you will not be corrected, nor leave off your vices, and that you will not follow the advice of Messire Otto nor of the wise men of your country, I want to be paid for my services to you, according to the promises made to me at Rivoli by the Marquis Jehan, your father. I'll tell you more; that if I'd seen that you had abandoned your evil conduct in favor of the good, as all seigneurs should do by reason, I would never have asked anything from you for undertaking those wars in defense of your country."[33]

When the marquis heard these words from the count, he was enraged, and replied "moult furieusement" that Amadeus had better reprimand his own children and not him. "And I am glad that you want to be paid, because I don't want to be endangered by you any longer." The count, naturally indignant at this added insult, replied, "Pour la mort Dieu, don't do me any other evil than paying me. But since you answer me this way, before you escape from me I shall have my pay." The count then commanded

---

[32] Servion, II, 183; Cabaret, p. 192 *dorso*.

[33] Servion, II, 183–184; Cabaret, pp. 193–194. Both texts are corrupt here and I have used both in attempting to translate the meaning of this passage as accurately as possible, without basing the translation upon either text alone.

his treasurers to come forth with his war accounts, and it was discovered that he had spent more than 70,000 florins on the defense of the marquisate.[34] As security for payment of this sum, the marquis turned over to the count a number of towns and fortresses, but according to the Savoyard version, Amadeus chivalrously gave orders that Secondotto might come and go as he pleased in any of these places. The result was that the marquis and some of his men went to visit the Savoyard castellan at Chivasso, and while they were at dinner with him, they suddenly fell upon him and threw him and his men out of the town.

This account, while it confirms other versions of Secondotto's character and correctly indicates a rupture of relations between the marquis and the count, appears to be in error regarding Chivasso. This city had been taken from Montferrat by the Visconti some years before and had remained in the hands of the latter, who apparently never did surrender it even after subsequent treaties in which they promised to do so. Whether the stormy interview between the Green Count and his cousin actually took place or not, Amadeus did emerge from his negotiations with Giangaleazzo well armed to cope with the "ingratitude" of the marquis. In a treaty of 29 August 1378 drawn up "in the bedchamber of Lady Blanche de Savoie at Pavia,"[35] Giangaleazzo agreed to permit Savoyard annexation of the whole northern part of the Vercellese and the region around Ivrea, in return (it was tacitly understood) for Savoyard acquiescence in the Visconti seizure of Asti. Two days later another agreement reaffirmed the mutual friendship and fraternal love henceforth to reign between uncle and nephew. Giangaleazzo agreed to mediate in the dispute between Amadeus and Secondotto over the towns to be awarded as security to the count for the reimbursement of his expenses during the marquis' minority.[36] On 19 October 1378, Secondotto, still deceived into thinking that Giangaleazzo was his best friend, agreed to accept the latter's arbitration. Amadeus retired to Turin

[34] Cabaret says 60,000 florins.

[35] *AST, Trattati diversi*, I, doc. 34. Reconfirmation on 27 March 1379. *Ibid.*, doc. 36. The treaty states that the count was to have permanently all the places in the dioceses of Vercelli and Ivrea which were once held by Galeazzo, and which were in the hands of the count at the time of the treaty.

[36] *AST, Ducato Monferrato*, mazzo V, docs. 3, 4.

with the prince of Achaea to await the results of the deception.[37]

The count did not have long to wait. In November he was notified that the lord of Pavia was about to hand down his impartial decision, and Secondotto and Amadeus both appeared for the occasion. The marquis then learned that if he did not pay what he owed to the count of Savoy within a few short weeks, he would lose what amounted to most of the western part of his marquisate. Chivasso, Riva, Poirino, and suzerainty over San Giorgio, Mazzè, Monardo, Mercenasco, Castiglione di Cándia, Orio, Rivara, Rocco di Corio, and Fávria—all were to go to the Green Count unless the money were paid.[38] At almost the same moment, the unhappy marquis learned that a new treaty had just bound Savoy and Pavia still more strongly in an offensive-defensive military alliance.[39]

In a panic Secondotto escaped from Pavia and fled toward central Lombardy, avoiding both his own lands and the territories of Giangaleazzo. If he could get to the court of Bernabò, who had long viewed his nephew's actions with suspicion, Secondotto could perhaps find a protector, just as the marquis of Saluzzo had done in earlier days. But the marquis never reached the other Visconti court. Under circumstances which remain obscure, he was stabbed to death by one of his soldiers near Langhirano in the Piacentino. The assassin was a victim of Secondotto's own brutality, according to most accounts, and may have chosen this means of avenging himself; but suspicion naturally fell at once, and has ever since, upon Giangaleazzo, who, it was rumored, had the marquis murdered in order to prevent his drawing the dreaded Bernabò into Piedmont affairs.[40]

Secondotto left no heirs, and his much-abused bride, Violante Visconti, returned home until such time as her brother might choose another husband for her. Three brothers of the late marquis were still alive, and all were minors. The eldest, who now became Marquis Giovanni III, was placed in the custody of Otto of Brunswick, who returned from Naples to participate in the new ar-

[37] Gabotto, *Età*, p. 247.

[38] *AST, Ducato Monferrato*, mazzo V, doc. 5.

[39] On 21 November 1378. *AST, Trattati diversi*, I, doc. 35.

[40] No evidence has ever been produced to support this charge, however suspicious the circumstances.

rangements required by the death of Secondotto. Brunswick maintained his authority as regent of the children of Giovanni II, but in the treaties resulting from months of diplomatic maneuvering, all that could be accomplished was a compromise with Giangaleazzo. Asti remained in his hands and so did Giovanni's next younger brother, Teodoro, who was to be brought up at the court of Pavia.[41] The Green Count did not get Chivasso as he had desired, but he apparently did get control of most of the other places awarded to him under the arbitral decision of the previous year.

At this point events in Rome commanded the attention of all of Western Christendom. No sooner had the news of the death of Gregory XI on 27 March 1378 reached the ears of the Roman population than they began to make their sentiments known. According to the Savoyard version, the Romans ran through the streets "murmurant & criant" that they wanted a Roman pope "who will live among us and not at Avignon; and if we don't get one who is Roman or Italian, you will have done your duty badly."[42] In Froissart's account the threat was that they would make the cardinals' heads redder than their hats if they did not get their Italian pope, and the chronicler commented that this frightened the cardinals greatly, for they much preferred to die confessors than martyrs.[43]

Gregory XI had foreseen that the disorders of the city might well make the selection of his successor a difficult task. He had attempted prior to his death to make provisions to guarantee an orderly election. The cardinals were given full authority to choose both the time and the place for the event. In accordance with the ordinances of Pope Nicholas II in 1059, it was expressly stated that no papal election was valid if it resulted from intimidation by outsiders, and the cardinals had the right to move out of the Eternal City if its turbulence hampered their freedom of choice. There were sixteen cardinals present for the election, of whom eleven were French, four Italian, and one Spaniard. The usual rivalries reigned among them on this occasion, but the population of the city was convinced that if the cardinals were ever permitted to leave Rome, the French influence would once again triumph and the new pope would return to Avignon. As the

[41] Cf. Gabotto, *Età*, pp. 250–251; *AST, Ducato Monferrato*, mazzo V. doc. 6.
[42] Cabaret, pp. 219 *dorso*, 220.
[43] Froissart, *Oeuvres*, IX, 50.

deliberations continued day after day, the uproar of the populace increased, and the cardinals were constantly threatened with violence unless they chose an Italian, preferably a Roman, pope.

At last on 8 April 1378, unable to agree upon one of their own number and frightened as well as fatigued by the clamor surrounding their deliberations, the cardinal of Limoges arose and proposed the name of Bartholomeo Prignani, archbishop of Bari, who was elected. But by now the Romans seemed absolutely bent upon having not just an Italian, but a Roman; and the cardinals found it necessary to persuade the cardinal of St. Peter to dress up in what looked like papal robes and show himself at one of the windows of the palace. Then, while the jubilant crowds hailed their newly acquired Roman pope and rushed off to sack the cardinal's palace, as was the strange usage on the election of a pontiff, the cardinals managed to escape from the hall of the conclave and take refuge in their fortresses in or outside the city.

The Romans were momentarily furious when the ruse was discovered, but by then most of the cardinals were beyond their grasp, and the fact that the archbishop of Bari was after all an Italian soon appeased the popular fury. The cardinals gradually returned and on Easter Day, the new pope, entitled Urban VI, was crowned in St. John Lateran. The extent to which popular agitation had in fact determined the choice of Prignani is uncertain, but until the cardinals had become better acquainted with the character of Urban VI some months later, they showed no inclination to deny the validity of his election.

A power struggle soon developed, however, between the elegant French cardinals and their austere Italian pope, who was determined to free himself from French influence. When Urban VI threatened to create enough Italian cardinals to end once and for all the predominance of the French, the latter resolved upon extreme measures. In August 1378 at Anagni the French cardinals issued a manifesto in which they declared that they had been forced to elect Prignani out of fear for their lives, thinking that he would never accept so obviously illegal an offer. "But he was unmindful of his own salvation and burning with ambition, and so, to the great scandal of the clergy and of the Christian people, and contrary to the laws of the church, he accepted this election which was offered to him, although not all of the cardinals were present at the election, and it was extorted from us by threats and demands of the officials and people of the city."[44]

At Fondi on 20 September 1378 the French cardinals, in response to Urban's recent creation of twenty-six new cardinals, met and elected one of their own number, a cousin of the count of Savoy, Robert de Genève, who took the title of Clement VII.[45] The Great Schism was to divide the Christian church of Europe for the next generation. The kings of Castile, Aragon, Navarre, Scotland, and France eventually accepted the second election and henceforth threw the weight of their support behind Clement VII and the papal court which followed him to Avignon. England, the Empire, and most of the rest of Latin Christendom accepted the Roman pope, although for the first several months most of the powers of Italy were divided. The Visconti held aloof, while Naples shifted from Urban to Clement. Naturally the Green Count ensured the recognition of his cousin's authority throughout the dominions of Savoy.

One of the first results of the Schism locally was a new treaty between Giangaleazzo and Montferrat, largely owing to the efforts of Clement VII, who needed peace among possible allies for his cause. On 22 January 1379 at Santhià, a truce was established for the next two years, and "illustrious Prince Lord Amadeus, count of Savoy" was instituted as a sort of guardian of the peace. Giangaleazzo was expressly forbidden to make any private arrangements with the count of Savoy or with Teodoro of Montferrat at the expense of his elder brother and Otto of Brunswick.[46] Soon after, Gui Flotte was installed as governor of Montferrat for young Giovanni III, and Otto of Brunswick returned to Naples, taking with him both the eldest and the youngest of the three Montferrat brothers.

[44] Cited from O. J. Thatcher and E. H. McNeal, *Source Book for Medieval History* (New York, 1905), doc. 167.

[45] Robert de Genève, the cardinal of Geneva, was the youngest of the five sons of the Green Count's late guardian, Amadeus III, who had died in January 1367. His eldest son and successor, Aymon, was with Amadeus VI on the crusade at the time, and he died shortly after his return, in August 1367. He was succeeded by his remaining three brothers: Amadeus IV, Jean, and Pierre, who died in 1392. Robert was bishop of Thérouanne in 1361–1368 and bishop of Cambrai 1368–1372.

[46] *AST, Ducato Monferrato*, mazzo V, docs. 6, 7.

# The Later Years

By the spring of 1380 the war with the sire of Beaujeu in which the Green Count's son had involved himself two years earlier was becoming a more serious affair than the Savoyards had expected. Young Amadeus' truce with his adversary was soon to expire, and Edward of Beaujeu had made it clear that since no settlement had been reached, he intended to recover the castles taken from him by force of arms.[47] Amadeus junior seemed to be looking forward to the reopening of hostilities, which he made inevitable by forcing certain nobles in Dombes to do homage to him on the grounds that he had replaced Beaujeu as suzerain of their fiefs there. War engines were constructed, quantities of red and white cloth were purchased for flags with the arms of Savoy on them, and war trumpets were adorned with silk fringe. A fleet was built for the Saône with the object of cutting off Beaujeu's towns in Dombes from their source of reinforcements across the river.

What distinguished this campaign from the earlier one was the participation of Amadeus senior. The Green Count had apparently decided that the annexation of Beaujeu's territories in the Empire might be accomplished by an all-out effort, and the idea of consolidating Savoyard holdings in Bresse and the Valbonne in this way appealed to him more than the idea of arbitrating the dispute. On 25 May the count and his son were camped before the gates of Montmerle, and by early June both Thoissey and Montmerle had fallen into their hands. Their progress was interrupted at this point by an envoy from the king of France, the seneschal of Rouergue, who succeeded in imposing a year's truce upon the combatants. The duke of Burgundy was again to arbitrate the dispute, despite the distinctly modest success of his earlier efforts in that capacity. The castles captured by the Savoyards were again to be turned over to neutrals, and again they were not, for the Bressan accounts annually report the revenues collected in these places for the count of Savoy.[48] These questions were not really

---

[47] The castles captured by Savoy in the fighting in 1378 had apparently neither been returned nor even consigned to neutral Burgundians, as the truce terms had stipulated. Cordey, pp. 234ff. has a full account of this war.

[48] *ADCO*, B 7363 (Bresse, *judicature*) includes revenues from Montmerle, Thoissey, and Lent. B 7023 is the account of a Savoyard castellan at Beauregard-sur-Saône, Ars, and Billon for 1380–1383.

settled until May 1383, when the sire of Beaujeu did homage to the new count of Savoy for all of the territories which he held on the imperial side of the Saône, and those taken from him were given back in fief.

In the autumn of 1380 the Green Count was obliged to visit his possessions in the Val di Susa and to settle disorders among his vassals in the Canavese.[49] On his way back to Savoy in November, he passed through the Val d'Aosta. His officers in the newly acquired barony of Cly were accused of oppressing his subjects there with unjust exactions, and a commission was charged with investigating the matter.[50] In July the *bailli* had granted to the citizens of Aosta the exclusive right to transport their merchandise without hindrance from their town in all directions: down the valley of the Dora to Ivrea, up the valley of the Dora to La Thuile, and up the valley leading to the Mont-Joux. The inhabitants of St-Rémy and Etroubles protested, however, that they had always enjoyed the right to transport merchandise across the Mont-Joux pass and down through the Val d'Aosta as far as Ivrea. Living as they did high up on the slopes of the pass, they represented to the count that if they were deprived of their exclusive transport privileges, they would be obliged to emigrate, for the country was too poor to support them otherwise. Amadeus granted their petition, but the resistance of the Aostans was not easy to break. The following January the count was obliged to reaffirm the privileges of St-Rémy and Etroubles, and to instruct his officers in the Val d'Aosta to see that they were respected.[51]

From Aosta the count probably crossed the Mont-Joux to the valley of the Rhône, for he was at Morges on Lake Geneva by mid-December. Political developments made such a route advisable, for in 1380 the Valaisans had risen up and driven out their new Savoyard bishop, Eduardo de Savoie. In keeping with his Valais policies of the past twenty years, the Green Count attempted to deal with these indomitable Swiss by negotiation rather than by war. In this intention he was vigorously supported by the Avignon pope, Clement VII, who was anxious to settle the matter so that his cousin of Savoy might join the forces which

---

[49] Details in Gabotto, *Età*, p. 258.

[50] Duc, IV, 81. Inquiry proved the complaints justified, and the officers involved were sternly rebuked.

[51] *Ibid.*, pp. 87, 90.

Clement was gathering for a campaign to drive his rival from Rome and put an end to the Schism. In the convention which permitted the bishop to return to Sion, the Green Count agreed to surrender all of the castles which he occupied in the Valais proper in return for an annual pension of 10,000 florins from the tithes collected in the territories of Savoy over the next ten years.[52] The Church thus paid the cost of protecting the Valaisans from the threat of Savoyard domination, and the Green Count emerged from nearly thirty years of warfare with a financial return considerably more secure and more substantial than his control of the Valais could possibly have been. The Great Schism was assuredly not without advantages for the house of Savoy.

### SAVOY AND THE GREAT SCHISM. PIEDMONT ADVANCES: ASTI, GENOA, CUNEO

The Great Schism, however, was creating a momentous chain of events which would all too soon involve the count of Savoy in less fortunate consequences. Clement VII, after an unsuccessful effort to drive Urban VI from Rome in the autumn of 1378, had fled to Naples. He had been welcomed by the queen, but the hostility of the population had made it unwise for him to remain in the kingdom. In May 1379 he had gone by sea to France and had reestablished the papal seat at Avignon, where the object of his efforts henceforth was a "crusade" against the "Anti-Christ," Urban VI. Even before his departure from Italy, Clement had received ambassadors from Louis, duke of Anjou, the eldest brother of Charles V, who agreed to aid the pope against his Roman rival in return for a "kingdom of Adria" to be carved out of the papal patrimony.[53]

In the meantime, Urban VI was disposing of kingdoms in quite another manner. Seeing that Queen Giovanna remained steadfast in her support of his rival, Urban solemnly deposed her from the throne of Naples. He then appealed to Charles of Durazzo, the least well-endowed of the Angevin branches which had sprung from Charles II of Naples. Charles of Durazzo had long had designs upon the kingdom of Naples, and the papal appeal was exactly the opportunity for which he had been waiting.

---

[52] Cognasso, *Il Conte Verde*, pp. 233–234.

[53] Léonard, p. 461. See this author generally for further details on this subject.

This move on the part of Urban VI naturally created alarm at the court of Naples, and the queen began to seek allies. Ambassadors were sent to Avignon to lend a note of urgency to the formation of an anti-Urban league, and the terms offered to the duke of Anjou were made more attractive. The queen now proposed to make Louis of Anjou her adoptive son and heir, and she invited him to come at once to help in the struggle to preserve his new inheritance from Durazzo. In June 1380 the official act of adoption was signed, and Anjou was given the title of duke of Calabria, the title traditionally reserved for the heir apparent to the kingdom.

Two important developments interferred with Anjou's preparations for an expedition to Naples. The first was the steady deterioration of relations between France and England in the course of 1380. The war in Brittany between rival contenders for the ducal throne was rapidly drawing the two kingdoms into conflict again because the French and the English were supporting different candidates. In the summer of 1380 an army under the command of Edward III's youngest son landed on the continent and began a systematic plundering expedition which devastated the prosperous countrysides of Champagne, Gâtinais, Beauce, and Anjou, describing a wide circle around Paris and heading at last for Brittany.

In an attempt to stop the progress of the invaders, Charles V summoned his vassals, including the count of Savoy and the duke of Anjou. But on 16 September 1380, before either the duke of Anjou or the Savoyards could reach the capital to join the royal host, the forty-two-year-old monarch was dead. The dauphin, who now became King Charles VI, was only twelve years old, and the eldest of the royal uncles, Louis of Anjou, was named regent. The duke was soon involved in a power struggle with his brothers the dukes of Burgundy and Berry, and the Neapolitan expedition was indefinitely postponed.

The Green Count went to Savoy briefly in the spring of 1381 for the arrival of Bonne de Berri, his daughter-in-law, who had come at last to live with her husband in the Alps. But the tide of Italian affairs which dominated the closing years of Amadeus VI's career very soon drew him across the mountains again. Since the winter of 1379, he had become increasingly disturbed by a war which had broken out between the great maritime republics of Genoa and Venice. Among the principal reasons for this war was the competition between them for control of the Byzantine trade. In the civil wars which had broken out in Byzantium since the count's departure in 1367, the Italian maritime powers favored opposite sides and exploited the weakness of both to secure advantages for themselves. The struggle now centered around the strategic island of Tenedos, commanding the entrance to the Dardanelles, which had fallen into the hands of the Venetians.

What concerned the count of Savoy was not the outcome of this struggle for power in the East, but rather the effects of the war in northern Italy. Each side sought allies, and Genoa had no difficulty securing the support of the king of Hungary, who had already given his cousin, Charles of Durazzo, Hungarian troops for an attack upon the mainland possessions of Venice in 1378. Archduke Leopold of Austria, hoping to extend his authority into the Friulian march, also joined the allies of Genoa, as did the Carrara of Padua and the patriarch of Aquileia, whose power had long been threatened by Venetian expansion on the mainland. The Venetians had the stronger allies in the East, but they felt obliged to draw closer to the Visconti as a counterweight to the power of their enemies in Italy. Bernabò was willing to join Venice because of his designs on eastern Lombardy; Giangaleazzo was willing because of his designs on Genoa.

At Pola in 1379 the Genoese inflicted a terrible defeat upon their rivals, and not long after, they seized the island of Chioggia in the Venetian lagoons. The proud islanders were faced with one of the most desperate moments in their history. During the winter of 1379–1380, peace negotiations were set on foot at Cittadella near Padua, but as usual when fortune smiles too brightly upon one party, it was impossible to secure from the winning side terms which could be accepted by the losers. To redress the balance Venice concluded a pact with the two Viscontis in April 1380, and in a short time armies of the latter were moving toward the territories of Genoa.

The count of Savoy was alarmed by this development, but it was hardly out of anguish at the spectacle of warfare between two great Christian powers.[54] To dwell upon this aspect is to miss

[54] Cf. Cibrario, *Storia*, III, 256–257, and Marie-José, pp. 227–228, for this interpretation. Marie-José says that Amadeus wanted the peace in order to free

the whole significance of the "Peace of Turin." What really concerned the Green Count was the balance of power in northern
Italy, threatened as always by the activities of the Visconti. Quite
apart from the international implications of the struggle, which
probably concerned him very little, Amadeus saw only that both
Bernabò and his nephew were taking advantage of the situation
to increase their own power. The Venetian alliance was only a
cloak for what was clearly an attempt to engulf the whole of
northern Italy by seizing the dominions of the Carrara in eastern
Lombardy and the possessions of Genoa in the west. Should the
attempt succeed, there was little doubt in the count's mind that
the Piedmont would be next.

As early as February and March of 1380, Amadeus had sent
envoys to his friend Federigo Cornaro, a prominent Venetian,
and to the bishop of Torcello, offering his services as mediator
in a war so dangerous for all.[55] The Venetians had just inflicted
a crushing defeat upon the Genoese at Chioggia, and the time
was ripe for peacemaking. The Green Count saw that his best
chance of preventing further Visconti expansion into his sphere
of influence would be to preside over a peace settlement himself
and to exclude, if possible, any Visconti part in it. In the course
of the winter of 1380–1381, he redoubled his efforts to interpose
himself as arbiter, and at last he succeeded. Cornaro used his influence in ruling circles at Venice, and the allies of Genoa—the
king of Hungary, the patriarch of Aquileia, the lord of Padua—
all expressed their willingness to accept the judgment of the count
of Savoy.[56]

Ambassadors of the various powers met at the castle of the
princes of Achaea in Turin in April 1381. The Visconti were
predictably angry at the willingness of the Venetians to negotiate
a peace without consulting them. Bernabò sent both his chancellor
and his son Ludovico to the count to represent his indignation at

---

his hands for an expedition to Naples, but there is no proof that he had committed himself to one at this point.

[55] Correspondence in Cibrario, *Storia*, III, 346ff. Cornaro had rented galleys
to Amadeus for the crusade and had loaned him substantial sums in 1367 for
the return trip.

[56] *Ibid.*, Cornaro's letter of 18 February 1380. I can find no basis for Cognasso's
assertion (*Il Conte Verde*, p. 235) that the initiative came from the allies, rather
than from the count of Savoy.

being thus ignored, but to no avail. On 8 August 1381 the treaty was completed and was subsequently accepted by all parties represented at the conference. This was the "Peace of Turin," often hailed as proof of the Green Count's pacific inclinations and of his skill as a diplomat. Amadeus VI was only pacifically inclined when it was to his advantage to be so, but certainly a peace settlement which reconciled such varied interests was a very creditable diplomatic accomplishment.

In the treaty the Genoese agreed to reopen Black Sea markets closed to Venetian shipping. Venice was to surrender the island of Tenedos to officers of the count of Savoy within the next two and a half months, and a large sum of money deposited by the Venetians at Florence was to be forfeited to the Genoese in case of noncompliance with the treaty terms.[57] The king of Cyprus was asked to surrender the city of Famagousta to the Genoese, and other provisions accommodated the interests of the patriarch of Aquileia, Louis of Hungary, and their allies. A final clause bound both Genoa and Venice to furnish military aid, if need be, to compel the emperor of Byzantium to "abjure the schism." This clause, taken with the count's efforts to secure the island of Tenedos, has awakened the suspicion that he was contemplating a second expedition to Byzantium to accomplish what the first had failed to do.[58] Whether the Green Count really had any such intention is difficult to affirm, but it is at least clear that he had not forgotten the unfulfilled promises of his imperial cousin.[59]

The Green Count had won the friendship of two powerful Italian states by thus mediating their differences, and he had established contacts which he hoped would prove useful in the future. For the moment it was enough to have broken up the Visconti-Venetian alliance so dangerous to his Piedmont interests, and at the same time to have cut the ground from beneath the campaign which his nephew was waging in the Genoese hinterland. The events of the summer, however, demonstrated that this was not enough. No sooner had hostilities ceased in the spring

[57] Cf. A. Segre, *Delle Relazioni Tra Savoia e Venezia da Amadeo VI a Carlo II (III)*, extract from *Accademia Reale delle Scienze di Torino* (Turin, 1899), pp. 5ff.

[58] For example, Cognasso, *Il Conte Verde*, p. 236; Cibrario, *Storia*, III, 259–260.

[59] The Venetians did not actually surrender the island to Savoyard officers until the summer of 1383.

of 1381 than Charles of Durazzo marched through the territory of Friuli to Rome. On 1 June 1381 he was proclaimed king of Naples by Urban VI, who received his oath of homage and presented him to the population of Rome as the champion of the Holy See. "Charles of the Peace," as he was called, then marched southward to take possession of his kingdom. He defeated the army of Otto of Brunswick at Anagni, and on 16 July entered the city of Naples almost without resistance. The queen took refuge in the Castelnuovo, where she hoped to hold the invaders at bay until either her husband or her adopted son, the duke of Anjou, came to her aid. Louis of Anjou could not come, however, and on 25 August, Otto of Brunswick was again defeated in battle. Young Giovanni III of Montferrat was killed, and his youngest brother, Guglielmo, was captured along with Brunswick himself. When the queen received this news, she gave herself up and was imprisoned by her conqueror first in the Castelnuovo, then at Nocera, where her chances of escape were more remote.

The news of these developments was disturbing to the Green Count not because of their importance for the kingdom of Naples, but because of their implications for the Piedmont. Now that Giovanni III was dead, the new marquis of Montferrat was his brother Teodoro, who had been brought up at Pavia and was at the time in the custody of Giangaleazzo. The latter had already concluded an alliance with Teodoro in August 1381, and in January 1382 the new marquis was obliged to cede Asti permanently to the Visconti as the price of peace and protection for his marquisate.[60] Amadeus had foreseen such a move, however, and he had by no means remained inactive. On 7 September 1381 a secret treaty was concluded between Savoy, Genoa, and Venice in which each agreed to aid any one of the others against any commune or prince in Lombardy that attacked him.[61] This pact was to last for ten years, and it was supplemented by a separate alliance between Savoy and Genoa. On 7 November the count and the Genoese swore perpetual friendship and defense against all powers "de provincia Lombardie," except the pope, the emperor, and the king

---

[60] D. M. Bueno de Mesquita, *Giangaleazzo Visconti*, (Cambridge, 1941), p. 18; *AST, Ducato Monferrato*, mazzo V, doc. 14.

[61] Cognasso, *Il Conte Verde*, p. 236.

of Hungary.[62] This was an obvious effort to checkmate the Visconti seizure of Novi and Serravalle, which commanded the passes through the Ligurian mountains from Giangaleazzo's stronghold of Alessandria to Genoa.[63]

Amadeus also began to intrigue with the Guelf exiles from Genoa, aiming at a Savoyard protectorate over the Republic that would block at one masterstroke the progress of Visconti infiltration in the region. To do this required popular support among the Genoese, and the count resolved to build upon the goodwill which his work at the Peace of Turin had won for him. The king of Cyprus had not been represented at the Peace of Turin conferences, and he was not disposed to accept the treaty stipulations concerning him. Savoyard negotiators were sent to Cyprus and to Genoa during the winter of 1381–1382, and in February 1382 a peace was concluded between the two powers which preserved the privileged position of the Genoese on the island. News of this accord greatly enhanced the prestige of the count of Savoy, and in March his machinations with the Guelf party bore inviting fruit. Amadeus received letters from Nicolo and Carlo Fieschi, counts of Lavagna and leaders of the Guelf faction which was struggling for domination of the city. The letters were a formal invitation, signed by about twenty of the leading Guelf nobles, asking the Green Count to become the protector of the Republic of Genoa and to assume the title of doge.[64]

This was not the only triumph for Savoyard diplomacy in 1382. The Green Count soon had even his nephew on the defensive against the rapid expansion of his influence. A considerable party of Astigiani were bitterly opposed to the seizure of their city and were resolved to throw off the Visconti yoke. Since the marquis of Montferrat was only a child and entirely under the control of Giangaleazzo, the rebels' only hope lay in the count of Savoy, who was now the only real champion against Visconti power in

---

[62] *AST, Trattati diversi*, II, doc. 3. The count commissioned his envoys at Ivrea on 13 September 1381, and the treaty was to be made public on 6 January 1382.

[63] Novi and Serravalle had been seized in August 1381.

[64] Cf. Federigo Donaver, *Storia della Repubblica di Genova*, 3 vols. (Genoa, 1913), I, 363; Eugène Jarry, *Les Origines de la domination française à Gênes 1390–1402* (Paris, 1896).

the Piedmont. Naturally Amadeus listened to their grievances, and a considerable number of Astigiani congregated at Rivoli in the spring of 1382.[65] On 23 March they proclaimed the count of Savoy "count of Asti" and laid down the conditions on which they hoped he would become their lord. The most important of these obligated him to govern the city jointly with the "society of San Secondo" (the Guelf or popular party), and to restore to Otto of Brunswick his part of the city upon reimbursement of the count's expenses in wresting it from the Visconti.[66] Neither the declaration of 23 March nor the letters from the Guelfs of Genoa meant that these cities had passed under Savoyard dominion, for the Guelf faction did not control Genoa, and the serpent banners still waved defiantly from the towers of Asti. But formidable groundwork had been laid against the day when Savoyard arms should lend the weight of steel to these promises.

On 10 April 1382 the Green Count's Piedmont ambitions were advanced more substantially when a lesser town placed itself under his authority. Cuneo on the Stura had been the most distant outpost of Visconti penetration in the years between 1357 and 1373, when the town had been captured by the count of Savoy. On that occasion Amadeus had been forced to turn it over to officers of the queen of Naples, since Cuneo was among the towns that once comprised the short-lived Angevin county of Piedmont. The collapse of Giovanna's power in Naples now made it necessary for the inhabitants to seek another protector, and the pro-Savoyard faction in the town had worked diligently to bring the commune over to the count of Savoy. The charter of dedication which resulted obligated Amadeus to protect the town from its enemies and to help the citizens recover territories once subject to them but since lost to powerful neighbors.[67]

[65] They included Antonio Turco, lord of Montemagno; Bonifacio, lord of Pralormo, Priocca, and Montà; and Antonio Asinari, lord of Costigliole d'Asti, Balangero, San Marzano, Canelli, etc. Gabotto, *Età*, p. 264.

[66] Treaty text in Cibrario, *Storia*, III, 265–267. Amadeus was to confirm all previous franchises of the commune, and to rest content with an annual tax of 6,000 florins and military service from the citizens for one month per year within the district of Asti only.

[67] Other clauses limited the commune's liability for past debts and required the count to promise never to alienate the commune or its territory. Amadeus confirmed previous franchises and agreed to choose his vicar from a list

The acquisition of Cuneo was not only an increase in the power of the count of Savoy; it was also a blueprint for Piedmont policy in the future, although Amadeus VI would not live to see it carried out. Only one of the places which the dedication charter obligated him to recover for their mutual advantage was already in his possession—Caraglio and its castle. The others were held by a former officer of the queen of Naples, the marquis of Saluzzo, and the marquises of Ceva and Montferrat.[68] To recover them all was a large order, but the count of Savoy had large ambitions. And already a possible means of realizing those ambitions presented itself: on 15 January 1382, Louis of Anjou at last announced his imminent departure to rescue the queen of Naples.

### INVOLVEMENT IN THE NEAPOLITAN SUCCESSION, 1382

The duke's resolution was supported by his brothers Berry and Burgundy, who were happy to relieve him of the burdens of the regency. Clement VII was counting upon the expedition to expel his rival from Rome and end the Schism in his favor. The aid of the count of Savoy was highly desirable, not only because the duke would need as many experienced warriors as he could find, but also because the Savoyard passes would thus be available to his army. Anjou's plan was to cross Lombardy en route to Naples, gathering into his host all who might be induced to join it.

In February 1382, while the Green Count was engineering his tactical victories in Genoa and Asti, envoys of the duke had encountered others from Savoy at Lyon and had drawn up the contract laying down the conditions on which Amadeus would agree to take part in the enterprise.[69] The conditions were not easy, for the count meant to be satisfied that his absence from the Piedmont at such an important moment was made well worth

---

of three persons chosen by the commune from among his or the prince of Achaea's subjects. Details in *ibid.*, pp. 272–274.

[68] The Angevin officer held Centallo and its castle in fief; Saluzzo held Valgrana, Montaurosio, Montemalo, Pradleves, and Castelmagno; Ceva had Andonno, Entracque, Valdieri, Noasca, Roccavione, and Robilante; and Montferrat held Brusaporcello, Boves, Peveragno, Bene Superiore, Margarita, and Morozzo.

[69] *AST, Traités anciens*, VI, docs. 24, 25.

his while. Louis of Anjou was forced to sign over to the count of Savoy almost all of the Angevin rights in the Piedmont: claims to Asti, Alba, Mondovì, Tortona, Cherasco, and even Alessandria, together with their dependencies; Cuneo and its district; and the homages of the Ceva family.[70] Since most of these places were now held by the Visconti, it would be necessary to secure them by force. This is probably the real explanation for the duke's promise that once the conquest of Naples was completed, he would furnish the count with 1,000 lances "for enterprises and conquests by him to be designated."[71] The Green Count intended to make certain that the promise of the Angevin heritage in Piedmont did not remain simply a promise. In return Amadeus agreed to assist Louis of Anjou in conquering the kingdom of Naples by providing an army of 2,000 lances at the duke's expense. The count would receive 5,000 gold francs for his personal service.

In May, Amadeus crossed the mountains to Savoy, and on 21 May he left "by boat and by horse" from Chambéry for Avignon.[72] According to the chronicles, Clement was "moult joyeulx" to see the count and at once exhorted him to participate in the Neapolitan expedition.[73] After the pope had finished outlining the reasons why Amadeus should join in this great effort "to remove the poison from the Holy Church" by expelling Urban VI from Rome, the count is supposed to have objected that he had already committed himself to an expedition to Jerusalem.

[70] *AST, Comptes . . . des guerres*, doc. 21, is the chief source for the count's participation in the Neapolitan expedition. Extracts are published by S. Cordero de Pamparato in *RS* (1902, pp. 101–115, 147–163, 247–289) in an article entitled "La dernière campagne d'Amédée VI, comte de Savoie." Item 29 is a gratuity given at Avignon on 4 June to the duke's secretary for drawing up the treaty granting to the count the "comitatu Pedemontii." Only Demonte was to remain in Angevin hands.

[71] Cognasso, *Il Conte Verde*, p. 240, thinks Amadeus wanted them exclusively for a crusade, which probably places too much trust in the chronicle versions.

[72] Pamparato, item 27. The count was lodged at the papal palace on arrival. His economical inclinations were again in evidence: he bought a boat at Chanaz for the trip down the Rhône, then sold it when he got there for fourteen gold francs, eighteen *denarii gros. tournois.* Item 4.

[73] Servion II, 226; Cabaret, p. 220 *dorso.* In fact Amadeus had already agreed to participate in the Neapolitan campaign as of February 1382.

After he had driven the Turks from the Holy City and entrusted it to the safekeeping of the knights of Rhodes, the count planned to bring the holy sepulcher back to Savoy, deposit it at Montgelat, and build a monastery to house it. In this monastery he intended to retire to end his days, while Bonne de Bourbon withdrew from the world into a nunnery.[74] The count claimed to have already at his disposal a large fleet of Venetian and Genoese galleys for this expedition, but he promised to assist the duke of Anjou and the pope on his return from the Holy Land.

Naturally this idea brought protests from both the pope and the duke. Anjou reminded the count that he would have plenty of time in the future to make the projected trip to Jerusalem, but that the most urgent necessity for the cause of the True Faith was the ending of the Schism. "I beg you to decide to come with me . . . to Rome," the duke is supposed to have argued. "We will drive out the intruder, and after that our holy father . . . will come, and we shall place him upon the throne of Saint Peter; and from there we will go to Naples, and when I have been crowned king, I promise you that I will give you one thousand men-at-arms, paid for one year, who will serve you at my own expense." Clement was equally persuasive. "Biau filz de Savoie, after I am in Rome and you wish to undertake your voyage to Jerusalem, I will give you on behalf of the Church the galleys and ships necessary to carry the soldiers which . . . Anjou will give you." At this Amadeus is supposed to have agreed to place the expedition to Rome and Naples before that to Jerusalem.

How much truth there is in this account is hard to say, but it is impossible to dismiss out of hand the contention that the Green Count was thinking of another crusade. His alliances with Genoa and Venice, his occupation of the island of Tenedos, his negotiations with the king of Cyprus—all these facts suggest that he may well have had such a plan. That he ever really planned to attempt such an enterprise before he had satisfied his Piedmont ambitions or had helped to end the papal schism, however, may be doubted. Amadeus was much too realistic to suppose that these

[74] This is an interesting idea, considering that Amadeus' grandson, Amadeus VIII, some twenty years after this chronicle was written, did abdicate his throne and retire into a monastery.

matters would resolve themselves to his liking during his absence. The first use which he intended to make of Anjou's promised 1,000 lances was certainly the conquest of the Piedmont territories ceded to him in the treaty at Lyon. But he might indeed have had a second use for them in mind as well. To fight the infidel on the walls of Jerusalem the Golden may well have been the glorious climax which the Green Count envisioned for his career.

In Savoy there was apparently some reluctance to participate in the expedition to Naples. According to Servion, certain barons feared for their own and for the count's safety. "Silence!" the count is supposed to have replied, "I will hear no more. I will fulfill what I have promised, even if it means my death."[75] This put an end to the complaints, and during the next several weeks the Savoyards put themselves "in a great state of arms and of horses, of tents and pavillions and other necessary things."[76] But the barons' premonition was all too true. When he set out for Avignon in May 1382, the Green Count had seen for the last time the white peaks and green valleys of his Alpine homeland.

[75] Servion, II, 228.

[76] At Chambéry on 22 May 1382, Amadeus certified having received from the treasurer of the duke of Anjou the sum of 45,000 gold francs, his pay for the first three months of the campaign. Pamparato, item 11, p. 105.

XI

# The Last Campaign

## 1382-1383

THE Green Count remained at Avignon with the pope and the duke of Anjou until early June. On 29 May he hired the sire of Pierre with eighty lances, and four days later the treasurer of the duke gave him most of the money with which to pay them. Amadeus then spent five days at Carpentras "for the most part at the expense of the bishop," and on 16 June the Savoyards arrived at Briançon.[1] The following day they crossed the Mont Genèvre, dined at Ulzio (at the expense of the *prévôt*), and that evening reached Susa, where they would await the arrival of the duke of Anjou. The abbey of Susa, where the count decided to stay, was swept out, and seven carpenters were hired to furnish the place properly for the duke's coming. Claret was made; bacon, beef, pork, and mutton were amassed in quantity, and sweets were imported from Turin.[2]

On the evening of 19 June, Anjou arrived at last with his "militibus et comitiva," for whom the Green Count broke open the stores of wine and claret and bought 259 pounds of fish.[3] At the outset the Neapolitan expedition had a decidedly festive quality about it, owing no doubt to the presence of so many old friends of the count—Pierre of Geneva, Boniface and Amadeus de Chal-

---

[1] Pamparato, items 11, 27. On 1 June, Amadeus received 2,630 francs from Anjou at Avignon; the sire of Pierre cost 2,800. Several other documents concerning this expedition, besides the treasury accounts, are published in this article.

[2] *Ibid.*, items 49–51. The *prévôt* of Ulzio made the count a present of eleven sheep. A quantity of spices were purchased for the cuisine: "xviii lib gingiberis pisti . . . xx lib pulveris communis . . . vi lib piperis . . . vi lib grane paradisi . . . x lib canelle . . . iii lib saffrani de Orta . . . ii lib nucis muscati . . . xxx lib zucari Babilonie," etc.

[3] *Ibid.*, item 51.

lant, Gaspard de Montmayeur, Etienne de la Baume, Richard Musard, and many others. Once again war seemed a joyous thing, and after much feasting to emphasize that view, the ever-growing host moved on to dine at San Ambrogio (at the expense of the abbot of San Michele) before reaching Rivoli. The next three weeks were spent largely at Rivoli and Turin, where each day saw the arrival of more troops, "for all wished to go with [the count] and serve him, for love of the prowess and munificence that they admired in him."

In the meantime, the count acquired supplies and equipment for himself and his entourage. He ordered twelve saddles in green, along with bridles, breastpieces, stirrups, and cruppers in green; and from a saddler in Chambéry he ordered four more sets, complete with protective coverings of boiled leather ornamented with "Hungarian ribbon knots."[4] For himself he also purchased emerald green silk for a surcoat with the red and white arms of Savoy on it, and three pages and a groom were outfitted with green shoes, hoods, and tabards.[5] Twenty-four barrels were required to contain the count's wine supply, and two baskets of cheeses were given to him by the monks of the Grande Chartreuse. Bernabò Visconti, now on his best possible behavior, sent Amadeus two warhorses and four suits of mail—princely gifts indeed, for chain mail manufactured at Milan was expensive and highly prized.[6]

Once again the army which the Green Count commanded was essentially a paid feudal army, not a mercenary host. By 11 July the men and their equipment had been carefully registered by the marshals of the Savoyard army, Gaspard de Montmayeur and Etienne de la Baume. Of some 1,100 nobles and captains listed in the accounts, over half were vassals from the count's own dominions, and half of the remainder were vassals of the house

[4] So I have ventured to translate "garnitis tassis allotis Ungarie." *Ibid.*, item 72.

[5] As usual, sufficient funds were lacking, and at Chambéry, on orders from the count in July 1382, Bonne de Bourbon pawned crown jewels worth 400 florins and 160 gold francs. *AST*, inv. 16, doc. 35 (1382–1385). The count's letter was dated at Turin on 7 July 1382.

[6] Amadeus also made many gifts to churches and shrines in almost every town through which he passed, to "pauperes Christi" encountered on the road, and even to a priest for the burial of a poor man found dead near Turin. Cf. Pamparato, item 71.

of Savoy from adjacent principalities. Mercenary companies contributed only 227 lances out of the 1,100 listed.[7] About ninety lances comprised the count's personal command, the "gentes armorum hospicii domini," and of these nearly all were Savoyards or Genevois. As Servion rightly pointed out, it was an army composed of knights and squires "de nom et darmes."[8]

The time for departure was approaching. On 12 July the Savoyards and the duke of Anjou, whose army was some 15,000 strong, moved to Moncalieri, where the citizens presented them with two cartloads of wine.[9] A few days later on the road to Piacenza, the host encountered Bernabò and Giangaleazzo, accompanied by members of the Visconti family. In order to secure safe passage for his army across Lombardy, Louis of Anjou had agreed to the betrothal of his eldest son to Lucia Visconti, one of Bernabò's daughters. While final arrangements were being made for the payment of Lucia's immense dowry, Amadeus hired a boat to haul his "magnum pavaillonum" down the river to Piacenza.[10]

Since the Republic of Florence had remained faithful to Urban VI and hostile to the Angevin pretender to Naples, it was necessary to skirt Tuscany and follow the ancient Via Emilia past Bologna to the Adriatic coast. The trip across Lombardy toward Ravenna was a sort of triumphal progress for the Green Count, with liveried heralds and minstrels bearing gifts and compliments from local rulers and communes at every crossroads. Warhorses were sent with the good wishes of the lords of Verona and the marquis of Ferrara; sacks of bread were given by the commune of Bologna; wine was offered by the lords of Imola, the Ordelaffi

---

[7] To be sure, all participants in the campaign were paid. The rate was thirty gold francs for a knight's lance, fifteen for a squire's or "qualibet aliarum lancearum," and one franc to the captain of a company for each lance in it per month, "tam milite quam scuttifero." *Ibid.*, p. 154.

[8] Amadeus' household for this trip consisted of the secretaries, a chaplain, five minstrels, two trumpeters, a "doctor de fatras," an archer, Theodoric ("king of the Heralds of Savoy"), a chamberlain, a master of the pantry, a master of the "bottlery," and a "forrerius domini," who was a quartermaster sergeant who went ahead of the army to arrange for his master's food and lodging. *Ibid.*, pp. 248–249.

[9] Fifteen thousand men rather than the 40,000 affirmed by Servion.

[10] This was a great tent with a green covering and twelve shields with the red and white emblem of Savoy decorating the sides. Pamparato, item 123.

of Forlì, and the Polenta of Ravenna; a herd of sheep was contributed by Bernabò's wife, and a straw hat with pearls in it by Bernabò's favorite mistress.[11] The Green Count responded in kind, generously rewarding those who brought the gifts and continuously giving alms to the poor, to religious establishments, and to prostitutes in distress.[12] He also attempted to restrain the predatory habits of his men and reimbursed individuals who had been robbed by them. By mid-August the army was camped near Ravenna, where the count received 20,000 ducats from the duke of Anjou, the monthly salary for the services of himself and his 1,100 lances.

From now on the expedition increasingly lost its initial festive quality. At least three of the count's vassals were so ill that they had to be left behind at Ravenna, and already at Parma, two weeks before, the lord of Venton had died. South of them lay the dominions of the Malatesta, supporters of Urban VI and Charles of Durazzo. While Galeoti Malatesta was not prepared to dispute their passage, he was at best an untrustworthy neutral who would not scruple to take advantage of their first sign of weakness.[13] By taking the Adriatic route instead of following the Tuscan seacoast, they had lost contact with the fleet which Clement VII had sent to keep them in provisions. And finally, by now they had surely received the news that Queen Giovanna had been murdered in her prison at Muro in the Basilicata.[14] The army was revictualled near Ancona during the last week of August, then headed into the mountains of the interior.

Now an important decision had to be made. The leaders of the expedition were in contact with informants in Rome and knew that the Florentines, fearing for their own safety, had not

[11] *Ibid.*, items 135, 124. Servion calls her Bernabò's "dame per amours." Her name was Donnina Porri.

[12] *Ibid.*, items 125–127, 134.

[13] Amadeus and Malatesta exchanged several letters, and when the count's men captured one "dicto Pellerin, cavalcatori domini Galeoti Malateste" near Pésaro on 21 August, Amadeus paid his ransom and set him free. This may have been a gesture intended to win good will upon which he might need to draw later on. *Ibid.*, item 142.

[14] The exact date of Giovanna's death (27 July 1383) was given by Charles of Durazzo in a letter to the Florentines. She may not have been brutally strangled by four Hungarians under Durazzo's personal supervision, as Anjou later declared, but Charles was certainly responsible for her death.

yet sent John Hawkwood and his company south to help defend
Urban VI, as they had promised to do. If Anjou would march
directly upon Rome before Hawkwood could get there, the city
might be taken. The Savoyard chroniclers assert that the Green
Count very much favored such a move, but that others persuaded Louis of Anjou to reject his advice and to place the conquest of Naples before the ending of the Schism.[15] In any case,
the army bypassed the road to Rome and on 17 September made
a triumphal entry into the city of Aquila, the first important town
within the boundaries of the kingdom. Louis of Anjou was graciously received and accepted as king by the duke of Montorio, an
adherent of the late queen.

Almost a whole week was spent at Aquila. Louis of Anjou
never did learn the importance of moving swiftly toward his objectives. More than a month was required to reach Caserta, and
the duke remained inactive there for over two weeks before withdrawing into the interior to Montesarchio on the road to Benevento. This unaccountable delay in marching upon Naples enabled Hawkwood's company to reach Charles of Durazzo by the
end of November, and all chance of a speedy and successful campaign was lost. The strength of the enemy and the winter season
convinced Louis of Anjou that nothing more could be done. The
Savoyards accordingly moved into winter quarters at Montesarchio on 21 November and remained there until February 1383.
It was a miserable winter, for supplies were low and, owing to the
"corrupt air," illness was spreading in the army. Amadeus was
obliged to pawn valuables and to borrow from some of his nobles
in order to make ends meet. Louis of Anjou sank into one of his
typical fits of depression and spent Christmas Day at Benevento
drawing up his last will and testament.

Despite his own ill health, the Green Count was not prepared
to give up and do nothing.[16] War having failed, he insisted upon
trying the weapons of negotiation. As early as 10 December he
was in touch with Hawkwood, and on 4 January he met with
the constable of the king, Hawkwood, and the count of Campania

---

[15] Servion, II, 233–234. This was not the only instance in which, according
to Savoyard chroniclers, Amadeus was dissatisfied with Anjou's leadership. Cf.
*ibid.*, 232.

[16] Amadeus' ill health in late October is indicated in Pamparato, item 174.

to treat of peace between Anjou and Charles of Durazzo.[17] Amadeus was already convinced that Anjou's cause was hopeless. In return for the duke's abandoning his claims to the throne of Naples, the count proposed that Durazzo allow them all safe conduct to the coast so that they could return home by ship, and that he agree to surrender the county of Provence to Anjou. Charles was now certain of victory, however, and he would not accept such terms. The negotiators accordingly resorted for awhile to the tactic of demanding a duel between the two rivals. As usual, the challenges were duly exchanged and accepted by both sides, and as usual, no duel ever took place.

By now the sickness in the army was reaching dangerous proportions. Sometime in mid-January, Jean-Philippe de Montbéliard, an important Burgundian vassal, died, and this was only the beginning. Guillaume de Luyrieux, Archimand de Grolée and his brother, Jean de Rossillon, and Jean de Montbel fell sick and died in a short span of time. On 1 February, Amadeus withdrew his troops from Montesarchio, where the plague was rife, and the dispirited Savoyards moved farther into the interior. Perhaps the count had decided to try to lead his men out of what had become a deadly impasse by heading across the mountains to the Adriatic coast. In any case he conferred with Louis of Anjou at Carreto and was nearing Campobasso when, on 15 February, he was himself struck by the disease that had been taking such a terrible toll among his men. His followers carried him to Santo Stefano and lodged him in a house near Castropignano.

On 27 February, sensing the approach of death, the Green Count made his will, instituting his son as his heir universal and his wife as regent of Savoy. Then Amadeus asked for his chaplain, to whom he confessed himself "moult plainement," had mass celebrated before him and communicated "tres benignement," and received the holy oil "moult paciement." After providing alms for the Church and for the poor and asking that his body be returned to Savoy that it might be laid to rest beside his ancestors at Hautecombe, the Green Count uttered his last words. "He recommended to . . . Louis of Savoy [Achaea] and to his barons, knights, and squires, Countess Bonne his wife and Amadeus his son, and begged them to counsel and aid them as loyally as they

---

[17] *Ibid.*, items 177, 180.

had done for him . . . and lastly, he handed the ring of Saint Maurice to Messire Gaspard de Montmayeur, one of his marshals, asking him to deliver it to his son Amadeus. And these words ended, he raised his eyes toward Heaven, joined together his hands, and recommending himself to the blessed Trinity and to the virgin maiden Mary, returned his soul unto its creator."[18]

When the duke of Anjou, who had been summoned posthaste from Benevento, saw that the Green Count was dead, he burst into tears and began naming the many virtues of which the world was deprived by his death. Pierre Voisin sadly began his last treasurer's account: ". . . on which first day of the month of March . . . at about midnight, in the presence of Louis [of France], duke of Calabria and Anjou, Lord Pierre, count of Geneva, Jean de Bueil, and many nobles, knights, and squires of the lord, and other foreigners, our aforesaid Lord Amadeus, Lord Count of Savoy, who auspiciously traversed this life with greatest honor and was held by Christians to be bold, prudent, and gentle among rulers . . . with true confession, satisfaction, and devotion did remove from this world. May his soul rest in peace, centuries without end. Amen."

THE RETURN TO SAVOY · THE FUNERAL AT HAUTECOMBE

Death would reap a dreadful harvest among the Savoyards, who found themselves deprived of their master thousands of miles from their homeland in a country as inhospitable as its inhabitants. To the living now remained the duty of fulfilling the count's last wish to be buried beside Lake Le Bourget in the shadow of friendlier mountains. His body was embalmed in wine and aromatics and placed in a cypress casket, while Gaspard de Montmayeur rode to Naples to secure safe conduct from Charles of Durazzo. The king not only complied, but paid his own respects to his fallen adversary by sending the Company of San Giorgio to escort the Savoyards as far as Capua. A considerable number of the count's vassals now detached themselves from the ill-fated Louis of Anjou, who was destined to survive the count of Savoy by scarcely over a year, in order to accompany the body of their master to its final resting place.

Easter morning, 22 March 1383, found the forlorn company at

18 Servion, II, 236–237.

Tripergoli on the bay of Pozzuoli near Naples. Raising money to finance the homeward trip was no easy matter, and many of the nobles found themselves obliged to advance sums which they could hardly spare. The sea voyage alone required two weeks and was a nerve-wracking experience for all. A few days before passing the isle of Monte Christo in early April, a storm buffeted them so violently that Ludovico de Savoie ordered mass said on board the ship. On 7 April they landed at the island of Gallinara off Albenga, grateful to be on solid ground once again, and that evening all but the attendants of the casket went ashore to spend the night in a hostelry. At the same time, it was discovered that the passes behind Albenga were controlled by the marquis of Carretto (of the house of Saluzzo), who was unfriendly to Savoy. It would be necessary to disembark elsewhere and try to find a safer route through the Ligurian mountains to the Piedmont. Another ship was hired to take the Savoyards to Savona, where they arrived two days later. On 10 April the news came that Gaspard de Montmayeur, who had been left behind at Albenga because of illness, was dead.

The ring of Saint Maurice and responsibility for getting the count's body back to Savoy now passed to Ludovico of Achaea, who at last got the whole company reassembled at Savona. There was not enough money to continue the journey, so two men were sent to Genoa to pawn more of the late count's jewels.[19] Messengers were sent over the passes to the Piedmont to notify the prince of Achaea of their arrival and to make sure that the route was safe. The plague still ravaged the company, and before the end of the month Richard Musard, like Montmayeur a faithful companion of the Green Count for twenty years, followed his master to the grave.[20] Black suits were made at Savona for the mule drivers and the two valets accompanying the funeral litter, and for four of the late count's pages.

After what must have seemed an interminable wait, the castellan of Villafranca finally arrived from the Piedmont to notify them that the passes were safe. The few hundred survivors, escorting a black-draped litter drawn by eight mules, began the trip across the mountains in the last week of April. At Ceva the

---

[19] Pamparato, item 194.

[20] Musard was buried in the church of the Hospitallers of Saint John at Savona.

# The Last Campaign

Franciscans, to whom Amadeus had always been so generous, allowed the casket to rest overnight in their church, and at Fossano the prince of Achaea, the bishop of Turin, and a large assemblage of barons and bourgeois were on hand to pay their last respects— and the remaining costs of the trip. At Vigone the body lay in state until the end of the month, when the final stage of the journey was undertaken across the Mont Cenis and through the Maurienne, forty torchbearers flanking the funeral litter.

On 8 May the casket, now draped in black velvet and cloth-of-gold, was escorted by 120 torchbearers through the gates of Chambéry to the shores of Lake Le Bourget. The funeral barge crossed the dark waters in the shadow of the mountain to the abbey of Hautecombe, that "threshold of eternal night" for the princes of Savoy, in the words of Lamartine. In the presence of the court of Savoy, the archbishop of Tarentaise, and dignitaries from France, Lombardy, and Savoy, the body of Amadeus VI was placed beside the remains of his predecessors, amid the "great tears, lamentations, and weeping of his subjects."

As was the custom, the funeral services did not take place until forty days after the burial. Messengers had been sent to neighboring lands, and for some weeks those who wished to attend gathered at Chambéry. On 15 June twenty-four prelates, the princes and princesses of the mountain dynasty from both sides of the Alps, several foreign ambassadors, and a large crowd of local Savoyards congregated at the abbey of Hautecombe. The curious ceremony which now took place provided a fitting conclusion to the Green Count's career, for the bright colors that had been so much a part of his life were permitted to act out the final pageant. Two knights appeared with the blue banner of the Virgin Mary, followed by two more pairs of knights mounted upon warhorses and carrying the banners of Saint George and Saint Maurice.[21] A squire of the prince of Achaea came next, holding the sword of justice, followed by the prince, who carried the count's battle sword, which he symbolically held by the point. The procession continued with the count's warhorses fitted out as they would have been when Amadeus himself was mounted upon them, caparisoned in green, scarlet, and white trimmed with silver

[21] Details taken from household, treasury, and castellany accounts for 1383 in *ADS* and *AST*, invs. 16, 38, 39.

and gold. One mounted knight wore the count's falcon-crested helmet and his tournament armor decorated with *lacs d'amour*; another, mounted upon Amadeus' favorite tournament horse, carried a broken sword in his hand. The bright banners representing the saints in whom Amadeus had placed his trust were set on either side of the bier before the altar, while the symbols of earthly power—the swords, the armor, the shields, the collar of his knightly order—were laid at the foot of the altar. At the end of the procession came a carriage drawn by four black horses bearing four black knights holding four black banners. The somber hue of death had triumphed over the bright colors of life.

THE SIGNIFICANCE OF THE ERA OF THE GREEN COUNT

For the Green Count life had come to an end, but for Savoy a new era had begun under his leadership. The reign of Amadeus VI was a particularly fortunate epoch in the history of the Savoyard state, which presents in this respect a striking contrast with most of its neighbors. While England, France, and Burgundy were torn with foreign and civil wars which periodically resulted in an almost complete breakdown of law and order, transalpine Savoy after 1355 achieved a degree of internal peace almost unparalleled in its history. While Italy was suffering from economic recession and the power struggles that would gradually create the precarious political equilibrium of the fifteenth century, the rulers of Savoy were slowly and steadily extending their sway over an increasingly large part of the western Alps between Lombardy and France. The fourteenth century is usually regarded as a period of retrogression and disaster in European history generally, but it was a period of glory for Savoy and of prosperity for its princes.

The striking territorial expansion of the Savoyard state during the era of the Green Count is the most obvious reflection of this fact. The annexation of the Valbonne, the barony of Faucigny, the Pays de Gex, and the Pays de Vaud on the western side of the Alps was paralleled by the subordination of the Piedmont and the acquisition of the Canavese, the northern Vercellese, and the district of Cuneo in Italy. Territorial growth was accompanied by a corresponding increase in comital power, for more land meant new sources of revenue and more men for the count's armies. Such a long period of aggressive and successful "foreign policy" also enhanced the power of the prince by placing him in direct command over his subjects, who were repeatedly called upon to serve and to obey. Possible rivals for authority within the state were kept constantly occupied and constantly subordinated.

The reasons for the success of the Green Count's political and military policies are not difficult to determine. To a considerable extent Amadeus VI was favored by otherwise unfortunate circumstances of his times. The French involvement in the Hundred Years War made the Valois monarchy a somewhat less potent threat to the lesser princes on its eastern frontier. In northern Italy the expansion of the Visconti state of Milan gave rise to a succession of anti-Visconti leagues among the other powers of Lombardy and Piedmont. The dynasty of Savoy, solidly rooted in its transalpine dominions, was soon in a position to play one side against the other to its own advantage. Amadeus VI revealed unusual skill in profiting from these situations. In the West he extracted the advantageous Treaty of Paris from royal cousins eager for his assistance against the English. In Italy he utilized his reputation as a benevolent and militarily successful ruler to become the protector of communes fearful of falling under the domination of local or neighboring tyrants. The appearance of the Great Companies in the Piedmont and elsewhere also worked to the Green Count's advantage, for the destruction and terror which they spread frequently induced communes and nobles alike to sacrifice, if necessary, political liberty for personal security.

As elsewhere in Europe, the geographical expansion of the Savoyard state was accompanied by the development of organs of centralized government. The judicial hierarchy was reorganized, and an attempt was made to draw up a code which would facilitate equal application of the law throughout the greater part of the count's dominions. Wherever possible, independent judicial authorities, whether lay or ecclesiastical, were eliminated or curtailed. Institutions such as the "advocatus pauperum" and the privileges obtained from the emperor were both efforts to extend the scope of the count's authority at the expense of barons and bishops alike. Yet at the same time, the Green Count took care not to antagonize the local population by trampling upon local custom, as his policies in the Val d'Aosta and in the annexation of Biella and Cuneo illustrate.

Amadeus VI was particularly resourceful in securing the money he needed for his expensive political and military enterprises. Innovations in collection and accounting techniques widened the financial bases upon which the *chambre des comptes* operated, and enabled the count to exploit the fiscal advantages of his feudal status more effectively than ever before. Subsidies were accounted for separately after 1331, and a resident branch of the *chambre des comptes* was fixed at Chambéry in 1355. Tax collectors and treasury officers were subject to surveillance and discipline, as the investigations of 1356 and the trial of Pierre Gerbais reveal. The Green Count soon discovered that as feudal lord and suzerain he could often extend the taxable population to include those hitherto financially responsible only to their immediate lords. He also discovered that cheaper sources of ready money than the usurers were the office-holders of his government, who often found themselves obliged to advance loans when the count was in need of immediate funds. The *Cour des Monnaies* created in 1358 enabled Amadeus VI to coordinate minting operations within his dominions and to make them a source of additional revenue.

The need for money to finance the vastly expanded bureaucracy of the Savoyard state under the Green Count required him to ask for general subsidies rather more frequently than his predecessors had done. Under his successors, general assemblies similar in composition to the "parliaments" elsewhere in Europe were convoked, and by the sixteenth century Savoy had a fairly well-established "Trois Etats." During the lifetime of the Green Count, however, no such assemblies seem to have existed as an integral part of comital government. Amadeus VI negotiated for his subsidies directly through his officers in each of the chief castellany towns, bailliage by bailliage. The duty of the count's subjects to furnish him with "aid and counsel" in monetary form seems to have been the prevailing concept in Savoy, which did not develop parliamentary bodies capable of restricting the power of the crown in return for granting subsidies, as occurred at least briefly elsewhere in fourteenth-century Europe.[22]

In military affairs, the day of the feudal army composed of part-time peasant-soldiers and captained solely by nobles who had inherited their commands was passing. Paid professional soldiers

[22] See Commentary, X.

were gradually becoming a necessity for military success, particularly on the Italian side of the Alps, and Amadeus VI reluctantly accepted this fact. The great disadvantage of the commercial soldier, however, was precisely the commercial character of the contract which bound him to his employer. Some mercenary captains would not desert their employer before the expiration of their contracts, as Amadeus himself discovered in 1368–1369, when he attempted to bribe the Monk of Hecz to desert first Filippo of Achaea, then Federigo of Saluzzo. The Green Count naturally preferred men upon whom he could rely to stay with him even when their pay was in arrears and their length of service ended.[23] Although the count began to employ mercenaries on a scale hitherto unknown among his predecessors in Savoy, he still sought to safeguard his own position by relying upon feudal traditions whenever he could. With rare exceptions Amadeus VI's armies were chiefly composed of feudal vassals, even when mercenary companies were also present. And even when the men-at-arms were commercial soldiers essentially, the count ordinarily kept all important commands in his own hands and in those of trusted Savoyard vassals, in order to assure himself of the loyalty of the military leadership.

A century and a half later Machiavelli wrote that the successful prince must rely upon native troops, otherwise his state could never be secure. Mercenaries, he declared, "are disunited, ambitious, undisciplined, and faithless, swaggering when among friends and cowardly in the face of the enemy; they have neither fear of God nor loyalty to men . . . they have no other interest or incentive to hold the field, save only their moderate pay, which is not enough to make them willing to die for you."[24] Machiavelli concluded with the declaration that the ruin of Italy was largely owing to the constant importation of mercenary troops, and that no state would be well defended unless its armies were recruited from among its subjects and captained by the prince himself. The conditions to which Machiavelli refers already existed in the fourteenth century, and the Green Count of Savoy is an excellent

---

[23] In most of Amadeus VI's municipal charters, the bourgeois were obliged to serve in his armies, within certain geographical limits, even beyond the expiration of their first forty days, provided that the count paid their expenses thereafter.

[24] Niccolò Machiavelli, *The Prince*, Chapter XII.

example of one who fully endorsed the Florentine writer's views on military affairs.

The Great Companies reflected a still larger trend of the age, the breakdown of feudalism before another system of values—or of payment—existed to replace it satisfactorily. Professional soldiers were more effective than the feudal levy, but their loyalty tended to be more readily transferrable. As Machiavelli pointed out, in many cases the financial resources of the state were not sufficient to retain that loyalty, and no adequate means of reabsorbing the military into the civilian population existed during the era of the Hundred Years War. The economic recession of the century played a role in depriving the soldiers of jobs to return to, with the result that every man was obliged to look out for himself. Economic necessity, as much as anything else, was what made the mercenaries "enemies of God, of pity, of mercy"— that is, rejectors of all traditional Christian and feudal values. In Amadeus VI's efforts to keep these people out of Savoy, there was much of the true conservative trying to maintain an older way of life which, if not without hardships and imperfections, had nevertheless meaning and a sense of direction.

The political stability of the Savoyard state during the Green Count's reign was also owing in part to his conscious policy of seeking the support of the various classes in his dominions. Transalpine Savoy did not escape from the Black Death which occurred in 1348–1352 and periodically thereafter, but it did largely avoid the ravages of war. Amadeus VI deserves most of the credit for this fact, and it probably explains why—in an era noted for peasant rebellions and communal uprisings—the count's dominions were singularly free of such unrest, except in contested frontier regions like the Valais and parts of the Piedmont. Certainly the count's policies, as well as his power, contributed to this result. He was not only the most effective guardian of the peace and safety of merchant caravans traveling between the valley of the Po and France; he also preserved and extended municipal franchises and facilitated some bourgeois penetration of aristocratic ranks by readily employing members of the middle class in his administration. The count's suppression of the prince of Achaea's merchandise tolls in 1356–1357 is the best, but not the only, illustration of his interest in minimizing obstacles to transalpine traffic through his territories. His efforts at pacification both in the Val d'Aosta and in the Valais often involved the investigation of offenses against merchants who complained of extortion or robbery.[25]

The count's continuous traveling through his territories brought him into frequent contact with his humbler subjects also, and his concern for their welfare was reflected in nearly every castellany and household roll throughout his career—gratuities to local people for services rendered, remission of fines, exemption from taxes for "poor and miserable persons," correction of officers guilty of misbehavior, and many other acts of paternalism. No doubt economic hardship, plagues, and depopulation weakened the agricultural and commercial classes, and deprived them of the means of opposing the count's authority, but there is no real evidence that they were inclined to do so. Only in the Valais, where the Green Count's power to pursue his own policies was limited by the rights of the bishop, and where the peasants were awakened by the neighboring Forest Cantons to a desire for political independence, did Amadeus VI's paternal government fail to win the support of the population.

The factors which weakened the peasants and townsmen also weakened the position of both lay and ecclesiastical magnates, and help to explain the count's success in bringing the latter under his control. The depopulation of town and country meant a diminution in manorial revenues for the nobles as well as for the count, whose drive to annex lands and subjects was doubtless motivated in part by a desire to make up for such losses. As elsewhere in Europe, the Savoyard nobles were not able to remedy their financial difficulties as effectively as the count because their subordinate position deprived them of the kinds of opportunities which he enjoyed. The result was a significant movement of the aristocracy into comital service as the most effective way of participating in the advance of comital power. This movement meant the loss of the feudal independence of an earlier age, but most nobles found the social and economic advantages more than adequate compensation. For many of the younger members of baronial families, careers in the count's service opened far more in-

---

[25] See, for example, in Van Berchem, pp. 98ff., and in Gremaud, doc. 1993, the case of Palmeron Turchi, a merchant of Asti, on whose behalf the count was negotiating with the Valaisans in the 1340's.

345

teresting and lucrative possibilities than a more independent but isolated life on the family estates could have done.

The decline in the prestige of the Church Universal and of the papacy in the fourteenth century opened ecclesiastical immunities to attack, and Amadeus VI contrived to profit substantially from the situation. Neither the pope nor the emperor was in a position to protect the bishops from the count's encroachments, and only the bishops of Geneva and Lausanne were able to maintain some measure of independence among the prelates in the dominions of the count of Savoy.[26] On the local level the count's officers continually infringed upon episcopal prerogatives, and although the count himself had no right to interfere in episcopal elections, Amadeus VI was fairly successful in securing the appointment of relatives or friends to the major sees. These were in turn often partially transformed into ministers of state when they accepted seats on the count's executive and judicial councils.

A natural concommitant of the political and social changes taking place in fourteenth-century Savoy was an ideology to justify and support them. Thus the era of the Green Count also witnessed a great flowering of knightly institutions and the spread of chivalric ideas, particularly on the Franco-Burgundian side of his Alps. Amadeus VI promoted these developments, for he saw in them the means of combating what he regarded as the moral degeneration of his times—the buying and selling of human loyalty, the insubordination of vassals toward their suzerain (as in the cases of Hugues de Genève-Anthon, Filippo of Achaea, Federigo of Saluzzo), and the spectacle of undutiful subjects (such as those in the Valais and the Canavese). To protect his nobles from the degrading commercialism of the times, the Green Count fostered the ideals of an aristocratic brotherhood. His vassals must be kept aware of their special status among humankind

[26] Guillaume de Marcossay, bishop of Geneva in 1366–1377, was the most effective of Amadeus VI's episcopal opponents. By 1370 he had surrounded his city with new walls and towers, and, after excommunicating Savoyard officers who were trying to enforce the count's vicarial rights despite the emperor's revocation of them, the bishop confiscated the subsidy money the count was collecting for his *viagio ultramarino* of 1366–1367. In a treaty of 18 March 1371, Amadeus finally gave up his vicarial rights at Geneva in return for his subsidy money. Cf. Muratore, "Carlo IV," p. 188, note 5. The count maintained his appellate judge at Lausanne, however, despite the bishop's protests.

and of the special privileges and responsibilities that went with their rank. In order to promote a sense of knightly solidarity through public display of fine sentiments and noble qualities, the Green Count organized frequent tournaments in which nobles might meet and develop mutual esteem as members of an exclusive kind of club. Amadeus VI created two knightly orders to the same end, and the Order of the Collar has survived to this day in Italy as the *Sanctissima Annunziata.*

In an artificial and ideal atmosphere such as that temporarily created by tournaments and knightly orders, it was easier to repair the damage which cruel reality so often does to honor. The loyalty of man to man, of knight to suzerain, could be renewed as religious faith is renewed through participation in religious services. The collapse of traditional feudal institutions could be denied through a reaffirmation of feudal values, just as the Christian hermit could deny nature through a reaffirmation of his belief that Christ had transcended nature. The impressive ceremonies surrounding special events such as the reception of the duke of Clarence and the visit of Emperor Charles IV were other occasions on which the Green Count was able to recognize publicly his knightly brothers "en armes et en foi," thereby rewarding their loyalty and inspiring others with a desire to emulate their example.

Amadeus VI's fame as a champion of the True Faith was probably also in part the result of a calculated effort to win the regard of churchmen in his dominions through preeminence in their own field. The most spectacular means to this end was the crusade to Constantinople, but it was by no means the only one. From childhood the Green Count had demonstrated exemplary piety beyond the call of duty, and his assiduous attention to visiting shrines and giving alms was a notable characteristic throughout his life. In the creation of his famous knightly order, he was careful to make much of its dedication to the Virgin Mary, whose banner was always prominently displayed whenever the knights appeared in public. The Green Count's success in disarming the prelates of his mountains and even in usurping many of their traditional privileges was no doubt facilitated by the great reputation for Christian piety which he enjoyed. Even churchmen who resisted, such as the bishops of Lausanne and Geneva, could not count upon the unreserved support of the pope, who more often than not regarded Amadeus VI as his "chiefest delight" and a "dearest son" of the Holy Church.

If the Green Count's championing of knighthood and the True Faith was intended to win him the support primarily of nobles and church leaders, other activities seemed mainly designed to please humbler subjects and to build a glorious reputation generally. The population was ordinarily pleased by splendid appearances; such colorful spectacles as the *Grandes Chevauchées* for the annexation of the Pays de Vaud and the Pays de Gex clearly had this effect, as did the count's festive visits to the Val d'Aosta for the convocation of the *Audiences générales*. Probably the selection of a single color for his own garments and for those of his entourage, which created the "Green Count" of the chronicles, was also calculated to convey to one and all the idea that their lord was no ordinary man, but a grand personage deserving honor and obedience. Practical measures such as redress of local grievances or relief for local disaster areas usually accompanied the pageantry to convince friend and foe alike of the count's beneficence. This mixture of pomp and paternalism was an important aspect of government under the Green Count, whose example in this regard was not infrequently repeated by his successors. In the eighteenth and nineteenth centuries the rulers of Savoy-Piedmont generally enjoyed a considerable reputation in Europe for liberal and enlightened government.

Amadeus VI was not a literary man, but he did imitate to some degree his French and Visconti relatives who were patrons of the arts. Galeazzo Visconti revived the university of Pavia, and the Green Count secured imperial letters patent founding a university at Geneva, although nothing came of the scheme during his lifetime. Savoy did not witness any real flourishing of art or literature under Amadeus VI, but at Ripaille, Bonne de Bourbon was helping to create an atmosphere favorable to cultural activities. The only Savoyard of the century to enjoy an international reputation in literature, the poet Othon de Grandson (d. 1396) from the Pays de Vaud may be considered in part a product of this atmosphere and the vogue for chivalric literature which the Green Count helped to create. Certainly Amadeus VI recognized artistic and literary merit when he encountered it, as his generosity to Froissart and Guillaume de Machaut bears witness. The count may not have been much of a connoisseur himself, but his frequent subsidies to painters and musicians in Savoy and abroad show that he considered such patronage to be among his princely obligations.

Like the despots of the Italian Renaissance, the Green Count of Savoy thus promoted the cult of the individual—the magnificent prince, the benevolent ruler, the victorious warrior, the champion of the Christian religion. While creating a reputation which enhanced his prestige and advanced his power, Amadeus VI also developed the machinery of a centralized government that would perpetuate his accomplishments beyond the limits of his own lifetime. He could be coldly realistic if circumstances so required, but he cared about the ideals he espoused. In the end he succeeded in his aim to be remembered for the ideals he championed, rather than for his deviations from them. The sharp political opportunist who so effectively matched wits and methods with the ruthless despots of Lombardy lies in the shadow of the cloisters at Hautecombe. The daylight of history falls rather upon the prince in emerald green, "moult chevaleureux et vaillant en son temps."

349

COMMENTARY

# Commentary

## I · THE CHRONICLES OF SAVOY

Jehan Servion, *Gestez et Croniques de la Mayson de Savoye*, was first published in *MHP,* III, *Scriptores* I, in 1840. A later edition was published in two volumes by Frederic-Emmanuel Bollati di Saint-Pierre (Turin, 1879). Servion composed his chronicles between 1464–1465 and relied heavily upon the earliest of the chronicles of Savoy which include mention of Amadeus VI, that of Jean d'Oronville (or Orville), "dit Cabaret," who was the official chronicler at the court of Amadeus VIII and wrote between 1417–1419. I have used Servion most of the time simply because his chronicle is available, while Cabaret's is not. I have, however, carefully checked the passages used in this work against the Cabaret manuscript at the *AEG* (historical manuscript no. 161). Much of Servion is word for word the same, but whenever discrepancies of any importance occur, I have so indicated in the footnotes.

## II · HUMBERT AND OGIER DE SAVOIE

Humbert was probably in his late 'teens or early twenties at the time of Amadeus' birth, for as early as 1338 he was sire of Ecluse and castellan of Tarentaise, and in 1339 he accompanied Count Aymon to Paris for the expedition against the English at Buironfosse. (Cf. Cordey, *Les Comtes,* p. 51, note 5; *ADS,* castellany, Tarentaise, 1338–1343.) Humbert's father married him to the heiress of the seigneurie of Arvillars near Montmélian, where he founded a noble dynasty of his own. During the reign of his half brother, he served as castellan of Chillon on Lake Geneva, of Maurienne, of Châtelard-en-Bauges, and of Tarentaise, successively. In 1357 he became *bailli* of Savoy and castellan of the key fortress of Montmélian, posts which he held until his death in 1374.

Ogier de Savoie's career was somewhat less distinguished, for although he was relied upon frequently, the posts he held were not so important. He was probably nearer Amadeus in age, as the household records show expenses of clothing for him along with those for the count's other children, and the earliest date at which Ogier can be definitely separated from the family foyer is 1353,

353

when he was made castellan of Faverges. (For example, *ADS,* castellany, Chambéry, 1347–1348, expenses "pro una penna ad for-randum corseti Ogerii fratrem naturalem domini.") Two years later he was castellan of Conflans, commanding the confluence of the Arly and the Isère in the Tarentaise, and he served more or less as the count's representative in that valley for most of the rest of his life. Marie-José, pp. 60–61, gives the date of Ogier's death as 1372. This is disproved, however, by *ADS* (castellany), Montmélian, 17 March 1373–11 January 1375, *librata* section for 1374: "expensis . . . in festo epiphanie ubi fuit de mandato domini quia dominus ipsum misit apud castellanum Bonitiarum pro morte domini Ogerii bastardi de Sabaudie." The same author reports that Ogier was married to one "N. de Meyria." This is possible, but Jacqueline Roubert (p. 163), following the *Armorial et Nobiliaire* of Foras (I, 326), states only that Ogier married Bernarde de Cevins, heiress of the vast territories of her father in the Tarentaise. The marriage must have been after 1364, since Bernarde's first husband, Emeric de Montfalcon, was still living in that year. In 1376 (at least) Bernarde married Antelme de Miolans, having apparently had no children from her marriage to Ogier de Savoie.

III · THE CASTELLANIES AND BAILLIAGES OF SAVOY, CA. 1350

1. *Bailliage of Savoy*: Montmélian, Chambéry, Le Bourget, Montfalcon, Cusy, Châtelard-en-Bauges, Faverges, Entremont (in the massif of the Grande Chartreuse), Les Marches, Tournon, Ugine, Conflans, Tarentaise (seat at Salins), Maurienne (seat at Hermillon), Aiguebelle, La Rochette, and Les Mollettes. The cas-tellan of Montmélian was *bailli* of Savoy, since Montmélian had been the "capital" of the counts of Maurienne-Savoy before their purchase of Chambéry in 1232 (insofar as they had a capital at all). Montmélian is more strategically located than Chambéry, commanding as it does the entrance to the Maurienne and Taren-taise routes to Italy.

2. *Bailliage of Chablais*: Chillon-Villeneuve, Geneva (castle of the Bourg-de-l'Ile in the Rhône), Versoix, Corbière, Yvoire-La Ravorée, Thonon-Allinges, Evian-Féternes, St-Maurice-d'Agaune–Monthey (after 1350, Monthey is accounted for as a separate castel-lany), Saxon, Sembrancher, Entremont (in the valley leading up

to the Great St. Bernard pass from Martigny; Entremont was sometimes combined with Saxon, sometimes styled "Entremont-Sembrancher," since the castellan's seat was apparently at Sembrancher), Conthey-Saillon, La Tour-de-Vevey, Châtel-St-Denis-en-Fruence, Payerne, and Morat in the Pays de Vaud. The castellan of Chillon was *bailli* of Chablais.

3. *Bailliage of Bresse*: Dullin's handling of this bailliage (p. 27) is very misleading. In 1285, Bresse contained thirteen castellanies: Bourg, Bâgé-le-Châtel, Pont-de-Veyle, Pont-de-Vaux, Châtillon, St-Martin-le-Châtel, St-Trivier-de-Courtes, St-André-en-Revermont, Treffort, Coligny, St-Etienne-de-Bois, Jasseron, and Marboz. Between 1330 and 1348 four of these were detached to form the dower lands of Countess Blanche de Bourgogne, widow of Count Edward. Upon her death in 1348, the bailliage was reconstituted and received three additions: Pont-d'Ain, Foissiat, and St-Laurent-les-Mâcon. The castellan of Bourg-en-Bresse was *bailli* of Bresse.

4. *Bailliage of Bugey* (in 1343): St-Germain-d'Ambérieux, St-Rambert, Ambronay, Rossillon, Lompnes, Balon, Seyssel, Billiat, Léaz-l'Ecluse (sometimes combined with Billiat), and Ordonnaz. Cf. *AST*, inv. 38, folio 43, doc. 2. The castellan of St-Germain was *bailli* of Bugey.

5. *Bailliage of Novalaise*: Pont-de-Beauvoisin, St-Genix-d'Aosta, Pierre-Châtel, Yenne-Chanaz in Novalaise proper; south of the Guiers: Voiron, St-Laurent-du-Pont, Dolomieu, and Ile-de-Ciers. The castellan of Voiron was *bailli* of Novalaise.

6. *Bailliage of Viennois*: St-Georges-d'Esperanche, Châbons, Septême, St-Symphorien-d'Ozon, St-Jean-de-Bournay, La Côte-St-André–Boczosel, La Verpillière, Azieu, and Jonage. The *bailli* was castellan either of St-Georges-d'Esperanche or of Côte-St-André.

7. *Bailliage of Aosta*: Aosta, Châtelargent, Bard-Donnas, Montalto, and Ivrea. The *bailli* was castellan either at Aosta or at Châtelargent; and Ivrea was only technically a part of the bailliage, since it was governed by a *podestà* with special powers.

8. *Bailliage of Susa*: Susa, Avigliana, Rivoli. The *bailli* was castellan either at Avigliana or at Rivoli. After 1359 three more castellanies were added to the bailliage—those of Caselle, Cirié, and Lanzo. They had been detached to form the dowry of Marguerite de Savoie on her marriage to Giovanni II, marquis of Montferrat,

and they returned to Savoy at her death since her marriage was childless.

## IV · THE ROLE OF THE NOBILITY IN COMITAL ADMINISTRATION

By the fourteenth century, one of the most striking features of comital administration on the higher levels is the role played in it by the Savoyard nobility. The *baillis* of the count's dominions were without exception nobles, and so were the great majority of castellans. Even an occasional *juge-mage* came from the noble class, although judicial offices were by now occupied almost exclusively by professional jurists, the "legum doctores," for whom careers in the magistracy were often a means of achieving noble rank. (Notable examples, drawn from the headings of castellany accounts in *ADCO* and *ADS*, were the Ravais, the Berre, the Montgelat, and the Murs of Montmélian.) Of the twenty nobles on the council of regency in 1343, at least ten had recently held or were holding, at the time of their appointment, posts as castellans and *baillis*; and six others had relatives holding such posts.

Guillaume d'Entremont was castellan-*bailli* at Chillon in 1342–1343; Pierre d'Urtières was castellan of Châtelard-en-Bauges in 1341–1344; Pierre Mareschal was castellan of Avigliana in 1333–1338; Pierre de Montgelat was castellan of Susa, 1344–1345; Amadeus de Beauvoir was castellan-*bailli* at St-Germain-d'Ambérieux in 1337–1338; Girin de St-Symphorien was castellan-*bailli* at Montmélian in 1341–1343, succeeding Jean de Saint-Amour, who was transferred to St-André-en-Revermont for 1342–1343. Pierre de Saillon was castellan of Saxon-Entremont in 1336–1340 (at least); Rodolph de Blonay was castellan of Thonon-Allinges in 1338–1342, then of Conthey-Saillon in 1343. Corgenon, Fromentes, La Baume, Montbel, Miribel, and Challant all had brothers or cousins serving as castellans in 1343. Cf. *ADCO, ADS, AST,* castellany accounts for places and dates listed above. The documents make it clear that this drafting of the nobility into the administrative framework of the state had long been a conscious policy of the counts of Savoy, who relied not only upon the lesser, but also upon the greater baronial families, and upon senior members as well as cadets.

To discover well over fifty families among the lesser nobility that consistently furnished officers in comital administration over the century is not surprising. Nor is it surprising to find examples of bourgeois who attained noble status in the count's service, as happened in the cases of the Bonivards of Chambéry, the Macets in Bresse, the Rigauds and Gerbais of Belley. The number of officers drawn from the great families over the same period, however, proves that exalting the lesser at the expense of the mighty was not the objective. How then could the counts prevent the great barons from turning to their own advantage these posts as castellans in regions where the barons' own territorial interests lay? For although later statutes indicate an awareness of this problem (statutes of 1379 and the *Statuta Sabaudiae* of 1430 are examples) and sometimes decree that castellans shall not be appointed to posts located in their home regions, the rule was more honored in the breach than in the observance in the fourteenth century.

The truth is that the noble could not always be prevented from advancing his own interests above those of the count, and this undoubtedly was a part of the reason why the post of castellan or *bailli* was so desirable. There were, on the other hand, important factors in the count's favor. These posts were salaried and non-hereditary. Each castellan took an oath to report all revenue faithfully on pain of a substantial fine, and instances are not wanting to show that such fines were imposed and collected. The salary was supplemented by a portion of judicial fees and various traditional perquisites. As manorial revenue declined, owing to repeated disasters of plague and famine during the fourteenth century, many a noble came to depend financially upon the income from his office. He was therefore anxious to avoid incurring fines or the loss of his office through dishonesty or disobedience; and he knew that the officers at the *chambre des comptes* were checking his accounts thoroughly.

To prevent the creation of vested interests, the tenure of office was usually limited to five years or fewer, and castellans were frequently transferred from one place to another. (To offer a few examples of these "career officers," many from great baronial families: Gaspard de Montmayeur, head of one of the oldest and most powerful families in the Maurienne, was castellan of Châtelard-en-Bauges in 1353 and 1355–1358; of La Rochette, 1358–1360 and 1364–1369; of Tarentaise, 1369–1383, when he died. Aymon of Challant, lord of Fenis and Aymaville in the Val d'Aosta, was castellan of Lanzo, 1331–1348 and 1350–1357; of Avigliana, 1350–

1354; of Susa, 1355–1357; of Chambéry, 1355–1370; of Tarentaise, 1357–1365; *Podestà* of Ivrea, 1363-1365; castellan of Sallanches, 1373–1380. Jean Mareschal of Montmélian was castellan of Montfalcon in 1316–1319; of Jasseron, 1319–1320; of Bâgé, 1324–1336; of Rossillon, 1336–1343. Lancelot of Châtillon-en-Michaille, seigneur of Cule, was castellan of Thonon in 1346–1347, of Avigliana in 1347–1349; he was castellan-*bailli* of Aosta in 1350–1353; castellan of St-Laurent-les-Mâcon in 1353-1354; of Lompnes in 1354-1355; of Bâgé in 1353-1355; of Châteauneuf-en-Valromey and *bailli* of Bugey and Valromey in 1355–1356; castellan of Avigliana and *bailli* of the Val di Susa in 1356–1364. Nicod François was castellan of Conflans in 1343–1345; of Maurienne in 1351–1354 and 1355–1356; of Lanzo in 1357–1358; of Bâgé, 1359–1366; of St-Germain and *bailli* of Bugey and Novalaise in 1366–1370; castellan of Châtillon-Cluses and *bailli* of Faucigny in 1370–1375. This information and much more on this question is to be found in the castellany accounts for the above regions in the departmental archives at Dijon, Chambéry, and Turin.)

There are some instances of castellans succeeded in their office by a son or heir—usually only for a year or two—to complete the accounts; but there are virtually no cases in which a grandson succeeds in retaining the same office held by his forebears. There is a trend over the century toward somewhat longer tenures of office, but this is not really a problem during the reign of Amadeus VI, when the movement of officers from post to post is the more striking characteristic. Dullin's affirmations (cf. pp. 41ff.) are therefore not really valid for most of the fourteenth century, and they rest for the most part upon a few isolated examples. It was rather Amadeus VII and his son's regents who kept the Green Count's appointees and their heirs in the same castellanies for decades.

Thus the counts of Savoy, unlike neighboring rulers in France and the Piedmont, did not rely upon the bourgeois in the struggle to curb the power of the nobility. The instances of castellans from the bourgeois class are relatively few, probably because this class was simply less prominent and less numerous in Savoy than elsewhere in the fourteenth century. The counts therefore continued to draw upon the nobles and sought, by the various means described above, to mold them into an obedient and dependable class of civil servants. Even the greatest baron was relegated to a distinctly subordinate role to the extent that he consented to serve as one of the count's officers. He was responsible for seeing that his revenues were accounted for down to the last *denarius,* and the scrupulous care with which irregularities are explained in the accounts suggests that castellans were not anxious to risk prosecution from the *chambre des comptes.* The baron-castellan was obliged to submit to constant surveillance and to follow orders from the count or his officers. While the heads of baronial families led their warriors into the field under the count's banners, their lieutenants (who were often relatives) or their cadets often remained behind to collect the count's moneys, enforce his rights, and manage his estates. In all of these ways the Savoyard nobility was being absorbed into the administrative framework of the Savoyard state.

### V · THE ORDER OF THE BLACK SWAN · 1350

The text of the Ordinances of the Order of the Black Swan as published in Luigi Cibrario, *Opuscoli* (Turin, 1841), pp. 75-77 are given as follows:

> La Companie du Cigne Noir se sera par la maniere que sensuit.

Premierement. Quilz porteront dargent au Cigne Noir le pied et le bec roge. Et soyent tenuz de porter le en armes et an aultre maniere en roubez quilz porteront en escucel ou en aultre maniere en entreseigne que appareisse quilz le portent si quil soit appareissant quilz sont de la Compaignie.

Item. Que li Compaignons soyent tenuz et jurent de siegre ung laultre a lour propre despens en contre tous seigneurs et vassaulx et parans jusques a gra de cusin germain.

Item. Quil soyent ordene certain Chevallier par les marches qui receivent les Compaignons de lordre et quil ne receivet negun qui ne puisse avoir cheval ou coursier et roncin et puisse servir viii jours a ses despens toutes les fois seroit besoing et tantes fois com le besoing seroit es Compaignons de lordre.

Item. Que si aucons Compaignons de cest Ordre avoit a faire li uns avec aultres ou par parolles ou par aultre chose quelle quelle soit Quilz ne soyent tenuz ne puissent mourre guerre li uns encontre laultre mais que les Chevalliers ordenes es marches ainsi dict est le puissent accorder. Et ilz soyent tenuz de faire et attendre tout ce que les ditz Chevalliers en vouldrent ordener et cougnoistre. Et ou cas en que lune des parties ne vouldroyent tenir lordenance des Chevalliers Que en celi cas sans rompre sairement les Compaignons de lOrdre puissent aider a laultre partie a lordenance des ditz Chevalliers a garder et deffendre sa raison.

Item. Se aucons des Compaignons avoit ne riote ne guerre a un aultre qui ne fut du sairement Quil ne puisse ne doive mourre guerre sans la voulente des Chevalliers nommez en la marche et li dictz Chevalliers soyent tenuz de somer celi qui ne seroit du sairement pour avoir raison de li et selon ce que bon lour sembleroit et ou cas que lon ne la pourroit avoir que les aultres du sairement soyent tenuz daider a celi qui seroit lour Compaignon a lordenance des Chevalliers.

Item. Que tuit li Banneret receuz a cest sairement soyent tenuz ou Escuyer soyent tenuz a mettre chascun an viii escus dor et Chevallier simple iiii et Escuyer i et soit mis ces argens en la main daulcon religious est a scavoir ceulx des marches de Savoye et Genevois Aultecombe, ceulx de Bresse et de Bourgoingne en mont Merlo et ceulx de la marche de Vienne en une aultre religion et le Chevalliers de les marches soyent tenus de ces choses soliciter et bailler largent en la main de lun des Religious et ces argens ne se puisse despendre si ce nest par lordenance des Chevalliers des marches et des Compaignons qui pourrent avoir et se face le payement at la Saincte Andre. Et est lentent des Compaignons que ces argens ne se puisse despendre se ce nestoit par estreordinaire tel qui fut accorde par les Compaignons.

Item. Que tuit le riche home qui seront receu du dict sairement soyent tenuz payer une somme dargens a lordenance des Chevalliers selon lour puissance.

Item. Que tuit le Compaignons de lordre soyent tenuz de servir les grans seignours qui seroyent de lordre a ses despens des ditz seigneurs de lour personnes. Et les seigneurs soyent tenuz de servir dune quantite le ditz Compaignons a lour despens a lordenance des Chevalliers.

# Commentary

Ce sont cil qui sont entre en lordre de la Compaignie du Cine:

Premierement Monsieur de Savoye
           Monsieur de Geneve
           Monsieur Galeaz Visconte
           Monsieur de la Sarree en Savoie
           Monsieur Pierre du Bullons eliz Chevallier en sa
               marche des dessus nommez.
           Monsieur Jean Ravoire eliz Chevallier en sa
               marche
           Monsieur Berlioz de Foraz
               Forreis de Tornonz
           Monsieur Pierre de Compois
               Serteauz de Mombrion
               Jean de Sollier
               Aimonet La Cue
           Monsieur Pierre de Crange
               Ame de Rogimont

I have not been able to identify all of those named in the above list with certainty. Pierre de Compeys was castellan of La Rochette in 1342–1349, and Viffred Fourrier de Tournon (d. 1372) was castellan of Versoix in 1343–1345, of Sallanches in 1355–1360, of Samoëns in 1360–1370, and of Sallanches again in 1370–1372. Berlion de Foras was a prominent vassal of the counts of Geneva and Savoy, a frequent participant in Amadeus VI's campaigns, and a future knight of the Order of the Collar. Serteauz de Mombrion might be Sorcel de Montbrun, seigneur of Creyssieu and castellan of Montfalcon in 1344–1349. *ADS,* Chambéry (castellany 1341–1342) identifies one "Sorcelli de Montebrieno" as "magister Amadei filii domini," i.e. young Amadeus VI. There is an Aymon de Rougemont who served as castellan of St-Germain-d'Ambérieux in 1364-1365. The Rougemonts were a prominent noble family with extensive holdings in Bugey and Bresse. The Ravoires came from near Chambéry, and there is a Jean de la Sarre who was castellan of Tarentaise in 1337–1338. Jean de Sollier may be "de Solerio," a family from Ivrea which furnished many important officers in the count's administration: Antoine de Solerio was castellan of Yenne-Chanaz in 1331–1343 and 1350–1351; Raymond de Solerio was castellan of Evian in 1344-1345 and judge of Bugey in 1343-1346; and Georges de Solerio was

361

judge of Bugey-Novalaise in 1336–1339, castellan of Chambéry and chancellor of Savoy in 1343–1350. If Pierre de Crange is the same as Pierre de Crangeat, then he was castellan of Pont-de-Vaux in 1351–1356 and 1359–1364, and castellan of Montluel in 1356–1357.

## VI · THE TOURNAMENT OF THE GREEN COUNT

The place and date of the famous "tournament of the Green Count" have been the subject of much debate and a variety of conclusions. According to Perrin, *Histoire de Savoie* (p. 88), Cordey (pp. 100–101), and R. Paquier, *Le Pays de Vaud* (II, 9), the tournament took place in 1348 at Chambéry; Plaisance, *Histoire des Savoyens* (I, 199) chooses 1351, while others have suggested 1344, 1352, and 1353. The Cabaret chronicle gives 1 May as the date, and all of the chroniclers place the event after the Valais expedition—though this cannot be considered conclusive, given the numerous errors of chronology of which the chroniclers stand convicted.

The castellany accounts for Chambéry do show that tournaments were held there in 1344 and 1348, but they do not attest to the count's participation in them. This is hardly surprising when it is recalled that Amadeus was only ten years of age in 1344. Moreover, there is no record of any purchases of green cloth for the count or any members of his entourage in those years. For the Christmas season of 1352–1353, however (hence the festive season immediately following the victorious Valais campaign), the sources prove that tournaments were held, that the young count participated in them, and that he had recently purchased green clothing. *AST*, inv. 38, folio 21 (hôtel du comte), doc. 60 (2 July 1352–29 March 1353) reveals that between 24 December 1352 and 9–10 January 1353 a total of 1,460 horses were at Bourg-en-Bresse, and that in addition to numerous items "pro expensas jostarum," thirty-four hogs, twelve oxen, and great quantities of cheeses and fish were purchased for the banquets which took place. (It is also clear that Amadeus was not at Bourg during the whole Christmas season, but that he moved from place to place in Bresse. He does seem to have been at Bourg on 24 December and 9–10 January, at least. *AST*, inv. 38, folio 1, doc. 11 [1352–1354]: "libravit domino in ludo in vigilia feste Natalis

Domini quo inceperunt currente anno [1353]," thirteen florins; item, "libravit menestreriis et eyraudis existentibus ad astraludia Burgi quando dominus fuit ibidem anno presente," forty florins.) There is also a gift to a minstrel of Thibaut de Neuchâtel, one of the knights mentioned in the chronicles as participating in the jousts, which suggests that he was indeed present on this occasion. *ADS* (castellany), Chambéry, 1352–1353, proves that Bourg-en-Bresse, not Chambéry, was the place: "in locagio unius roncini cum valleto portandi lanceas domini ad jostandum de Chamberiaco apud Burgum-in-Breyssia ... ut per litteram domini datam Burgi 29 Dec. 1352." *ADCO*, B 7104 (Bourg, 1352–1353) furnishes other details: "librata domino Amadeo de Villeta, militi, qui gravatus in jostis Burgi nuper preteritis et stetit ibidem infirmus, per litteram domini de mandata" dated Pont-de-Veyle, 21 January 1353. Also in the same account Amadeus VI replaces a horse lost by Pierre Crochet of Bourg "ex ictu magni equi domini diebus quibus dominus fecit justas apud Burgum," letter dated from St-Martin-le-Châtel, 16 January 1353.

The crucial item, however, is to be found in *AST*, inv. 38, folio 21, doc. 60, which reports that in November or December 1352, after the Valais expedition while the count was at Vevey on Lake Geneva, he had green silk jackets made for himself and his cousin, Aimone de Savoie (a younger brother of Prince Giacomo): "libravit in emptione vii oytanorum sirici viridis empti apud Turrim [Vevey] pro malescottis domini et domini Aymonis de Sabaudia factis de panno viridi et duarum unciarum de filo pro eodem. Et in emptione vi ulnarum fustanei et dimidiam ulne tele tinte pro ipsis maliscottis forrandis, xxx s. x d. laus[anne]." Green cloth was also purchased for hoods to go with the "maliscottis": "libravit in emptione v ulnarum et [¾] pagni viridis emptis apud Viviacum pro dictis malecottis domini et domini Aymonis de Sabaudia et pro capuciis dupplicibus ipsorum ... xv s. lausan." Green cloth was also purchased for their shoes, but striped cloth for three valets of the count's *camera*. No precise date is given for these purchases, but the clerks try to place expense items in chronological order, and these fall between items dated 11 November 1352 and 2 January 1353.

Cordey picks 1348 as the date of the tournament and says that only after that date do the count's household records list purchases of green cloth in conspicuous quantity. But he produces no items earlier than 1353 as proof, and I have found only one after examining household and castellany accounts in considerable detail. This is an item in *AST,* inv. 16, doc. 15 (2 July 1349–25 June 1351), *librata* section: "Alloquatur sibi per litt. domini demandato data Burgeti die ultima Aprilis anno predicto [1351] . . . pro precio unius pecie cendalis viridis empte ab ipso [Jean Picard of Chambéry] pro paramento domini in astulidiis Rumilliaci, viii flor. boni ponderis." This proves that the tournament at Bourg-en-Bresse was not the first such occasion on which Amadeus wore a green outfit, but it does not require us to place the tournament of the Green Count at Rumilly in 1351. The data, scattered and incomplete as it is, most strongly singles out the Christmas season of 1352–1353 as the one time during these years when there was a really full-scale tournament in which the count himself clearly participated after having recently purchased green clothing for himself and others, a tournament in which Amadeus had two very special reasons for celebrating: his first battlefield victory and his knighting. Cognasso (p. 20) and Cibrario (*Origine e Progressi delle Istituzioni della Monarchia di Savoia,* (2nd edn., Florence, 1869), Part II, p. 117) have also chosen January 1353, but without explaining the basis for their choice.

As for the significance of the color chosen, I have offered in the text the conclusions I think most likely. Ménabréa, *Chambéry,* MS, Book IV, Chapter VII, says that green was the color of the "anciens preux" of Charlemagne, but offers no proof for this contention, and I have been unable to find any. If it could be shown that Savoyard versions of the Charlemagne tales ascribed this color to him or to his peers, then Amadeus' choice of the color could very probably be accounted for in this way; but unfortunately the missing link is still missing. It should be pointed out that to identify oneself with a particular color was by no means unusual in the fourteenth century. The Black Prince of Wales is a famous example but not the only one. Jean de Châlon IV (1337–1370) was known as the "chevalier blanc," and his brother, Louis de Châlon, count of Tonnerre, went by the name of "le chevalier vert." Cf. Ernest Petit, *Histoire des Ducs de Bourgogne de la Race capétienne,* Dijon, 9 vols., 1885–1905, V, genealogical charts. Richard Musard was known as the "Black Squire," and in the house of Saluzzo at this time there was a "scudiero verde." Cf. Gabotto, *Eta,* p. 196.

VII · THE VALUE OF THE TERRITORIES EXCHANGED IN 1355

The Dauphinois author in question, Mathieu Thomassin, less than a century after the Treaty of Paris, wrote in his *Registre delphinal*: "Messire Ayme, conte de Savoye, appelé le Conte-Vert, voyant qu'on luy avait baillé fort et puissant adversaire, et que, pour le temps advenir, luy ne ses successeurs ne pouvoient espérer de résister à la France, se prouposa d'y pourveoir, et profitant des grandes tribulations du royaulme, procura par divers moyens, promesses et corruptions, de tirer à luy plusieurs gens et officiers par l'entremise desquelx furent faicts les eschanges et permutations qui s'ensuyvent." Then, after enumerating the clauses of the treaty of 1355, Thomassin added: "Esdictz eschanges, monseigneur le daulphin et messeigneurs ses successeurs se trouverent grandement grévez, car ce qui fut baillé audict conte valoit, chascun an, XXV mille florins dor, saulf le plus, et ce qui fut baillé du costé de Savoye ne valoit pour lors, chascun an, que mil V cens florins, et aujourd'hui vault moins. Et aultres lesions y a qui seroient trop longues à réciter, que l'on pourra mettre en avant quand besoing sera." (Cited in Ménabréa, "Faucigny," p. 193.)

Thomassin was writing on the orders of the dauphin, the future King Louis XI, who was seeking a pretext for military action against the duke of Savoy. Thomassin's views were expected to provide such a pretext and can therefore hardly be taken at face value, as they too often are. His estimate of the revenues of the Viennois castellanies given to the dauphin in 1355 was certainly too low, just as his estimate of the value of the territories ceded to the count of Savoy was very probably too high. Unfortunately, many of the documents which would have permitted an accurate solution to this problem have disappeared, and I have found only fragmentary evidence to go on. The importance of the question seems to me to warrant presenting what evidence I do have, however incomplete.

1. *The castellanies.* Two full accounts survive for St-Georges-d'Esperanche, and they reveal that that castellany yielded (in round numbers) 1,780 florins in 1352–1353 and 2,550 florins *boni ponderis* in 1346–1347. A subsidy collected from some 400 inhabitants of the castellany between 1331 and 1334 brought in an average of

216 florins per year (*ADI,* B 3628, B 3626, B 3620, *rouleaux*). A register entitled "Etat de la recette générale de Dauphiné," dated ca. 1365 (*ADI*, IX, B 143, pp. 48ff.) gives the amount for which four more of the castellanies formerly belonging to Savoy were farmed out: Côte-St-André went for 400 florins in 1363–1364; St-Symphorien-d'Ozon went for 600 florins in 1362–1363; Azieu for 56 florins in 1357–1358; Châbons for 50 florins in 1358–1359. The same register states that the "pedagium per aquam" at St-Symphorien was worth 1,200 florins in 1358, and the "pedagium per terram" was evaluated at 100 florins. The castellany of Les Avenières was sold in 1347 (later repurchased at the same price) for 6,000 florins, which suggests annual revenues in the vicinity of 500 florins. (Chevalier, *Regeste*, VI, docs. 35300 and 35330.) If one estimates these six castellanies, exclusive of *péage* and subsidies, as worth about 3,500 florins annually (on the basis of the above information), then the remaining eight castellanies ceded to the dauphin are likely to have been worth between 3,500 and 4,500 florins more per year. This suggests that the regular castellany revenues for the places ceded to the dauphin in 1355 were between 7,000 and 8,000 florins per year at the least.

2. *Judicature*. Between 1330 and 1349, Voiron, Avenières, Dolomieu, and St-Laurent-du-Pont, then forming part of the Savoyard judicature of Bugey-Novalaise, yielded roughly 100 florins per year in judicial fees (*ADS,* inv. 156, SA 1563, 1564, 1565, 1567). Two judicature accounts for the Viennois reveal that in 1338–1339 (one year, eleven weeks, one day) the income was 544 florins, and in 1347–1348 (forty-five weeks, five days), the yield was 122 florins (*ADI*, B 3627, B 3623, rouleaux). The reasons for this discrepancy are not clear, but in each case no revenue was received from Ecluse or St-Jean-de-Bournay because they were in the hands of others. While this information is too scanty to provide the basis for calculations as to what the judicial rights ceded to the dauphin by the count of Savoy were worth, they do give some idea of what their value was.

Thomassin's assertion that the lands which the dauphin received from Savoy in 1355 were only worth 1,500 florins per year is obviously false. I consider 7,000–8,000 florins per year to be a conservative estimate as to what these territories were really worth.

VIII · THE SUBSIDY OF 1356

For example, *ADS* (*subsides*), Maurienne, 1356–1359: ". . . subsidio concesso domino de gracia speciali per banneretos, religiosos, et nobiles ac alios homines eiusdem castellaniae pro tres annis inceptis festo paschie [1356] viz. pro qualibet persona focum faciende in dicta castellania iiii denarii gros. turn. . . . exceptis focis nobilium et aliorum . . . habentes homines in quantitate qui nichil solvit pro suis focis propriis." Elsewhere, such as at Evian and Thonon, noble hearths are exempted but without reference to those "having men in quantity," which I take to be a definition (for fiscal purposes) of "nobles," as opposed to bannerets.

The total revenues from the first term of the 1356 subsidy, as accounted in *AST,* inv. 38, folio 1, doc. 13 (1356–1357) by Aymon de Challant were: (1) Bresse and Valbonne: 209 libri fortis escutellis, 1,759 florins boni ponderis, 175 florins parvi ponderis; (2) town and castellany of Susa: 362 florins boni ponderis; (3) castellany of Avigliana and the Val di Susa: 120 florins boni ponderis, 47 solidi 8 denarii grossis turonensis; (4) "Hominibus et subdittis" of monastery of St. Just of Susa (487 *foci*): 162 florins boni ponderis and 4 denarii grossis turonensis; (5) bailliages of Savoy and Faucigny: 1,366 libri 15 solidi fortis escutellis, 380 libri gebennensis, 532 florins boni ponderis, 200 florins parvi ponderis; (6) officials and castellans of Bresse and Valbonne: 96 libri fortis escutellis, 500 florins boni ponderis, and 500 *moutones auri*. Smaller additional sums came in from men belonging to the abbey of "Stamedei," the priory of Novalaise, the chapter of Maurienne, and the lord of Aiguebellette.

IX · THE COUR DES MONNAIES OF 1358

Prior to the fourteenth century there had been three mints in the territories of Savoy, the oldest being at St-Maurice-d'Agaune in the defiles of the Rhône above Lake Geneva. A second mint at Chambéry was almost as old and served the needs of Savoy proper, while a third at Nyon on the shores of Lake Geneva was in existence by 1284. Count Aymon had recognized the need for further minting facilities and had established four more mints, all of them in the westernmost territories of Savoy—an indication perhaps of the increased commercial importance of these areas by the fourteenth century. One was located at Pont d'Ain in 1338, and another was established about the same time at Bourg-en-Bresse. A third was at St-Genix-d'Aoste on the route of the Mont Cenis via Grenoble to Lyon, and the fourth was on the Rhône valley route from Lyon to Geneva at Pierre-Châtel. Cf. F. Rabut, "Notice sur quelques monnaies de Savoie," *MARS* (2nd series I, 1851) pp. 165–166. At each mint there was a master, an essayer, an engraver, two guardians, a "counter-guardian," a procureur-fiscal, and a secretary. Often the same individual exercised the same function at more than one mint. The new *Cour des Monnaies* was an effort to control and standardize minting operations now that they had been so greatly expanded. The first coin issued under Amadeus VI was minted at Chambéry in June 1349, but only in subsequent coin issues does his distinctive design appear. Amadeus VI was the first count of that name to put the shield of Savoy on the face of his coins, with a large "A" surrounded by four stars on the reverse.

### X · "ESTATES" IN THE DOMINIONS OF SAVOY IN THE FOURTEENTH CENTURY

On the subject of the development of "parliaments" or "estates" in the territories ruled by the house of Savoy, the reader should consult the definitive study by Armando Tallone, *Parlamento Sabaudo* (10 vols., 1928ff.), particularly *Parte Prima: Patria Cismontana 1286–1385* (Bologna, 1928), and *Parte Secunda: Patria Oltramontana* (Bologna, 1935). My comments here are intended only as a brief summary of Mr. Tallone's principal findings.

Tallone has shown that the name of "Three Estates" does not appear before the end of the third decade of the fifteenth century; assemblies in the thirteenth and fourteenth centuries were usually referred to as a "colloquium" or occasionally as a "parlamentum." The first real proof of such an assembly which clearly included representatives of the non-noble classes is a summons issued by Louis I of Vaud from Lyon on 15 January 1285 ordering "universis nobilibus, civibus, burgensibus et aliis quibuscumque in terra Pedemontis a Monte Cinisii versus Lombardiam superius" to attend an assembly scheduled to meet in Piedmont on 24 May 1285. During the reign of Amadeus VI, there were repeated convocations of the nobles and communes of the Piedmont when men and money were needed; and during the regency of the Green Count in Piedmont between 1368–1377, representatives from both the count's and the prince's territories met together for the first time. (Cf. *Patria Cismontana,* pp. cii, ciii.) Amadeus VI always distinguished between those from his own territories, i.e. the lands north of the Po and the Dora Riparia (Canavese and Val di Susa) and one-half of Chieri, and representatives from lands belonging to the prince of Achaea. Tallone says that 12 February 1370 was the first time such an assembly was convoked, and that by 1374 (at least) an assembly had taken place under the aegis of the Green Count in which representatives from both sides of the Alps participated. Doc. CLXXXVI refers on 4 July 1374 to a previously held "consilio plurium fidellium nostrorum citra et ultra montes comorencium," and on 27–28 May 1375, Amadeus (doc. CCXIV) used the expression "habere nostrum parlamentum generale" in asking Turin and Moncalieri to send two "ambaxiatores" each to Rivoli on 5 June. On 19 September 1377 the assembly convoked at Rivoli for the reception of Amadeo of Achaea included representatives from all of the Piedmont towns, which chose their ambassadors in a "pleno et generali consilio . . . convocato in palatio comunis . . . ad sonum campane ut moris est de mandato . . . castellani et . . . judicis." At Moncalieri the ambassadors were elected by majority vote, "facto partito ad tabulas albas et nigras ut moris est"; elsewhere the communities voted to allow the "clavarios" to choose their ambassadors.

In Savoy there is no proof of an assembly comparable to that summoned by Louis of Vaud for the Piedmont in 1285 until 1388; but Tallone argues (*Patria Oltramontana,* pp. xxxixff.) that general assemblies existed as early as the first half of the thirteenth century. There is no proof that representatives of the communes participated in these assemblies, however, at least not before 1388. Those for which Tallone cites evidence are clearly convocations of nobles and officers of the Savoyard state mostly intended to swell the ranks of the resident council or the count's *curia* when some especially weighty matter required consideration. Tallone admits that the phraseology used in the subsidy accounts is not proof that any assembly really took place; indeed, the accounts do not state that one did, but merely that the various classes of the population have "graciously conceded" the subsidy requested by the lord count.

The earliest "Estates" in Bresse date from 1385 perhaps, but only from 1399 with any certainty. In the Pays de Vaud, Pierre II had his statutes of 1263 or 1264 approved by "nobiles et innobiles," probably at an assembly at Moudon; but the famous document of 1264 in which he created the Three Estates of the Pays de Vaud has been shown never to have existed (p. cli). There seem to have been occasional assemblies of barons and probably of communal representatives in the Pays de Vaud during the fourteenth century, but there is no real proof of what can be called representative assemblies on anything resembling a regular basis until after the death of the Green Count.

### XI · GUILLAUME DE GRANDSON AND THE LANZO EPISODE OF 1361

This is another instance in which the Savoyard chronicles of Cabaret and Servion must be accorded more credence than they have hitherto received. Grandson does not appear to have fought with the English in Gascony, as the chroniclers state (cf. H. J. Hewitt, *The Black Prince's Expedition of 1355–1357,* Manchester, 1958; D. L. Galbreath, "Les Grandsons d'Angleterre," *AHS,* 1927, pp. 56–69). But Froissart (*Oeuvres,* Lettenhove ed., VI, 222) names Guillaume de Grandson along with other Francs-comtois who participated in Edward III's invasion of Champagne and Burgundy in 1359–1360, and Aimé Chérest, *L'Archiprêtre, Episodes de la Guerre de Cent Ans* (Paris, 1879), pp. 125–128, has positively identified him as Guillaume de Grandson, sire of Sainte-Croix. There was an English branch of the Grandson family, cousins of Guillaume, who had entered the service of the English kings in the thirteenth century and who were prominent figures among the English nobility by the fourteenth century. Two of them, Othon de Grandson (d. 1359) and his son, Thomas (d. 1375), whose exploits are celebrated by Froissart, did participate in the English campaigns in Flanders, Picardy, Normandy, and Brittany in the 1340's and 1350's. According to Chérest, Guillaume de Grandson had joined his English cousins by this time, and he was chosen by the English king in the summer of 1360 as one of Edward's ambassadors to the duke of Bungundy. He signed the treaty of 1 January 1361 at Beaune on behalf of the English, along with Nicolas Tamworth.

Thus the Savoyard chronicles are correct in stating that Guillaume had fought with the English side recently and that he knew many of the English captains. Since some of the English mercenaries in northern Italy in 1361 following the Peace of Bretigny were also veterans of the same campaigns, it is entirely possible that Guillaume was on friendly terms with some of the leaders of the Lanzo attack. Guillaume's presence at Lanzo on this occasion is proved by an item in the castellany accounts for Lanzo (*AST,* mazzo VI, doc. 28, 1361–1362, p. xxiiii): "libravit ad expen. domini Guilla de Grandissono et Anselmi de Portenton equorum et familie ipsorum factas in Lanceo certis temporibus et diebus quibus ibidem fuerunt in infirmitate gravati ratione vvulnerium receptarum et substentorum per eos ab Anglicis in invasione loci." (The count's letter ordering payment of these expenses is dated Rivoli, 15 February 1362.) Another letter, dated Rivoli, 24 December 1361, authorizes the castellan of Lanzo to deduct expenses of the count and his household who were "apud Lanceum pluribus diebus finitis die XI Novembris [1361]." There are also the expenses for increasing the garrison at Lanzo for one year and thirteen weeks beginning 12 November 1361, the day of the count's departure.

The fact that no trace exists of any ransom paid for the release of the count of Savoy at Lanzo lends additional weight to the essential truth of the Savoyard version of what happened.

### XII · THE DATES OF THE ORDER OF THE COLLAR

The date and place of the founding of the Order of the Collar have been the subject of much dispute. J. Letanche in "La Chartreuse-forteresse de Pierre-Châtel," *MDSS,* XLVII (1909), 428, follows earlier writers in dating the foundation of the Order in 1362, which he says accords better with the castellany accounts of Pierre-Châtel, where he affirms the ceremony to have taken place. But there is no proof that it did take place there, and I can find no items in the castellany accounts to which he refers that support his choice of either the place or the date. Terrier de Loray, *Jean de Vienne, amiral de France 1341–1396* (Paris, 1877), p. 36, note 1, argued for 1366 on the grounds that neither Hugues de Châlon nor Jean de Vienne, two members of the new order, can be shown to have been in Savoy before that date. They could very well have been at Avignon, however; and in any case, Loray is quite wrong concerning Jean de Vienne. *AST*, inv. 16, docs. 23 (1360–1363) and 26 (1364–1365) prove that Jean de Vienne, referred to as "consanguineus domini [comitis]," was in the service of the count at least by 1360, and that he was with Amadeus at Lanzo in 1361. By 1364 he was receiving an annual pension of 100 florins from the comital treasury.

Mr. Vittorio Prunas Tola in his handsome two-volume anniversary edition, *L'Ordine Supremo della SS. Annunziata 1362–1962* (Milan, 1963, 1964) supports his choice of 1362 for the founding of the Order by uncritically listing all previous writers who chose that date, and by an erroneous reference to the item in the Hotel accounts in which Amadeus ordered " . . . quindecim colariis argenti deaurati factis ad devisam domini. . . ." Mr. Prunas Tola is correct in thus suggesting that this item constitutes the only solid evidence we possess for dating the founding of the Order of the Collar, but his citation is entirely incorrect. The correct reference is *AST,* inv. 38, folio 21, doc. 63 (1361–1365), p. xxxviii; and the date of the crucial item is not 1362, but January 1364. Much the best study of the founding of the order and its membership is that of Dino Muratore, "Les Origines de l'Ordre du Collier," *AHS*, XXIII and XXIV (1909–1910), whose conclusions seem to me most consistently in accord with the evidence.

### XIII · THE KNIGHTS OF THE COLLAR

Cabaret, Servion, and Paradin are in exact agreement on the list of knights, except that the Geneva manuscript of Cabaret's chronicle omits number five entirely (Aymon de Genève-Anthon), probably a copyist's error. Cognasso, *Il Conte Verde*, pp. 140–141, writes "Amadeo" of Geneva for Aymon de Genève-Anthon, and "Gaspare di Montléon" instead of Gaspard de Montmayeur for number eleven, but cites no proof whatever for these changes. Cibrario, in *Origine e Progressi delle Istituzioni della Monarchia di Savoia* (2nd ed., revised, Florence, 1869), Part II, *Specchio Cronologico,* p. 129, does not include Count Amadeus himself in the list, but adds the sire of Saint-Amour, not mentioned in the chronicles, to make fifteen. Letanche, "Pierre-Châtel," p. 429 gives number thirteen as "Thennard de Menthon," and Cibrario, *Origine e Progressi,* lists "Francesco di Menthon"; but A. de Foras in the *Armorial et Nobiliaire de l'Ancien Duché de Savoye* (4 vols., 1863–1900) shows (I, 410, and IV, 124) that no such member of the famous Menthon family is known to have existed, whereas one "François, dit Chivard (ou Thennard) de Monthouz" did exist at just this time and died in 1381.

### XIV · SUZERAINTY OVER THE MARQUISATE OF SALUZZO

The Dauphinois historians Chorier (seventeenth century) and Valbonnais (eighteenth century) argued that the dauphins were correct in asserting that they were the earliest princes to receive the homage of the whole marquisate of Saluzzo when, in 1210, Adelaide, regent for Marquis Manfredo, her grandson, threatened by Count Thomas of Savoy, did homage to the dauphin in return for his protection (Nicholas Chorier, *Histoire générale de Dauphiné*, Valence, 1869, II, 91). In an act of 1210 listed in Chevalier, *Regeste,* II, doc. 6108, a Marquis Tommaso did homage to the dauphin and claimed that he held his marquisate in free alod, "dependent upon no lord."

However this may be, the claims of Savoy to suzerainty over the marquisate are at least equally valid, following the documents preserved in *AST, Saluzzo Marchesato,* 4th categoria, mazzi I and II. An act of arbitration by the marquis of Montferrat on 6 December 1169 awarded the homage of the marquis of Saluzzo to the count of Savoy (I, doc. 1). On 3 August 1210, Countess Adelaide of Piedmont did homage for the marquisate to her uncle, Gui de Vienne, the dauphin (I, doc. 3), while in 1216 (I, doc. 2) and 1223 (I, doc. 5), Count Thomas invested the marquis of Saluzzo with at least part of his possessions, notably those in Piedmont: Barge, Fontanile, Roncaglia, Busca, and others. Then on 27 August 1305, Marquis Manfredo of Saluzzo did homage to Count Amadeus V of Savoy for the whole marquisate and its dependencies (I, docs. 14 and 15), and this act was renewed following the accession of Count Edward of Savoy, in 1325 (I, doc. 22).

In the course of a bitter war between young Marquis Tommaso II and his uncle for the marquisate of Saluzzo, Tommaso fled to the Dauphiné and did homage to the dauphin on 31 October 1343. On 1 January 1347, however, Amadeus VI invested Tommaso with Barge, Scarnafigi, Busca, Bernezzo, and all other fiefs held from Savoy, and this act was repeated in May of the following year (II, docs. 6, 8, and 10). This would seem to indi-cate that the count of Savoy had acquiesced in the marquis' homage for the marquisate proper to the dauphin, although it is more likely that he was biding his time until he should be in a position to do something about it. It was not until 1363 that the count again demanded the marquis' homage for the marquisate as well as for his Piedmont holdings.

GENEALOGIES

BIBLIOGRAPHY

INDEX

# THE HOUSE OF SAVOY:

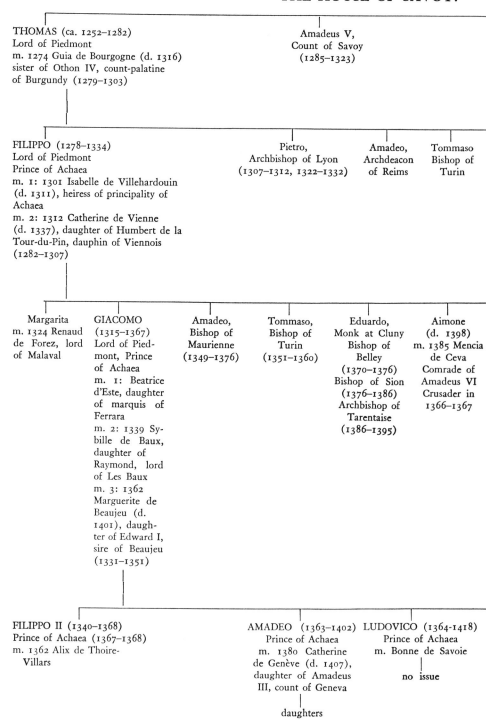

THOMAS (ca. 1252–1282)
Lord of Piedmont
m. 1274 Guia de Bourgogne (d. 1316)
sister of Othon IV, count-palatine
of Burgundy (1279–1303)

Amadeus V,
Count of Savoy
(1285–1323)

FILIPPO (1278–1334)
Lord of Piedmont
Prince of Achaea
m. 1: 1301 Isabelle de Villehardouin
(d. 1311), heiress of principality of
Achaea
m. 2: 1312 Catherine de Vienne
(d. 1337), daughter of Humbert de la
Tour-du-Pin, dauphin of Viennois
(1282–1307)

Pietro,
Archbishop of Lyon
(1307–1312, 1322–1332)

Amadeo,
Archdeacon
of Reims

Tommaso
Bishop of
Turin

Margarita
m. 1324 Renaud
de Forez, lord
of Malaval

GIACOMO
(1315–1367)
Lord of Pied-
mont, Prince
of Achaea
m. 1: Beatrice
d'Este, daughter
of marquis of
Ferrara
m. 2: 1339 Sy-
bille de Baux,
daughter of
Raymond, lord
of Les Baux
m. 3: 1362
Marguerite de
Beaujeu (d.
1401), daugh-
ter of Edward I,
sire of Beaujeu
(1331–1351)

Amadeo,
Bishop of
Maurienne
(1349–1376)

Tommaso,
Bishop of
Turin
(1351–1360)

Eduardo,
Monk at Cluny
Bishop of
Belley
(1370–1376)
Bishop of Sion
(1376–1386)
Archbishop of
Tarentaise
(1386–1395)

Aimone
(d. 1398)
m. 1385 Mencia
de Ceva
Comrade of
Amadeus VI
Crusader in
1366–1367

FILIPPO II (1340–1368)
Prince of Achaea (1367–1368)
m. 1362 Alix de Thoire-
 Villars

AMADEO (1363–1402)
Prince of Achaea
m. 1380 Catherine
de Genève (d. 1407),
daughter of Amadeus
III, count of Geneva

daughters

LUDOVICO (1364-1418)
Prince of Achaea
m. Bonne de Savoie

no issue

# PIEDMONT-ACHAEA BRANCH

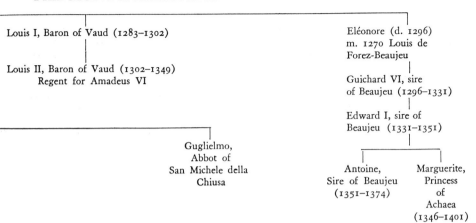

Louis I, Baron of Vaud (1283–1302)

Louis II, Baron of Vaud (1302–1349)
Regent for Amadeus VI

Guglielmo,
Abbot of
San Michele della
Chiusa

Eléonore (d. 1296)
m. 1270 Louis de
Forez-Beaujeu

Guichard VI, sire
of Beaujeu (1296–1331)

Edward I, sire of
Beaujeu (1331–1351)

Antoine,
Sire of Beaujeu
(1351–1374)

Marguerite,
Princess
of
Achaea
(1346–1401)

Alice (d. 1368)
m. 1: 1324
Manfredo del
Carretto
m. 2: Antelme
de Miolans, sire
of Urtières

Eleonora
(d. 1350)
m. Manfredo di
Saluzzo-Cardé

Jeanne
(d. 1352)
m. Amédée
de Poitiers,
lord of St-
Vallier

Isabelle
m. Jean I
de la
Chambre,
viscount
of
Maurienne

Béatrice
(d. 1340)
m. 1331 Hum-
bert, lord of
Thoire-Villars

Agnès
m. Jean II
de la
Chambre, vis-
count of
Maurienne
(1326–1372)

# THE HOUSE OF SAVOY

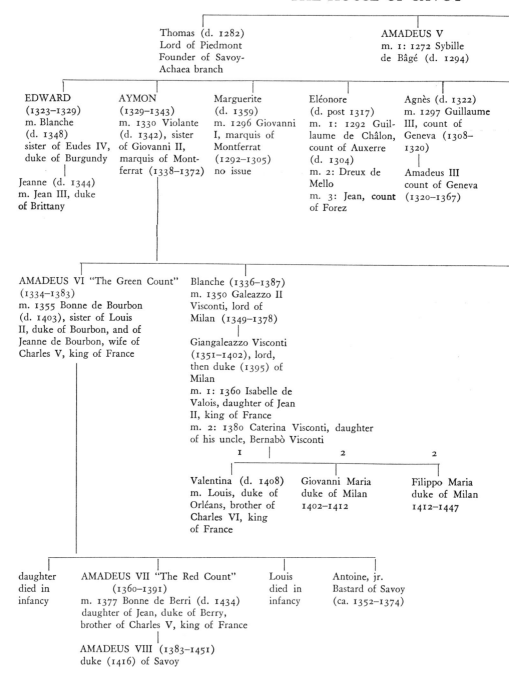

Thomas (d. 1282)
Lord of Piedmont
Founder of Savoy-
Achaea branch

AMADEUS V
m. 1: 1272 Sybille
de Bâgé (d. 1294)

EDWARD
(1323–1329)
m. Blanche
(d. 1348)
sister of Eudes IV,
duke of Burgundy

Jeanne (d. 1344)
m. Jean III, duke
of Brittany

AYMON
(1329–1343)
m. 1330 Violante
(d. 1342), sister
of Giovanni II,
marquis of Mont-
ferrat (1338–1372)

Marguerite
(d. 1359)
m. 1296 Giovanni
I, marquis of
Montferrat
(1292–1305)
no issue

Eléonore
(d. post 1317)
m. 1: 1292 Guil-
laume de Châlon,
count of Auxerre
(d. 1304)
m. 2: Dreux de
Mello
m. 3: Jean, count
of Forez

Agnès (d. 1322)
m. 1297 Guillaume
III, count of
Geneva (1308–
1320)

Amadeus III
count of Geneva
(1320–1367)

AMADEUS VI "The Green Count"
(1334–1383)
m. 1355 Bonne de Bourbon
(d. 1403), sister of Louis
II, duke of Bourbon, and of
Jeanne de Bourbon, wife of
Charles V, king of France

Blanche (1336–1387)
m. 1350 Galeazzo II
Visconti, lord of
Milan (1349–1378)

Giangaleazzo Visconti
(1351–1402), lord,
then duke (1395) of
Milan
m. 1: 1360 Isabelle de
Valois, daughter of Jean
II, king of France
m. 2: 1380 Caterina Visconti, daughter
of his uncle, Bernabò Visconti

1                          2                   2

Valentina (d. 1408)
m. Louis, duke of
Orléans, brother of
Charles VI, king
of France

Giovanni Maria
duke of Milan
1402–1412

Filippo Maria
duke of Milan
1412–1447

daughter
died in
infancy

AMADEUS VII "The Red Count"
(1360–1391)
m. 1377 Bonne de Berri (d. 1434)
daughter of Jean, duke of Berry,
brother of Charles V, king of France

AMADEUS VIII (1383–1451)
duke (1416) of Savoy

Louis
died in
infancy

Antoine, jr.
Bastard of Savoy
(ca. 1352–1374)

# IN THE FOURTEENTH CENTURY

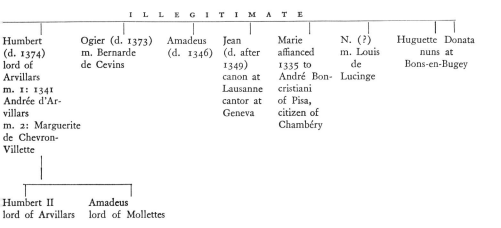

"The Great" (1285–1323)
m. 2: 1297 Marie
de Brabant, sister of John II,
    duke of Brabant

Louis (d. 1302)
Baron of Vaud
Founder of Savoy-
Vaud branch

Bonne
m. Hugues de
Bourgogne, brother
of Othon IV,
count-palatine
of Burgundy
(1279–1303)

Marie
m. 1309 Hugues
baron of Faucigny,
brother of Jean II,
dauphin of
Viennois
(1307–1319)

Catherine (d. 1326)
m. 1315 Leopold of
Habsburg, land-
grave of Alsace

Béatrice
m. 1328 Henry
of Habsburg,
duke of
Carinthia

Jeanne (d. 1360)
m. 1325 Androni-
cus III, emperor
of Byzantium
(1328–1341)

John V,
emperor of Byzantium
(1341–1376, 1379–1391)

ILLEGITIMATE

Humbert
(d. 1374)
lord of
Arvillars
m. 1: 1341
Andrée d'Ar-
villars
m. 2: Marguerite
de Chevron-
Villette

Ogier (d. 1373)
m. Bernarde
de Cevins

Amadeus
(d. 1346)

Jean
(d. after
1349)
canon at
Lausanne
cantor at
Geneva

Marie
affianced
1335 to
André Bon-
cristiani
of Pisa,
citizen of
Chambéry

N. (?)
m. Louis
de Lucinge

Huguette Donata
nuns at
Bons-en-Bugey

Humbert II
lord of Arvillars

Amadeus
lord of Mollettes

Addison, Joseph. "Remarks on Several Parts of Italy, Etc.," *Miscellaneous Works of Joseph Addison*. Ed. Guthkelch. 2 vols. London, 1914.

Atiya, Aziz. *The Crusade in the Later Middle Ages*. London, 1928.

Bédier, Joseph. *Les Légendes épiques*. 4 vols. Paris, 1926–1929.

Bernard, Félix. *Histoire de Montmélian*. Chambéry, 1956.

Besson, J. A. *Mémoires pour servir à l'histoire écclesiastique des diocèses de Genève, Tarentaise, Aoste, et Maurienne et du Décanat de Savoie*. Moûtiers, 1871.

Binz, Louis. "La population du diocèse de Genève à la fin du Moyen Age," *Mélanges d'histoire, éonomique et sociale* (offered to Antony Babel, Geneva, 1963).

Blondel, Louis. "Le Bourg de Viège," *Valesia* (1957).

———. "Le Château des de la Tour-Châtillon à Bas-Châtillon," *Valesia* (1951).

———. "L'Architecture militaire au temps de Pierre II de Savoie," *Geneva*, XIII (1935).

Bollati de Saint-Pierre, Frederic-Emmanuel. *Illustrazioni della Spedizione in Oriente di Amadeo VI* in *BSI*, V (1900).

Bouquet, Jean-Jacques. "Remarques sur l'idée de croisade dans l'expédition d'Amédée VI de Savoie à Constantinople," *Bulletin annuel de la Fondation Suisse* (University of Paris, VII, 1958).

Bowsky, W. M. *Henry VII in Italy*. Lincoln, 1960.

Bruchet, Max. *Le Château de Ripaille*. Paris, 1907.

———. *La Savoie d'après les anciens voyageurs*. Annecy, 1908.

Bueno de Mesquita, D. M. *Giangaleazzo Visconti*. Cambridge, 1941.

Burney, Charles. *Dr. Burney's Musical Tours in Europe*. 2 vols. Vol. I: *An Eighteenth Century Tour in France and Italy,* ed. P. A. Scholes. Oxford, 1959.

Cabaret (Jean d'Oronville, "dit Cabaret"). *Chronique de la Maison de Savoye* (1417–1419, historical manuscript 161 in *AEG*).

Chapperon, Timoléon. *Chambéry à la fin du XIVe siècle*. Paris, 1893.

Chérest, Aimé. *L'Archiprêtre, Episodes de la Guerre de Cent Ans*. Paris, 1879.

Chevailler, Laurent. *Recherches sur la Réception du Droit romain en Savoie des Origines à 1789*. Annecy, 1953.

Chevalier, Ulysse. *Mémoires pour servir à l'histoire des comtes de Valentinois et de Diois*. Paris, 1897–1906.

———. *Regeste Dauphinois,* VI. Valence, 1923.

Chorier, Nicholas. *Histoire générale de Dauphiné*. Valence, 1869.

Cibrario, Luigi. *Della Economia Politica del Medio Aevo*. 2 vols. Turin, 1861.

——. *Opuscoli*. Turin, 1841.

——. *Origine e Progressi delle Istituzioni della Monarchia di Savoia*. 2nd ed., Florence, 1869.

——. *Storia della Monarchia di Savoia*. 3 vols. Turin, 1844.

Cipolla, Carlo. "Clemente VI e Casa Savoia," *MSI* (3rd series, V, 1900).

——. "Innocenzo VI e Casa Savoia," *MSI* (3rd series, VII, 1902).

Cognasso, Francesco. *Il Conte Verde*. Turin, 1926.

——. *Umberto Biancamano*. Turin, 1937.

Cook, A. S. "The Last Months of Chaucer's Earliest Patron," *Transactions of the Connecticut Academy of Arts and Sciences* (Vol. 21, 1916).

Cordero de Pamparato, S. "La dernière campagne d'Amédée VI, comte de Savoie," *RS* (1902).

Cordey, Jean. *Les Comtes de Savoie et les Rois de France pendant la Guerre de Cent Ans* (Bibl. de l'Ecole des Hautes Etudes, fasc. 189, Paris, 1911).

——. "L'Acquisition du Pays de Vaud par le Comte Vert, 1359," *MDR* (2nd series, VI, 1907).

Corio, Bernardino. *Storia di Milano*. Eds. Butti and Ferrario. 3 vols. Milan, 1856.

Costa de Beauregard, J. H. "Documents inédits pour servir à l'histoire de la ville de Chambéry," *MSRS,* XI (1843).

*Cronaca latina Sabaudiae* in *MHP, III, Scriptores,* I (Turin, 1840).

Datta, Pietro. *Storia dei Principi di Savoia del Ramo d'Acaia*. 2 vols. Turin, 1832.

——. *Spedizione in Oriente di Amadeo VI*. Turin, 1826.

Della Chiesa, Gioffredo. *Cronaca di Saluzzo* in *MHP,* V (ca. 1430).

Donaver, Federigo. *Storia della Repubblica di Genova*. 3 vols. Genoa, 1913.

Duc, J. A. *Histoire de l'Eglise d'Aoste*. 10 vols. Aosta, 1901–1915.

Dufour, A., and F. Rabut. "La Rénonciation du Comte Amédée VI de Savoie au mariage arrêté entre lui et Princesse Jeanne de Bourgogne," *MSI,* XVII (1878).

Dullin, Etienne. *Les Châtelains dans les domaines de la Maison de Savoie en deçà des Alpes*. Grenoble, 1911.

Duparc, Pierre. *Le Comté de Genève, IX–XVe siècles*. Geneva, 1955.

Faure, Claude. "Contribution à l'histoire du Faucigny au XIVe siècle," *RS* (1909).

Foras, Amédée de. *Armorial et Nobiliaire de l'Ancien Duché de Savoie.* 4 vols. Grenoble, 1863–1900.

Forel, F. "Chartes communales du Pays de Vaud," *MDR* (2nd series, XXVII, 1872).

Fournier, Paul. *Le Royaume d'Arles et de Vienne 1138–1378.* Paris, 1891.

Froissart, Jehan. *Oeuvres de Froissart.* Ed. Kervyn de Lettenhove. 25 vols. Brussels, 1867–1877.

————. *Poésies.* Ed. Auguste Scheler. 3 vols. Brussels, 1870–1872.

Gabotto, Ferdinando. *L'Età del Conte Verde in Piemonte* (*MSI*, XXXIII, 1895).

————. "Pinerolo ed il Pinerolese dal 1356 al 1363," *BSBS*, IV–VI 1899).

————. "Nuovi contributi alla storia del Conte Verde," *BSBS*, IV 1899).

————. "La Guerra del Conte Verde contro i Marchesi di Saluzzo e di Monferrato nel 1363," *Piccolo Archivio Storico da Saluzzo* (1901).

Galbreath, D. L. "Les Grandsons d'Angleterre," *AHS* (1927).

Gerbaix de Sonnaz, A. de. "Mémoire historique sur Louis II de Savoie, sire de Vaud, sénateur de Rome (1310–1312), de 1275 à 1349," *MARS* (5th series, I, 1908).

Gibbons, H. A. *The Foundations of the Ottoman Empire 1300–1403.* Oxford, 1916.

Gilliard, Charles. *Moudon sous le Régime savoyarde* (*MDR*, 2nd series, XIV, 1929).

Gray, Thomas. *Correspondence of Thomas Gray.* Eds. Toynbee and Whibley. Oxford, 1935.

Gremaud, J. *Documents rélatifs à l'histoire du Vallais* in *MDR*, XXIX–XXXIII (1875–1884) and XXXVII–XXXIX (1893–1899).

Grenus-Saladin, F. T. L. de. *Documents rélatifs à l'histoire du Pays de Vaud.* Geneva, 1817.

Gros, Adolphe. *Histoire du Diocèse de Maurienne.* 2 vols. Chambéry, 1948.

Guichenon, Samuel. *Histoire généalogique de la Maison royale de Savoie.* 3 vols. Lyon, 1660.

Guiffrey, J. J. *Histoire de la Réunion du Dauphiné à la France.* Paris, 1868.

Guigue, G. *Récits de la Guerre de Cent Ans: Les Tard-Venus dans le Lyonnais, Forez et Beaujolais (1356–69).* Lyon, 1886.

Guigue, M-C. *Topographie historique du département de l'Ain.* Trevoux, 1873.

# Bibliography

Hayward, Fernand. *Histoire de la Maison de Savoie.* 2 vols. Paris, 1941.

Hewitt, H. J. *The Black Prince's Expedition of 1355-1357.* Manchester, 1958.

*Histoire de Genève des Origines à 1789* (Société d'Histoire et d'Archéologie de Genève, 1951).

Huizinga, J. *The Waning of The Middle Ages.* Doubleday, 1954.

Jarrett, Bede. *Emperor Charles IV.* London, 1935.

Jarry, Eugène. *Les Origines de la domination française à Gênes 1390–1402.* Paris, 1896.

Jorga, Nicholas. *Philippe de Mézières et la croisade au XIVe siècle.* Paris, 1896.

Lamartine, Alphonse de. *Lamartine et la Savoie.* Ed. G. Roth. Chambéry, 1927.

Lange, Augusta, *Le Udienze dei Conti e Duchi di Savoia nella Valle d'Aosta 1337–1351.* Paris and Turin, 1956.

Lateyssonnière, A. C. N. *Recherches historiques sur le département de l'Ain.* 4 vols. Bourg, 1838–1843.

Léonard, E. G. *Les Angevins de Naples.* Paris, 1953.

Letanche, J. "La Chartreuse-forteresse de Pierre-Châtel," *MDSS,* XLVII (1909).

Marie-José. *La Maison de Savoie: Les Origines, Le Comte Vert, Le Comte Rouge.* Paris, 1956.

Ménabréa, Léon. *Histoire de Chambéry.* Chambéry, 1846. Unfinished *MS* in *ADS.*

———. "L'Organization militaire au Moyen Age," *MARS* (2nd series, I, 1851).

———. "L'Occupation du Faucigny par le Comte Vert," *MARS* (2nd series, I, 1851).

Mugnier, François. "Lettres des Visconti de Milan et divers autres personnages aux comtes de Savoie Amédée VI, Amédée VII, et Amédée VIII (1360–1415)," *MDSS* (2nd series, XXXV, 1896).

Muir, Dorothy. *A History of Milan under the Visconti.* London, 1924.

Muratore, Dino. "Bianca di Savoia e le sue nozze con Galeazzo II Visconti," *ASL,* VII (1907).

———. "L'Imperatore Carlo IV nelle Terre Sabaude nel 1365 e il Vicariato Imperiale del Conte Verde," *MAS* (2nd series t. XVI, Turin, 1906).

———. "La nascita e il battesimo del primogenito di Gian Galeazzo Visconti e la politica viscontea nella primavera del 1366," *ASL,* XXXII (1905).

————. Les Origines de l'Ordre du Collier," *AHS*, XXIII and XXIV (1909–1910).

————. "Una Principessa sabauda sul trono di Bisanzio" in *MASBAS* (4th series, XI, 1909).

Naef, A. *Le Château de Chillon.* 2 vols. Lausanne, 1929, 1939.

Nani, C. *Gli Statuti del 1379 di Amadeo VI, Conte Verde* in *MSI* (2nd series, XXII, 1884).

Ostrogorsky, George. *History of the Byzantine State.* New Brunswick, 1957.

Paradin, Guillaume. *Cronique de Savoye.* Lyon, 1552.

Paquier, Richard. *Le Pays de Vaud des origines à la conquête bernoise.* 2 vols. Lausanne, 1943.

Pérouse, Gabriel. *Inventaire sommaire des Archives départementales de la Savoie antérieures à 1793, Archives communales,* I. Chambéry, 1911. Introduction.

Perrin, André. *Histoire de Savoie des origines à 1860.* Chambéry, 1900.

Perroud, M. "Les Grandes Compagnies en Bresse et en Dombes," *Annales de la Société d'Emulation de l'Ain* (Bourg, 1874).

Perroy, Edouard. *The Hundred Years War.* Bloomington, 1959.

Petit, Ernest. *Histoire des Ducs de Bourgogne de la Race capétienne.* 9 vols. Dijon, 1885–1905.

Plaisance, Emile. *Histoire des Savoyens.* 2 vols. Chambéry, 1910.

Portail, Jean. *Contes et Légendes de Savoie.* Paris, 1960.

Previté Orton, C. W. *The Early History of the House of Savoy 1000–1233.* Cambridge, 1912.

Prou, M. *Etude sur les relations politiques du pape Urbain V avec les rois de France Jean II et Charles V.* Paris, 1888.

Rabut, F. "Notice sur quelques monnaies de Savoie," *MARS* (2nd series, I, 1851), 165–166.

Richard, Jean. "L'Accession de la Maison de La Tour au Dauphiné de Viennois," *Bulletin philologique et historique* (1951–1952).

Ricotti, Ercole. *Storia delle Compagnie di Ventura in Italia.* 4 vols. Turin, 1844–1846.

Robinson, J. H., and H. W. Rolfe. *Petrarch.* N.Y., 1914.

Rodd, Rennell. *The Princes of Achaia and the Chronicles of Morea.* 2 vols. London, 1907.

Roubert, Jacqueline. *La Seigneurie des Archevêques-comtes de Tarentaise du Xe au XVIe siècles* in *MASBAS* (6th series, V, 1961).

Rousseau, Raymond. *La Population de la Savoie jusqu'en 1861.* Paris, 1960.

Saint-Genix, Victor de. *Histoire de Savoie.* 3 vols. Paris, 1868–1869.

Scarabelli, Luigi. *Paralipomeni di Storia Piemontese dall'Anno 1285 al 1617* in *ASI,* XIII (1847).

Sclaffert, Thérèse. "Comptes de péage de Montmélian 1294–1585," *Revue de Géographie Alpine,* XXI (1933).

Segre, A. *Delle Relazioni Tra Savoia e Venezia da Amadeo VI a Carlo II (III),* extract from *Accademia Reale delle Scienze di Torino.* Turin, 1899.

Servion, Jehan. *Gestez et Croniques de la Mayson de Savoye.* Ed. F-E. Bollati di Saint-Pierre. 2 vols. Turin, 1879.

Tabacco, Giovanni. *Lo Stato Sabaudo nel Sacro Romano Impero.* Turin, 1939.

Tallone, Armando. *Parlemento Sabaudo.* 10 vols. Bologna, 1928ff.

Temple-Leader, J., and G. Marcotti. *Sir John Hawkwood.* London, 1889.

Terrier de Loray. *Jean de Vienne, amiral de France 1341–1396.* Paris, 1877.

Thatcher, O. J., and E. H. McNeal. *Source Book for Medieval History.* New York, 1905.

Tucoo-Chala, Pierre. *Gaston Fébus et La Vicomté de Béarn.* Bordeaux, 1960.

Valbonnais, Monet de Bourchenu de. *Histoire de Dauphiné.* 2 vols. Geneva, 1772.

Van Berchem, Victor. *Guichard Tavel, Evêque de Sion* (Extr. *Jahrbuch für Schweizerische Geschichte,* 1899).

Villani, Matteo. *Cronaca.* Ed. Florence, 1825.

Wilkins, E. H. *Petrarch's Eight Years in Milan.* Cambridge, 1958.

Young, George. *Constantinople.* London and New York, 1926.

MEDIEVAL persons are indexed by dynastic names except for counts of Savoy, kings of France and England, Holy Roman Emperors, and popes, who are listed by Christian name or title. Abbreviations used are: abp. = archbishop; bp. = bishop; ct. = count; cty. = county; dy. = duchy.

# Index

menestrerii, 53, 101, 119, 363

Menthon family, 372-73; Saint Bernard de, 80; Thomas de, 131n

mercenaries in Savoyard service, 99-100, 109-11, 163, 171-72, 209, 210, 220n, 262-63, 331-33; attitude of Amadeus VI toward, 161-63, 280; significance of, 343-44

merchants, 10-11. *See also* routes, tolls

*merum et mixtum imperium* in Piedmont, 128

Mesembria, 224, 226-29, 230, 231n, 234

mestral, 44, 121-22, 306

Mézières, Philippe de, 170n, 177, 178, 184, 204

Michaele, Aimone, 220

Milan, *see* Visconti

military service in Savoy, 42, 50, 99-100, 108-11, 130, 171-72, 181-82, 331-33, 343, 344; crusading army, 207-209; military operations, 100, 108-11

mints and coinage, 66, 124n, 129, 131, 367-68

Miolans, Antelme de, sire d'Urtières, 23n, 66, 255, 354

Miribel, siege of (1348), 72-73; Amadeus, sire of, 36n; Guillaume de, sire of Faramans, 36n

Mistral, Jean, *legum doctor*, 112

Moncalieri, charter of (1360), 141

Montagnieu, Henri de, 112, 113n

Montbel, Pierre de, seigneur of Les Echelles, 36n

Montbéliard, Jean-Philippe de, 336

Mont Cenis pass, 3, 4, 6, 7, 10, 19, 124-25, 150, 250

Montesarchio, 335

MONTFERRAT, Giovanni II, marquis of (d. 1372), 62, 63, 71, 125-26, 127n, 128, 143-44, 154, 170, 174, 205n, 255, 257, 261, 264, 355; sons of, 313, 314, 316

   Giovanni III, marquis of (d. 1381), 313, 316, 324

      Guglielmo de, 324

      Secondotto, marquis of (d. 1378), 262, 264, 265, 274n, 296, 297n

Teodoro I, marquis of (d. 1338), 12

   Teodoro II, marquis of (d. 1418), 314, 316, 324

   Violante de, countess of Savoy, 12-15, 23n, 31-32

Montfort, Jean de, 54, 55

Montgelat family, 356; François de, 193n, 227, 236; Pierre de, 36

Montgenèvre pass, 3

Monthey, commune of, 92

Monthoux, battle of (1332), 56n

Monthoux, François "Chivard" de, knight of the Collar, 181, 183, 255n

Montichiari, battle of (1373), 277-78

Mont-Joux, 67, 83, 318. *See also* Great St. Bernard

Montjovet, *see* Challant

Montmayeur, Gaspard de, 135, 172, 255, 258n, 357; knight of the Collar, 181, 182, 193n, 372; on crusade, 208n, 211, 219, 223, 229; on Neapolitan expedition, 332, 336, 338

Morat, 191, 192, 355

Morea, *see* Greece

Morges, 136

Mortgarten, battle of (1315), 88n

Moûtiers, siege of (1335), 47

municipal government, 48-50. *See also* communes

Murad, Turkish sultan, 217, 219

Murs family, 356; Pierre de, 255, 256n

Musard, Richard, knight of the Collar, 181, 183, 207, 208n, 228, 236, 252, 262, 280, 298, 332, 338, 364

musicians in Savoy, 53, 288-89

Namur, Guillaume the Rich, ct. of, 132-33, 135

NAPLES, André of, 62

   Charles d'Anjou, king of (d. 1285), 20n

   Charles II, king of (d. 1309), 62, 319

   Giovanna I, queen of (d. 1383), 62, 126, 155, 168, 267, 310n, 319-20, 326, 334

# Index

397

# Index

travel, difficulties of, 6, 11

treasury, *see chambre des comptes*

Treaty of Paris (1355), 76, 103ff, 112, 365; execution of, 118-19, 168, 187, 247, 294; significance of, 174, 288

Turenne, Raymond of, nephew of Gregory XI, 279

Turin, bp. of, 23, 124; city of, 140; Peace of (1381), 322-23, 325

Turks, *see* Ottoman Turks

universities, 348; of Geneva, 198-99; of Pavia, 273

Unterwalden, *see* Forest Cantons

Urban V (1362-70), election of, 168n; and Great Companies, 148, 197-98, 202; and crusade, 169, 170, 178, 197-98, 208, 238; anti-Visconti policies, 174, 261, 262; relations with Amadeus VI, 180, 186, 206-207

Urban VI (1378-89), 315, 316, 319-20, 324, 328, 333, 334, 335

Uri, *see* Forest Cantons

Urtières, Antelme d', 211, 229; Pierre d', 36, 356

usurers, 34, 130

Valais, nobles of, 36; and Savoy, 46, 87-92; expeditions of Amadeus VI, 89-90, 92, 95-96; rebellions in, 120-21, 245, 289-92, 318-19; treaties with, 92, 96, 152-54, 192

Valbonne, annexed by Savoy, 103, 104, 106, 340

Val d'Aosta, *see* Aosta

Valentinois, Aymar de Poitiers, ct. of, governor of Dauphiné, 102n, 103n, 104, 111, 112, 113n

Valleise family, 84ff, 123, 135

VALOIS, Isabelle de, daughter of Philippe V, 25n

   Isabelle de, daughter of Jean II, 144-46, 209n, 250

   Marguerite de, mother of Philippe VI, 22. *See also* Charles V, Charles VI, Jean II, Philippe V, Philippe VI

Valois-Visconti marriage (1360), 144-46

Valromey, annexed to Savoy, 100, 103, 136, 303n

Varey, battle of (1325), 26, 38, 93, 101

Varna, 224-26, 228

VAUD, Catherine de, 109, 132

   Louis I, baron of (d. 1302), 21, 132n, 182n, 368, 369

   Louis II, baron of (d. 1349), 13, 33, 36-37, 71, 132; as regent of Savoy, 57, 59-60, 61, 66, 68. *See also* Châlon-Arlay, Isabelle de

Vaud, barony of, origins, 21, 45, 132; military service from, 99, 109; annexation by Savoy, 131-37, 340

Veissy, Roland de, knight of the Collar, 181, 183-84, 188, 223

Venice and crusade of 1366-67, 178, 204, 205, 208, 210-13; relations with Genoa, 218, 321-23; treaty with Savoy, 324

Vercelli, bp. of, 282n, 297, 298; and Visconti, 71, 125, 268

Verona, lords of, 333

*via publica*, rights of, 46, 84, 88

vicariate, imperial, 123-24, 194-95, 197, 201, 240, 245, 246n, 289

*vidomnat* in Geneva, 46

Vienne, Gautier de, 211; Henri de, 103n; Jean de, knight of the Collar, 181, 184, 211, 224, 371-72

VIENNOIS, Gui, dauphin of, 373

   Guigues VIII, dauphin of (d. 1333), 23, 24, 25, 26, 31, 37, 54, 93

   Hugues de, baron of Faucigny, 22

   Humbert II, dauphin of (d. 1355), 24-27, 29-31, 56, 61-62, 67, 71, 72-75, 106n, 179, 206. *See also* Charles V

Viennois, bailliage of, 31, 39, 101, 106, 355; barons of, 36; castellanies dispute, 107, 118, 168, 246-47, 294-95, 365-66; dauphins of, 21, 23

Villa de la Tour de Gressan, barons of, 81, 83n

Villani, Matteo, Florentine chronicler, 160, 189-90

399